# TV
## THE TELEVISION ANNUAL
## 1978-79

STEVEN H. SCHEUER is the author of the best-selling *Movies on TV* and *The Movie Book* and is known throughout the TV industry as one of its most knowledgeable and articulate observers. He edits and publishes "TV Key," a syndicated service that appears daily in over 200 newspapers, and is frequently consulted by the networks for information on current and past events in the medium. Besides the two-hour ABC special that gave rise to this book, he has produced an award-winning series, "All About TV," for airing on cable channels and PBS. He is on the faculty of New York's New School for Social Research, where he teaches the history of American television.

# TV

## THE
## TELEVISION ANNUAL
## 1978-79

A Complete Record of American Television
from June 1, 1978 through May 31, 1979

CONCEIVED AND EDITED BY

# STEVEN H. SCHEUER

Collier Books
A Division of Macmillan Publishing Co., Inc.
NEW YORK

Collier Macmillan Publishers
LONDON

Macmillan Publishing Co., Inc.
866 Third Avenue, New York, N.Y. 10022
Collier Macmillan Canada, Ltd.

ISSN 0194-1933

First Collier Books Edition 1979

*TV: The Television Annual 1978-79* is published in a hardcover edition
by Macmillan Publishing Co., Inc.

PRINTED IN THE UNITED STATES OF AMERICA

*Design by Antler & Baldwin, Inc.*

# ILLUSTRATION CREDITS

No book about the television season would be complete without numerous illustrations. The following have graciously supplied and given permission to reprint the photographs in this book. (Because of the large number of photographs and the limited amount of space, the page location, not the subject, of the photograph is given.)

*Cover*

Front: (left) Ed Friendly Productions and National Broadcasting Company, Inc.; (center) photo by Jim Britt, © 1979 Television Production Division, Paramount Pictures Corporation, and American Broadcasting Companies, Inc.; (right) "The Incredible Hulk," Copyright © 1979 Marvel Comics Group, a Division of Cadence Industries Corp., all rights reserved.

Back: (left) Tandem Productions and National Broadcasting Company, Inc.; (center) CBS News Inc.; (right) "The Rockford Files," Universal Television, a Division of Universal City Studios, Inc., and American Broadcasting Companies, Inc.

*Black and white photographs*

ABC Circle Films: 85 (left) photo by Gene Stein

ABC News (© American Broadcasting Companies, Inc.): 131, 140, 141 (right)

AKAI, Inc.: 190

Alan Landsburg Productions: and Columbia Broadcasting System, Inc., 52 (left); and National Broadcasting Company, Inc., 95 (right)

Artemis Productions: and American Broadcasting Companies, Inc., 62 (photo by Peter Miller)

Bennet-Katleman Productions and Columbia Pictures: 52 (right)

Cates Brothers Company and National Broadcasting Company, Inc.: 60 (left)

CBS News (Columbia Broadcasting System, Inc.): 135, 144 (left)

Charles Fries Productions and Columbia Broadcasting System, Inc.: 55 (right), 75

© 1979 Children's Television Workshop: and Columbia Broadcasting System, Inc., 73; and Muppets, Inc., 175

Cinerama Releasing Corporation: 119 (right)

Clasart Films, Inc., and National Broadcasting Company, Inc.: 60 (right)

Columbia Broadcasting System, Inc.: 123

Columbia Pictures: 109 (left), 109 (right), 117 (bottom, left)

Columbia Pictures Television: and Columbia Broadcasting System, Inc., 83 (right), 100 (left), 129 (bottom, left), 129 (bottom, right); and National Broadcasting Company, Inc., 127 (right)

David L. Wolper Productions and Warner Brothers Television: 54 (center) photo by Gene Stein, 54 (right) photo by Chic Donchin

Dick Clark Motion Pictures: 81 (left) photo by Bob Coburn

Dick Clark Productions and National Broadcasting Company, Inc.: 26 (left)

Don Fedderson Productions and Columbia Broadcasting System, Inc.: 89 (left)

Filmways International and Columbia Broadcasting System, Inc.: 81 (right)

Four D Productions and American Broadcasting Companies, Inc.: 21 (right)

Golden West Television: 146

Hopewell Productions-SFM Media Services Corporation: 1, 163

Jocar Productions and Columbia Broadcasting System, Inc.: 58 (left)

Labine-Mayer Productions and © 1979 American Broadcasting Companies, Inc.: 128

Lorimar Productions: and © 1979 American Broadcasting Companies, Inc., 27 (right); and Columbia Broadcasting System, Inc., 25 (left), 54 (left); and National Broadcasting Company, Inc., 46 (right), 55 (center)

Magnavox Consumer Electronics Company: 189

Marble Arch Productions: 83 (left) photo by Peter Sorel

Medcom Company and National Broadcasting Company, Inc.: 34 (right)

Media Productions and National Broadcasting Company, Inc.: 55 (left)

Metromedia Producers Corporation and National Broadcasting Company, Inc.: 87 (left)

MGM-TV: 11 (photo by Gene Stein); and National Broadcasting Company, Inc., 24 (left)

Michael Klein Productions and Columbia Broadcasting System, Inc.: 95 (left)

MTM Productions, Inc., and Columbia Broadcasting System, Inc.: 49 (left), 49 (right)

National Broadcasting Company, Inc.: 58 (right), 134, 195

NBC News (National Broadcasting Company, Inc.): 148

New York Post Corporation: 197; and Paul Rigby, 142

Osmond Productions and American Broadcasting Companies, Inc.: 26 (right)

© Paramount Pictures Corporation: and American Broadcasting Companies, Inc., 21 (left), 31 (left), 34 (left) photo by Bob Coburn, 38 (photo by Bruce Birmelin), 45 (left) photo by Jim Globus, 102 (right); Columbia Broadcasting System, Inc., 104 (left), 107 (right), 111 (right), 117 (bottom, right); and National Broadcasting Company, Inc., 22 (left), 30 (right), 35 (left), 50 (left), 111 (left)

Procter & Gamble Productions and Columbia Broadcasting System, Inc.: 127 (left), 129 (top, left), 129 (top, right)

Public Broadcasting Service: 20 (left), 24 (right), 29 (right), 30 (left), 30 (center), 33 (left), 33 (right), 36 (left), 36 (right), 39 (left), 40 (left), 43 (right), 46 (left), 48 (left), 50 (right)

RCA American Communications, Inc.: 186

RCA Corporation: 193

The Register and Tribune Syndicate, Inc., and Bil Keane: 192

For Berta Kaslow

With profound thanks for more than two decades
of extraordinary dedication, rare talent,
and that precious quality—loyalty.

# ACKNOWLEDGMENTS

The preparation of this first edition of *The Television Annual* was a massive undertaking that could not have been completed without the generous advice and assistance of many people throughout the television industry.

At the networks, we are grateful for the support and cooperation of: Barry Richardson and his CBS colleagues Harry Feeney, Helen Chiotes, Ellen Ehrlich, Gail Plautz, and Susanna Martin; NBC's George Hoover and his colleagues Owen Comora, Jack Van Buskirk, Betty Jane Reed, and Joe Riccuiti; Tom Mackin of ABC and his colleagues Dan Rustin, Audrey Fecht, Rick Giacalone, and Gloria Nappi; and Julie Osler and Donna Williams of PBS.

For their assistance in researching photographic materials, we wish to thank Ella Pesin of *Newsweek* and Don Bowdin of World Wide Photos.

For assistance in the collection and management of the masses of factual material contained herein, we thank our assistant editor, Joel Altschuler; and our editorial assistants from the undergraduate division of the Department of Communications, Brigham Young University, Alice Tate, David Heylen, and Linda Barr.

My sincere thanks to Charles Levine, a discerning and supportive editor; and special thanks to Rayanna Simons, who made this book a reality.

Steven H. Scheuer, *Editor*
Kim Gantz, Harry Zerler, *Associate Editors*
Charles Witbeck, *Hollywood Editor*

# CONTENTS

# PREFACE

**T**HOUSANDS of newspaper and magazine articles, and by now hundreds of books, have expounded upon television's enormous impact upon virtually every phase of American life. Many Americans have at least some modest understanding of this revolutionary phenomenon. A miniscule number, however, realize that this already staggering and all-pervasive grip on American society will *increase* in the 1980's, as American network television moves into its fourth decade. Television is clearly the major shared experience of our time.

Yet, astonishingly enough, there is remarkably little reliable, insightful, or accessible reference material concerning American television. (For example, to date there is only one serious history of American TV, Erik Barnouw's *The Golden Web*.) There has been, up till now, no comprehensive record of any given season or programming year in American TV. *TV: The Television Annual 1978-79* is expressly designed to fill this long recognized but unfilled need. This is the first in a series of forthcoming yearbooks covering the most significant aspects of American network television, and, increasingly, the fascinating and rapidly enlarging galaxy of global telecommunications.

In the 1950s and '60s, when television scheduling was more genteel and orderly, the season ran from September through the Christmas holidays. There were special one-shot programs after that, of course, but practically no weekly series debuted after the first of the year. In the early and mid-'70s a few new weekly series were warily premiered in January during what was then referred to as the "second season." By the end of the '70's, new weekly series were routinely introduced throughout the winter and spring, with some hopefuls getting a trial run as late as May.

For this and other reasons *Television Annual 1978-79* covers the broadcast year from June 1, 1978 through May 31, 1979. It combines reference listings, qualitative reviews, and essays laced with a wide range of black and white and color photographs, and some droll cartoons.

But *The Television Annual 1978-79* is more than a mere tabulation of archival material. It contains numerous essays by experts in specific areas of this vast, complex industry. Tom Shales, the perceptive television critic of the *Washington Post*, sets the tone with a lucid, witty analysis in "Walking on Water into the '80s." Wall Street analyst Anthony Hoffman explains the business of TV including how and why this incredibly profitable industry can afford to pay the two stars of a hit situation comedy $75,000 each for every episode produced. The unique characteristics of this particular television season is extensively chronicled—from the frantic juggling of prime-time shows to an update on technology to the major news stories covered by the evening newscasts of CBS, NBC, and ABC.

A chapter is devoted to "Other Voices," a selection of some of the best articles written about television during the year. They range from the light-hearted "How'd You Like to Pick the Nation's Programs?" to a serious discussion of alternatives to the present lamentable ratings system.

In addition to the primary emphasis on programming, especially prime-time programming, there is substantial coverage of important political and regulatory issues, court decisions, the Carnegie II Report on the future of public broadcasting, new developments in cable and pay TV, research, etc.

Considerations of both time and space have precluded more exhaustive coverage of such topics as broadcast journalism, program syndication, and emerging public policy issues. The changing regulations and policies formulated in Washington, D.C., and around the world will determine not only the nature and quality of American television in the 1980s and '90s, but will, in a very real sense, determine how we communicate with each other between now and the year 2000, both how we receive and *send* information.

Work on the next volume in this series, *The Television Annual 1979-80*, is already under way. I would welcome readers' suggestions concerning how *The Television Annual* could be improved to best serve the needs of both TV industry professionals and interested viewers. Please write to me c/o the Macmillan Publishing Company, 866 Third Avenue, New York, New York 10022.

Steven H. Scheuer
July 1979

# 1

# SEASON

# OVERVIEW

# WALKING ON WATER INTO THE '80s

by Tom Shales*

FOR the television networks, the 1978-79 season was decorated with lights that flickered—and many that failed. "Battlestar Galactica," the most expensive weekly series in TV history, went out in a burst of rueful smithereens. Mary Tyler Moore flopped not just once but twice, in separate musical-variety formats. The ceaselessly ballyhooed "Supertrain" proved a veritable Three Mile Island on wheels. And NBC president and chief executive officer, Fred Silverman, was unable to fulfill the expectations of those who assumed that, at the very least, he would walk on water in the fountain at Rockefeller Center in New York City.

Beyond all the more or less superficial phenomena of the season, however, there were deeper, more ominous, and, in several cases, actually encouraging signs of cosmic change in television: the emerging semiwonderland of American and global telecommunications. A combination of social, economic, regulatory, and, most of all, technological developments loomed on the horizon of the '80s, making the decade ahead look like an Emerald City of promise and adventure—at least in comparison to the decade behind.

That's a romantic interpretation, of course, but not even television has been able to kill all hope. Indeed, the '80s began to look positively cluttered with possibilities, and mere odds would suggest that a few might turn out to be glorious. At the very least they portend an end to the network era of American television, a system dominated by networks to a degree which some angry Hollywood producers have labeled a monopoly.

Unquestionably the commercial-network sphere of influence is on the decline, and if 1978-79 can't accurately be called the twilight of the networks, it is at least apparent that television has entered a purgatorial twilight zone. When it emerges into the ultraelectrified, wired-up, multi-channeled living room of the '80s, it is going to be another medium; it is going to be reinvented, and the network share of the American pie will get smaller.

Threats to the networks were everywhere during the season—little threats, big threats, and, above all, a growing national consensus that television hadn't worked out quite so wonderfully as expected. In particular, a *Washington Post* poll conducted in midseason revealed that 53 percent of American TV viewers say they're watching less TV now than they did five years ago—the highest such figure ever recorded. Similarly, a *TV Guide* survey, published in May, found five out of ten people saying that they watch less TV "than they used to."

Network nabobs naturally dismissed such heresy. The National Association of Broadcasters' (NAB) Television Information Office issued its annual and predictable Roper poll, this one insisting that "television viewing time has increased to peak levels for college-educated and upper-income viewers, as well as the general public," and that, just for the record, "a four-to-one majority of the American public favorably views the concept of commercially sponsored television."

Nielsen figures also showed viewing at all-time highs. So why the discrepancy with the published surveys? The networks explained that people *claimed* to watch less TV than they actually do, so the figures

PRECEDING PAGE: *Donna Pescow (left), Conrad Bain, and Lee Meriwether lead the singing as the 1978–79 TV season "graduates," and then reviews its past highlights on "The Television Annual" TV special.*

*Tom Shales is the television editor and chief television critic of the *Washington Post*.

were inconsistent. And yet if more people than ever were *lying* about how much TV watching they did, that at least indicated that TV watching is considered more of a social stigma than ever—something one does rather furtively and doesn't admit to later. Like masturbation.

Responses further indicated a growing eagerness for such options as cable and pay-cable channels to liberate viewers weary of the limited alternatives provided by the network-dominated system. Home Box Office, the largest pay-cable distributor, grew to serve a population of over two million subscribers on 900 affiliated systems in 50 states, Puerto Rico, and the Virgin Islands. These people were paying monthly fees, partly to escape the free TV that network honchos insisted was as popular and dear to America's heart as ever.

Cable continued apace, with one out of five American homes now hooked up to cable TV. Its growth rate is projected at 11 percent per year by the National Cable Television Association (NCTA). This could be an under-estimate to avoid the "blue-skying" that haunted cable during its first 20 over-regulated years. Perhaps by or before 1984 cable will reach that magical 33 percent penetration figure which, according to at least one Madison Avenue sage, will mean it has truly arrived as a force whose growth will "snowball" from there. From blue sky to snowball has been a long trek for cable, but in April the FCC removed another potential shackle from its progress by refusing to disallow satellite transmission to cable systems.

Former NBC vice president Paul L. Klein predicted that if a theatrical motion picture played on cable TV, an average loss of 3 rating points would be seen when it was later shown on a commercial network.

Many of the "new" technologies that appeared to be just around the corner or already in America's lap had something to do with cable. Some of these, like fiber optics and digital transmission, remained largely in the sci-fi realm, but others were either on hand or imminent: one-half-inch video cassette recorders (introduced the previous season), over-the-air subscription television, an exploding market of video games, satellite-linked cable networks, video disc players (test marketed meekly by MCA Inc.), and the new "Super Stations" that bounced their signals off satellites and into millions of homes through hundreds of cable systems.

Ted Turner, flamboyant yachtsman-broadcaster and owner of WTCG in Atlanta, said that since he had invented the term "Superstation" he had the one and only "Superstation" in existence. But others were beaming up, just the same. Turner told a press conference in Washington, D.C.: "The effect of the networks' push for 100 percent of the audience, and their selecting programming designed to reach the lowest common denominator, has the ultimate result of driving the people of this nation down intellectually."

He said parents spent thousands of dollars sending their kids to college only to have television turn their brains to pudding when they got out.

Turner was subject to fits of rhetoric and his syntax could be on the broken side, but he was tapping a vein of discord that seemed genuinely to be growing. Everybody was unhappy with the system. It was the season of hate-the-network. Frustrated viewers were angered by the ratings war that produced feast-or-famine program choices depending on whether it was a sweep month (a major ratings month) or not. Hollywood producers were infuriated by escalated last-minute, counter-programming, and scattershot schedule juggling.

Hit-maker Garry Marshall, for example, was enraged when ABC president Fred Pierce shuttled Marshall successes like "Happy Days" all over the schedule in order to zap whatever the opposition was trying to do. It became an absurd game of million-dollar video pong.

Network execs made their usual dull, self-serving speeches warning against premature acceptance of new technologies. In fact, they had more to fear than just cable, Qube (the two-way cable system Warner Communications pioneered in Columbus, Ohio, and planned to export to Houston and other cities), and Ted Turner's Superstation. There were other more specific economic threats. CBS suffered substantial revenue losses when 15 of the network's affiliates were among those to sign up for "Edward the King," a high-toned, imported, British series sponsored and syndicated by Mobil Oil; it was slotted for Wednesdays, 8 P.M. (EST), in all markets where it played. That knocked out the CBS pulp series apportioned to that hour, "The Incredible Hulk."

Other subnetworks or instant networks sprang up for sports coverage and for a dubious collection of lackluster but plot-packed (and, inevitably, bosomy) serials produced and syndicated by mammoth Universal TV, as part of an alternative programming plan known as "Operation Prime Time."

Clearly enough, this was to have been a transitional season. The day, moreover, may not be far off when the national audience is so fractionalized, so subject to exploring other forms of television, that the networks will merely be one source among many—not a dominant, decisive presence—and viewers will return en masse perhaps only for live news and sports events of national importance and scope.

In the meantime the FCC was continuing to press on at its usual pokey pace with an inquiry into network practices. On Capitol Hill, legislators on the House and Senate sides toiled away over rewrites of the Communications Act of 1934, that tattered Magna Carta of broadcasting which had set parameters for federal regulation. Lionel Van Deerlin (D-Ca.), chairman of the House Communications Subcommittee and sponsor of the House version of the bill, was surprised and dismayed to find that his bill had brought the people together—they all hated it. H.R. 3333 was trounced by the broadcasting industry—which panicked at the thought of a spectrum-use fee requiring them to pay for the public airwaves they'd long squatted on for free; by consumer activists such as Ralph Nader and Nicholas Johnson; and by everybody, in fact, from the National Education Association to the United Auto Workers to a coalition of nuns.

Suddenly, or so it seemed, television was no longer just a medium with an audience. It was a power center fought over by innumerable and often conflicting constituencies.

In the midst of all this, as if they weren't getting enough grief, the embattled networks faced new attacks from the Hollywood community; producers decried the nutty, breakneck, cutthroat, slit-wrist competition that led to rushed production, hectic schedule-juggling, and obsessive imitation of prevailing sitcom hits.

Things became so zany that "60 Minutes" embarked on that rarest of rarities, a televised report on television. But, as Mike Wallace complained at a party given to celebrate the show's tenth anniversary, none of the top network executives he wanted were willing to be interviewed on camera, not even CBS's own programming boss Robert A. Daly. "It's such horseshit," Wallace said succinctly.

It was also such madness. "MADNESS"—as the survivor says at the end of *The Bridge on the River Kwai*.

For the producers of "Battlestar Galactica," it was such madness that some episodes were not finished and delivered to ABC until the Saturday morning preceding that Sunday night's telecast. "Galactica," which the usually prescient ad agency Dancer-Fitzgerald-Sample had called "the season's most promising new program," was originally intended as a 7-hour miniseries. It "went to series" late and the quality of the first episodes couldn't be maintained. The show made an unexpected crash dive after only one season.

For the producers of "Mrs. Columbo," it was such madness that one scheduled episode simply could not be finished on time, so NBC ran two "Quincy" episodes in a row. Programs were going on the air "wet"; promos were made from such rough cuts of shows that viewers could see scratches running across the face of the film.

For producer Dan Curtis, it was such madness that after working weeks and weeks of 14-hour days to get NBC's "Supertrain" on the tracks, he was fired by the network soon after the premiere so NBC could change the direction of the show.

Madness, madness, madness. Who could end this madness? Who could lead network television out of the wilderness it had constructed for itself? Who could take television across the threshold of technological revolution and into the ultra '80s?

Up in the sky—on the silver screen—it was the year of *Superman*. Up on the air—on the funny little screen—it was the year of Silverman. Fred Silverman became the most talked-about, joked-about, denounced, and celebrated TV executive in network history. The man who had helped shape programming at CBS and then ABC was now not only president and chief executive officer of NBC, but also somehow a personification of all that people thought was wrong, and some of what people thought might be right, about American television.

Silverman had been hired by RCA chairman Edgar Griffiths to rescue NBC from third-place embarrassment and declining profits, but Silverman inherited problems that may have been more formidable than he imagined. Since 1972, 36 stations had changed their affiliation to ABC, the network Silverman made number one—21 defected from CBS and 15 from NBC. NBC would lose another before Silverman's first season was through. Meanwhile, parent corporation RCA had failed to adequately invest in program development for years, and Silverman had to start almost from scratch. In fact, at midseason he blitzkrieged every new program that had been introduced the preceding fall. "NBC stands for Nine Bombs Canceled," quipped Johnny Carson the night the axings were announced.

NBC, the oldest network, was also the one most encrusted in bureaucratic barnacles and beset at various levels by a certain fey indolence. The cobwebs had been sufficient for awhile to conceal masses of funds being diverted to private use by some of the network's unit managers, but the scandal broke just after Silverman came aboard. And then, as if all this weren't enough, late-night star Johnny Carson became noisily restless in the second half of the season and decided he wanted out of his "Tonight Show" contract before its expiration date, April 1981. Though Carson's ratings had eroded over the years in the face of increased late-night competition from the other networks (both of them using reruns of old NBC shows, among other attractions), the "Tonight Show" still represented a huge chunk of NBC profits and Silverman had to face an angry RCA stockholders' meeting soon after the story broke.

But did Silverman break? Though there were many tales of inter-office screaming sessions and executive tantrums, Silverman remained to all appearances confident and good-humored, even to the point of accepting a scalp full of "noogies" from manic Bill Murray at a party celebrating the fourth season of NBC's unthreatened smash, "Saturday Night Live."

Murray to Silverman: "Get out of here, you knucklehead." Silverman laughed. One couldn't help imagining the response if this sort of thing had happened to august William S. Paley of CBS or poker-faced Pierce of ABC. Silverman was still the most engagingly human of all top network executives.

But people weren't expecting human. They were expecting super human. The New York press jabbed at Silverman mercilessly; he was held responsible for not only everything that went wrong at NBC, but for virtually everything bad on television. In *Esquire,* eastern liberal Richard Reeves had welcomed Silverman to NBC with a lacerating harangue that stopped short only of accusing him of genocide. The *New York Post* kept up a steady stream of Silverman rumors, including the allegation that he was feuding with his own hand-picked NBC board chairman Jane Cahill Pfeiffer, nicknamed "Attila the Nun" by the press because of a fling with religion in her past.

Pfeiffer swept through the network on a cost-cutting binge that may have produced more resentful squawks and hurt feelings than productive results. In the meantime, Silverman reorganized the NBC board, gave the entire bureaucracy a vacuum-cleaning, and still found time to read many pilot scripts and personally look at all pilot tapes and films.

On the air, though, the master programmer did not exactly manage instant renaissance. In his defense, the "Supertrain" fiasco was really Paul Klein's baby more than Silverman's and, in March, Klein left the network. Silverman had said, weeks prior to its premiere, that the situation comedy "Diff'rent Strokes" would be "the first Fred Silverman show" on NBC, and despite merciless counterprogramming from ABC's Pierce (still smarting over Silverman's defection to NBC), "Strokes" became NBC's first big hit since "CHiPs." Silverman still had the touch.

And yet not even Silverman may be able to save the networks from their own folly and their own twilight. If Nick Johnson and Ralph

Nader couldn't raise the public consciousness about the evils of no-holds-barred network competition, maybe the networks could do it themselves. The trend reached its Gotterdammerung on the night of Sunday, February 11, 1979, amid the hellzapoppin' chess match of the Nielsen sweeps. On that night viewers had to choose between the new three-hour movie *Elvis* on ABC, the television premiere of *One Flew Over the Cuckoo's Nest,* winner of five Oscars, on NBC, and the second telecast in history of the motion picture classic *Gone With the Wind* on CBS. The ratings were so close, from a network standpoint, and considering the huge number of sets in use that night, everybody "won"— everybody but the viewers. The night became a reference point for those who decried the frenzy of network competition, of win-at-any-cost.

And while Silverman made bold promises to Hollywood producers about giving them increased lead time to prepare their shows—veteran writer-producer Larry "M*A*S*H" Gelbart was given a whole year to develop a project of his own choosing—Silverman's later trips to the Coast were decidedly on the hell-bent-for-leather side. He reportedly ordered up George Schlatter's "Real People" series at the very last minute after looking at 20 minutes of tape in his Beverly Hills hotel suite. Schlatter could later be seen running around his offices like a mad man, loaded down with video cassettes full of material for the show.

And still it was said over and over by insiders and enlightened outsiders alike: Fred Silverman was the one man who could take network television out of the '70s and into the '80s; he was one of the few network leaders to propose *adapting* to new technologies and program sources rather than going into hysterics over them. As the season ended, it was too early to judge Silverman's performance, but that didn't keep a lot of people from judging it just the same.

If the network era is ending, as it appears to be, it should be said that there is no absolute guarantee that what follows will be nirvana; cable and its refinements could just mean a multiplicity of mediocrities. Then, too, the passing of the network era also meant the phasing out or shift into low profile for a vanishing breed, the gentleman-broadcaster —men like Julian Goodman, deposed NBC chairman, David C. Adams, longtime RCA vice president, and even CBS chairman William S. Paley himself, who insisted on remaining active but whose autobiography, *As It Happened,* was in the nature of a farewell to the good old days. Paley's suggestion, in the book, that all three networks set aside their swords for one night a week of plowshares, during which they would program nonrated "quality" material, not only got hoots or silence from the other networks, but was even ridiculed by the less visionary and more hard-bitten businessmen in Paley's own shop. The pioneers who built American broadcasting didn't do it in secret. The whole nation was watching. It is ludicrous to claim now we were all bamboozled while they made fortunes.

Nor can it be claimed that the 1978-79 TV season was a thorough-going disgrace or uninterrupted parade of imbecilities. Though at mid-season 15 of 18 new shows introduced were comedies or programs with high comedy content, a television season that included programs of the caliber of "Taxi" (ABC), "Lifeline" (NBC, canceled), "The White

Shadow" (CBS), and "Kaz" and "The Paper Chase" (both CBS, both canceled) can hardly be labeled worthless.

In addition to these outstanding regular series, prime-time network television showed remarkable improvement in the area of films made for television. With the number of available theatrical titles dwindling and their purchase prices skyrocketing, made-for-TV movies increased in quantity and, perhaps surprisingly, in quality as well. More and more of them dealt with high-tension contemporary issues, often in a manner more intelligent than that of Hollywood theatrical features, and some showed a genuine sense of style as well as mission.

So that while movie folk congratulated themselves on bravely facing the Vietnam war in movies like *The Deer Hunter*, television made the war a much more immediate, gripping, and thoughtful experience for millions more Americans with ABC's *Friendly Fire*, an adaptation by Fay Kanin of the C.D.B. Bryan book about a middle-American family's reaction to their boy's death in Vietnam. The film, which starred Carol Burnett and Ned Beatty, also proved that material that appeared downbeat or discouraging on the surface—that brought up unpleasant American realities—could attract a huge audience if done well.

Many other TV movies dealt realistically or at least earnestly with social problems; these included ABC's *Like Normal People, A Question of Love*, and the acquisition *Who Are the DeBolts? And Where Did They Get 19 Kids?*, as well as *Dummy* on CBS and, on NBC, *Battered* and *Son-Rise: A Miracle of Love*. There were other outstanding films: NBC's *The Winds of Kitty Hawk; Ishi, The Last of His Tribe; Rainbow; Amateur Night at the Dixie Bar and Grill;* and *Too Far to Go*, from the Maples stories of John Updike. NBC also televised a respectable and earthy adaptation of James T. Farrell's *Studs Lonigan* and an earthier than respectable remake of *From Here to Eternity*, both in six-hour miniseries formats.

(Drawing by Stevenson; © 1977 The New Yorker Magazine, Inc.)

Superior CBS movies included *Like Mom, Like Me; Murder by Natural Causes;* and Katharine Hepburn in George Cukor's new version of Emlyn Williams's *The Corn Is Green.* On ABC, the 14-hour sequel to *Roots,* called *Roots: The Next Generation,* was emotionally the equal of and artistically superior to the original, record-breaking program.

For public television, many of the season's main events took place beyond the screen, where, as in years past, the interlocking, overlapping, or combatant bureaucracies of the system struggled to restructure or merely preserve themselves. The long-awaited, 401-page sequel to the first Carnegie Commission report arrived with due fanfare and with the predictable recommendations that funding of the system be substantially increased. But discussion of the report seemed to flare up quickly and then die out, partly because CPB and PBS were both working on reorganizational schemes and reorganization of public TV was also a part of Van Deerlin's much-debated, but unlikely to pass, rewrite bill.

Public TV audiences increased considerably according to ratings reports, but the system remained plagued by bureaucratic rivalries and incredibly muddled priorities. While the arrival of "The Shakespeare Plays" was a commanding cultural event, it was probably of less real importance to public TV as an alternative medium than the less promoted arrival of "Non Fiction Television," a series of independently made documentaries channeled through New York's WNET.

The first of these, "Paul Jacobs and the Nuclear Gang," about the health hazards of radiation, was televised just two days before HEW Secretary Joseph A. Califano made a public statement on the subject and only weeks before revelations about the lingering dangers of fallout from atomic tests and the earthshaking nuclear accident at Three Mile Island.

On May 6 another group of independents—these video makers, not film makers—made another breakthrough in public television when, for $1199.50, they rented three hours on a PBS satellite channel so that any public TV station that wanted it could air, live from Washington, "Nuclear Power: The Public Reaction," a report on a huge antinuclear rally held in front of the U.S. Capitol. Only 15 stations picked up the telecast, but it marked the first time a live event produced by independents made it onto the PBS system, and it gave new hope to independent film and video makers who had considered the PBS bureaucracy impenetrable.

The group that produced the May 6 telecast, a hastily assembled coalition called Public Interest Video, had 100 volunteers, some on busman's holidays from network news divisions, working with them; their telecast was praised by PBS president Lawrence K. Grossman, even though the Washington PBS station, WETA, had refused to carry it.

As the season ended, the future, the purpose, and the operations of the public television system were still in a state of perpetual acrimony —the local stations both needing and despising the idea of a central program source in Washington (or New York, or wherever), PBS and CPB at loggerheads, and producers of public-affairs programs bemoaning the fact that underwriters gravitate toward operas, ballets, and British imports, leaving public affairs critically neglected and underrepresented on the system.

As with most years, it isn't easy to pinpoint the pivotal, seminal moments of the 1978-79 television season. It began with one giant step for President Jimmy Carter, though, on September 17, 1978, at 10:30 P.M. (EST), when he interrupted the premiere of "Battlestar Galactica" to announce preliminary establishment of a kind of peace in the Mideast, signing accords in the White House with his costars Menachem Begin and Anwar Sadat. After about 20 minutes of peace, the warfare of "Galactica" merrily resumed, on a night that attracted one of the largest aggregate audiences of the year.

As usual in television, there were steps forward and steps back. Sometimes they seemed concurrent; in April 1979 researchers at the University of Pennsylvania revealed that violence in weekend children's-television programming had risen to "near-record levels" on all three networks the preceding fall.

The study, said investigator George Gerbner, was even more disturbing for "the clear message of unequal power and victimization" it showed in programming. The "mean-world" syndrome Gerbner had spotted earlier was increasing among young people who watch large amounts of television. They are more likely to see the world as a hostile place full of threatening people than are those who watch less TV, the study showed; women and members of minority groups continue to be "overrepresented" as victims in TV programs.

And then, after the season had ended, the Justice Department dropped one of the most outrageous bombshells of all. It sued the NAB over its mild and only minimally effective self-regulatory advertising code, charging that this was a monopolistic practice that drove up the cost of ads and excluded some firms from buying television time. Just when the issue of on-air clutter was becoming a widespread industry concern, the Justice Department arrived on the scene with a recipe for more clutter and more frequent and annoying commercials than anyone had ever dreaded.

Madness, madness. Too much madness even for "Weekend," the NBC news magazine that had tried to keep a level head in a topsy-turvy world, including the very topsy-turviness of television, where it was moved from its comfy late-night spot to a prime-time berth, shunted about, praised by Silverman as "the finest thing" he'd seen on NBC soon after he arrived there, and then, ignominiously and, as is the custom, without apology, canceled.

The cancellation was another sign that mass network prime-time television remained an inhospitable environment for the maverick, iconoclastic, and personal touch of someone like producer Reuven Frank, who with his colleagues had manned a classy little bastion of reason, irreverence, and curiosity over what makes things tick and why.

"Weekend" stopped ticking early in 1979 to make way for graying golden boy Tom Snyder and his bombastic revue. On the last "Weekend" show on April 22, host Lloyd Dobyns, still somehow capable of bemusement at It All, looked into the camera and said, "It has been fun. It is now over. And so it goes."

And so it went.

# PRIME-TIME

# VIEWING

# THE YEAR OF THE JIGGLE AND THE JUGGLE

by John N. Goudas and Berta Kaslow*

THE 1978-79 television season was easily the most competitive in recent memory. The three commercial networks juggled their schedules at the drop of a rating point and canceled shows after just one or two weeks on the air. This practice caused viewers a great deal of confusion, making it difficult for them to establish regular viewing patterns.

Adding to the viewers' dilemma of what to watch and when to watch was the ploy of "blocking" another network's potential hit series by scheduling a very strong entry opposite it. For instance, "Battlestar Galactica" took off with impressive ratings and looked as if it was on its way to becoming a hit when CBS moved "All in the Family" and "Alice" up an hour to block ABC's would-be winner—and it worked. "Battlestar" went into a nosedive never to recover. The blocking maneuver was employed against specials, too. ABC often scheduled two episodes of "Laverne & Shirley" or "Mork & Mindy" back to back in order to ensure heavy competition for a potentially potent special.

On February 11, 1979, the networks locked horns in a multimillion-dollar three-way ratings showdown. ABC scheduled its three-hour TV movie *Elvis!;* CBS attacked head on with the first part of the classic film *Gone With the Wind;* and NBC countered with the network debut of the Oscar-winning film, *One Flew Over the Cuckoo's Nest* (*Elvis!* got higher ratings than *Cuckoo* and Scarlett and Rhett but viewers were so evenly divided among the three shows that all networks could feel that they "won").

Situation comedies led the successful series of each network, beginning with number-one-ranked ABC, which suffered from an embarrassment of riches. Bolstered by their established hits such as "Laverne & Shirley," "Three's Company," "Happy Days," "The Love Boat," "Eight Is Enough," and "Barney Miller," it came up with the megahit "Mork & Mindy," which understandably and deservedly made Robin Williams a star in a matter of weeks. "Mork & Mindy" became the greatest breakaway hit in recent years. Riding the crest, ABC also hit pay dirt with "Taxi," another new entry of the season, produced by alumni of the old "Mary Tyler Moore Show" production team.

At midseason, ABC introduced two sitcoms—"Angie" and "The Ropers," which was a spin-off from "Three's Company"—and both found immediate favor with the viewing audience. As the season progressed it became apparent that series aimed at the black viewing audience were declining in popularity: ABC's "What's Happening!," previously a consistently high-rated show, slipped and eventually went off the air; "Carter Country" seemed to share the disfavor of its presidential namesake. CBS's "Good Times" never rallied from a decline that began last season, despite the return of Esther Rolle in the role of the mother of the Evans clan. Even "The Jeffersons" started to slip, although to a lesser degree.

ABC was not without its flops, too. It tried for an *Animal House* clone called "Delta House," also produced by *National Lampoon*ers, but the show failed to excite the audience that flocked to see the feature film. And there was "Salvage I," which couldn't be; "Makin' It," which didn't; and "Apple Pie," which couldn't cut it. "Donny and Marie" was

PRECEDING PAGE: *James Arness hangs tough in the saddle in* How the West Was Won.

*John Goudas and Berta Kaslow are television columnists for TV Key, a syndicated news service.

floundering and called in their kin for "The Osmond Family Hour," to no avail; "Welcome Back, Kotter" lost the services of star Gabe Kaplan in many shows while he was making his movie debut in *Fastbreak*, and the show went down the drain; "Family" moved around but never found the right time slot (it was scheduled to return in January 1980) and "The Hardy Boys" and "Starsky and Hutch" also called it a day when their popularity diminished. Oh, yes, Kate Jackson was canned from "Charlie's Angels" and her replacement is Shelley Hack, the blonde from all those "Charlie" perfume commercials. Now if Jaclyn Smith ever decides to leave, there'll be a whole new triumvirate.

CBS, the middle network in the ratings war, tried just about anything and everything this season. Very little worked. It tried hip nuns and bewildered priests running a community center for underprivileged youths ("In the Beginning") and failed; sexy stewardesses in "Flying High" failed; dewy-eyed newlyweds in "Married: The First Year" failed; liberated unwed mothers in "Miss Winslow and Son" failed; a TV incarnation of the pop magazine *People* failed; amiable street gangs in "Flatbush" failed; sexy investigative reporters known as "The American Girls" failed; "The New Adventures of Wonder Woman" and "Spider-Man" failed; a junior Walter Mitty in "Billy" failed; and two, count 'em, two, Mary Tyler Moore variety outings: failed and failed. Mary was so keen to have a shot at being Carol Burnett and Julie Andrews rolled into one that CBS was willing to let her have her way. The first outing, "The Mary Tyler Moore Hour," employed a cast of regulars who assisted Mary in sketches and production numbers, but it added up to little, and after a few weeks the show left the air for a revamping. Sometime later, "Mary" emerged, with a fresh look: guest stars, and a gimmick used successfully by Jack Benny for many years, putting on a show about putting on a show . . . but it was only a slight improvement, and by the spring of 1979, Mary took off her dancing shoes for good (or so she says).

CBS's consistently high ratings winner was "60 Minutes," the one program in the season's Top Ten which wasn't a situation comedy. In addition to the popular "60 Minutes," CBS presented established hits including "All in the Family," "One Day at a Time," "M*A*S*H," "Alice," "Lou Grant," "Barnaby Jones," "Dallas," "Hawaii Five-0," and "The Incredible Hulk." A new series which surprisingly clicked with audiences was "The Dukes of Hazzard," reminiscent of the "Green Acres" or "Beverly Hillbillys" brand of country hokum. Two handsome lads played the Hazzard boys, who jus' luv wimmen an' fast cars. "WKRP in Cincinnati," a funny show about a band of misfits who run a radio station, started off big, faltered, and was dropped, but then returned later in the season. "Kaz," which benefited from the charm and talent of Ron Leibman in the title role, jumped all over the schedule, seemingly managed to avoid cancellation, but was finally dumped. "Stockard Channing in Just Friends" was a midseason entry that captured some attention, thanks largely to its star. CBS is to be commended for sticking with "The Paper Chase," a beautifully produced and well-acted series about academic life at a leading law school. The show just never got off the ground, but CBS gave it every conceivable chance . . . it lasted the whole season, which is a victory any way you look at it.

"Rhoda" ran its course and departed, and "The Waltons" seemed to be on its last legs (though it's been renewed for next season, anyway). Two sports-themed shows debuted in midseason: "The White Shadow," about the coach of a ghetto high school basketball team; and "The Bad News Bears," about the grizzled coach of a suburban Little League baseball team. While "The White Shadow" was decidedly the better of the two, both were scheduled to return to CBS next season. CBS managed to hold on to second place, and they certainly tried harder.

NBC, which some wags say now stands for "Nothing but Clinkers," had a dismal season, staying in the cellar most of the year and coming up with one flop after another. The big news at the start of the season was Fred Silverman's move from head of programming at ABC to the presidency of NBC. All of NBC's hopes were pinned on Silverman, but his strategy did little to help the network hang on during its slide to the bottom of the ratings. Granted, many of the programs were scheduled prior to Silverman's arrival at NBC, but his own choices later on weren't any more successful.

His first act as NBC's new programmer was to cancel "Coast to Coast," another stewardess opus, and replace it with "Lifeline," a cinema-verité-style documentary series which followed the on-and-off-duty experiences of a different physician each week. The show was innovative in content and well produced, but the viewing public was used to Robert Young as "Marcus Welby, M.D.," and they didn't want to tune in week after week to the real thing. Another of Silverman's choices, which fared a bit better, was "Diff'rent Strokes," about two black kids placed in the posh home of a Park Avenue millionaire, played with bewildered charm by Conrad Bain. The star of this predictable sitcom was pint-sized Gary Coleman, who displayed the comedic timing and delivery of a cross between Jack Benny and Pearl Bailey. "Hello, Larry" was McLean Stevenson's second series in one season (remember "In the Beginning"?), which seemed to finally catch on and will return next season. Another new show that didn't do too badly was "Mrs. Columbo," with former soap-opera star Kate Mulgrew in the title role as the heretofore unseen but all-knowing wife of Peter Falk's slouching sleuth. A final footnote to the NBC madness was the re-run of *Aspen,* a miniseries fraught with sexually disturbed characters. For its repeat, NBC found fit to retitle the affair (in hopes of attracting a better audience than on the first go-round), and it went on the air as *The Innocent and the Damned.*

On the hit side were "Little House on the Prairie" (NBC's best ratings scorer); "The Rockford Files," still coasting on James Garner's presence; "Quincy," staring Jack Klugman as an inquisitive medical examiner; "CHiPs," with handsome Erik Estrada on a motorcycle for the teenaged girls; and "The Wonderful World of Disney," which just rolls along season after season.

Now for the list of "clinkers," beginning with "Silverman's folly," more commonly known as "Supertrain." This multimillion-dollar series was expected to become a big hit, but it got thoroughly derailed. It tried for the same audience that flocks to "The Love Boat" each week, but the lure of train travel couldn't compare with the romance of an

*"This is my husband, Taylor. His brain has turned to mush from too much television."*
(Drawing by Weber; © 1978 The New Yorker Magazine, Inc.)

ocean cruise. Then there was "Brothers and Sisters," another dim-witted and unfunny imitation of *Animal House.* "Cliffhangers" was made up of three separate serial-like shows with cliffhanging finales each week . . . evidently no one cared enough to tune in again to find out what happened to Susan Anton or Count Dracula. "Sword of Justice" was a pretentious title for another adventure yarn about a guy bent on revenge. "Turnabout," based on Thorne Smith's tale of a husband and wife wishing each were the other, then awakening one morning to find that they were, displayed some promise and wit, but never lasted long enough to find out if the far-out premise might have worked. "W.E.B." was intended to blow the lid off the behind-the-scenes drama of TV networks, as in the feature film *Network,* but it was an obvious phony from the start and died a merciful death after three weeks. The real bottom-of-the-barrel scrapings were "Sweepstakes," a feeble reworking of the old "Millionaire" gimmick; and "Whodunnit," a combination mystery-game show with Ed McMahon as host. And then there were Joe Namath in "The Waverly Wonders" and "Dick Clark's Live Wednesday," of which the less said the better.

In spite of the hysteria which has marked the scheduling, unscheduling, and rescheduling of many network programs in their mania for ratings, it is amazing, not to say surprising, that each network managed to offer, if only occasionally, miniseries, made-for-TV films, specials, and documentaries of quality and distinction. ABC's contributions were considerable, with the widely anticipated *Roots: The Next Generation* leading the way. *Roots II,* as it was known, came close to duplicating the phenomenal success of last season's miniseries, and was perhaps closer to home for the contemporary audience, portraying the racial problems of the black soldier, the black job-seeker, and the black writer. It also made stars of Dorian Harewood, in the role of Simon Haley (Alex's father), and of Stan Shaw, who played Alex's grandfather.

Another ABC miniseries, *IKE*, brought General Dwight D. Eisenhower, the sensitive but indomitable leader of the Allied forces in Europe during the Second World War, vividly to life in the performance of Robert Duvall, aided by Lee Remick who charmingly portrayed Kay Summersby, his driver, secretary, and aide.

Among the made-for-TV films of merit seen on ABC were *The Jericho Mile*, in which Peter Strauss gave an outstanding performance as a convicted murderer serving a life sentence who developed into an Olympic-class runner in prison; *A Question of Love*, dealt with the fight of a woman to retain custody of her child after it was revealed that she was living with another woman in a romantic relationship, beautifully underplayed by two fine actresses, Gena Rowlands and Jane Alexander; *The Child Stealer*, presented another strong contemporary theme concerning divorced parents kidnapping their own children from their former spouses; *The Cracker Factory*, in which Natalie Wood gave a brutally honest portrayal of a young woman whose violent behavior sent her at regular intervals to a sanitarium; and the outstanding *Friendly Fire*, starring Carol Burnett and Ned Beatty in a true story of the ordeal of the parents of a young soldier killed in Vietnam by our own troops.

ABC's award-winning series of "Afterschool Specials" for younger viewers continued a tradition of excellence with many of its presentations. *One of a Kind*, for example, told a story of child abuse by an overworked single mother that was particularly effective. And the "ABC News Close-Up" series of documentaries was frequently distinguished . . . its report titled "Asbestos: The Way to Dusty Death" is a memorable case history of an industrial killer abounding in our environment, filled with a history of warning signals that both government and industry had ignored for years. Another "Close-Up," "Youth Terror: The View from Behind the Gun" provides startling revelations through a series of talks with, and observations of, American teenagers growing up in the gang's battlegrounds on the streets of the South Bronx and Brooklyn.

CBS offered a miniseries based on John Dean's book about his experience as one of the Watergate cover-up conspirators. *Blind Ambition*, starring Martin Sheen and Rip Torn, turned out to be a riveting drama despite the familiarity of the material, hindered only by too many repetitive scenes of a personal nature between John and Maureen. Among the made-for-TV films, CBS's version of Emlyn Williams's stage and screen success, *The Corn Is Green*, was a triumph for the wonderful Katharine Hepburn, who dominated the scene amid the visual grandeur of location filming in Wales under the impeccable direction of George Cukor. Another fine entry in this category was a new production of Victor Hugo's classic *Les Miserables*, capturing the grimness, the relentlessness, and finally the irony of the confrontations between its hero, portrayed by Richard Jordan, and his nemesis, played by Anthony Perkins.

Other fine made-for-TV films were *Lovey, a Circle of Children,
Part 2,* a moving study of severely emotionally disturbed children,
made memorable by the superb performance of Jane Alexander as their
teacher; and *First You Cry,* in which Mary Tyler Moore proved her
talent with a sensitive dramatic performance as TV newswoman Betty
Rollin, dealing with the trauma of undergoing a radical mastectomy,
and her spirited recovery.

Among the documentaries, "CBS Reports" about the tragedy of
Southeast Asia's "Boat People," the dangers of "The Politics of Abortion," and the little-known story of guerrilla forces in "The Battle for
South Africa" were quite well handled, and "Anyplace but Here" was
an exceptional report on the difficulty of finding a home for the mentally retarded; the last three mentioned were covered by Bill Moyers,
reporting more memorably than in any of his "Bill Moyers' Journal"
programs on PBS this season.

NBC made varied attempts at presenting miniseries of quality,
with uneven but worthy results. Among the finest were *Backstairs at the
White House,* adapted from Lillian Rogers Parks's autobiography de-
tailing several generations of service to the nation's first families. It
presented an engaging picture of the black house staff, and occasionally
memorable portraits of presidents or first ladies, held together by the
excellent performance of Olivia Cole, who was a star of last season's
*Roots.* Also notable was *A Woman Called Moses,* in which Cicely Tyson portrayed Harriet Tubman, an ex-slave who became the driving
force behind the Underground Railroad which carried many blacks to
freedom. *From Here to Eternity,* based on the novel by James Jones,
offered earthy, oversexed portrayals hardly reminiscent of the characters portrayed in the fine Burt Lancaster-Deborah Kerr film, but the
performances of William Devane and Natalie Wood were dramatically
viable just the same. James T. Farrell's depression-era classic *Studs
Lonigan* tended to be dangerously repetitious in its development of
Studs's mistaken, lonely road to ruin, but managed at last to arouse
one's sympathy through the embattled, flailing performance of Harry
Hamlin as Studs. And the Hallmark Hall of Fame production of Arthur
Miller's *Fame,* a mildly entertaining and ultimately intriguing tale
about the effect of sudden success upon a writer, really came to life with
the arrival on the scene of Jose Ferrer playing an erratic Italian film
director.

NBC presented a great many made-for-TV films, filling the gaps
left by the decimation of its ranks of prime-time series. They included
one of the loveliest dramas of the television season, *Summer of My
German Soldier,* luminously acted by Kristy McNichol and Bruce Davison, which told a tender, yet terrifying story of the loving relationship
between a teenaged Jewish girl and an escaped anti-Nazi German prisoner of war stationed in her bitterly prejudiced small Southern town.

We note in passing the rather curious presentation by NBC of a
theatrical film titled *Two-Minute Warning,* an undistinguished caper
flick concerning a sniper with a vantage point at a crowded pro-football
game, who opens up on the packed spectators before being killed himself. NBC decided there was too much violence and profanity and edited down the original 115 minutes by half an hour, leaving 85 minutes

which, including commercials, would have been ample by itself. But NO-o-o-o-o-o-o! the powers that be decided to film a new subplot and attach it to the original footage. In the revised version, the sniper is now part of a gang of art thieves, who send him on his dastardly mission to create a diversion from their big heist. The original was no gem, but who needed this "improvement"? The film's director, Larry Peerce, was reportedly furious with NBC for its tampering.

In other programming, NBC's monthly "Special Treat" for youngsters was a fine series with a few outstanding productions: Geraldine Fitzgerald starred in *Rodeo Red and the Runaway,* creating a vigorous picture of a weathered farm woman, warm enough to offer a runaway girl a haven, but wise enough to put her on notice.

NBC's "Weekend" news-magazine series, a success as a once-a-month substitute for "Saturday Night Live" was actually buried once it became a weekly Sunday night feature at 10:00 P.M. (EST). In an occasional documentary special NBC offered a few programs of note, particularly Edwin Newman's report on "Reading, Writing, and Reefer," an eye-opening evaluation of teaching practices in our schools and the amount of misleading information about marijuana current among school-age kids; and a fine study of modern-day China with the well-informed reportage of NBC correspondent Jack Reynolds.

The Public Broadcasting Service has the honor of being dominated by quality programs, whether they hail from Britain or are home-grown products of production units based in local PBS affiliates all over the United States. Leading the way are the "Masterpiece Theatre" productions for the 1978-79 season. *Poldark II,* that flamboyant period adventure story about the trials and tribulations of a handsome, honest man of means bedeviled by circumstances, made of Sunday nights a Robin Ellis festival. It was followed by Thomas Hardy's *The Mayor of Casterbridge,* a doleful story of a morally guilty man, brilliantly portrayed by Alan Bates. *The Duchess of Duke Street* followed with a bang, in a tale about an extraordinary young cockney woman, based upon the true story of Rosa Lewis, who ran and ruled a unique hotel in a posh section of London catering to a very distinguished, and frequently eccentric, clientele. Gemma Jones was heroic as the lady in question. A few slightly sordid but rare tales of passion by British short-story masters H.E. Bates and A.E. Coppard followed under the omnibus title "Country Matters," until the arrival of *Lillie,* in the exquisite person of Francesca Annis, regaled us with details of the life of a "professional beauty" during the Victorian and Edwardian eras, displaying a remarkable range of poise, spirit, and unfailing elegance.

"Great Performances" always promised a special evening, and it is a delight to note that the majority of these shows are domestic productions of the highest calibre. Some were presented "Live from Lincoln Center," such as the operas *Tosca, Otello, The Bartered Bride,* and *Luisa Miller,* and the historic dual recital by reigning operatic superstars Luciano Pavarotti and Joan Sutherland. At other times, "Great Performances" presented "Dance In America," a remarkable series utilizing television's unique capabilities to open our eyes to the magic of the art of dance. These programs included performances choreographed by George Balanchine, featuring the New York City Ballet company, The American Ballet Theatre, The Eliot Feld Dance Company, and a particularly impressive performance of Martha Graham's *Clytemnestra*.

Drama was not neglected, as "Great Performances" presented a five-part production of Eugene O'Neill's *Mourning Becomes Electra*, filled with stark, unforgettable performances by Joan Hackett, Roberta Maxwell, and Bruce Davison.

Not as brilliant, yet memorable, in a slightly flawed production, were Meg Foster, John Heard, and Kevin Conway starring in a multipart dramatization of Nathaniel Hawthorne's *The Scarlet Letter*.

In one of television's most monumental undertakings, Public Broadcasting presented the first season of the BBC/Time-Life coproduction of "The Shakespeare Plays," an enormously ambitious six-year project during which every one of the Bard's 37 plays will be broadcast. Uneven though the initial half-dozen productions proved to be, each had some quality, and Derek Jacobi's "Richard II" was outstanding.

Documentaries and special programs on a variety of subjects frequently met the highest standards of television excellence, covering a variety of subjects from "The Faces of Communism" and "Black's Brittania" to "The Priceless Treasures of Dresden" and Boston's "Southie." Public Broadcasting continues to demonstrate that you don't have to be the biggest to be the best.

This summary of highlights of prime-time viewing during the 1978-79 season would not be complete without mention of the distinguished syndicated series *Edward the King*, magnificently cast in every role, but dominated by what would seem to be the definitive portrayal of Edward VII by Timothy West. The critical acclaim for this production was such that a number of network affiliates preempted their regularly scheduled programming to present this outstanding production.

# PRIME TIME SERIES

---

**ACADEMY LEADERS** (PBS)

Movie buffs and film fans in general savored this new series, which showcased cinematic shorts of varying lengths that have either won Oscars or been nominated, but were generally neglected by TV. Norman Corwin, celebrated radio, TV, and film writer, hosted, setting the tone for the offbeat film shorts which ran the gamut from arty to silly to serious.

HOST: Norman Corwin   EXECUTIVE PRODUCER: Pierre Sauvage   PRODUCER: Mark Waxman   DIRECTOR: Jerry Hughes   PRODUCTION COMPANY: KCET (Los Angeles)

**ALICE** (CBS)
*Sunday 9:30-10:00 P.M.*

Two ladies on the series—Linda Lavin and Polly Holliday—still make this show tick with their endearingly breezy ways as offbeat waitresses in Mel's Diner. Third season for this high-rated CBS entry.

STARS: Linda Lavin, Vic Tayback, Polly Holliday, Beth Howland
PRODUCERS: Madelyn Davis, Bob Carroll, Jr.   CREATED BY: Robert Getchell   EXECUTIVE STORY EDITOR: Tom Whedon   DIRECTOR: Bill Asher   PRODUCTION COMPANY: Warner Bros. Television

**ALL IN THE FAMILY**
(CBS)
*Sunday 9:00-9:30 P.M.*

Gloria and Mike left the series, but the ninth season bounced along without a hitch. In fact, Archie and Edith were never better in a group of well-defined episodes. Nine-year-old Stephanie, played by Danielle Brisebois, was added to the cast, but she didn't add anything. The two hundredth episode prompted a special which offered excerpts of some of the best scenes from one of TV's all-time great series.

Show debuted on January 12, 1971.

STARS: Carroll O'Connor, Jean Stapleton    EXECUTIVE PRODUCER: Mort Lachman    PRODUCER: Milt Josefsberg    DIRECTOR: Paul Bogart    WRITERS: Various    PRODUCTION COMPANY: Tandem Productions

**THE AMAZING SPIDER-MAN** (CBS)
*Various times*

Limited series which popped up sporadically through the season with Nicholas Hammond as press photographer Peter Parker, alias the Spider-Man. A show only the younger kiddies enjoyed.

STAR: Nicholas Hammond    EXECUTIVE PRODUCERS: Charles Fries, Dan Goodman    PRODUCERS: Ron Satlof, Bob Janes    DIRECTORS: Various    PRODUCTION COMPANY: Charles Fries Production, in association with Dan Goodman Productions

**THE AMERICAN GIRLS** (CBS)
*Saturday 9:00-10:00 P.M.*

A ridiculous, offensive opus about two female reporters covering the U.S.A. in a fancy van for a TV magazine show ("60 Minutes" should sue). Priscilla Barnes was the blonde, Debra Clinger was the brunette. Their hairdresser had all the talent.

STARS: Priscilla Barnes, Debra Clinger, David Spielberg    PRODUCER: Simon Muntner    DIRECTORS: Various    WRITERS: Various    PRODUCTION COMPANY: Bennett/Katleman Productions, Inc., in association with Columbia Pictures Television

**ANGIE** (ABC)
*Thursday 8:30-9:00 P.M.*

This old yarn about people from opposite sides of the track who meet, fall in love, and get married is revamped in this comedy which relies heavily on its star, Donna Pescow, and Doris Roberts, as her mother. It became a TV hit soon after its debut in February 1979.

STARS: Donna Pescow, Robert Hays, Doris Roberts   PRODUCERS: Alan
Eisenstock, Larry Mintz, Bruce Johnson   CREATED BY: Garry K. Marshall,
Dale McRaven   DIRECTORS: Various   WRITERS: Various   PRODUCTION
COMPANY: Miller-Milkis Productions, Inc. and Henderson Production
Company, Inc. in association with Paramount Television

The Waltons faced the Depression of the thirties with a stiff upper lip, but the
Hollyhocks breezed through the era with an air of controlled lunacy. It had
possibilities but was whisked off the air in a couple of weeks, after it debuted
in September 1978.

**APPLE PIE** (ABC)
*Saturday 8:30-9:00* P.M.

STARS: Rue McClanahan, Dabney Coleman, Jack Gilford   PRODUCER/
WRITER: Charlie Hauck   CREATED BY: Norman Lear, Charlie Hauck
DIRECTOR: Peter Bonerz   PRODUCTION COMPANY: T.A.T. Communications
Company

Fourth lively season for this entertaining Texas-produced musical series, fea-
turing the best artists in progressive country music, such as Tom T. Hall,
Lightnin' Hopkins, Leon Redbone, Tom Waits, Taj Mahal, and Norton
Buffalo.

**AUSTIN CITY LIMITS**
(PBS)

STARS: Various   PRODUCERS: Terry Lickona, Delia Gravel   DIRECTOR: Clark
Santee   PRODUCTION COMPANY: KLRN-TV (Austin)

The popular movie was turned into a midseason TV series starring Jack Warden as the cantankerous Little League coach, the role created by Walter Matthau. The comedy seemed forced and Warden, usually a fine actor, can't compare with Matthau.

**THE BAD NEWS
BEARS** (CBS)
*Saturday 8:00-8:30* P.M.

STARS: Jack Warden, Catherine Hicks, Phillip R. Allen   EXECUTIVE
PRODUCERS: Arthur Silver, Bob Brunner   PRODUCERS: John Boni, Norman
Stiles, Jeffrey Ganz   DIRECTOR: Bruce Bilson   WRITERS: Arthur Silver, Bob
Brunner   PRODUCTION COMPANY: Huk, Inc. and Frog Productions, Inc., in
association with Paramount Television

LEFT: *Donna Pescow
(center) starred as
"Angie," a mid-season
winner featuring (clock-
wise from left) Debralee
Scott, Doris Roberts, Robert Hays, Sharon Spel-
man, Diane Robin, and
Tammy Lauren.*

RIGHT: *The late Jack Soo
as Detective Nick Yemana
offers oriental wisdom to
star Hal Linden in
"Barney Miller."*

**BARNABY JONES** (CBS)
*Thursday*
*10:00-11:00* P.M.

Seventh season for Buddy Ebsen's sleuth Barnaby Jones—a series that just goes on forever and ever. Maybe someday a TV historian or perhaps a cultural anthropologist will explain why?

STARS: Buddy Ebsen, Lee Meriwether, Mark Shera   EXECUTIVE PRODUCER: Philip Saltzman   PRODUCER: Robert Sherman   DIRECTOR: Walter Grauman WRITERS: Various   PRODUCTION COMPANY: Quinn-Martin Productions

**BARNEY MILLER** (ABC)
*Thursday 9:00-9:30* P.M.

Fifth season and going strong. Hal Linden's Barney Miller and his 12th Precinct crew face an array of weirdos for a weekly festival of funny one-liners. Jack Soo, who played Nick Yemana, passed away during the year, and there was a special show paying tribute to the veteran actor.

STARS: Hal Linden, Max Gail, Ron Glass, Jack Soo   EXECUTIVE PRODUCER: Danny Arnold   PRODUCERS: Tony Sheehan, Rhinehold Weege   DIRECTOR: Noam Pitlik   WRITERS: Various   PRODUCTION COMPANY: Four D Productions

**BILL MOYERS'**
**JOURNAL** (PBS)

Moyers is, arguably, American television's most thoughtful and articulate broadcast journalist. He returned to public television after a two-year stint at CBS with a full season of his "Journals," ranging in scope from the remarkably human study of two New York City social workers, who opted for the harsh life of farming in North Dakota ("Harvest"), to a powerful and disturbing examination of women prisoners in Dade County Women's Detention Center in Miami, Florida ("Women Inside"), plus provocative interviews with presidential hopeful California Governor Jerry Brown; historian Henry Steele Commager on Tocqueville; and the fascinating philosopher Mortimer Adler, among others. Some of the films were made by independent filmmakers, a pattern commercial television would be well advised to adopt.

HOST: Bill Moyers   EXECUTIVE EDITOR: Bill Moyers   PRODUCTION COMPANY: WNET (New York)

**BILLY** (CBS)
*Monday 8:00-8:30* P.M.

Evidently TV fans weren't ready for a 19-year-old Walter Mitty. Clumsily derived from the British movie hit, *Billy Liar,* this show, transferred to an American setting, leaves the eccentricity of the characters dangling in midair. Overly eager Steve Guttenberg as Billy didn't help. The writing and acting were uniformly terrible.

LEFT: *William Windom (left) watches Jon Cutler demonstrate on Mary Crosby the cave-man approach to love and marriage in an episode of "Brothers and Sisters."*

RIGHT: *Kate Jackson, Jaclyn Smith, and Cheryl Ladd were one of television's prettiest and best-known trios in "Charlie's Angels."*

STAR: Steve Guttenberg  PRODUCER: John Rich  DIRECTOR: John Rich
WRITERS: Dick Clement, Ian La Frenais  PRODUCTION COMPANY: John Rich
Productions, in association with Twentieth Century-Fox Television

A silly premise about a free-wheeling Southern trucker and his pal, a chimp called Bear, pulled big ratings as a TV film, so NBC scheduled it for a run. Handsome, easy-going Greg Evigan as the footloose BJ appeals to the teenage girls, and the action is fast-paced, if mindless.

**BJ AND THE BEAR** (NBC)
*Saturday 9:00-10:00 P.M.*

STARS: Greg Evigan and *Sam*  EXECUTIVE PRODUCERS: Glen A. Larson, Michael Sloan  DIRECTORS: Various  WRITERS: Various  PRODUCTION COMPANY: Glen Larson Productions in association with Universal Studios

Slapdash midseason replacement comedy on fraternity-house hijinks starring Lemmon's boy, Chris, and Bing Crosby's daughter, Mary, among others. It's noisy and frantic as the kids bungle about looking for character and direction.

**BROTHERS AND SISTERS** (NBC)
*Friday 8:30-9:00 P.M.*

STARS: Chris Lemmon, Jon Cutler, Randy Brooks, Mary Crosby  EXECUTIVE PRODUCERS: Bob Brunner, Arthur Silver  PRODUCERS: Nick Abdo, Jerry Mayer  DIRECTORS: Various  WRITERS: Various

The Clinton Corners Police Department chalked up its last season with Chief Mobey (Victor French) running into more than a usual number of mishaps.

**CARTER COUNTRY** (ABC)
*Various times*

STARS: Victor French, Kene Holliday, Richard Paul, Guich Koock  EXECUTIVE PRODUCERS: Austin and Irma Kalish  PRODUCERS: Douglas Arango, Phillip Doran  DIRECTORS: Various  WRITERS: Various  PRODUCTION COMPANY: TOY Productions

The third season of this popular "T&A" show introduced Cheryl Ladd, saw Farrah Fawcett-Majors return for a few episodes, and ended up with Kate Jackson being fired. By the way, the trio of beauties managed to overcome another year of trite scripts.

**CHARLIE'S ANGELS** (ABC)
*Wednesday 9:00-10:00 P.M.*

STARS: Kate Jackson, Jaclyn Smith, Cheryl Ladd, David Doyle  EXECUTIVE PRODUCERS: Aaron Spelling, Leonard Goldberg  PRODUCERS: Edward J. Lakso, Ronald Austin, James Buchanan  DIRECTORS: Various  WRITERS: Various  PRODUCTION COMPANY: Spelling/Goldberg Productions

Erik Estrada and Larry Wilcox were back for their second season, zipping from one adventure to the next as police on their shiny motorcycles along California's freeways. As usual, there were plenty of subplots and fast-paced action. However, there was a minimum of violence here, which was a plus.

**CHiPs** (NBC)
*Saturday 8:00-9:00 P.M.*

STARS: Larry Wilcox, Erik Estrada  PRODUCER: Cy Chermak  CREATED BY: Rick Rosner  WRITERS: William D. Gordon, James Doherty  PRODUCTION COMPANY: MGM-TV in association with NBC-TV

NBC gambled with an old chestnut—movie-type serials—and all three of them bombed. A blonde photographer (Susan Anton); an 1880s lawman who has dropped into an underground futuristic kingdom; and Dracula posing as a college professor were the featured acts.

**CLIFFHANGERS** (NBC)
*Tuesday 8:00-9:00 P.M.*

STARS: Susan Anton, Ray Walston, Geoffrey Scott, Michael Nouri  EXECUTIVE PRODUCER: Kenneth Johnson  PRODUCERS: Richard Milton, Paul

Samuelson, Bill Sandefur   DIRECTORS: Various   WRITERS: Various   PRODUCTION COMPANY: Universal Television, in association with NBC Entertainment

**CONGRESSIONAL OUTLOOK** (PBS)

Pending Congressional issues were the focus of this informative series produced in cooperation with Congressional Quarterly, the Washington-based news and research service.

HOST: Patrick Tyler   PRODUCERS: Bob Gilbert, Gene Walz   PRODUCTION COMPANY: WCET (Cincinnati) in cooperation with Congressional Quarterly

**THE COUSTEAU ODYSSEY** (PBS)

Captain Jacques Cousteau and his son Philippe embarked on a series of four specials, which lacked the excitement of previous seasons, particularly the ponderous premiere show, "Blind Prophets of Easter Island," which chronicled their journey to the "loneliest" island in the Pacific.

STAR: Jacques Cousteau   EXECUTIVE PRODUCERS: Jacques Cousteau, Philippe Cousteau   PRODUCTION COMPANY: The Cousteau Society in association with KCET (Los Angeles)

**DALLAS** (CBS)
*Saturday 10:00-11:00 P.M.*

Prime-time soap opera which found an audience this season after a false start last year. The Ewing family has enough problems collectively to supply the plots for a dozen daytime dramas. Somehow it works.

STARS: Barbara Bel Geddes, Jim Davis, Patrick Duffy, Larry Hagman, Victoria Principal, Linda Gray, Charlene Tilton   EXECUTIVE PRODUCERS: Lee Rich, Philip Capice   PRODUCER: Leonard Katzman   DIRECTORS: Various WRITERS: Various   PRODUCTION COMPANY: Lorimar Productions, Inc.

**DAVID CASSIDY, MAN UNDERCOVER** (NBC)
*Thursday 10:00-11:00 P.M.*

Prompted by the high ratings of a two-hour movie, NBC cast the former singing TV idol as the baby-faced undercover cop. Cassidy looked uncomfortable, shorn of his long locks and songs. It evidently didn't matter to his former fans, who have also grown up.

STAR: David Cassidy   EXECUTIVE PRODUCER: David Gerber   PRODUCERS: Mel Swope, Mark Rodgers   DIRECTORS: Various   WRITERS: Various PRODUCTION COMPANY: Columbia Pictures Television in association with NBC-TV

Brenda Vaccaro was better than her material in this cop show inspired by a French film by director Philipe DeBroca. Brenda plays a police detective sergeant and her sense of style is used to advantage here, but the scripts let her down most of the time.

STAR: Brenda Vaccaro    PRODUCERS: Dean Hargrove, Roland Kibbee
DIRECTOR: Dean Hargrove    WRITERS: Roland Kibbee, Dean Hargrove
PRODUCTION COMPANY: Kibbee/Hargrove Productions in association with Viacom, Inc.

**DEAR DETECTIVE**
(CBS)
*Wednesday*
*9:00-10:00 P.M.*

The laughs hadn't died down from the movie hit, *National Lampoon's Animal House,* when TV rushed this blurred carbon copy to the home screen. Fans expecting another *Animal House* were sorely disappointed. The humor was pedestrian and the antics exaggerated. The executive producers for this were also responsible for developing *Animal House.*

STARS: John Vernon, Stephen Furst, Bruce McGill, James Widdoes, Josh Mostel    EXECUTIVE PRODUCERS: Matty Simmons, Ivan Reitman
PRODUCER: Edward J. Montagne    DIRECTOR: Alan Myerson
WRITERS: Various    PRODUCTION COMPANY: Matty Simmons-Ivan Reitman in association with Universal Television

**DELTA HOUSE** (ABC)
*Saturday 8:00-8:30 P.M.*

LEFT: *Linda Gray, Larry Hagman, and Jim Davis are members of the troubled Ewing clan in the series "Dallas."*

RIGHT: *The fraternity brothers of "Delta House" were played by (clockwise from lower left) Jamie Widdoes, Bruce McGill, Josh Mostel, Peter Fox, Stephen Furst, and Richard Seer.*

Dick's show was like the Ed Sullivan Show resurrected though less skillfully produced. Headliners stepped into the spotlight for their turns, and Dick reminded his audience that each guest was his close, personal friend. The gimmick was a live show, but this particular format has been dead for some time.

STAR: Dick Clark    EXECUTIVE PRODUCER: Dick Clark    PRODUCER: Bill Lee
DIRECTOR: John Moffitt    PRODUCTION COMPANY: Dick Clark Productions for NBC-TV

**DICK CLARK'S LIVE WEDNESDAY** (NBC)
*Wednesday 8:00-9:00 P.M.*

NBC's strongest new show this season. Two black kids from Harlem move into a high-living apartment house on Park Avenue following the death-bed wish of their new white guardian's housekeeper, who happened to be their mother. The kids are cute—especially Gary Coleman, who's the whole show as the mischievous Arnold.

**DIFF'RENT STROKES** (NBC)
*Friday 8:00-8:30 P.M.*

LEFT: *Dick Clark tried to revive Ed Sullivan-style variety programming on "Dick Clark's Live Wednesday."*

CENTER: *Conrad Bain plays it straight with mini-sized superstar Gary Coleman on one of NBC's most popular new shows, "Diff'rent Strokes."*

RIGHT: *Donny and Marie Osmond were stars of the musical variety series "Donny & Marie."*

STARS: Conrad Bain, Gary Coleman, Todd Bridges   EXECUTIVE PRODUCER: Budd Grossman   PRODUCERS: Howard Leeds, Herbert Kenwith   DIRECTOR: Herbert Kenwith   WRITER: Ben Starr   PRODUCTION COMPANY: Tandem Productions, Inc., in association with NBC Entertainment

**DONNY & MARIE**
(ABC)
*Friday 8:00-9:00 P.M.*

The glitter and glow was still there as the famous singin' and struttin' siblings began their third season, but the magic was gone and they flopped. They came back with the rest of the clan for "The Osmond Family Hour" later, but there wasn't any strength in numbers.

STARS: Donny and Marie Osmond   EXECUTIVE PRODUCERS: The Osmond Brothers   PRODUCER: Art Fisher   DIRECTOR: Art Fisher   WRITER: Phil Hahn   PRODUCTION COMPANY: Osmond Productions

**THE DUKE** (NBC)
*Friday 10:00-11:00 P.M.*

After his sturdy performance as Pasquinal in *Centennial* this season, Robert Conrad turned his attention to the starring role of a private eye in this spring replacement series. Although the character was tailor-made for Conrad, playing a former prize fighter turned private eye, the ratings were disappointing and the series went down for the count.

STARS: Robert Conrad, Larry Manetti, Red West   EXECUTIVE PRODUCER: Stephen J. Cannell   PRODUCERS: Alex Beaton, Don Carlos Dunaway   DIRECTOR: Larry Doheny   WRITER: Stephen J. Cannell

**THE DUKES OF HAZZARD** (CBS)
*Friday 9:00-10:00 P.M.*

Mindless rural comedy for the young'uns from the network that gave you "The Beverly Hillbillies" and "Green Acres." The Duke brothers are fun-loving country boys, happiest behind the wheel of a car. Screeching car chases seem to take up half the hour.

STARS: Tom Wopat, John Schneider, Catherine Bach, Denver Pyle, James Best   EXECUTIVE PRODUCERS: Paul R. Picard, Philip Mandelker   PRODUCERS: Gy Waldron, Bill Kelley   CREATED BY: Gy Waldron   DIRECTOR: Rod Amateau   WRITER: Gy Waldron   PRODUCTION COMPANY: Paul R. Picard Productions and Piggy Productions in association with Warner Bros. Television

This series dealt with the impact of national and world events on the economic well-being of the average citizen, exploring such complicated issues as inflation, tax reform, energy conservation, and others. The guests of series' host Marina v. N. Whitman express opposing views on most issues, making for an informative, lively discussion.

HOST: Marina v. N. Whitman   EXECUTIVE PRODUCER: Robert Chitester
PRODUCER: Craig Perry   PRODUCTION COMPANY: WQLN (Erie, Pennsylvania)

**ECONOMICALLY SPEAKING** (PBS)

The best thing about this series was its star, Vincent Baggetta, an engaging New York actor, who played the mystery-solver Capra, a character out of the Columbo mold.

STAR: Vincent Baggetta   EXECUTIVE PRODUCER: Peter S. Fischer
PRODUCER: James McAdams   DIRECTORS: Various   WRITERS: Various
PRODUCTION COMPANY: Universal Studios for NBC-TV

**THE EDDIE CAPRA MYSTERIES** (NBC)
*Sunday 10:00-11:00 P.M.*

The Bradford family was back for season three, all hale and hardy. However, the stories focused on little Nicholas to the point of tedium, but it still was well done.

STARS: Dick Van Patten, Betty Buckley, Grant Goodeve   EXECUTIVE PRODUCERS: Lee Rich, Philip Capice   PRODUCERS: Gary Adelson, Greg Strangis   DIRECTORS: Various   WRITERS: Various   PRODUCTION COMPANY: Lorimar Productions, Inc.

**EIGHT IS ENOUGH** (ABC)
*Wednesday 8:00-9:00 P.M.*

This durable and amiable summer series began five seasons ago under the baton of Boston Pops conductor Arthur Fiedler and enjoyed another entertaining run, with guest stars running the gamut from violin virtuoso Itzhak Perlman to dancing genius Ben Vereen, with pop singer Tony Bennett and soprano Clamma Dale in between.

STAR: Arthur Fiedler, conductor   PRODUCER: William N. Cosel   DIRECTORS: David Atwood, Russell Fortier, Richard Heller, William N. Cosel
ORCHESTRAL CAMERA TREATMENT: Jordan M. Whitelaw   PRODUCTION COMPANY: WGBH (Boston) and the Boston Symphony Orchestra

**EVENING AT POPS** (PBS)

LEFT: *Anne Francis and Robert Loggia guest-starred, with Vincent Baggetta in the title role, on "The Eddie Capra Mysteries."*

RIGHT: *One of television's most popular families are The Bradfords, on "Eight Is Enough." Dick Van Patten and Betty Buckley (center) starred with (clockwise from top center) Grant Goodeve, Diane Kay, Connie Newton, Lani O'Grady, Adam Rich, Willie Aames, Laurie Walters, and Susan Richardson.*

**EVENING AT SYMPHONY** (PBS)

Season five focused on the Boston Symphony Orchestra under the spirited conducting of Seiji Ozawa, with an impressive lineup of guest soloists including violinist Itzhak Perlman, pianist Murray Perahia, and soprano Barbara Hendricks.

STAR: Seiji Ozawa, conductor and music director  PRODUCER: Jordan M. Whitelaw  DIRECTORS: David Atwood, Russell Fortier, Richard Heller  ORCHESTRAL CAMERA TREATMENT: Jordan M. Whitelaw  PRODUCTION COMPANY: WGBH (Boston) and the Boston Symphony Orchestra

*"Family" starred Gary Frank, Meredith Baxter-Birney, Kristy McNichol, Quinn Cummings, James Broderick, and Sada Thompson.*

**FAMILY** (ABC)
*Thursday*
*10:00-11:00* P.M.

Still one of TV's best series, even if the plots have become predictable. How many times can Willie fall in love, and will Kate ever get really angry? Quinn Cummings was introduced into the family as the little orphan Annie Cooper, but she added very little in the final analysis.

STARS: Sada Thompson, James Broderick, Meredith Baxter-Birney, Gary Frank, Kristy McNichol, Quinn Cummings  EXECUTIVE PRODUCERS: Aaron Spelling, Leonard Goldberg  PRODUCER: Nigel McKeand  DIRECTORS: Various  STORY CONSULTANT: Carol Evan McKeand  PRODUCTION COMPANY: Spelling/Goldberg Productions in association with Mike Nichols

**FANTASY ISLAND** (ABC)
*Saturday 10:00-11:00* P.M.

Second season for this ridiculous series, which invites the fantasies of its guests to be played out on an island terrain. To call this escapist fare is redundant.

STARS: Ricardo Montalban, Herve Villechaize  EXECUTIVE PRODUCERS: Aaron Spelling, Leonard Goldberg  PRODUCER: Arthur Rowe  DIRECTORS: Various  WRITERS: Various  PRODUCTION COMPANY: Spelling-Goldberg Productions in association with Columbia Pictures Television

**FLATBUSH** (CBS)
*Monday 8:00-8:30* P.M.

Brooklyn was the setting of this inept youth-oriented sitcom in which the Fungos—that's right, the Fungos—own the "turf." Loosely inspired by the film, *The Lords of Flatbush,* but nowhere near as entertaining.

STARS: Joseph Cali, Adrian Zmed, Vincent Bufano, Randy Stumpf, Sandy Helberg, Antony Ponzini, Helen Verbit  EXECUTIVE PRODUCERS: Lee Rich, Philip Capice, Gary Adelson  PRODUCER: Norman Powell  DIRECTOR: William Asher  WRITER: Dennis Palumbo  PRODUCTION COMPANY: Lorimar Film-Und Fernsehproduktion, GmbH

CBS's highly publicized sexy stewardess series was a real bomb. In fact, the show debuted with guess what—a bombing yarn!

STARS: Kathie Witt, Pat Klous, Connie Sellecca, Howard Platt  EXECUTIVE PRODUCER: Mark Carliner  PRODUCER/WRITERS: Marty Cohan, Bob Van Scoyk  DIRECTORS: Various  WRITERS: Various  PRODUCTION COMPANY: Mark Carliner Productions, Inc.

**FLYING HIGH** (CBS)
*Friday 10:00-11:00* P.M.

Pete, Nancy, and Randy, three 11-year-old school children, as played by Charles Aiken, Jill Whelan, and Jarrod Johnson, were much better than the scripts which defeated them. This one should have worked, but a lack of subtlety killed it off early.

STARS: Charles Aiken, Jill Whelan, Jarrod Johnson  EXECUTIVE PRODUCERS: Aaron Spelling, Douglas S. Cramer  PRODUCERS: Bo Kaprall, Bob Sand, Cindy Dunne  DIRECTORS: Various  PRODUCTION COMPANY: Aaron Spelling Productions

**FRIENDS** (ABC)
*Sunday 7:00-8:00* P.M.

This probing series made an offbeat but serious attempt to relate problems concerning many Americans—the high costs of health care; the challenge of unemployment; the regulation of drugs, to cite a few—to the activities of government agencies that can do something about them . . . for better or for worse.

HOST: Tony Batten  EXECUTIVE PRODUCER: Tony Batten  PRODUCER CORRESPONDENTS: Christopher Koch, Gregg Ramshaw  DIRECTOR: Jay Zabriskie

**F.Y.I.** (PBS)

This series began with a three-part study on the fight for food, exploring the problems and policies that make hunger and starvation a fact of life for five-hundred million people. Part Three featured a debate on all aspects of the subject, with participating panelists including Robert Bergland, U.S. Secretary of Agriculture; Eugene Whelan, Canadian Minister of Agriculture; U.S. Representative Thomas Foley; U.S. senators George McGovern and Robert Dole; and moderator Julian Bond, Georgia state senator.

EXECUTIVE PRODUCER: Alvin H. Perlmutter  PRODUCER: Martin Carr, Robert Bendick  PRODUCTION COMPANY: WQED-TV (Pittsburgh)

**GLOBAL PAPER** (PBS)

LEFT: *Ricardo Montalban and Herve Villechaize starred as modern myth-makers on "Fantasy Island."*

RIGHT: *Christopher Koch, Linda Shen, and producer Tony Batten explored the role of government agencies in our lives on the series "F.Y.I."*

**GOOD TIMES** (CBS)
*Wednesday 8:00-8:30 P.M.*

Esther Rolle returned to launch season number six, which turned out to be the finale for the series which started out with some validity, but grew into a raucous showcase for the hypercomedy antics of Jimmie Walker as J.J.

STARS: Jimmie Walker, Esther Rolle, Ja'net DuBois, Ralph Carter, BerNadette Stanis   EXECUTIVE PRODUCER: Norman Paul   PRODUCER: Sid Dorfman
DIRECTOR: Gerren Keith

**GRANDPA GOES TO WASHINGTON** (NBC)
*Wednesday 9:00-10:00 P.M.*

Compared to some of the other NBC flops, this one showed early signs of promise. Jack Albertson as a gruff old college professor wins a seat in the U.S. Senate and takes a few swipes at politicians. The knock on politicians was soft-pedaled in the subsequent shows and the series dissipated into just another sitcom.

STAR: Jack Albertson   EXECUTIVE PRODUCERS: Arthur Fellow, Terry Keegan
PRODUCER: Robert Stambler   DIRECTORS: Various   WRITER: Lane Slate
PRODUCTION COMPANY: Paramount Television

LEFT: *"Great Performances" included music, drama, and outstanding presentations of dance. Shown: Peter Martins and Suzanne Farrell performing a pas de deux from "Diamonds," "Choreography by Balanchine."*
CENTER: *Paul Gallico's "Verna: U.S.O. Girl" starred Sissy Spacek and Sally Kellerman, another presentation on "Great Performances."*
RIGHT: *Jack Albertson starred in "Grandpa Goes to Washington."*

**GREAT PERFORMANCES** (PBS)

Under the umbrella title "Great Performances" the series presented a high-calibre assortment of the best the fine arts has to offer in drama, dance, opera, and concerts. "Live From Lincoln Center" presented such operas as *Tosca, Otello, The Bartered Bride,* and *Luisa Miller,* plus the memorable, vibrant dual recital by the reigning operatic superstars, Luciano Pavarotti and Joan Sutherland. The choice offerings of "Dance in America" included performances of Balanchine choreography by the New York City Ballet Company, highlighting the artistry of the remarkable Mikhail Baryshnikov; plus programs showcasing the American Ballet Theatre, the Eliot Feld Dance Company, and a particularly impressive performance of Martha Graham's *Clytemnestra.*

EXECUTIVE PRODUCER: Jac Venza   DIRECTORS: Various   WRITERS: Various
PRODUCTION/PRESENTATION: WNET-TV (New York)

**HAPPY DAYS** (ABC)
*Tuesday 8:00-8:30 P.M.*

Sixth season for Fonzie and his friends, and still going strong. Historians may be able to explain the reason for the popularity of this series, which makes most of the young people in the show act like total fools. Also, isn't Henry Winkler's Fonzie TV's oldest juvenile delinquent?

STARS: Ron Howard, Henry Winkler, Tom Bosley   EXECUTIVE PRODUCERS: Thomas L. Miller, Edward K. Milkis, Garry K. Marshall   PRODUCERS: Jerry Paris, Bob Brunner   DIRECTOR: Jerry Paris   WRITERS: Various   PRODUCTION COMPANY: Miller-Milkis Productions, Inc. and Henderson Production in association with Paramount Pictures Corp.

**THE HARDY BOYS MYSTERIES** (ABC)
*Sunday 7:00-8:00 P.M.*

This low-rated opus limped along for a second and last season. Shaun Cassidy's young fans were probably turned off when he was married and widowed in the season's two-part opener.

STARS: Shaun Cassidy, Parker Stevenson   EXECUTIVE PRODUCER: Glen A. Larson   PRODUCER: Christopher Crowe   DIRECTORS: Various   WRITERS: Various   PRODUCTION COMPANY: Glen A. Larson Production in association with Universal MCA

**HAWAII FIVE-0** (CBS)
*Thursday 9:00-10:00 P.M.*

Season number 11 for Jack Lord's tight-lipped McGarrett and his Hawaiian police series.

STAR: Jack Lord   PRODUCER: Leonard B. Kaufman   CREATED BY: Leonard Freeman   DIRECTORS: Various   WRITERS: Various   PRODUCTION COMPANY: CBS Television Network

**HEADLINERS WITH DAVID FROST** (NBC)
*Wednesday 9:00-10:00 P.M.*

Six mildly engaging "topical" specials, featuring live and taped segments, with the ubiquitous David Frost up front and center. On his first show, for instance, David interviewed the then-hottest young male star around, John Travolta, and rock superstars the Bee Gees. The whole show never really jelled.

HOST: David Frost   EXECUTIVE PRODUCER: David Frost   PRODUCER: John Gilroy   DIRECTOR: Bruce Gowers   WRITER: Tony Geis   PRODUCTION COMPANY: David Paradine Television, Inc. in association with NBC-TV

**HELLO, LARRY** (NBC)
*Friday 9:30-10:00 P.M.*

Bird dog McLean Stevenson never says die . . . here was his second series during the season. ("In the Beginning" on CBS was his first.) This time out Stevenson was a recently separated parent embroiled in facts-of-life talk with his two young daughters. The situation has been milked countless times, yet the dogged Stevenson hung in there. And so, for some inscrutable reason, did the network.

STARS: McLean Stevenson, Kim Richards, Donna Wilkes, Joanna Gleason, George Memmoli   EXECUTIVE PRODUCERS: Perry Grant, Dick Bensfield
PRODUCER: George Tibbles   DIRECTOR: Doug Rogers   WRITERS: Various
PRODUCTION COMPANY: T.A.T. Communications Company

**HIGHCLIFFE MANOR**
(NBC)
*Thursday 8:30-9:00 P.M.*

NBC combined character eccentricity with gothic pageantry, trying for a duplication of other mad-hatter series such as "Mary Hartman, Mary Hartman," and "Soap." What came out was unfunny and unpalatable.

STARS: Shelley Fabares, Stephen McHattie, Eugenie Ross-Leming
PRODUCER: Alan Horn   DIRECTOR: Nick Havinga   CREATED BY: Eugenie Ross-Leming, Brad Buckner   PRODUCTION COMPANY: T.A.T. Communications Company

**HIZZONER** (NBC)
*Thursday 8:00-8:30 P.M.*

This NBC springtime limited-run series had the dubious honor of premiering two weeks earlier than originally announced and never found an audience. (Consistently placed in the five lowest-rated shows.) David Huddleston, a fine character actor, starred as the mayor of an undesignated Midwestern city who is beset with problems, thanks to his wacky family.

STAR: David Huddleston   PRODUCER: David Huddleston   DIRECTOR: Joan Darling.   WRITER: Sheldon Keller   PRODUCTION COMPANY: Huddleston Productions

**HOW THE WEST WAS WON** (ABC)
*Monday 9:00-11:00 P.M.*

The well-produced saga of the Macahans returned after the football season for 11 two-hour episodes. James Arness and company kept the TV Western alive and interesting for three months.

STAR: James Arness   EXECUTIVE PRODUCER: John Mantley   DIRECTORS: Various   WRITERS: Various   STORY CONSULTANT: Calvin Clements
PRODUCTION COMPANY: John Mantley Productions in association with MGM-Television

**THE INCREDIBLE HULK** (CBS)
*Various times*

Second season for this comic-book adventure which appealed to the simple-minded of all ages. Muscleman Lou Ferrigno is the real draw despite Bill Bixby's billing as the star.

STAR: Bill Bixby   EXECUTIVE PRODUCER: Kenneth Johnson   PRODUCERS: Nicholas Corea, James G. Hirsch   DIRECTORS: Various   WRITERS: Various
PRODUCTION COMPANY: Universal Television

**IN THE BEGINNING**
(CBS)
*Saturday 8:30-9:00 P.M.*

Norman Lear flopped with this forced comedy entry about a priest and a nun who run a store-front mission, with McLean Stevenson and Priscilla Lopez. Clerical shows often have a tendency to offend some viewers and this one was true-to-form. It never made God laugh either.

STARS: Priscilla Lopez, McLean Stevenson   EXECUTIVE PRODUCER: Mort

Lachman   PRODUCER: Jim Mulligan   DIRECTORS: Various   WRITERS: Various   PRODUCTION COMPANY: T.A.T. Communications Company

The prolific author James Michener, hosted this series of travelogues to far-away places, beginning with "Poland: The Will to Be." Mr. Michener lacked the on-camera personality to make these visits stimulating.

**JAMES MICHENER'S WORLD** (PBS)

HOST: James Michener   PRODUCERS: Albert Waller, Nan Segerman   DIRECTOR: Albert Waller   WRITER: Albert Waller   PRODUCTION COMPANY: Emlen House Productions, Inc.

Season number five and nothing's changed. George Jefferson's still running off at the mouth and his wife Louise always has the last word.

**THE JEFFERSONS** (CBS) *Wednesday 8:00-8:30 P.M.*

STARS: Isabel Sanford, Sherman Hemsley   EXECUTIVE PRODUCERS: Don Nicholl, Michael Ross, Bernie West   PRODUCERS: Mike Milligan, Jay Moriarty, Jack Shea   DIRECTOR: Jack Shea   DEVELOPED BY: Norman Lear   PRODUCTION COMPANY: T.A.T. Communications Company in association with NEW Productions

The situation comedy about a young Brooklyn couple seen in the spring of 1978 had a second chance as a January 1979 replacement series. Despite lots of disco dancing and cute stars—Paul Regina and Char Fontanne—it failed to ignite interest the second time around.

**JOE AND VALERIE** (NBC) *Monday 8:30-9:00 P.M.*

STARS: Paul Regina, Char Fontanne   PRODUCER: Bernie Kahn   DIRECTORS: Various   WRITERS: Various   PRODUCTION COMPANY: Hope Enterprises

Julia Child, television's hearty, cheery, inexhaustible cook, came back after five years off the air, with a delightful season of chatter and preparation of meals which made your mouth water.

**JULIA CHILD & COMPANY** (PBS)

STAR: Julia Child   PRODUCER: Russell Morash   DIRECTOR: Dave DeBarger   COLLABORATOR: Ruth Lockwood   PRODUCTION COMPANY: WGBH (Boston)

LEFT: *Pulitzer Prize-winning author James Michener shared insights into many different cultures on "James Michener's World."*

RIGHT: *Television's best-known chef put millions of Americans into the world of French cuisine on "Julia Child & Company."*

**KAZ** (CBS)
*Sunday 10:00-11:00* P.M.

Ron Leibman was excellent as Kaz, the ex-con lawyer battling prejudice right and left. Although the show was bounced around the CBS lineup, some of the faithful fans always found it, and the stories improved as the season progressed, before it was axed.

STARS: Ron Leibman, Patrick O'Neal  EXECUTIVE PRODUCERS: Lee Rich, Marc Merson  PRODUCER: Sam Rolfe  DIRECTORS: Various  WRITERS: Various  PRODUCTION COMPANY: Lorimar Productions, Inc.

**LAVERNE & SHIRLEY** (ABC)
*Tuesday 8:30-9:00* P.M.

The madcap duo kept slapstick comedy thriving in their third season. Penny Marshall and Cindy Williams are like having two Lucille Balls reliving the antics of "I Love Lucy," and that may just be the reason for their enormous popularity.

STARS: Cindy Williams, Penny Marshall  EXECUTIVE PRODUCERS: Garry K. Marshall, Thomas L. Miller, Edward K. Milkis  PRODUCERS: Arthur Silver, Tony Marshall  CREATED BY: Garry K. Marshall, Lowell Ganz, Mark Rothman  DIRECTORS: Various  WRITERS: Various  PRODUCTION COMPANY: Miller-Milkis Productions, Inc. and Henderson Production Company, Inc., in association with Paramount Television

LEFT: *Cindy Williams and Penny Marshall starred in one of the season's most popular series "Laverne & Shirley."*

RIGHT: *Dr. Judson Graves Randolph and a young patient were profiled on the high-quality but short-lived series "Lifeline."*

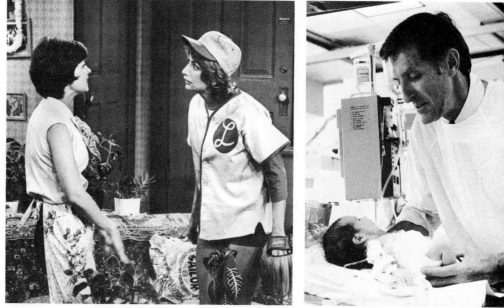

**LIFELINE** (NBC)
*Various times*

This nonfiction series featured real doctors at work and at home and was certainly innovative by the normal standards of prime-time commercial TV. However, the doctors on the job and at play tended to make you feel they were acting. After several months and some unusual scheduling—several episodes aired in one week—it was scrubbed.

STARS: Various  EXECUTIVE PRODUCERS: Thomas W. Moore, Robert E. Fuisz, M.D.  PRODUCER: Alfred R. Kelman  DIRECTOR: Alfred R. Kelman  PRODUCTION COMPANY: Tomorrow Entertainment/Medcom Company

**LITTLE HOUSE ON THE PRAIRIE** (NBC)
*Monday 8:00-9:00* P.M.

This western drama series, in its fifth season, deserved consistently high marks for the quality of its writing, acting, and production. The saga of the Ingalls family remained NBC's lone high-rated show. Star Michael Landon also wrote and directed many of the episodes.

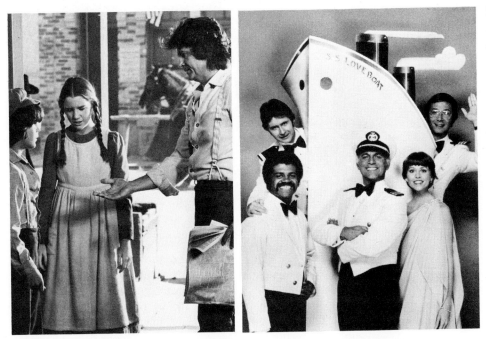

STARS: Michael Landon, Karen Grassle, Melissa Gilbert, Melissa Sue Anderson, Lindsay and Sidney Greenbush   EXECUTIVE PRODUCER: Michael Landon   PRODUCERS: Kent McCray, William F. Claxton   DIRECTORS: Michael Landon, William F. Claxton   PRODUCTION COMPANY: Ed Friendly Productions in association with NBC

Second season sailing for this water-logged comedy which has won favor with armchair travelers. The plots are totally absurd, but the glamorous setting and guest stars evidently are enough.

**THE LOVE BOAT** (ABC)
*Saturday 9:00-10:00 P.M.*

STARS: Gavin MacLeod, Bernie Kopell, Fred Grandy, Ted Lange, Lauren Tewes   EXECUTIVE PRODUCERS: Aaron Spelling, Douglas S. Cramer   PRODUCERS: Gordon and Lynne Farr, Henry Colman   DIRECTOR: Paul Stanley   WRITERS: Various   PRODUCTION COMPANY: Aaron Spelling Productions, Inc.

The limited-run series about a young man, raised by animals during his first 10 years, couldn't sustain interest any longer. The gimmick just petered out.

**LUCAN** (ABC)
*Monday 8:00-9:00 P.M.*

STAR: Kevin Brophy   EXECUTIVE PRODUCER: Barry Lowen   PRODUCER: Harold Gast   CREATED BY: Michael Zagor   DIRECTOR: Peter H. Hunt   WRITERS: Camille Marchetta, Rick Edelstein   PRODUCTION COMPANY: A Barry Lowen Production in association with MGM-Television

Remember those five orphans in the 1978 movie *Stickin' Together* who convinced a free-wheeling beachcomber in Hawaii to become their legal guardian? Well, they came back in this limited series in which the lush Hawaiian scenery turned out to be more interesting than the characters in the show.

**THE MACKENZIES OF PARADISE COVE** (ABC)
*Friday 8:00-9:00 P.M.*

STARS: Clu Gulager, Shawn Stevens, Lory Walsh, Sean Marshall, Randi Kiger, Keith Mitchell   PRODUCERS: William Blinn, Jerry Thorpe   DIRECTORS: Various   WRITERS: Various   PRODUCTION COMPANY: A Blinn/Thorpe Production in association with Viacom Enterprises

**MAKING IT** (ABC)
*Friday 8:30-9:00* P.M.

Another attempt to duplicate the popularity of a film that skyrocketed at the box office—namely *Saturday Night Fever*. This 10th carbon copy, however, failed to impress. David Naughton, as the leading character, wasn't enough to carry the show, and the supporting characters looked like rejects from "Laverne & Shirley."

STARS: David Naughton, Greg Antonacci, Denise Miller, Ellen Travolta
EXECUTIVE PRODUCERS: Mark Rothman, Lowell Ganz   PRODUCERS: David Duclon, Deborah Leschin, Jeff Ganz   DIRECTORS: Various   WRITERS: Various   PRODUCTION COMPANY: Miller-Milkis Productions, Inc., Henderson Production Company, Inc., The Stigwood Group, Ltd.

**MARIE CURIE** (PBS)

A superior five-part BBC series about the most famous woman scientist the world has ever known showed her as an intense, introspective, and determined human being, eloquently portrayed by Jane Lapotaire.

STAR: Jane Lapotaire   PRODUCER: Peter Goodchild   DIRECTOR: John Glenister   WRITER: Elaine Morgan   PRODUCTION COMPANY: The BBC and Time-Life Films

**MARRIED: THE FIRST YEAR** (CBS)
*Wednesday 8:00-9:00* P.M.

Is the first year of marriage the hardest or the easiest? This CBS entry took the middle course, and seldom got off the ground. Mainly, it was a sugary love story with pretty-boy Leigh McCloskey and newcomer Cindy Grover as the leads.

STARS: Leigh McCloskey, Cindy Grover   EXECUTIVE PRODUCERS: Lee Rich, Philip Capice   PRODUCER: David Jacobs   DIRECTOR: Robert Michael Lewis   WRITER: David Jacobs   PRODUCTION COMPANY: Lorimar Productions, Inc.

**MARY** (CBS)
*Sunday 8:00-9:00* P.M.

Mary Tyler Moore came back on weekly TV, headlining her own Sunday night variety hour, with the stress on comedy, for which she assembled a repertory company of comedic talents, headed by Dick Shawn. Mary sang and danced and clowned, but few of her fans seemed to care, and her show went off the air, only to return later as "The Mary Tyler Moore Hour."

STAR: Mary Tyler Moore   PRODUCERS: Tom Patchett, Jay Tarses
DIRECTOR: Rob Iscove   WRITERS: Various   PRODUCTION COMPANY: MTM

LEFT: *French actress Jane Lapotaire played the title role of the gifted and determined woman of science "Marie Curie."*

CENTER: *Alan Alda starred as Hawkeye in the popular series "M*A*S*H."*

RIGHT: *Francesca Annis played the title role in* Lillie *on "Masterpiece Theatre."*

Here's Mary again, after a production overhaul. However, the show was only a little better than her first outing, employing guest stars and the gimmick of doing a show about putting on a show. Mary finally called it quits in the singing and dancing arena, and will return in 1980 in a new sitcom.

STAR: Mary Tyler Moore   EXECUTIVE PRODUCER: Jim Hirschfeld
PRODUCER: Perry Lafferty   DIRECTOR: Robert Scheerer   WRITER: Arnie Kogan   PRODUCTION COMPANY: MTM

**THE MARY TYLER MOORE HOUR** (CBS)
*Sunday 10:00-11:00 P.M.*

The seventh season of this wonderful series went along in delightfully predictable fashion with Alan Alda's Hawkeye and company in top form. The series has lasted longer than the Korean War, which is the setting for this TV comedy classic.

STARS: Alan Alda, Mike Farrell, Harry Morgan   PRODUCER: Burt Metcalfe
DIRECTORS: Various   WRITERS: Various   PRODUCTION COMPANY: Twentieth Century-Fox Television

**M*A*S*H*** (CBS)
*Monday 9:00-9:30 P.M.*

PBS's most popular and diverting mainstay of its entire schedule continued to stimulate and entertain viewers, kicking off the season with *Poldark II*, the continuation of the saga of the flamboyant adventurer from Cornwall. It was followed by Thomas Hardy's *The Mayor of Casterbridge*, a sad story of a morally bankrupt man, brilliantly portrayed by Alan Bates. *The Duchess of Duke Street* followed, bringing the rags-to-riches tale of a Cockney woman's rise from cook to posh hotel proprietor. A few slightly sordid but rare tales of passion by British short story masters H. E. Bates and A. E. Coppard were presented under the omnibus title, "Country Matters." *Lillie* regaled viewers with the romantic yarn of real-life actress Lillie Langtry, played with great eccentricity and enormous charm by Francesca Annis.

**MASTERPIECE THEATRE** (PBS)

**Masterpiece Theatre:**
EXECUTIVE PRODUCER: Joan Sullivan   U.S. PRODUCTION COMPANY: WGBH (Boston)
**The Mayor of Casterbridge:**
PRODUCER: Jonathan Powell   DIRECTOR: David Giles   PRODUCTION COMPANY: BBC-TV
**The Duchess of Duke Street:**
PRODUCER: John Hawkesworth   DIRECTORS: Bill Bain, Cyril Coke, Simon Langton, Raymond Menmuir   PRODUCTION COMPANY: BBC-TV
**Country Matters:**
PRODUCERS: Derek Granger, Sylvia Narizzano   DIRECTORS: Barry Davis, Richard Everitt, Peter Wood   PRODUCTION COMPANY: Granada TV
**Lillie:**
EXECUTIVE PRODUCER: Tony Wharmby   PRODUCER: Jack Williams   DIRECTOR: John Gorrie   WRITER: David Butler   PRODUCTION COMPANY: London Weekend TV
**I, Claudius:**
PRODUCER: Martin Lisemore   DIRECTOR: Herbert Wise   WRITER: Jack Pulman   PRODUCTION COMPANY: BBC-TV

Darlene Carr played an unmarried mother who had to overcome numerous obstacles in order to create a life for herself and her baby. The series, based on the British show, "Miss Jones & Son," didn't fare well in its voyage across the Atlantic.

**MISS WINSLOW & SON** (CBS)
*Wednesday 8:30-9:00 P.M.*

*Robin Williams became the season's brightest new star as a far-out spaceman visiting Earth on "Mork & Mindy."*

STARS: Darleen Carr, Roscoe Lee Browne, Elliott Reid, Sarah Marshall EXECUTIVE PRODUCERS: Ted Bergmann, Don Taffner PRODUCER: Alan J. Levitt DIRECTOR: George Tyne WRITER: Alan J. Levitt PRODUCTION COMPANY: TTC Productions, Inc.

## MORK & MINDY
### (ABC)
*Thursday 8:00-8:30 P.M.*

The ingratiating, enormously talented, and inventive Robin Williams as Mork, the alien creature from the planet Ork, descended on earth, disrupted the life of a lovely lass named Mindy, and became a huge, phenomenal immediate TV hit —the biggest breakaway ratings winner in recent years.

STARS: Robin Williams, Pam Dawber, Elizabeth Kerr, Conrad Janis EXECUTIVE PRODUCERS: Garry K. Marshall, Tony Marshall PRODUCERS: Dale McRaven, Bruce Johnson EXECUTIVE STORY EDITOR: Tom Tenowich DIRECTORS: Various WRITERS: Various PRODUCTION COMPANY: Henderson Production Company, Inc. and Miller-Milkis Productions, Inc., in association with Paramount Television

## THE NEW ADVENTURES OF WONDER WOMAN
### (CBS)
*Friday 8:00-9:00 P.M.*

This was the second and final season for Lynda Carter's ageless Amazon princess. Although the show is geared for the kiddies, Ms. Carter's attributes were noticed by the older males.

STAR: Lynda Carter EXECUTIVE PRODUCER: Douglas S. Cramer PRODUCER: Charles B. FitzSimons STORY CONSULTANT: Anne Collins PRODUCTION COMPANY: Bruce Lansbury Productions, Ltd., in association with The Douglas S. Cramer Company, in association with Warner Bros. Television

## NOVA (PBS)

This distinguished series offered, during its sixth season, a strong array of fascinating documentaries, including one story about oil spills and the devastation they wreak; an offbeat story of Dr. Frederick Young, a poor Navajo Indian who is a nuclear physicist today; and a study of the life and work of the controversial behavioral psychologist B. F. Skinner.

EXECUTIVE PRODUCER: John Angier PRODUCTION COMPANY: WGBH (Boston)

This coproduction of Time-Life Television and the BBC offers a group of dramatized children's stories of varying lengths. The opener was *The Secret Garden*, a seven-part mystery about a little girl who mends her nasty ways after a frightening experience. Other segments included the lesser known *John Halifax Gentleman*, and an offbeat version of *Pinocchio*.

**EXECUTIVE PRODUCER:** Jay Rayvid   **PRODUCER:** James A. DeVinney
**DIRECTORS:** Various   **WRITERS:** Various   **PRODUCTION COMPANY:** Time-Life Television in association with the BBC

**ONCE UPON A CLASSIC** (PBS)

This was the fourth season go-round for Bonnie Franklin as a single parent raising two teenage daughters. The stories were less interesting this season, but the show's popularity holds up.

**STARS:** Bonnie Franklin, Mackenzie Phillips, Pat Harrington, Valerie Bertinelli   **EXECUTIVE PRODUCERS:** Jack Elinson, Alan Rafkin   **PRODUCERS:** Dick Bensfield, Perry Grant   **DIRECTOR:** Alan Rafkin   **WRITERS:** Various
**PRODUCTION COMPANY:** T.A.T. Communications Company and Allwhit, Inc.

**ONE DAY AT A TIME** (CBS)
*Monday 9:30-10:00 P.M.*

LEFT: *The grounded supertanker* Amoco Cadiz *threatened the environment with a deadly oil spill which environmental scientists worked to clean up in "Black Tide," an episode of "Nova."*

RIGHT: *Mackenzie Phillips, Valerie Bertinelli, and Bonnie Franklin tried to work things out on "One Day at a Time."*

This series bombed last year, but ABC was a glutton for punishment and brought it back, with a new crew. Slapstick ahoy!

**STARS:** Randolph Mantooth, Robert Hogan, JoAnn Pflug, Warren Berlinger, Hilary Thompson   **EXECUTIVE PRODUCERS:** Jeff Harris, Bernie Kukoff
**PRODUCER:** Michael Rhodes   **DIRECTORS:** Various   **WRITERS:** Various
**PRODUCTION COMPANY:** Boiney Stoones, Inc. (Bernie Kukoff/Jeff Harris)

**OPERATION PETTICOAT** (ABC)
*Various times*

After "Donny & Marie" failed to click with fans, the entire Osmond family was called on camera to bolster the ratings. They didn't help a bit.

**STARS:** Donny, Marie, Jimmy, Jay, Wayne, Merrill, Alan, George, and Olive Osmond   **EXECUTIVE PRODUCERS:** The Osmond Brothers, Dick Callister
**PRODUCERS:** Alan Osmond, Phil Hahn   **DIRECTOR:** Walter C. Miller
**WRITERS:** Earl Brown, Steven Adams, Bruce Kirschbaum   **PRODUCTION COMPANY:** Osmond Productions

**THE OSMOND FAMILY SHOW** (ABC)
*Sunday 7:00-8:00 P.M.*

LEFT: *Intrigue and Romance ruled the day in* The Pallisers *starring Philip Latham as Plantagenet and Susan Hampshire as Cora.*

RIGHT: *John Houseman prepares to "shroud" law student James Stephens in academic ignominy in this scene from "The Paper Chase."*

**THE PALLISERS** (PBS)

A handsomely mounted 22-part series on Victorian England based on six books by 19th-century novelist Anthony Trollope. Susan Hampshire and Philip Latham starred as the aristocratic British family whose saga would rival any royal family's complex history. Expert British production.

STARS: Susan Hampshire, Philip Latham    PRODUCER: Martin Lisemore
DIRECTORS: Hugh David, Ronald Wilson    WRITER: Simon Raven
PRODUCTION/PRESENTATION: WNET-TV (New York)

**THE PAPER CHASE**
(CBS)
*Various times*

A generally superior series based on the fascinating movie of the same name. John Houseman was perfection itself as the formidable law professor Charles W. Kingsfield, Jr., a role for which he won an Academy Award, and James Stephens turned out to be equally delightful as the student determined to gain his attention and respect. CBS eventually tried to find the right time slot somewhere for this worthy entry other than opposing "Laverne & Shirley" and "Happy Days," but it never found a substantial audience. It did, however, run for the full season.

STARS: John Houseman, James Stephens    EXECUTIVE PRODUCER: Robert C. Thompson    PRODUCER: Robert Lewin    PRODUCTION COMPANY: Twentieth Century-Fox Television

**PEOPLE** (CBS)
*Monday 8:00-8:30 P.M.*

Trying to duplicate the breezy style of the magazine with the same title, this series had two chances and failed miserably both times. The segments were often too short, too rapid, and convoluted, and Phyllis George just ain't no Barbara Walters.

HOST: Phyllis George    EXECUTIVE PRODUCER: David Susskind    PRODUCER: Charlotte Schiff Jones    DIRECTOR: Merrill Mazuer    PRODUCTION COMPANY: Time-Life Television

**PREVIN AND THE PITTSBURGH** (PBS)

The charming and enormously talented conductor-composer Andre Previn hosted his third season of this wonderful music series, which encompassed classical, opera, movie, and contemporary music. Only Previn could bridge the vast musical gap with ease. The opener for this season with Ella Fitzgerald was a perfect example of the superior quality of this series.

STAR: Andre Previn, conductor    EXECUTIVE PRODUCERS: Jay Ravid, Dale Bell
PRODUCER: Stephen Dick    DIRECTOR: Hugh Downing    PRODUCTION
COMPANY: WQED (Pittsburgh)

**THE PRIME OF MISS JEAN BRODIE** (PBS)

An excellent six-part adaptation of Muriel Spark's valentine to a talented, progressive, and outspoken school teacher in a conservative British girls' school during the thirties. Geraldine McEwan didn't strike a single false note in her impeccable characterization of the magnificent teacher.

STAR: Geraldine McEwan    WRITER: Jay Presson Allen    PRODUCTION
COMPANY: Scottish Television Limited

**PROJECT U.F.O.** (NBC)
*Sunday 8:00-9:00 P.M.*

After premiering last midseason, this adventure series returned with a new chief investigator played by stoic Edward Winter. However, the return was short-lived for this show about government probings of UFO sightings.

STARS: Edward Winter, Caskey Swaim    EXECUTIVE PRODUCER: Jack
Webb    PRODUCERS: Col. William T. Coleman, USAF, Ret., Robert
Blees    DIRECTORS: Jack Cooperman, Harry L. Wolf, A.S.C.    CREATED BY:
Harold Jack Bloom    PRODUCTION COMPANY: A Mark VII Ltd. Production for
NBC-TV

**QUINCY** (NBC)
*Thursday 9:00-10:00 P.M.*

Jack Klugman's gruff performance as Quincy, the conscientious medical examiner who is never satisfied with just determining the cause of death of the corpses that come his way, kept viewers interested for a successful third year.

STAR: Jack Klugman    PRODUCER: Peter Thompson    DIRECTORS: Various
WRITERS: Various    PRODUCTION COMPANY: Glen A. Larson Production in
association with Universal Studios

**REAL PEOPLE** (NBC)
*Wednesday 8:00-9:00 P.M.*

Producer George Schlatter, who was responsible for bringing "Laugh-In" to television, gave vent to his imagination and originality and came up with this potpourri. Live and taped segments dot the hour which is peopled by a variety of American personalities doing their own thing. Fred Willard, Sarah Purcell, Skip Stephenson, John Barbour, and Bill Rafferty were co-hosts.

STARS: John Barbour, Sarah Purcell    WRITERS: Digby Wolfe, Kendis
Rochlen    PRODUCTION COMPANY: George Schlatter Production in association
with NBC-TV

LEFT: *Jack Klugman and Robert Ito are crime-solving medical examiners on "Quincy."*

RIGHT: *James Garner and James Luisi in "The Rockford Files."*

**RHODA** (CBS)
*Saturday 8:00-8:30 P.M.*

The fifth and last season for Rhoda and her struggle to cope with life, TV sitcom style. Valerie Harper may never find a role better suited for her offbeat comedy style. Also, Nancy Walker, as her mother Ida Morgenstern, shared some comic gems during the five seasons.

STAR: Valerie Harper  PRODUCER: Bob Ellison  DIRECTORS: Various  WRITERS: Various  PRODUCTION COMPANY: MTM

**THE ROCKFORD FILES** (NBC)
*Friday 9:00-10:00 P.M.*

Fifth season and still going strong, James Garner's amiable private eye Jim Rockford remains the chief lure for fans.

STAR: James Garner  EXECUTIVE PRODUCER: Meta Rosenberg  PRODUCERS: David Chase, Charles F. Johnson  DIRECTORS: William Wiard, Ivan Dixon, and others  WRITERS: Stephen J. Cannell, Juanita Bartlett, David Chase, and others  PRODUCTION COMPANY: A Roy Huggins/Public Arts Production in association with Cherokee Productions, Universal Television, and NBC-TV

**THE ROPERS** (ABC)
*Tuesday 9:30-10:00 P.M.*

Audra Lindley and Norman Fell, as the bickering Ropers in "Three's Company," sold their apartment house and moved into a new neighborhood for their own series. The show was a resounding hit right from the spin-off. Forced comedy, but well played.

STARS: Audra Lindley, Norman Fell  EXECUTIVE PRODUCERS: Don Nicholl, Michael Ross, Bernie West  PRODUCER: George Sunga  DIRECTOR: Dave Powers  WRITERS: Johnnie Mortimer, Brian Cooke  PRODUCTION COMPANY: The NRW Company in association with TTC Productions, Inc.

**SALVAGE I** (ABC)
*Monday 8:00-9:00 P.M.*

Even Andy Griffith couldn't "salvage" this one, about a team of adventurers who go anywhere, including outer space, to retrieve junk worth a lot of money. Tossed on the scrap heap.

STARS: Andy Griffith, Joel Higgins, Richard Jaeckel  EXECUTIVE PRODUCERS: Harve Bennett, Harris Katleman  PRODUCER: Ralph Sariego  DIRECTOR: Gene Nelson  WRITER: Ruel Fischman  PRODUCTION COMPANY: Bennett/Katleman Productions in association with Columbia Pictures Television

**THE SCARLET LETTER** (PBS)

Nathaniel Hawthorne's classic American novel, published in 1850 and set in 17th-century Boston, was dramatized in a strikingly honest but ultimately lackluster four-part production. Meg Foster as Hester Prynne was too stoic to enlist more than passing sympathy, but John Heard was sensitive and extremely vulnerable as her pastor, and Kevin Conway was hauntingly dangerous as her husband.

STARS: Meg Foster, Kevin Conway, John Heard  EXECUTIVE PRODUCER: Herbert Hirschman  PRODUCER: Rick Hauser  DIRECTOR: Rick Hauser  PRODUCTION COMPANY: WGBH (Boston)

**THE SHAKESPEARE PLAYS** (PBS)

This is the first season for an extraordinary venture in which all 37 of The Bard's plays will eventually be produced by the BBC and Time-Life Television and shown over the next six years. This season's six selected plays: *Julius Caesar, As You Like It, Romeo and Juliet, Richard II, Measure for Measure,* and *Henry VIII* were as diverse in quality as they were in their plotlines.

Perhaps the worst production was *Julius Caesar,* which lacked fire and passion. On the other hand, an impeccable mounting of the ingratiating *As You Like It,* with a luminous performance by Helen Mirren as Rosalind, and the seldom produced *Henry VIII* struck a promising note for the remaining productions.

**The Shakespeare Plays:**
EXECUTIVE PRODUCER: Jac Venza  SERIES PRODUCER: Cedric Messina
PRODUCTION COMPANY: BBC-TV in association with Time-Life Television, Inc.
**Julius Caesar:**
STARS: Richard Pasco, Keith Mitchell, Charles Gray  DIRECTOR: Herbert Wise
**As You Like It:**
STARS: Helen Mirren, Brian Stirner, Richard Pasco, Angharad Rees
DIRECTOR: Basil Coleman
**Romeo and Juliet:**
STARS: Patrick Ryecart, Rebecca Saire, Celia Johnson, John Gielgud
DIRECTOR: Alvin Rakoff
**Richard II:**
STARS: Derek Jacobi, John Gielgud, Jon Finch, Wendy Hiller  DIRECTOR: David Giles
**Measure for Measure:**
STARS: Kenneth Colley, Kate Nelligan, Tim Pigott-Smith  DIRECTOR: Desmond Davis
**Henry VIII:**
STARS: John Stride, Timothy West, Michael Poole  DIRECTOR: Kevin Billington

This series, produced in Chicago and hosted by critics Gene Siskel and Roger Ebert, focused on new film releases but tended to be overly "cute" and geared for the cinemaphiles rather than the average potential moviegoer.

**SNEAK PREVIEW** (PBS)

HOSTS: Roger Ebert, Gene Siskel  EXECUTIVE PRODUCER: Thea Flaum
PRODUCTION COMPANY: WTTW (Chicago)

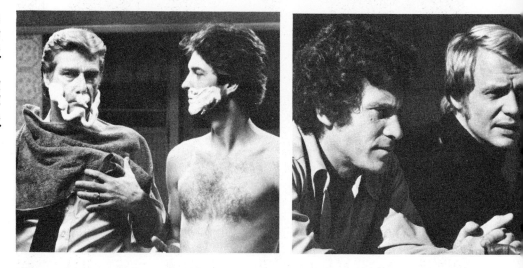

LEFT: *Richard Mulligan and Ted Wass share the washbasin in a scene from "Soap."*

RIGHT: *Paul Michael Glaser and David Soul were a detective team on "Starsky and Hutch."*

**SOAP** (ABC)
*Thursday 8:30-9:00* P.M.

Insane fun lasted throughout season two as the Tates and the Campbells played out their eccentricities to the delight of their fans. Impeccable comedy ensemble of actors.

STARS: Billy Crystal, Cathryn Damon, Robert Guillaume   EXECUTIVE PRODUCERS: Paul Junger Witt, Tony Thomas   PRODUCER: Susan Harris DIRECTOR: Jay Sandrich   WRITERS: Susan Harris, Jordan Crittenden PRODUCTION COMPANY: A Witt/Thomas/Harris Production

**SOUNDSTAGE** (PBS)

Fifth season for the Chicago-based musical series which runs the gamut from pop, rock, jazz, R&B, and country music. The series maintained its entertaining format with enterainers such as Leo Sayer, Freddie Fender, and Emmy Lou Harris.

PRODUCER: Ken Erlich   DIRECTOR: Dick Carter   PRODUCTION COMPANY: WTTW-TV (Chicago)

**STARSKY AND HUTCH**
(ABC)
*Tuesday 10:00-11:00* P.M.

The fourth and last season limped along with the show's ingredients intact. Paul Michael Glaser and David Soul looked as if they were playing their roles by rote.

STARS: David Soul, Paul Michael Glaser   EXECUTIVE PRODUCERS: Aaron Spelling, Leonard Goldberg   PRODUCER: Joseph T. Naar   CREATED BY: William Blinn   DIRECTORS: Various   WRITERS: Various   PRODUCTION COMPANY: A Spelling/Goldberg Production

**STOCKARD CHANNING IN JUST FRIENDS** (CBS)
*Sunday 9:30-10:00* P.M.

Stockard Channing tackled a situation comedy playing the Boston housewife who comes to Los Angeles to begin life on her own. Ms. Channing is a charmer and carries the whole show.

STAR: Stockard Channing   EXECUTIVE PRODUCER: David Debin PRODUCER: Al Rogers   DIRECTORS: Robert Drivas, Rich Bennewitz   WRITERS: Nick Arnold, Eric Cohen

**SUPERTRAIN** (NBC)
*Various times*

NBC's super chief Fred Silverman's call for fans to come aboard this "Loveboat" on rails fell on deaf ears. It cost a fortune to produce and repeated revamping and rescheduling couldn't save it from derailing.

STARS: Various   EXECUTIVE PRODUCER: Dan Curtis   DIRECTORS: Various   WRITERS: Various   PRODUCTION COMPANY: An NBC Production in association with Dan Curtis

Bottom-of-the-barrel scrapings. The personal stories of ticket holders vying for a million-dollar sweepstake was embarrassingly bad on all counts. So bad, it made you crave for reruns of the old "Millionaire" series.

**SWEEPSTAKES** (NBC)
*Friday 10:00-11:00 P.M.*

STARS: Ed Byrnes   EXECUTIVE PRODUCER: Robert Dozier   PRODUCER: Ben Kadish   DIRECTORS: Various   WRITERS: Various   PRODUCTION COMPANY: Miller-Milkis Productions in association with Paramount Pictures Corp.

Action series starred Dack Rambo as a curly-headed, swaggering type who makes the tricks he learned in prison pay off while getting even with the businessmen who ruined his dad. Formula stuff, dressed up with a pretentious title.

**SWORD OF JUSTICE** (NBC)
*Friday 10:00-11:00 P.M.*

STARS: Dack Rambo, Bert Rosario, Alex Courtney   EXECUTIVE PRODUCER: Glen A. Larson   PRODUCERS: Joe Boston, Herman Groves   DIRECTORS: Various   WRITERS: Various   PRODUCTION COMPANY: An NBC-TV Production in association with Glen A. Larson and Universal

The members of the Sunshine Cab Company of New York City shaped up as a very entertaining group. Created and produced by former members of the old Mary Tyler Moore group, the fast-paced, glib series stars likable Judd Hirsch and a talented supporting cast. The show became an instant hit, and rightly so!

**TAXI** (ABC)
*Tuesday 9:30-10:00 P.M.*

STAR: Judd Hirsch   EXECUTIVE PRODUCERS: James L. Brooks, Stan Daniels, David Davis, Ed Weinberger   PRODUCERS: Glen Charles, Les Charles   DIRECTOR: James Burrows   WRITERS: James L. Brooks, Stan Daniels, David Davis, Ed Weinberger   PRODUCTION COMPANY: John Charles Walters Productions in association with Paramount Studios

LEFT: *Andy Kaufman brought a unique comic style to TV in his role as an immigrant mechanic on "Taxi."*

RIGHT: *"Three's Company" starred (left) Suzanne Somers, John Ritter, and Joyce DeWitt as roommates.*

**13 QUEENS BLVD.**
(ABC)
*Tuesday 10:30-11:00 P.M.*

Funny midseason domestic sitcom in which the woman's point of view was stressed. Eileen Brennan was wonderful as a Queens (New York) housewife, and, if given a chance, she and the show would probably have caught on.

STARS: Eileen Brennan, Jerry Van Dyke, Marcia Rodd  EXECUTIVE PRODUCERS: Bud Yorkin, Bernie Orenstein, Saul Turteltaub  PRODUCER: Sue Nevens  DIRECTOR: Kim Friedman  WRITERS: Cyra McFadden, Linda Marsh, Margie Peters  PRODUCTION COMPANY: TOY Productions

**THREE'S COMPANY**
(ABC)
*Various times*

It's season number two for the Big Three. The comedy settled into a predictable groove, but John Ritter's antic performance kept things moving along, with a little bit of help from Suzanne Somers and Joyce DeWitt.

STARS: John Ritter, Joyce DeWitt, Suzanne Somers, Norman Fell, Audra Lindley  PRODUCERS: Don Nicholl, Michael Ross, Bernie West  DIRECTOR: Bill Hobin  WRITER: Richard Orloff  PRODUCTION COMPANY: The NRW Company in association with TTC Productions, Inc.

**TIME EXPRESS** (CBS)
*Thursday 8:00-9:00 P.M.*

On paper, this one must have really sounded great—Vincent Price and his elegant wife, Coral Browne, as a charming host and hostess of a mysterious train which takes passengers on a journey to their past. However, in execution, the "express" derailed.

STARS: Vincent Price, Coral Browne  EXECUTIVE PRODUCERS: Ivan Goff, Ben Roberts  PRODUCER: Leonard Kaufman  DIRECTOR: Arnold Laven  WRITER: Gerald Sanford  PRODUCTION COMPANY: Warner Bros. Television

**TURNABOUT** (NBC)
*Friday 9:00-9:30 P.M.*

A sprightly touch of whimsy in this version of Thorne Smith's 1930s comedy about a married couple whose spirits trade bodies. Husky-voiced Sharon Gless and John Schuck managed to give it some style, but it still flopped. (Avid moviegoers may recall a 1940 film version of this tale starring the late Carole Landis and John Hubbard.)

STARS: John Schuck, Sharon Gless  EXECUTIVE PRODUCER: Sam Denoff  PRODUCER: Arnold Kane  DIRECTORS: Various  WRITERS: Various  PRODUCTION COMPANY: Universal Television in association with NBC Entertainment

LEFT: *Felicia Lowe and Gerri Lange reported on the special problems of women in contemporary America in the PBS series "Turnabout."*

RIGHT: *Joe Namath played a hapless basketball coach in the short-lived series "The Waverly Wonders."*

Second season for this potpourri magazine-format show with the focus on women, hosted by Gerri Lange. The best portions dealt with the everyday woman functioning in her special role or job, rather than the name guest-star interviews.

**TURNABOUT** (PBS)

STAR: Gerri Lange  EXECUTIVE PRODUCER: Martna Glessing  DIRECTOR: Louisa Lo  WRITER: Roxanne Russell  PRODUCTION COMPANY: KQED-TV (San Francisco)

A new slick action series about a smooth-operating private investigator named Dan Tanna in Las Vegas relied heavily on the magnetism of its star, Robert Urich, and he delivered the audience.

**VEGA$** (ABC)
*Wednesday*
*10:00-11:00* P.M.

STARS: Robert Urich, Tony Curtis  EXECUTIVE PRODUCERS: Aaron Spelling, Douglas S. Cramer  PRODUCER: E. Duke Vincent  DIRECTOR: Harry Falk  WRITER: Burton Armus  PRODUCTION COMPANY: Aaron Spelling Productions, Inc.

It's a pity that this was the last season for this often remarkably adventuresome drama series which brought some excellent dramas and comedies to the screen and encouraged new writers for the TV medium. Unfortunately, funding ran out for this milestone series. It generally was well produced by executive producer Barbara Schultz. It's a national scandal that funding for this much needed public television series could not be secured. "Visions" should be a weekly fixture on the airwaves, providing much needed access for young writers and filmmakers.

**VISIONS** (PBS)

EXECUTIVE PRODUCER: Barbara Schultz  PRODUCTION COMPANY: KCET-TV (Los Angeles)

This series, in its seventh season with PBS, is unquestionably one of the most popular on public television. Host Louis Rukeyser and his guest experts cover the economic scene, both fact and theory, as it relates to the investment problems and opportunities of viewers.

**WALL STREET WEEK** (PBS)

HOST: Louis Rukeyser  EXECUTIVE PRODUCER: John Davis  DIRECTOR: George Beneman  WRITER: Dennis Moore  PRODUCTION COMPANY: The Maryland Center for Public Broadcasting

Season number seven began to show signs of wear and tear. Not only is Will's Grandpa sorely missed, but Michael Learned's Olivia also left before the season ended. However, she'll be back for frequent appearances next season. Season eight may be its last.

**THE WALTONS** (CBS)
*Thursday 8:00-9:00* P.M.

STARS: Ralph Waite, Michael Learned  EXECUTIVE PRODUCERS: Lee Rich, Earl Hamner  PRODUCER: Rod Peterson  DIRECTORS: Various  WRITERS: Various  PRODUCTION COMPANY: Lorimar Productions, Inc.

In January 1969, "Washington Week in Review" became the first program produced by a local station to be aired by the newly organized Public Broadcasting Service. The free-wheeling, informal discussion of current events by top news correspondents provides incisive and sometimes unexpected insights into both the news and the newsmakers.

**WASHINGTON WEEK IN REVIEW** (PBS)

LEFT: *Pamela Bellwood starred as Ellen Cunningham, a woman network executive on "W.E.B."*

RIGHT: *PBS's longest-running and most popular program is "Washington Week in Review"; shown here are regular panelists Neil MacNeil of* Time *(left), Charles Corddry of the* Baltimore Sun *(right), and series moderator Paul Duke (center).*

HOST: Paul Duke    PRODUCER: Elvera Ruby    PRODUCTION COMPANY: WETA (Washington)

**THE WAVERLY WONDERS** (NBC)
*Friday 8:00-8:30 P.M.*

Football's Joe Namath fumbled as Harry Casey, an ex-basketball star who became a high school history teacher and coach. His acting matched the high school gym floor—wooden!

STAR: Joe Namath    COPRODUCERS: Bruce Kane, Steve Zacharias DIRECTOR: Dick Martin    WRITERS: Various    PRODUCTION COMPANY: Lorimar Productions, Inc.

**W.E.B.** (NBC)
*Thursday 10:00-11:00 P.M.*

Intended as an inside view of high-level TV network life, more or less inspired by the movie *Network*. It turned out to be a real bore. Even actress Pamela Bellwood's young TV executive failed to sustain consistent interest.

STAR: Pamela Bellwood    EXECUTIVE PRODUCER: Lin Bolen    PRODUCER: Chris Morgan    DIRECTORS: Various    WRITERS: Various    PRODUCTION COMPANY: A Lin Bolen Production

**WELCOME BACK, KOTTER** (ABC)
*Various times*

Gabe Kaplan and his cantankerous, lovable sweathogs played out their swan song in their fourth season. Kaplan was gone for a good part of the season, making a movie, *Fast Break*. His absence hurt the show.

STAR: Gabriel Kaplan    EXECUTIVE PRODUCER: James Komack    PRODUCERS: Bill Richmond, Gene Perrett    CREATED BY: Gabriel Kaplan, Alan Sacks    DIRECTOR (SEASON PREMIER): Norman Abbott    WRITERS: Bill Richmond, Gene Perrett    PRODUCTION COMPANY: A Production of the Komack Company, Inc. and Wolper Productions

**WHAT'S HAPPENING!!** (ABC)
*Various times*

The sitcom about three black teenagers fizzed out during its third and last season. The antics got broader, and sillier, and the cast mugged it up outrageously. They were funnier and less frantic when they started in 1976.

STARS: Ernest Thomas, Haywood Nelson, Fred Berry, Danielle Spencer, Mabel King, Shirley Hemphill    EXECUTIVE PRODUCERS: Bud Yorkin, Bernie Orenstein, Saul Turtletaub    DIRECTORS: Various    PRODUCTION COMPANY: A TOY Production

A well-done series about a washed-up pro basketball star who coaches a bunch of kids who've been goofing off at an L.A. high school. An earnest attempt to portray high school youngsters, mostly black, reacting to a man who loves the game of basketball. Rangy Ken Howard is excellent as the coach who really cares about his charges.

STARS: Ken Howard, Robin Rose, Jerry Fogel  EXECUTIVE PRODUCER: Bruce Paltrow  PRODUCER: Mark C. Tinker  DIRECTOR: Jackie Cooper  WRITER: Bruce Paltrow  PRODUCTION COMPANY: MTM

**THE WHITE SHADOW** (CBS)
*Monday 8:00-9:00 P.M.*

In NBC's scramble for ratings, they initiated this combination game show and mystery, sort of a cross between "Let's Make a Deal" and "Ellery Queen." Ed McMahon was the host of the short-run mess.

HOST: Ed McMahon  EXECUTIVE PRODUCER: Martin Starger  PRODUCERS: Bill Carruthers, Doris Quinlan  DIRECTORS: Bill Carruthers, Doris Quinlan, Don Wallace  WRITERS: Jeremy Lloyd, Lance Percival, Bill Mitchell  PRODUCTION COMPANY: Marble Arch Production

**WHODUNNIT?** (NBC)
*Thursday 8:30-9:00 P.M.*

LEFT: *Ken Howard has an encounter with Thomas Carter in the series "The White Shadow."*

RIGHT: *Gordon Jump (left), Tim Reid, and Gary Sandy tried to salvage a sinking radio station on "WKRP in Cincinnati."*

A dud from sitcom wizard Garry Marshall ("Happy Days" and "Laverne & Shirley"). A pair of nice Vegas showgirls are raising a 15-year-old troublemaking brother and his bright 9-year-old sister. Thoroughly bland comedy.

STARS: Caren Kaye, Larry Breeding, Scott Baio, Tammy Lauren, Lynda Goodfriend  EXECUTIVE PRODUCERS: Garry Marshall, Tony Marshall  PRODUCERS: Martin Nadler, Gary Menteer  PRODUCTION COMPANY: Henderson Productions in association with Paramount Television and NBC-TV

**WHO'S WATCHING THE KIDS** (NBC)
*Friday 8:30-9:00 P.M.*

This jaunty, good-natured comedy series about the running of a radio station in Cincinnati comes from the MTM stable, and the emphasis is on characters rather than on situations. An expert cast of players, especially Howard Hesseman as DJ Johnny Fever, keeps it lively. The show had a rough time, being shuffled around the CBS schedule, taken off the air, and brought back.

STARS: Gary Sandy, Gordon Jump  PRODUCER: Hugh Wilson  DIRECTORS: Various  STORY EDITORS: Tom Chehak, Bill Dial, Blake Hunter  PRODUCTION COMPANY: MTM

**WKRP IN CINCINNATI** (CBS)
*Monday 8:30-9:00 P.M.*

LEFT: *In a dream sequence, young Frankie, Scott Baio, sees himself as a millionaire toasting Memphis O'Hara, played by Lorrie Mahaffey, in an episode of "Who's Watching the Kids."*

RIGHT: *"Chachaji: My Poor Relation," a segment of "World," was author Ved Mahta's reminiscence of family life in India.*

**THE WONDERFUL WORLD OF DISNEY** (NBC) *Sunday 7:00-8:00 P.M.*

Although Mickey Mouse turned 50, the Disney TV show is only half that age— it reached its 25th year on the air this season (18 years on NBC). The series continues to offer staples of family entertainment, focusing on a blend of new productions from the Disney camp, as well as vintage Disney theatrical features.

SERIES EXECUTIVE PRODUCER: Ron Miller   DIRECTORS: Various
WRITERS: Various   PRODUCTION COMPANY: Walt Disney Productions in association with NBC-TV

**WORLD** (PBS)

A generally fine 14-part series of documentaries produced throughout the world. Among the best entries was "Chachaji: My Poor Relation," a study of old customs conflicting with the new way of life in India, and "Inside Europe: F-16: The Arms Sale of the Century," a thought-provoking program which succinctly detailed the high-level wheeling and dealing involved in a multibillion dollar jet fighter sale to four European nations.

EXECUTIVE PRODUCER: David Fanning   PRODUCTION COMPANY: WGBH-TV (Boston)

# MINISERIES

**BACKSTAIRS AT THE WHITE HOUSE** (NBC)

Superb acting, good scripts, and a handsome production made this nine-part miniseries about various presidents and their families, as seen through the eyes of the servants on the White House staff, a memorable one. Based on the book *My Thirty Years at the White House,* by Lillian Rogers Parks and Frances Spatz Leighton, Olivia Cole as the dignified Maggie Rogers—the first black maid to work in the White House—is the backbone of the series, along with Leslie Uggams, as her daughter Lillian.

STARS: Olivia Cole, Leslie Uggams, Louis Gossett, Jr.   DIRECTOR: Michael O'Herlihy   WRITERS: Gwen Bagni, Paul Dubov   PRODUCTION COMPANY: Ed Friendly Production

**THE BEST PLACE TO BE** (NBC)

Glossy four-hour miniseries which brought Donna Reed out of retirement. She shouldn't have bothered, since this was prime-time soap-opera melodrama without a trace of any real or human emotion. Patented pap from the Ross Hunter stable.

STARS: Donna Reed, Efrem Zimbalist, Jr., Betty White    PRODUCERS: Ross Hunter, Jacque Mapes    DIRECTOR: David Miller    WRITER: Stanford Whitmore    PRODUCTION COMPANY: Ross Hunter-Jacques Mapes Productions

The Watergate scandal as seen through the eyes of White House counsel John Dean, based on books written by Dean and his wife Mo, and augmented by transcripts from the Oval Office, was dramatized as an eight-hour series. It was very uneven, with too much emphasis placed on John and Mo's boring love story, but the White House office scenes, with Martin Sheen as Dean and Rip Torn as Nixon, were dramatically sound despite the familiarity of much of the material, and the lame table decision to "launder" the conversation of the foul-mouthed President Nixon. Rip Torn, playing Nixon, captured much of Nixon's unctuous quality.

**BLIND AMBITION**
(CBS)

STARS: Martin Sheen, Michael Callan, Lonny Chapman, Rip Torn    EXECUTIVE PRODUCER: David Susskind    PRODUCERS: George Schaefer and Renee Valente    CREATED BY: Ben Edwards    DIRECTOR: George Schaefer    WRITERS: John Dean and Maureen Dean    PRODUCTION COMPANY: A Time-Life Television Production

This rambling 26-hour adaptation of James Michener's *Centennial* was an uneven affair, at best. Michener took us from the late 1700s, when French-Canadian trappers paddled along the Platte River to hunt beaver and trade with the Indians, to today, when a historian appeared to compile the history of the town of Centennial.

**CENTENNIAL** (NBC)

Best performances were given by Richard Chamberlain, as a romantic Scot, and Robert Conrad, as a French trapper in the early chapters. Ambitious effort, meticulously produced.

STARS: Robert Conrad, Richard Chamberlain, Michael Ansara, Raymond Burr, Sally Kellerman    EXECUTIVE PRODUCER: John Wilder    DIRECTOR: Virgil Vogel    CREATOR/WRITER: James A. Michener's novel adapted for television by John Wilder    PRODUCTION COMPANY: Universal Studios Production in association with NBC-TV

LEFT: *Martin Sheen portrayed John Dean, Rip Torn was Richard Nixon, and Lawrence Pressman was H.R. Haldeman in the miniseries adapted from Dean's book about the Watergate cover-up conspiracy,* Blind Ambition.

RIGHT: *Richard Chamberlain played Alexander McKeag in the twenty-five-hour miniseries adapted from James Michener's best-seller,* Centennial.

**THE CHISHOLMS** (CBS)   An appealing six-hour miniseries about the wagon trains of the wild old West in the middle of the 19th century, graced by a fine cast—Rosemary Harris, Robert Preston, and Charles Frank—and a rousing musical score by Elmer Bernstein. What held it together was the sense of family that existed among the Chisholms.

STARS: Robert Preston, Rosemary Harris, Ben Murphy   EXECUTIVE PRODUCERS: Alan Landsburg, David Dortort   PRODUCER: Paul Freeman DIRECTOR: Mel Stuart   WRITER: Evan Hunter   PRODUCTION COMPANY: Alan Landsburg Productions

**THE CRITICAL LIST** (NBC)   A routine four-hour medical drama loosely based on the novel of the same name by Marshall Goldberg, starring Lloyd Bridges as the battling hero of the tale. Malpractice suits formed the core of the drama, but no new light was shed on the subject.

STARS: Lloyd Bridges, Robert Wagner, Buddy Ebsen   EXECUTIVE PRODUCER: Jerry McNeely   DIRECTOR: Lou Antonio   WRITER: Jerry McNeely PRODUCTION COMPANY: MTM Enterprises

**FROM HERE TO ETERNITY** (NBC)   Bristling dialogue straight from the hard-hitting James Jones novel; brazen sexuality from Natalie Wood and William Devane's characterizations made this three-part TV adaptation of the book fairly worthwhile. Admiring fans of the 1954 movie weren't won over, but the whole quality of this miniseries was gutsy and compelling.

STARS: Natalie Wood, William Devane   EXECUTIVE PRODUCERS: Harve Bennet, Harris Katelan   PRODUCER: Buzz Kulik   DIRECTOR: Buzz Kulik WRITERS: Don Mcguire, Harold Gast   PRODUCTION COMPANY: Bennet-Katleman Production in association with Columbia Pictures TV

LEFT: *Jimmy Van Patten, Rosemary Harris, and Stacey Nelkin were members of a frontier family in* The Chisholms, *a four-part miniseries.*

RIGHT: *Natalie Wood and William Devane starred in the miniseries based on James Jones's novel,* From Here to Eternity.

This four-part miniseries on various legends of the Bible suffered from a lack of imagination. The language of the familiar stories was everyday English and the casts were made up of secondary talents.

**GREATEST HEROES OF THE BIBLE** (NBC)

STARS: Lew Ayres, Robert Culp, John Carradine, John Marley  DIRECTOR: James Conway  WRITERS: Brian Russell, S.S. Schweitzer, Stephen Lord, Martin Roth  PRODUCTION COMPANY: Sunn Classic Films

The six-hour presentation of Dwight D. Eisenhower's World War II experiences was a frequently engaging drama. Robert Duvall as Eisenhower presented a portrait of a man of unswerving integrity to the army, but capable of personal warmth he tried desperately to conceal. His caustic, witty, but always conscientious driver, Englishwoman Kay Summersby, was magnificently portrayed by Lee Remick.

**IKE** (ABC)

The question of whether Ike did or did not bed down with Summersby, and whether or not Ike was impotent as Summersby states in her book, was conveniently avoided.

STARS: Robert Duvall, Lee Remick, Dana Andrews  EXECUTIVE PRODUCERS: Melville Shavelson, Louis Rudolph  PRODUCER: Bill McCutchen  DIRECTORS: Melville Shavelson, Bill McCutchen  WRITER: Melville Shavelson  PRODUCTION COMPANY: ABC Circle Films

Louisa May Alcott's classic about the March family during the Civil War has been dramatized brilliantly many times before. This four-hour adaptation successfully evoked some of the flavor of the novel, especially in the casting of Susan Dey as the rebellious and temperamental writer, Jo March.

**LITTLE WOMEN** (NBC)

STARS: Susan Dey, Meredith Baxter-Birney, Eve Plumb, Ann Dusenberry  PRODUCER: David Victor  DIRECTOR: David Lowell Rich  WRITER: Suzanne Clauser  PRODUCTION COMPANY: Universal TV in association with NBC

A six-hour World War II espionage miniseries with a winning lady spy to its credit. The spy network involved is run on several levels by David Niven, yet the fragile lady spy, played by Barbara Hershey, stole the show.

**A MAN CALLED INTREPID** (NBC)

STARS: David Niven, Michael York, Barbara Hershey, Paul Harding  DIRECTOR: Peter Carter  WRITER: William Blinn

Oscar-winner William Goldman penned this laconic four-hour two-part Western about the legendary scout Tom Horn, the man who captured the famous Apache warrior, Geronimo. This Western was meant to correct the white man's hero image, but it was too laborious, and David Carradine in the leading role gave new meaning to the word monotonous.

**MR. HORN** (CBS)

STARS: David Carradine, Richard Widmark, Karen Black  EXECUTIVE PRODUCER: Lee Rich  PRODUCER: Robert L. Jacks  DIRECTOR: Jack Starrett  WRITER: William Goldman  PRODUCTION COMPANY: Lorimar Productions, Inc.

This slick, "sexy," predictable six-hour miniseries dealt with the days just before and after the attack on Pearl Harbor on December 7, 1941. Writer Stirling Silliphant concocted a familiar potboiler, combining a set of readily

**PEARL** (ABC)

identifiable dramatic characters, an exotic locale, and the emotion-charged atmosphere of war.

STARS: Angie Dickinson, Dennis Weaver, Robert Wagner, Lesley Ann Warren   EXECUTIVE PRODUCERS: Stirling Silliphant, Frank Konigsberg   PRODUCER: Sam Manners   DIRECTOR: Hy Averback   WRITER: Stirling Silliphant   PRODUCTION COMPANY: Silliphant/Konigsberg Company in association with Warner Bros. Television

LEFT: *David Carradine portrayed adventurer Tom Horn in the mini-series* Mr. Horn.

CENTER: *Georg Stanford Brown carries on an age-old family tradition in a dramatic moment from* Roots: The Next Generations.

RIGHT: *Irene Cara, leaving home for the first time, bids farewell to her anxious parents Bever-leigh Banfield and Stan Shaw in a scene from* Roots: The Next Generations.

## ROOTS: THE NEXT GENERATION (ABC)

Riveting saga of Alex Haley's ancestors continued in another highly dramatic four-hour series, focusing on the years after the Civil War up to Alex's rise as a writer. Haley's painstaking search for the facts of his heritage, which would eventually become his celebrated book, *Roots,* was extremely interesting. When Haley finally met the oral historian in Africa who corroborated the abduction of Kunta Kinte by slave traders, the screen literally ignited with elation of joy. Satisfying sequel to the original landmark series.

STARS: Georg Stanford Brown, Lynn Moody, Debbi Morgan, Henry Fonda, Olivia de Havilland   EXECUTIVE PRODUCER: David L. Wolper   PRODUCER: Stan Margulies   DIRECTOR: Charles S. Dubin   WRITERS: Teleplay by Ernest Kinoy based on the book *Roots* by Alex Haley   PRODUCTION COMPANY: A David L. Wolper Production in association with Warner Bros. Television

## THE SACKETTS (NBC)

Feuding and fighting time out West for the Sackett boys added up to a rousing miniseries set in Colorado gold country, based on Louis L'Amour's novels. Cowboy fans had a treat in this lively two-parter.

STARS: Jeff Osterhage, Tom Selleck, Sam Elliott   PRODUCER: Douglas Netter   DIRECTOR: Robert Totten   WRITER: Jim Byrnes   PRODUCTION COMPANY: Media Productions, Inc.

## STUDS LONIGAN (NBC)

This six-hour miniseries, based on James T. Farrell's classic American trilogy about Studs Lonigan, the son of a lower-middle-class Irish Catholic family in Chicago in the 1920s and '30s, suffered from too many repetitive scenes. Harry Hamlin managed to make a good Studs, Reginald Rose's script was often too verbose, but this series captured more of the novel's enduring qualities than most such TV adaptations.

STAR: Harry Hamlin  EXECUTIVE PRODUCERS: Lee Rich, Philip Capice
PRODUCER: Harry S. Sherman  DIRECTOR: James Goldstone  WRITER:
Reginald Rose  PRODUCTION COMPANY: Lorimar Productions, Inc.

**WOMEN IN WHITE**
(NBC)

A patented four-hour miniseries about beleaguered women doctors in a Florida hospital, led by former soap-opera heroine, Susan Flannery. The plot was sudsy enough to make her feel right at home. Based on the novel by Frank Slaughter.

STARS: Susan Flannery, Stuart Whitman, Patty Duke Astin  EXECUTIVE PRODUCER: David Victor  PRODUCER: Robert F. O'Neill  DIRECTOR: Jerry London  WRITERS: Robert Malcolm Young, Irving Pearlberg  PRODUCTION COMPANY: Universal Television in association with NBC Entertainment

LEFT: *Marcy Hanson attracts the eye of Tom Selleck in the drama based on novels by Louis L'Amour,* The Sacketts.

CENTER: *Colleen Dewhurst, Harry Hamlin, and Charles Durning portrayed members of an embattled family in the miniseries adapted from James T. Farrell's* Studs Lonigan.

RIGHT: *Mario Scaccia portrayed a famous scholar whose reputation rests upon the authenticity of a fabulous archeological discovery in* The Word.

**THE WORD** (CBS)

Irving Wallace's best-selling trashy novel about the unearthing of an ancient document said to shed new light on religious beliefs was a ponderous, pretentious bore. David Janssen, Florinda Bolkan, John Huston, and James Whitmore were at the mercy of their sophomoric material.

STARS: David Janssen, Florinda Bolkan, John Huston, James Whitmore
EXECUTIVE PRODUCERS: Dick Berg, Charles Fries  PRODUCER: Robert
Markell  DIRECTOR: Richard Lang  PRODUCTION COMPANY: Dick Berg's
Stonehenge Productions in association with Charles Fries Productions

# SPECIALS

Listed below in alphabetical order are the top fifty specials of the 1978-79 season, in the opinion of the editors. For each of these we have identified the network, original air date, and available production credits, together with a brief description of the program.

Following the top fifty specials is a chronological listing, month by month, of all specials aired, listed by title in alphabetical order, with original air date and network identified.

## TOP FIFTY SPECIALS

**THE AMERICAN FILM INSTITUTE SALUTE TO ALFRED HITCHCOCK** (CBS)
*March 12, 1979*

The unquestioned master of suspense, whose 57-year career as director-and/or-producer of such classics as *The 39 Steps, The Lady Vanishes, The Man Who Knew too Much, To Catch a Thief, North by Northwest, Psycho,* and *Notorious* was honored with the "Life Achievement Award" bestowed upon him by the American Film Institute. Alfred Hitchcock never takes a back seat to his work, and he nearly stole the show with his caustic droll acceptance speech. Ingrid Bergman was very touching in her glowing remarks about the remarkable "Hitch."

STARS: Henry Fonda, Charlton Heston, John Houseman, Janet Leigh, Anthony Perkins, Ingrid Bergman, James Stewart PRODUCER: George Stevens, Jr. DIRECTOR: Marty Pasetta WRITER: Hal Kanter PRODUCTION COMPANY: The American Film Institute

**BAD BOYS** (PBS)
*October 29, 1978*

The video team of Alan and Susan Raymond offered this powerful, disturbing, low-cost, high-impact documentary essay on children and the society that so often brutalizes them, both in deep trouble. It focused on various children, male and female, black and white, all under 16, and their seemingly inexorable progression through three different institutions: public school, reform school, and finally a prison for juvenile offenders.

EXECUTIVE PRODUCER: David Loxton PRODUCERS: Alan and Susan Raymond PRODUCTION COMPANY: WNET (New York)

**BARYSHNIKOV AT THE WHITE HOUSE** (PBS)
*April 15, 1979*

The inimitable Mikhail Baryshnikov and his colleagues from the New York City Ballet performed in the East Room of the White House for President Carter and family. It was an hour of infinite beauty, grace, and skill ranging from virtuoso performances of Balanchine's ballet *Harlequinade* and *Rubies,* plus Jerome Robbins's elegant love dances to music by Chopin.

HOST: Edward Villella EXECUTIVE PRODUCER: Gerald Slater PRODUCER/ DIRECTOR: Emile Ardolino PRODUCTION COMPANY: WETA (Washington)

**THE BEST OF SATURDAY NIGHT LIVE** (NBC)
*January 10, 1979*

The wonderful comics of "Saturday Night Live" regaled fans with a recap of their three and a half seasons of late-night madness, a welcome second look at many of their best sketches in this raucously funny spree. Included were a look at their very first sketch performed in 1975 with John Belushi, Chevy Chase, and Michael O'Donahue; Steve Martin and Gilda Radner in their "Dancing in the Dark" take-off on Astaire and Charisse; the Coneheads at home; the Blues Brothers; and Belushi's great "Godfather" spoof.

STARS: Dan Akroyd, John Belushi, Chevy Chase, Jane Curtin, Garrett Morris, Bill Murray, Laraine Newman, Gilda Radner PRODUCER: Lorne Michaels DIRECTOR: Dave Wilson

**THE BODY HUMAN: THE SEXES** (CBS)
*May 21, 1979*

Narrator Alexander Scourby closed this vivid exploration of "the sexes" with the phrase: "He and she fascination never ends." Leading up to this previously disclosed fact, the documentary offered some extraordinary footage, made possible by recent technology, of the embryo's initial signs of sex; followed by the natural development of sexual differences; and the subsequent awakening of "the sexual time clock." A graphic, informative, adult hour. Remarkable cinematography credits due to Robert Elfstrom, Paul Goldsmith, Don Lenzer, and John L. Marlow.

NARRATOR: Alexander Scourby   EXECUTIVE PRODUCER: Thomas W. Moore
PRODUCERS: Robert E. Fuisz, M.D., Hank Whittemore, Alfred Kelman
DIRECTOR: Alfred Kelman   WRITERS: Robert E. Fuisz, M.D., Hank
Whittemore   PRODUCTION COMPANY: The Tomorrow Entertainment/
Medcom Company

By the time the evening was over, you savored the magic of this extraordinary opera diva as an artist and as a woman. On the occasion of what would have been Maria Callas's 55th birthday, Franco Zeffirelli lovingly narrated a 90-minute study of her remarkable life. Not only did we hear ecstatic but deeply individual tributes to the lady from such opera greats as Gian-Carlo Menotti, Zeffirelli, Tito Gobbi, and even Sir Rudolf Bing, who quarreled with her, but we also heard Callas in an enthralling 1968 interview with Lord Harewood.

**CALLAS** (PBS)
*December 2, 1979*

NARRATOR: Franco Zeffirelli   EXECUTIVE PRODUCERS: George Page, Jac
Venza   PRODUCERS: David Griffiths, Kenneth Carden, Peter Weinberg
DIRECTOR: Peter Weinberg   WRITER: John Ardoin   PRODUCTION COMPANY:
WNET (New York) in association with the BBC

C. S. Lewis's modern parable about four youngsters who accidently ventured into the magical land of Narnia was masterfully brought to life in this two-part animated fairytale, set among the wonders and mysteries of Narnia and its incredible inhabitants—the mighty Aslan, the Great Lion; the unscrupulous White Witch; and the lovable beaver family. Dazzling color and surrealistic animation contribute greatly to an unforgettable fantasy. Produced by the Children's Television Workshop, the creators of "Sesame Street."

**THE CHRONICLES OF NARNIA: THE LION, THE WITCH, AND THE WARDROBE** (CBS)
*April 1, 1979*

EXECUTIVE PRODUCER: David Connell   PRODUCER: Steve Melendez
DIRECTOR: Bill Melendez   ADAPTED BY : Bill Melendez, David Connell
PRODUCTION COMPANY: The Children's Television Workshop in association
with Bill Melendez Productions

The old reliable team of star Katharine Hepburn and director George Cukor are together once more in this remake of the celebrated Emlyn Williams play and equally successful film starring Bette Davis. With small reservations, this newest version of the story of the dedicated teacher, Miss Moffat, and her efforts to get at least one promising young man out of the Welsh coal mines and in to Oxford, works beautifully. Miss Hepburn's portrayal of the strong-willed Miss Moffat captured the nuances of a woman who will not be deterred from her goals. The supporting cast is perfect, and the physical production, shot on location in north Wales, adds greatly to the impact of this touching story.

**THE CORN IS GREEN** (CBS)
*January 29, 1979*

STARS: Katharine Hepburn, Ian Saynor, Bill Fraser, Anna Massey
PRODUCER: Neil Hartley   DIRECTOR: George Cukor   WRITER: Ivan Davis
PRODUCTION COMPANY: Warner Bros. Television

Carol Burnett proved in the past that she can team up with such diverse performers as Julie Andrews and Beverly Sills and come up with first-class entertainment. Dolly Parton joined Carol for a lively hour of wonderful songs and good-natured fun, taped at the Grand Ole Opry. Whether the two talented ladies were clad in jeans or glamorous gowns, they hit the bull's-eye each time, especially with a terrific medley of "heart" songs.

**DOLLY AND CAROL IN NASHVILLE** (CBS)
*February 14, 1979*

STARS: Carol Burnett, Dolly Parton   EXECUTIVE PRODUCER: Joe Hamilton

PRODUCERS: Ken Welch, Mitzie Welch, Joe Layton   DIRECTOR: Roger
Beatty   WRITERS: Ken Welch, Mitzie Welch, Joe Layton   PRODUCTION
COMPANY: Jocar Productions

LEFT: *Country-music star Dolly Parton gives a few pointers to Carol Burnett in their variety special "Dolly and Carol in Nash-ville."*

RIGHT: *Illusionist Doug Henning performed amazing feats on the holi-day special "Doug Hen-ning's World of Magic."*

**DOUG HENNING'S
WORLD OF MAGIC**
(NBC)
*December 14, 1978*

The marvelous illusionist Doug Henning unveiled his fourth live magic hour, revealing new mysteries and illusions. The flamboyant, appealing wizard's pièce de résistance was "The Miraculous Den of Tigers," in which Henning, hands tied, was dropped into a cage of growling tigers. Applause! Applause!

STARS: Doug Henning, Brooke Shields, Tom Bosley   EXECUTIVE PRODUCER:
Jerry Goldstein   PRODUCER: Walter C. Miller   DIRECTOR: Walter C. Miller
WRITERS: Buz Kohan, Doug Henning, Barbara DeAngelis Henning

**EINSTEIN'S
UNIVERSE** (PBS)
*March 13, 1979*

Peter Ustinov was the show's narrator, asking all the questions a poor, scientifically unschooled layman would ask of a group of brilliant research scientists involved in working on Einstein's theories. As Peter commented at the start, "confirming Einstein's ideas is now a global industry." This imaginatively conceived two-hour journey filled with mammoth telescopes, animation, and visual effects helped bring meaning out of scientific jargon, in the simple terms Einstein himself encouraged from the scientific community.

NARRATOR: Peter Ustinov   EXECUTIVE PRODUCER: Jo Gladstone
PRODUCER: Martin Freeth   DIRECTOR: Martin Freeth   WRITER: Nigel Calder

**FROM CHINA TO US**
(PBS)
*May 15, 1979*

This special gave us highlights of the tour made by the Performing Arts Company of the People's Republic of China during July and August of 1978. The program featured choreography filled with acrobatics, topped by excerpts from a Peking Opera production of a satire called "Monkey Makes Havoc in Heaven," in which marvelous pantomime, wildly dramatic makeup, and gorgeous costumes prevailed.

EXECUTIVE PRODUCER: Cyrus H. Bharucha   PRODUCER: Mark Lowry
DIRECTOR: Brian Large   COORDINATOR OF PRODUCTION: Stanley Dorfunson

All the talented performers connected with this concert, performed January 9, 1979, at the United Nations General Assembly Hall and telecast the next day, donated their services to UNICEF in the hopes of establishing a permanent fund for this organization. The roster included ABBA; the Bee Gees; Rita Coolidge; John Denver; Earth, Wind and Fire; Andy Gibb; Elton John; Kris Kristofferson; Olivia Newton-John; Rod Stewart; and Donna Summer.

**A GIFT OF SONG— THE MUSIC FOR UNICEF CONCERT** (NBC) *January 10, 1979*

EXECUTIVE PRODUCERS: Robert Stigwood, David Frost  PRODUCERS: Marty Pasetta and Ken Ehrlich  DIRECTOR: Marty Pasetta

This was an eloquent production of the classical ballet, *Giselle,* performed by members of the Bolshoi Ballet and filmed at the Bolshoi Theater in Moscow. Natalia Bessmertnova made an achingly lovely Giselle and Mikhail Lavrovsky a noble Count Albrecht.

**GISELLE** (NBC) *April 8, 1979*

STARS: Natalia Bessmertnova, Mikhail Lavrovsky, Vladimir Levashev
PRODUCER: E. Grigorian  PRODUCTION COMPANY: Gosteleradio (USSR) and LBA Associates

Fascinating documentary study of man's adventure with gold through the ages. The thoroughly absorbing hour detailed the difficulties of mining gold and the glories of working with it as jewelry of great beauty. A National Geographic Society entry.

**GOLD** (PBS) *January 1, 1979*

HOST: E. G. Marshall  PRODUCER: Irwin Rosten  ASSOCIATE PRODUCER: Sascha Schneider  DIRECTOR: Irwin Rosten  WRITER: Irwin Rosten
PRINCIPAL PHOTOGRAPHY: Andre Gunn  EDITED BY: David Saxon, A.C.E.
MUSIC BY: Lee Holdridge

The talented Hal Linden, TV's "Barney Miller," headlined his own musical special. The result was a stylish, clever, and original hour. Hal and his trio of TV-comedy leading ladies—Linda Lavin ("Alice"), Bonnie Franklin ("One Day at a Time"), and Cathryn Damon ("Soap")—entertained with a capital E. The special material was right on target at all times, and Hal's closing medley of songs from his Broadway musicals was super.

**THE HAL LINDEN SPECIAL** (ABC) *April 11, 1979*

STAR: Hal Linden  EXECUTIVE PRODUCERS: Jerry Levy, Paul Tush
PRODUCERS: Joe Layton, Ken Welch, Mitzie Welch  DIRECTORS: Kip Walton, Joe Layton  WRITERS: Stan Hart, Jules Tasca, Mitzie Welch  PRODUCTION COMPANY: INJA Productions, Inc., in association with Welch/Layton/Welch Productions

Playwright Arthur Miller wrote a lark of a play about fame and the absurdities that come from it, beautifully realized in this production starring Richard Benjamin and Jose Ferrer. There was a lightness of touch that made it frequently appealing, whether the suddenly famous writer, played by Benjamin, was seen shabbily dressed but recognized on the streets of New York; or badgered by an obtuse fool. Miller's originality and subtlety really come into play when Benjamin met an Italian filmmaker (Ferrer) and discovered whom he wanted to cast as the heroine of the film he had written. Linda Hunt, as the diminutive Mona, added a memorable bizarre quality to this comedy-drama.

**HALLMARK HALL OF FAME:** *Fame* (NBC) *November 30, 1978*

STARS: Richard Benjamin, Jose Ferrer, Raf Vallone  EXECUTIVE PRODUCERS: Gilbert Cates, Joseph Cates  PRODUCERS: Patricia Rickey, Marc Daniels
DIRECTOR: Marc Daniels  WRITER: Arthur Miller

LEFT: *Richard Benjamin enjoys the attentions of Shera Danese in Arthur Miller's* Fame, *a Hallmark Hall of Fame special.*

RIGHT: *Conductor Zubin Mehta and pianist Vladimir Horowitz at rehearsal for the special "Horowitz . . . Live!"*

**HERE TO MAKE MUSIC** (PBS)
*December 1, 1978*

This musical curio celebrated a chamber-music concert filmed almost a decade ago, performed by five instrumentalists who had made their mark by then, but whose careers have skyrocketed since: pianist-conductor Daniel Barenboim, then 26; cellist Jacqueline Du Pre, then 24; conductor Zubin Mehta (who plays double bass in the concert), then 33; violinist Itzhak Perlman, then 23; and violinist Pinchas Zukerman (who plays viola in the concert), then 21; playing Schubert's "Piano Quintet in A Major: The Trout."

PRODUCER: Christopher Nupen   DIRECTOR: Christopher Nupen
PRODUCTION COMPANY: Allergro Film

**HEROES OF ROCK 'N' ROLL** (ABC)
*February 9, 1979*

Rock 'n' roll fans savored this comprehensive look at the musical "fad" of the fifties, which became the dominant force of today's popular music. Tapping a variety of sources, producers Andrew Solt and Malcolm Leo compiled the most ambitious retrospective on the subject to date, featuring vintage film and tape of its most influential stars. A well-written script traced rock 'n' roll from its meager beginnings as a variation of rhythm and blues, to its present status as a worldwide billion-dollar industry. Of course, there was footage of the "biggies" like Elvis, plus the Beatles, Bob Dylan, and the Rolling Stones, but also on hand were memorable performances by Otis Redding, Buddy Holly, Chuck Berry, and Little Richard, and many many more.

HOST: Jeff Bridges   EXECUTIVE PRODUCER: Jack Haley, Jr.   PRODUCERS: Malcolm Leo, Andrew Solt   DIRECTORS: Malcom Leo, Andrew Solt
WRITERS: Malcolm Leo, Andrew Solt, Sam Egan   PRODUCTION COMPANY: Solt/Leo Productions in association with Twentieth Century-Fox TV

**HOROWITZ—LIVE!** (NBC)
*September 24, 1978*

From Avery Fisher Hall in New York City's Lincoln Center, music lovers everywhere were offered a special musical treat as Zubin Mehta conducted the New York Philharmonic in Rachmaninoff's "Third Piano Concerto," with world-famous pianist Vladimir Horowitz as soloist.

PIANIST: Vladimir Horowitz   EXECUTIVE PRODUCER: Herbert Kloiber
PRODUCER: John Goverman   DIRECTOR: Kirk Browning   PRODUCTION COMPANY: Clasart Films, Inc.

This special was taped December 3, 1978, before an invitational black-tie audience as a benefit for the Kennedy Center. Special tribute was paid to five of the world's most distinguished performing artists: Marian Anderson, Fred Astaire, George Balanchine, Richard Rodgers, and Arthur Rubinstein. Among those artists who performed for the honored quintet were violinists Itzhak Perlman and Isaac Stern; cellist Mstislav Rostropovich; composer-conductor Leonard Bernstein; blues singer Alberta Hunter; and Suzanne Farrell and Peter Martins of the New York City Ballet. A gala event! Highlights were clips of the wondrous Astaire dances, and the swinging Alberta Hunter, a great jazz singer "rediscovered" in her early eighties.

HONOREES: Marian Anderson, Fred Astaire, George Balanchine, Richard Rodgers, Arthur Rubinstein   PRODUCERS: George Stevens Jr., Nick Vanoff
DIRECTOR: Don Mischer   WRITER: George Stevens Jr.

**THE KENNEDY CENTER HONORS: A CELEBRATION OF THE PERFORMING ARTS** (CBS)
*December 5, 1978*

Touching, well-acted drama about a stubborn old man who won't cooperate with the plans of his children to place him in a convalescent home. Though the subject has been handled on TV many times before, the interest here was its focus on the point of view of the man's children, particularly that of the eldest son. It was the first TV production of work by a new playwright, George Rubino, and was headed by a fine cast including Tony Lo Bianco and Lee Strasberg, as son and father, respectively.

STARS: Tony Lo Bianco, Lee Strasberg, Christine Lahti   EXECUTIVE PRODUCER: Herbert Brodkin   PRODUCER: Robert Berger   DIRECTOR: Jud Taylor   WRITER: George Rubino   PRODUCTION COMPANY: Titus Productions, Inc.

**THE LAST TENANT** (ABC)
*June 25, 1978*

Leonard Bernstein was joined by an astonishing group of artists for a two-hour gala, live from Wolftrap Farm Park, in celebration of Mr. Bernstein's 60th birthday! The first part of the program was devoted to works by Mr. Bernstein including his "On the Waterfront"; and selections from *West Side Story, Wonderful Town,* and *Mass.* The second half, introduced by author Lillian Hellman, featured Mr. Bernstein conducting the final two movements of Beethoven's "Triple Concerto," performed by the National Symphony Orchestra, violinist Yehudi Menuhin, cellist Rostropovich, and pianist Claudio Arrau.

EXECUTIVE PRODUCER: David Griffiths   PRODUCER: Hal Hetkoff
DIRECTOR: Roger Englander

**LEONARD BERNSTEIN'S 60TH BIRTHDAY** (PBS)
*August 25, 1978*

A stimulating perceptive look at American architecture, past and present. Lewis Mumford, the 83-year-old architectural and social critic extraordinaire, takes a historical look at the mistakes we made since World War II, by building cold, abstract structures for people to live in, and inevitably creating slums out of our high-rise public housing. Mumford's advice, and that of corroborating architects, is build to a "human scale!"

EXECUTIVE PRODUCER: Ray Hubbard   PRODUCERS: Ray Hubbard, Mark Olshaker, Larry Klein   PRODUCTION COMPANY: Ray Hubbard Associates

**LEWIS MUMFORD: TOWARD HUMAN ARCHITECTURE** (PBS)
*May 22, 1979*

Hume Cronyn and Jessica Tandy remind us again how superbly talented they are. In this delightful stage presentation, taped before a live audience, Mr. Cronyn and Ms. Tandy cover the gamut of emotions about love, reading selections they have chosen from letters, plays, speeches, and poems.

**THE MANY FACES OF LOVE** (PBS)
*December 10, 1978*

STARS: Hume Cronyn, Jessica Tandy   PRODUCTION COMPANY: The Canadian Broadcasting Corporation

**MICKEY'S 50TH ANNIVERSARY**
*November 19, 1978*

Believe it or not, Mickey Mouse turned 50 years old. The event was celebrated with 90 minutes of nostalgia, full of vintage cartoons and anecdotes from celebrities. Everybody got into the act from former President Gerald R. Ford to Bette Davis, Raquel Welch, and Johnny Carson, with Elton John paying tribute to Mickey singing "Minnie's Yoo-Hoo."

DIRECTOR: Phil May   WRITERS: Nicholas Harvaey Bennion, Phil May
PRODUCTION COMPANY: Walt Disney Productions

**NORTH STAR: MARK DI SUVERO** (PBS)
*July 18, 1979*

The eccentric, individualistic sculptor, Mark di Suvero, was the subject of this interesting documentary, filmed by coproducer-director Francois de Menil over a two-year period in France and the United States. Whether or not you were taken by the massive di Suvero steel and iron structures, the 44-year-old bearded, outspoken, and sometimes naive artist who left the United States for France in 1971 as a protest of the Vietnam war, had stimulating remarks about his art and life. Also touched upon was di Suvero's tenacious fight back to health after a freak accident some years back which left him temporarily crippled. Provocative portrait of a highly unorthodox artist and man.

DIRECTED AND PHOTOGRAPHED BY: Francois de Menil   CONCEIVED AND WRITTEN BY: Barbara Rose

**ONE OF A KIND** (ABC)
*September 27, 1978*

This superbly acted, tender story confronted a difficult but appropriate subject for the afterschool set and their parents—child abuse! This poignant drama was produced by and starred Diane Baker as an overworked, single mother, grappling with her intense emotions while trying to provide for herself and her precocious daughter, all the while neglecting and abusing her child in the process.

STARS: Diane Baker, Ken Hill, Stephanie Brown   PRODUCER: Diane Baker   DIRECTOR: Harry Winer   WRITER: Marjorie Sigley   PRODUCTION COMPANY: Artemis Productions

*Stephanie Brown and Diane Baker starred in a sensitive family story "One of a Kind," one of the "ABC Afterschool Specials."*

Illuminating three-part documentary about the worldwide opium trade. Filmed in Burma, Hong Kong, the United States, etc.

**OPIUM** (PBS)
*October 1, 1978*

DIRECTOR: Adrian Lowell   WRITER: Elaine S. Svensson   PRODUCTION COMPANY: ATV, England

Not only was this a rare television opportunity to hear the Philadelphia Orchestra in rehearsal and performance, playing works by Debussy, Ives, Brahms, and Strauss, under the baton of its illustrious conductor Eugene Ormandy; but it was also an opportunity to see an American symphony orchestra on tour in Japan.

**ORMANDY AND HIS ORCHESTRA: JAPANESE ODYSSEY** (PBS)
*October 19, 1978*

PRODUCER: Allan Miller   DIRECTOR: Allan Miller   PRODUCTION COMPANY: WHYY (Philadelphia)

As eloquent and moving a human story as you're likely to find in a documentary, charged with unforgettable factual matter. The subject was the deadly long-term effects of low-level radiation, and the efforts of the United States government agencies to withold facts from the public over a period of twenty-five years. Paul Jacobs, the investigative reporter who died in January 1978, just a month after his last appearance in this documentary was filmed, was himself a victim of lung cancer attributed to low-level radiation he was exposed to during his early investigations of the subject, which he began in 1957.

**PAUL JACOBS AND THE NUCLEAR GANG** (PBS)
*February 25, 1979*

PRODUCER: Jack Willis   WRITERS: Jack Willis, Saul Landau   DIRECTORS: Jack Willis, Saul Landau

Fabulous art on display in this special highlighting some seven-hundred masterworks selected from eight Dresden collections dating back five-hundred years. The footage was taped in the museums and private collections of the East German city of Dresden and at the National Gallery in Washington, D.C. A feast for the eyes, as an endless array of ceramics, sculpture-jewels, furniture, and paintings were examined by the cameras in loving detail and definition.

**THE PRICELESS TREASURES OF DRESDEN** (PBS)
*June 27, 1978*

PRODUCER: Al Perlmutter   DIRECTOR: Sid Smith   WRITER: Lou Solomon

This is a highly recommended study of child abuse and neglect. Violent child abuse was discussed at some length by parents who felt inadequate and compensated by calling their children stupid or dumb, and by those who entered parenthood with fantasies about its joys and none of its responsibilities.

**RAISED IN ANGER** (PBS)
*January 11, 1979*

HOST: Ed Asner   PRODUCER: James Seguin   ASSOCIATE PRODUCERS: Sam Newbury, Margy Whitmer   DIRECTOR: James Seguin   WRITER: Stephen Dick   PRODUCTION COMPANY: WQED (Pittsburgh)

An enlightening sometimes irresponsible portrait of a man and his town, seen with his friends, as well as his detractors. Program was subtitled, "Documentary Melodrama," since it told the story of a man, adored by some of his South Philadelphia neighborhood pals, and despised by his political opponents who believe him to be a racist and a proponent of police violence in his zeal for law and order.

**RIZZO** (PBS)
*January 21, 1979*

PRODUCER: Heidi Trombert   DIRECTOR: Robert Mugge   PRODUCTION COMPANY: The Maryland Center for Public Broadcasting

**ROCKETTE: A HOLIDAY TRIBUTE TO THE RADIO CITY MUSIC HALL** (NBC)
*December 14, 1978*

A grand outing showcasing Ann-Margret in a wonderful array of musical numbers; with Gregory Peck, who was once an NBC page, on hand as the genial host. It's hard to single out the highlights of this well-paced musical special, but certainly Ben Vereen's high-stepping act with the Rockettes was one of them, as was his thirties-style tap routine with Ann-Margret. The awesome Rockettes were featured in some of their famous precision dance numbers, with Ann-Margret right at home kicking her shapely legs in the line.

STARS: Ann-Margret, Gregory Peck   PRODUCERS: Gary Smith, Dwight Hemion   DIRECTOR: Dwight Hemion

**RODEO RED AND THE RUNAWAY** (NBC)
*November 28, 1978*

Geraldine Fitzgerald has delighted us with her versatility in films, on stage, and on TV for years, and her performance in this afternoon drama confirmed her rare virtuosity again. She played a solid, Irish farm woman, who has maintained her inner and outer self with a rare compassion and strength as she makes a self-centered teenaged female runaway face her own selfishness.

STARS: Geraldine Fitzgerald, Marta Kober, Gil Rogers, Marlene Lustik
EXECUTIVE PRODUCER: Linda Gottlieb   PRODUCER: Doro Bachrach
DIRECTOR: Bert Salzman   WRITER: Bert Salzman   PRODUCTION COMPANY:
Highgate Pictures, a Division of Learning Corporation of America

**SARAH VAUGHAN IN CONCERT** (PBS)
*March 12, 1979*

This concert, taped during a performance at the Palace Theatre in Des Moines, Iowa, really gave "Sassy" Sarah's fans a special treat. Vaughan is one of the greatest jazz singers of all time and her miraculous voice was heard to good advantage.

STAR: Sarah Vaughan   PRODUCER: John Beyer   DIRECTOR: John Beyer
PRODUCTION COMPANY: The Iowa Public Broadcasting Network

**SHARKS: THE DEATH MACHINE** (NBC)
*September 6, 1978*

A well-photographed, absorbing account of a real shark hunt involving three businessmen. Includes a generous portion of stunning underwater sequences and closeups of those cruising beauties with the rows of pearly teeth.

EXECUTIVE PRODUCER: James W. Packer   PRODUCERS: Ken Shapiro, Nicholas Webster   DIRECTOR: Nicholas Webster   WRITER: Peter A. Lake   UNDERWATER PHOTOGRAPHY: Ron and Valerie Taylor

*Shirley MacLaine responds to a standing ovation at one of the world's most famous cabarets in the special "Shirley MacLaine at the Lido."*

Shirley MacLaine's enthusiasm for performing in this celebrated French cabaret set the tone for this high-powered hour of glittering production numbers set against Ms. MacLaine's ingratiating individual performing style. Shirley even got to do a dramatic recitation from her hit film *The Turning Point,* and it was quite moving.

STARS: Shirley MacLaine, Tom Jones   PRODUCERS: Dwight Hemion, Gary Smith   DIRECTOR: Dwight Hemion   WRITER: Buz Kohan   PRODUCTION COMPANY: Smith-Hemion Productions

**SHIRLEY MacLAINE AT THE LIDO** (CBS)
*May 20, 1979*

Extremely interesting historical review and analysis of South Boston, filmed in 1976 by an Irish TV network team, and originally broadcast in Dublin toward the end of 1977. What made the film so interesting was the way it captured the quality of life in this mostly Irish enclave, filled with people bound together by their religious faith and their pride in their community. In this homogeneous and highly traditional neighborhood the need for busing to accomplish school desegregation became a highly charged issue; the documentary probes for understanding of the shock of that struggle, and its lasting effect on South Boston.

PRODUCTION COMPANY: WGBH (Boston) and Irish Television

**SOUTHIE** (PBS)
*August 30, 1978*

An enjoyable show that celebrated Tin Pan Alley's great Irving Berlin classics. Steve and Eydie's guest Sammy Davis, Jr., mimed Bert Williams in a rendition of "Alexander's Ragtime Band"; Carol Burnett sang "Suppertime"; jazz pianist Oscar Peterson played "Cheek to Cheek"; and our hosts joined their guests in lengthy medleys. The obligatory clip of Bing Crosby intoning "White Christmas" was dutifully included.

STARS: Steve Lawrence, Eydie Gorme   EXECUTIVE PRODUCERS: Steve Lawrence, Gary Smith   PRODUCERS: Gary Smith, Dwight Hemion
DIRECTOR: Dwight Hemion   WRITER: Harry Crane   PRODUCTION COMPANY: A Stage-2 Production in association with Smith-Hemion Productions

**STEVE & EYDIE CELEBRATE IRVING BERLIN** (NBC)
*August 22, 1978*

A deliberately paced study of a strained relationship between a rigid mother and the daughter who left home 21 years ago to seek her independence. Emotionally satisfying thanks to the stalwart performances of Miss Rowlands as the fortyish daughter, and Bette Davis as her aging mother.

STARS: Gena Rowlands, Bette Davis   PRODUCERS: Robert W. Christiansen, Rick Rosenberg   DIRECTOR: Milton Katselas   WRITER: Michael de Guzman   PRODUCTION COMPANY: Chris-Rose Productions

**STRANGERS: THE STORY OF A MOTHER AND DAUGHTER** (CBS)
*May 13, 1979*

There was a sweetness and sensitivity about this story of the relationship between a young Jewish girl, luminously played by Kristy McNichol, and an escaped anti-Nazi POW, performed with tender restraint by Bruce Davison, that leaves an indelible impression on the viewer. Set in a small town in the Deep South during World War II, the play depicts the hatred of the townfolk for the german prisoners interned in their midst, and the bonds of friendship that develop between the girl and the young man.

STARS: Kristy McNichol, Bruce Davison, Esther Rolle   PRODUCER: Linda Gottlieb   DIRECTOR: Michael Tuchner   WRITER: Jane Howard Hammerstein   PRODUCTION COMPANY: Highgate Pictures in association with NBC-TV

**SUMMER OF MY GERMAN SOLDIER** (NBC)
*October 30, 1978*

LEFT: *Steve Lawrence, Lucille Ball, and Eydie Gorme in the special "Steve and Eydie Celebrate Irving Berlin."*

RIGHT: *Blythe Danner and Michael Moriarity starred in the dramatic special adapted from stories by John Updike, "Too Far to Go."*

**THE TAP DANCE KID**
(NBC)
*October 24, 1978*

Emmy-winning show. A warm, light-hearted tale about the trials and tribulations of an upper-middle-class black family named the Sheridans, superbly acted and produced. Cherubic newcomer James Pelham stole the show as the irrepressible "Tap Dance Kid," a feisty eight-year-old whose wish to dance in summer stock against his parents' orders is the premise of the show.

STARS: Danielle Spencer, James Pelham, Charles Blackwell, Anna Maria Horsford, Charles Honi Coles   EXECUTIVE PRODUCER: Linda Gottlieb
PRODUCER: Evelyn Barron   DIRECTOR: Barra Grant   WRITER: Barra Grant
PRODUCTION COMPANY: Highgate Pictures, A Division of Learning Corporation of America

**THE TELEVISION ANNUAL 1978-79** (ABC)
*May 14, 1979*

The broadcast side of this publication is "The Television Annual" TV special, produced in conjunction with the International Radio and Television Society, which debuted this season on ABC, and will rotate in future to each of the other networks. The program is a retrospective look at the highlights of the television season that made it unique, recalled for viewers by stars and industry figures from all the networks, joining for an evening of celebration and reminiscence.

EXECUTIVE PRODUCERS: Steven H. Scheuer, Jordan Ringel, Stanley Moger
PRODUCER: Robert Arthur   WRITER: Robert Alan Arthur
PRODUCTION COMPANY: SFM Media Service Corporation/Hopewell Productions

**THE THIRD BARRY MANILOW SPECIAL**
(ABC)
*May 23, 1979*

The effervescent pop star Barry Manilow seemed more comfortable in his third stylish network special, and his offbeat guest star, the low-keyed John Denver, worked out well, too. As always, Barry's solo selections were deftly staged, and his adoring fans were everywhere in evidence. Manilow's songs included "Ready to Take a Chance Again" and "What's on Your Mind?"

STAR: Barry Manilow   EXECUTIVE PRODUCER: Miles Lourie   PRODUCERS: Barry Manilow, Ernest Chambers   DIRECTOR: Don Mischer   WRITERS: Barry Manilow, Ernest Chambers   PRODUCTION COMPANY: Manilow Productions

**TOO FAR TO GO** (NBC)
*March 12, 1979*

Since 1956, John Updike has written 17 short stories about the life and times of Richard and Joan Maple. William Hanley deftly adapted them into a literate two-hour special starring Michael Moriarty and Blythe Danner as the suburban couple about to terminate their marriage of more than 20 years. Though the subject matter was familiar, this particular version was far better, thanks to the Updike dialogue, and quite engrossing. Skillfully conceived and executed by executive producer Robert Geller.

STARS: Michael Moriarty, Blythe Danner   EXECUTIVE PRODUCERS: Chris Schultz, Robert Geller   DIRECTOR: Fielder Cook   WRITER: William Hanley   PRODUCTION COMPANY: Sea Cliff Productions

The answer to the question about the DeBolts is that they're a near saintly couple who adopted and are rearing 19 children (20 at last count) of many races and backgrounds in their own home. What makes this generosity of mind and spirit even more remarkable is the fact that all the children are physically handicapped, some of them severely. This edifying example of generosity and love should have been telecast in its entirety, but even this much abbreviated version of the Academy Award-winning documentary was a most ennobling show.

**WHO ARE THE DeBOLTS—AND WHERE DID THEY GET 19 KIDS?** (ABC)
*December 17, 1978*

HOST: Henry Winkler   EXECUTIVE PRODUCERS: John Korty, Henry Winkler   PRODUCER: John Korty   DIRECTOR: John Korty   PRODUCTION COMPANY: Fair Dinkum Productions Inc., John Korty Films

Orson Welles narrated this two-part story starring Cicely Tyson as Harriet Tubman, a slave who escaped to freedom across the Mason-Dixon line, but returned many times to rescue other slaves via her Underground Railroad. The entire cast was excellent, and the development of Harriet's character wonderfully realized, especially in one dramatic scene in which her employer forces her to wear a harness and pull a wagon to amuse his guests. Part 1 concludes with her successful escape, while Part 2 focuses attention on Tubman's efforts as a free woman to help others to the North despite the efforts of a detective hired by wealthy plantation owners to kill her.

**A WOMAN CALLED MOSES** (NBC)
*December 11 and 12, 1978*

STARS: Cicely Tyson, Dick Anthony Williams, John Getz, James Wainwright   PRODUCERS: Ike Jones, Michael Jaffe   DIRECTOR: Paul Wendkos   WRITER: Lonne Elder, III   PRODUCTION COMPANY: Henry Jaffe Enterprises, Inc.

This intimate, engrossing series of interviews with a diverse group of American homosexuals was a provocative two-hour documentary. The candor of those interviewed was refreshing—viewers who might have found the subject hard to confront may have been drawn to many of these so-called "outcasts." Emotions ranging from guilt and sorrow to an overwhelming joy for life were frankly expressed. The documentary's most memorable subjects included Elsa Gidlow, a 79-year-old poet; and an extremely outgoing middle-aged former WAC whose ribald anecdotes are sprinkled with humor as well as pathos.

**WORD IS OUT** (PBS)
*October 10, 1978*

PRODUCER: The Mariposa Film Group   CONCEIVED BY: Peter Adair
PRODUCTION COMPANY: WNET (New York)

## CHRONOLOGICAL LIST OF ALL SPECIALS

**JUNE 1978**

"After Bakke: Who Gets Ahead?" (PBS) June 30
"America Salutes Richard Rodgers" (CBS) June 3
"Are You a Missing Heir?" (ABC) June 8
"Canal Zone" (PBS) June 26
"Circus of the Stars" (CBS) June 11

"College Can Be Killing" (PBS) June 27
"George Crumb: Voice of the Whale" (PBS) June 5
"Good Mornin' Blues" (PBS) June 20
"Jacques Lipchitz" (PBS) June 6
*The Last Tenant* (ABC) June 25
"McNamara's Band" (ABC) June 10
"Minnesota Orchestra 75th Anniversary" (PBS) June 13
"No Way to Run a Government" (PBS) June 30
"The People's Command Performance" (CBS) June 22
"The Priceless Treasures of Dresden" (PBS) June 27
"The Rosenberg-Sobell Case Revisited" (PBS) June 19
"Solzhenitsyn at Harvard" (PBS) June 8
"Tomorrow's Stars" (ABC) June 17
"Tony Awards Ceremonies" (CBS) June 4
"The Unwanted" (PBS) June 20
"Welfare" (PBS) June 5

JULY     "From Paris with Love: An Evening of French TV" (PBS) July 14
"Funny Business" (CBS) July 26
"Miss Universe Pageant" (CBS) July 24
"New Orleans Concerto" (PBS) July 1
"North Star: Mark di Suvero" (PBS) July 18
"The Rock Rainbow" (ABC) July 15

AUGUST     "An Architectural Odyssey With G. E. Kidder Smith" (PBS) August 2
*The Belle of Amherst* (PBS) August 29
"A Day to Remember: August 28, 1963" (PBS) August 27
"Down Home" (CBS) August 16
"Drum Corps International" (PBS) August 18
"The Fabulous 50s" (NBC) August 22
"Festival of the Stars" (CBS) August 15
"The Joffrey Ballet: Live from Art Park" (PBS) August 23
"The Leningrad Ice Show" (CBS) August 29
"Leonard Bernstein's 60th Birthday Celebration" (PBS) August 25
"Live from the Grand Ole Opry" (PBS) August 26
"Memories of Elvis" (NBC) August 29
"Oho: Zoo Gorilla" (PBS) August 30
*Out of Our Father's House* (PBS) August 2
"Paul Anka in Monte Carlo" (CBS) August 27
*The People vs. Inez Garcia* (PBS) August 8
"Ship Shape" (CBS) August 1
"Sinatra and Friends" (ABC) August 9
"Southie" (PBS) August 17
"Tut, The Boy King" (NBC) August 3
"TV on Trial" (PBS) August 15
"A Wilder Wilder" (PBS) August 30
"Winner Take All" (NBC) August 18

SEPTEMBER     "Dr. Strange" (CBS) September 6
"Echoes of Silver" (PBS) September 20
"Elvis: Love Me Tender" (ABC) September 9
"The Emmy Awards" (CBS) September 17
"Eric Hoffer: The Crowded Life" (PBS) September 7

"GE All Star Anniversary" (ABC) September 29
"John Denver in Alaska" (ABC) September 3
"Los Angeles Philharmonic at the Hollywood Bowl" (PBS) September 12
"Mark Russell Comedy Special" (PBS) September 26
"Miss America Pageant" (NBC) September 9
"Mstislav Rostropovich at the White House" (PBS) September 17
"The Popeye Show" (CBS) September 13
"Sharks: The Death Machine" (NBC) September 6
"Something for Joey" (CBS) September 8
"The 36 Most Beautiful Girls in Texas" (ABC) September 4
"Thracium: Gold" (PBS) September 14
"The Time of Your Life" (PBS) September 6
"Union Maids" (PBS) September 19
"Us Against the World" (NBC) September 9

"Bad Boys" (PBS) October 10
"Bix Beiderbecke Memorial Dance Festival" (PBS) October 1
"Bob Hope Special" (NBC) October 15
"Boston's Marathon Man" (PBS) October 19
*Bugs Bunny Howl-o-ween Special* (CBS) October 25
"California Reich" (PBS) October 22 and October 28
"The Country Music Association Awards" (CBS) October 9
*Dr. Seuss* (ABC) October 26
*Fat Albert's Halloween Special* (CBS) October 25
"Grease Band" (PBS) October 26
"Hee Haw 10th Anniversary" (NBC) October 22
"Leontyne Price at the White House" (PBS) October 8
"The Magic of David Copperfield" (CBS) October 27
"Opium: Part 1, The Warlords" (PBS) October 1
"Opium: Part 2, The Politicians" (PBS) October 2
"Opium: Part 3, White Powder Opera" (PBS) October 3
"Ormandy and His Orchestra: Japanese Odyssey" (PBS) October 19
"Pompeii: Frozen In Fire" (PBS) October 26
*Puff, The Magic Dragon* (CBS) October 30
"A Salute to American Imagination" (CBS) October 5
"Sinai Field Mission" (PBS) October 22
*Summer of My German Soldier* (NBC) October 30
"Superstars on Stage at Ohio Fair" (ABC) October 23
"U.N. Day Concert" (PBS) October 24
"Word Is Out" (PBS) October 10 and October 15

"Affair in the Air" (PBS) November 26
"All Star Family Feud" (ABC) November 6
"An Evening With Chuck Mangione" (PBS) November 2
"Battle of the Network Stars" (ABC) November 18
"Bobby Vinton's Rock 'n' Rollers" (CBS) November 20
"Cinderella at the Palace" (CBS) November 2
"Dean Martin's Celebrity Roast" (NBC) November 21
"Dick Clark's Good Old Days" (NBC) November 25
"Every Tub on Its Own Bottom" (PBS) November 22
*Fame* (NBC) November 30
"Frankie and Annette: The Second Time Around" (NBC) November 18
"Geraldine Fitzgerald at Reno Sweeney's" (PBS) November 9

"The Harpsichord Maker" (PBS) November 16
"Here to Make Music" (PBS) November 30
"Hollywood's Diamond Jubilee" (CBS) November 11
*How Bugs Bunny Won the West* (CBS) November 15
*Lil Abner in Dogpatch Today* (NBC) November 9
"The New Klan Image" (PBS) November 19
"Pat Boone Thanksgiving Special" (ABC) November 12
"Portrait of a Nurse" (PBS) November 8
"Race War in Rhodesia" (PBS) November 15
"Return Engagement" (NBC) November 17
"Sing-Sing Thanksgiving" (PBS) November 23
"The Star Wars Holiday Special" (CBS) November 17
"The Steve Martin Special" (NBC) November 22

**DECEMBER**  *Amahl and the Night Visitors* (NBC) December 24
"America Salutes the Performing Arts" (CBS) December 5
*The Bear Who Slept Through Christmas* (NBC) December 19
"Bing Crosby—The Christmas Years" (CBS) December 6
"A Birthday Party for Josef Strauss" (PBS) December 31
"Bob Hope Special" (NBC) December 3
"Bob Hope Special" (NBC) December 22
"The Carpenter's Christmas" (ABC) December 19
"Cedar Rapids Symphony Orchestra" (PBS) December 31
*A Charlie Brown Christmas* (CBS) December 18
"Christmas At the Grand Ole Opry" (ABC) December 13
"A Christmas Celebration" (PBS) December 20
"A Christmas Celebration" (PBS) December 23
"Christmas Eve on Sesame Street" (PBS) December 21
"Christmas Heritage" (PBS) December 21
"Christmas Heritage" (PBS) December 24
*The Christmas Miracle in Caufield, U.S.A.* (NBC) December 26
*Christmas Snows, Christmas Winds* (PBS) December 20
"A Conversation with the Carters" (ABC) December 14
"A Country Christmas" (CBS) December 7
"Dean Martin" (NBC) December 9
*Dr. Seuss's How the Grinch Stole Christmas* (CBS) December 16
"Doug Henning's World of Magic" (NBC) December 14
"Drugs in America" (PBS) December 2
"Elizabethan Christmas Celebration" (PBS) December 7
"Fifth Annual Bach Festival" (PBS) December 10
"Fifth Annual Bach Festival II" (PBS) December 17
*The Flintstones* (NBC) December 11
*Frosty's Winter Wonderland* (ABC) December 13
*The Gift of the Magi* (NBC) December 21
*The Girl with the Incredible Feeling* (PBS) December 13
"Hallmark: *Stubby Pringles Christmas*" (NBC) December 17
"Hanukkah" (PBS) December 12
"Holiday Tribute to Radio City Music Hall" (NBC) December 14
*The Homecoming—A Christmas Story* (CBS) December 23
"Jackie Gleason's Christmas" (ABC) December 10
"John Davidson Christmas Special" (ABC) December 22
"The Johnny Cash Christmas Show" (CBS) December 6
"The King Orange Parade" (NBC) December 29
*Les Miserables* (CBS) December 27

*Like the Wind* (PBS) December 16
*The Little Drummer Boy* (NBC) December 21
"Living Sands of Nambia" (PBS) December 10
*Lovey: A Circle of Children,* Part 2 (CBS) December 13
"Mac Davis Christmas Special" (NBC) December 19
"Mark Russell Comedy Special" (PBS) December 27
*Morning Blues* (PBS) December 7
*Nestor, the Christmas Donkey* (ABC) December 13
"The Nobel Prize" (PBS) December 12
*Nutcracker Suite* (CBS) December 24
*Once upon a Starry Night* (NBC) December 19
"Perry Como's Christmas" (ABC) December 13
*The Pink Panther's Christmas* (ABC) December 7
"The Priceless Treasures of Dresden" (PBS) December 28
*Rudolph's Shiney New Year* (ABC) December 9
*Rudolph the Red-Nosed Reindeer* (CBS) December 6
*Santa Claus Is Coming to Town* (ABC) December 10
*Simple Gifts: Six Episodes for Christmas* (PBS) December 17


"The Amazing World of Psychic Phenomena" (NBC) January 17      **JANUARY 1979**
"America Entertains Vice Premier Teng Xiaoping" (PBS) January 29
"The American Family: An Endangered Species" (NBC) January 1
"American Music Awards" (ABC) January 12
"The Best of Saturday Night Live" (NBC) January 10
"Bob Hope Special" (NBC) January 28
"The Challenge of the Super Heroes" (NBC) January 18
*Champions: A Love Story* (CBS) January 13
"Circus Highlights" (NBC) January 31
"Dean Martin" (NBC) January 19
"George Burns" (CBS) January 22
"Gift of Song" (NBC) January 10
"Gold" (PBS) January 7
*Happy Birthday, Charlie Brown* (CBS) January 5
"Hong Kong—A Family Portrait" (PBS) January 28
*It's Your First Kiss, Charlie Brown* (CBS) January 8
"The Making of a Myth" (PBS) January 6
"Mark Twain's America" (NBC) January 11
"Mr. Speaker: A Portrait of Tip O'Neill" (PBS) January 22
"The 9th Annual Entertainer of the Year Award" (CBS) January 10
*The Phenomena of Benji* (ABC) January 21
*The Puppy Who Wanted A Boy* (ABC) January 21
"Raised in Anger" (PBS) January 11
"Rizzo" (PBS) January 21
"Rona Barrett Special" (ABC) January 1
"The Talking Walls of Pompeii" (PBS) January 17
"Thieves of Time" (PBS) January 17
"Tony Orlando Special" (NBC) January 3
"A Tribute to Martin Luther King, Jr." (PBS) January 15
*The Two-Five* (ABC) January 7


"All Star Family Feud" (ABC) February 12      **FEBRUARY**
*Bugs Bunny's Valentine* (CBS) February 14
"Celebrity Challenge Of The Sexes" (CBS) February 25

"Circus Super Heroes" (NBC) February 1
"Dolly And Carol In Nashville" (CBS) February 14
"Dragons Of Paradise" (PBS) February 11
"DuPont Journalism Awards" (PBS) February 6
"Grammy Awards Ceremonies" (CBS) February 15
"The Heroes Of Rock 'n' Roll (ABC) February 9
*Langston* (PBS) February 7
"Leontyne Price at the White House" (PBS) February 3
"Liberace: A Valentine Special" (CBS) February 3
"Mark Russell Comedy Special" (PBS) February 26
"Mehta And His Music: A Tour Triumph" (PBS) February 24
"Paul Jacobs and the Nuclear Gang" (PBS) February 25
*The Popeye Valentine Special* (CBS) February 14
"Roots, Rock, Reggae" (PBS) February 7

MARCH  "AFI Salute to Alfred Hitchcock" (CBS) March 12
"All-Star Salute To Pearl Bailey" (CBS) March 14
"American Pop: The Great Singers" (PBS) March 17
"American Youth Awards" (NBC) March 2
"Andres Segovia at the White House" (PBS) March 11
"The Captain And Tennille Special" (ABC) March 26
"A Celebration Of Straus" (PBS) March 7
"Cleveland Orchestra 60th Anniversary" (PBS) March 27
"Einstein's Universe" (PBS) March 13
"The Four Freshmen In Concert" (PBS) March 7
"Just Call Me Maestro" (PBS) March 18
"Leopard of the Wild" (NBC) March 1
"Methadone: An American Way of Dealing" (PBS) March 27
"The People's Choice Awards" (CBS) March 8
"200th Episode Celebration of 'All In The Family' " (CBS) March 4
*Up In Rosebud Country* (PBS) March 20
*Wild Horses, Broken Wings* (PBS) March 8

APRIL  "An Americanism—Joe McCarthy" (PBS) April 24
"America's Junior Miss Pageant" (CBS) April 14
"Austin City Limits" (PBS) April 2
"Baryshnikov At The White House" (PBS) April 14
*Beauty and The Beast* (NBC) April 6
"Black Mans Land: Kenyatta" (PBS) April 5
"Black Mans Land: Mau Mau" (PBS) April 4
*The Bugs Bunny Easter Special* (CBS) April 13
"California's Public Workers: A Time of Crisis" (PBS) April 21
"Catching Salmon" (PBS) April 1
"The Cheryl Ladd Special" (ABC) April 9
"The Do It Yourself Messiah" (PBS) April 14
"Dorothy Hamill's Corner of The Sky" (ABC) April 23
*The Easter Bunny is Coming To Town* (ABC) April 14
"The 51st Annual Academy Awards Presentation" (ABC) April 9
"The First Easter Rabbit" (CBS) April 7
"The Great Midwest Hot Air Ballon Race" (PBS) April 18
*Happy Birthday, Donald Duck* (NBC) April 4
"Here Comes Peter Cottontail" (CBS) April 10
*It's The Easter Beagle, Charlie Brown* (CBS) April 9

*Aslan, the noble lion, sacrifices himself for the sake of the magical land of Narnia in the animated special "The Lion, the Witch, and the Wardrobe."*

"John Denver's Rocky Mountain Reunion" (ABC) April 29
"Library of Congress" (PBS) April 10
*The Lion, The Witch, and The Wardrobe* (CBS) April 1
"The Miss U.S.A. Pageant" (CBS) April 30
"Off Your Duff" (PBS) April 17
*On Vacation With Mickey Mouse And Friends* (NBC) April 11
"One of the Missing" (PBS) April 19
"Pat Boone and Family Easter Special" (ABC) April 14
"Perry Como's Springtime Special" (ABC) April 9
"Royal Heritage, The Medieval King" (PBS) April 13
"Royal Heritage, The Tutors" (PBS) April 20
"Running the Show" (PBS) April 1
*The Scarlet Letter* (PBS) April 2
"The 2nd Annual National Collegiate Cheerleading Championship"
   (CBS) April 16
"A Special Kenny Rodgers" (CBS) April 12
*Transplant* (CBS) April 17
"Who Killed Martin Luther King?" (PBS) April 7
*Who Remembers Mama?* (PBS) April 18

**MAY**

"Academy of Country Music Awards" (NBC) May 2
"Alan King" (ABC) May 24
"Alexander's Bachtime Band" (PBS) May 8
*An Apple, An Orange* (PBS) May 29
"Applachian Moods" (PBS) May 17
"Barbara Walters Special" (ABC) May 29
"Battle of The Network Stars" (ABC) May 7
"The Best of Saturday Night Live" (NBC) May 4
"Bob Hope" (NBC) May 30
*A Boy Named Charlie Brown* (CBS) May 26
"Chevy Chase" (NBC) May 10
"Dean Martin" (NBC) May 11

"From China to Us" (PBS) May 15
"Glen Campbell—Back To Basics" (NBC) May 20
"Gravity Is My Enemy" (PBS) May 17
"The Guiness Book of World Records" (ABC) May 20
"The Heifetz Concert" (PBS) May 23
"Irish Treasures" (PBS) May 12
"Johnny Cash Springtime Special" (CBS) May 9
"Lewis Mumford: Toward Human Architecture" (PBS) May 22
"The Lief Garrett Special" (CBS) May 18
"The London Palladium Anniversary Special" (NBC) May 14
"Meeting of Minds" (PBS) May 26
"The Muppets Go Hollywood" (CBS) May 16
"Once a Daughter" (PBS) May 9
"The Originals: Women in Art" (PBS) May 14
"Over Easy: Four Alone: The Older Women In America" (PBS) May 13
"Paul Lynde Goes Ma-a-a-d" (ABC) May 12
"Playboy 25th Anniversary" (ABC) May 7
"Rites of Spring" (PBS) May 20
"Roy Clark Flying Down to Provo" (ABC) May 5
"Run America, Run" (PBS) May 29
"Shirley MacLaine at the Lido" (CBS) May 20
*Snoopy, Come Home* (CBS) May 14
"Steve Martin: A Wild and Crazy Guy" (NBC) May 2
"The Television Annual 1978–79" (ABC) May 14
"Views of Asia: Thailand" (PBS) May 24
*Wild West Revisited* (CBS) May 9

# MADE-FOR-TV FILMS

**AMATEUR NIGHT**
**\* NBC**

Henry Gibson, Tanya Tucker

*Amateur Night* is an apt title. A Dixie roadhouse is the setting for this bomb examining the crowd that hangs out there and the help that serves them booze and small talk. Country music star Tanya Tucker made her acting debut as a singer stricken by stagefright during an amateur talent contest, with Henry Gibson trying too hard as her manager . . . but in the final analysis, who cares?

D\*: Joel Schumacher                                    104 minutes

**ANATOMY OF A**
**SEDUCTION**
**\*\*\* CBS**

Susan Flannery, Jameson Parker, Rita Moreno

The older woman-younger man love affair is explored with some moments of genuine emotion. Susan Flannery stars as the beautiful 40-year-old divorced mother who takes up with her best friend's 20-year-old son. Jameson Parker, in the pivotal role of the young man home from Princeton for the summer, shows the stuff that stars are made of. It's inevitable that the subject matter eventually sinks to the level of soap opera, but there are enough substantial scenes, good acting, and honest writing by Alison Cross to make it worthwhile.

D: Steven Hilliard Stern                                104 minutes

\*D means Director.

Blair Brown, David Ackroyd, Maggie Cooper

A show for the hardy. This true story about a gutsy young lady who survived an air crash in the Sierra Nevadas in 1976, written by the survivor herself, Lauren Elder, stars Blair Brown, who does her best in recreating Lauren's nightmare descent down the side of an icy precipice.

D: Billy Graham                                                 104 minutes

*Jeffrey Bravin and Sally
Struthers in a drama
about a deaf child,* And
Your Name Is Jonah.

Sally Struthers, James Woods

A heartbreaking, sometimes poignant story about a seven-year-old deaf child originally diagnosed as mentally retarded. Jeffrey Bravin, a deaf youngster in real life, gives a moving performance as the untrained, undisciplined Jonah, whose mom (Sally Struthers) painfully discovers the best way to cope with the situation. James Woods is especially effective as the boy's traumatized father, but this "Jonah" belongs to young Jeffrey.

D: Richard Michaels                                             104 minutes

**AND YOUR NAME
IS JONAH**
*** CBS

Kathleen Beller, Blythe Danner

An ordinary drama that strives to come to grips with an important subject: the rape of a high school girl by one of her classmates, and the social and legal aftermath which ensues. Unfortunately, the contrived script remains melodramatic, with young, pretty Kathleen Beller staked out, threatened by a series of menacing notes and phone calls, and brutally attacked.

D: Walter Grauman                                               104 minutes

**ARE YOU IN THE
HOUSE ALONE?**
*1/2 CBS

**BATTERED**
*** NBC

Karen Grassle, LeVar Burton, Mike Farrell

Powerful, disturbing drama about a national plague which has received little attention until recently—wife beating. Karen Grassle, best-known for her role in the NBC series "Little House on the Prairie," gets double credits and kudos. She researched and co-authored the screenplay with Cynthia Lovelace Sears, and she is seen to good advantage as a victim of wife beating. Scenario has some plot problems but it holds up and does explain some of the difficulties law-enforcement officers and victims have in combating this widespread inter-family violence.

D: Peter Werner                                                          104 minutes

**BEACH PATROL**
*1/2 ABC

Christine DeLisle, Richard Hill, Jonathan Frakes

A routine police story with a woman in the lead. Christine DeLisle is a member of a special police team in southern California that patrols the beaches in dune buggies. While trying to capture a drug pusher, she is menaced by a maniacal sniper.

D: Robert Kelljan                                                         90 minutes

**BETRAYAL**
**1/2 NBC

Lesley Ann Warren, Rip Torn

A true story of a psychiatrist who has an affair with his patient in the name of "therapy" becomes a sudsy made-for-TV film. Sexy Leslie Ann Warren plays the victim, and Rip Torn the villainous psychiatrist who knows how to put women under his spell. It may be seamy, chilling stuff, but Rip Torn has a field day playing the lie-down-now-we'll-talk-later lecher.

D: Paul Wendkos                                                         104 minutes

**BIG BOB JOHNSON AND HIS FANTASTIC SPEED CIRCUS**
1/2* NBC

Charles Napier, Maud Adams, Connie Forslund

A "greasy" story about the adventures of an auto-racing team, complete with a lady mechanic. A rich kid hires the team for a head-to-head Rolls-Royce race against uncle for the family booty. This one's for sappy kids or auto nuts: The wrenches and the transmissions give the best performances.

D: Jack Starrett                                                         104 minutes

**THE BILLION DOLLAR THREAT**
* ABC

Dale Robinette, Patrick Macnee, Ralph Bellamy

James Bond should sue! A blatant ripoff of the 007 adventure yarns, this time the agent is an American called Robert Sands, but his derring-do follows the Bond mode, down to the adversary who threatens to pierce the earth's ozone layer.

D: Barry Shear                                                           104 minutes

**BJ AND THE BEAR**
* NBC

Claude Akins, Greg Evigan

Shades of *Smokey and the Bandit!* Silly drivel about a guitar-playing trucker (Greg Evigan) who travels around with a pet monkey called Bear, and agrees to transport a group of girls across a county line only to discover the local sheriff is in hot pursuit. This was a pilot for a subsequent series on NBC.

D: John Peyser                                                          104 minutes

Buddy Hackett, Harvey Korman, Michelle Lee, Robert Reed

**BUD AND LOU**
\*\*\* NBC

This drama tells about the backstage lives and tumultuous careers of the famous comedy team Abbott and Costello, beginning with their burlesque and vaudeville days, through their highly successful movie career. *Bud and Lou*, a revealing and sometimes sad narrative, offers a candid glimpse of the true personalities of the team, particularly Lou Costello's troublesome and unsavory character. Buddy Hackett excels as the rotund and obnoxious Lou Costello; Harvey Korman is equally good as his browbeaten partner.

D: Robert C. Thompson                                         104 minutes

Reb Brown, Heather Menzies, Len Birman

**CAPTAIN AMERICA**
1/2\* CBS

The Marvel comic book hero, Captain America, tests the TV waters. Steve Rogers (Reb Brown) follows in the footsteps of his famous crime-fighting dad, with super powers thanks to the supersteroid FLAG—Full Latent Ability Gain for the ignorant. Rubbish!

D: Rod Holcomb                                         104 minutes

Bob Denver, Alan Hale, Jr.

**THE CASTAWAYS ON GILLIGAN'S ISLAND**
\* NBC

Strictly for fans of the witless series. Picking up from the conclusion of their last TV movie *Rescue from Gilligan's Island*, this opus chronicles the castaways' misadventures in attempting to be rescued once again. Ends with the Gilligan crew buying the island and turning it into an offbeat resort.

D: Earl Bellamy                                         104 minutes

Martha Scott, Lynne Moody, Delta Burke

**CHARLESTON**
\*\* NBC

Magnolias and melodrama, set in the post-Civil War South, which reminds one of a dozen other such movies including big chunks of the plot of *Gone With the Wind*. The leading roles are played by two relatively new faces, Delta Burke, as Stella Farrell, the Scarlett O'Hara role; and Patricia Pearcy as her wishy-washy cousin. Lynne Moody, as a black servant, has the best part in the film.

D: Karen Arthur                                         104 minutes

Beau Bridges, Blair Brown, David Groh

**THE CHILD STEALER**
\*\*\*1/2 ABC

The subject of a divorced parent abducting his children from his ex-wife is given a sensitive, honest, compelling treatment. Blair Brown is absolutely heart-wrenching as the divorced woman who has her two young daughters snatched by her desperate ex-husband, only to find the authorities can do very little to help her to find them. Beau Bridges, who invariably gives a fine performance, outdoes himself as the father who takes illegal measures when he feels his kids' love for him is being usurped by a new man in his former wife's life. There's not a wasted gesture or a superfluous scene in this gripping story.

D: Mel Damski                                         104 minutes

Jason Robards, Eva Marie Saint, George Parry, Joanne Woodward

**A CHRISTMAS TO REMEMBER**
\*\*\*1/2 CBS

Jason Robards is in top form playing a gruff, cantankerous, ailing old Minnesota farmer who treats his city-bred grandson with derision. Robards and young George Parry, as the grandson who must weather the initial shock of farm chores, make a grand pair. A moving script and splendid acting turn this into quality fare, beautifully adapted by Steven Stern from the novel by Glendon Swarthout.

D: George Englund                                          104 minutes

**CLONE MASTER**
*** NBC

Art Hindle, Ralph Bellamy, Robyn Douglas

One might have thought after all the media coverage about cloning and test-tube babies in 1978 that this Hollywood version might be just another ho-hum mystery in which the bad guys muscle in on brainy scientists, but happily that isn't the case. John D. F. Black, one of our better mystery writers, not only effectively dramatizes the act of cloning, but also shows us how clones might go through an identity crisis—all of them being exactly alike. This sci-fi mystery deserves a look because of its script, production values, and stars.

D: Don Medford                                            104 minutes

**THE COMEDY COMPANY**
** CBS

Jack Albertson, Lawrence Hilton-Jacobs, Michael Brandon

There are two well-known nightspots, one in New York City (The Improv), and one in Hollywood (The Comedy Store), which cater to new comics striving to develop their material and delivery; both clubs have spawned some of the brightest young comics of the '70s. This film tries to capture that process but fails. Jack Albertson plays an ex-vaudevillian who runs The Comedy Company, a Hollywood spot where young comics do their stuff. It's part drama, part comedy routines, and very uneven.

D: Lee Philips                                            104 minutes

**COTTON CANDY**
**1/2 NBC

Charles Martin Smith, Clint Howard

Try a little nepotism . . . perhaps that explains this youthful entry directed by Ron Howard of "Happy Days" and written by and starring his younger brother Clint. A teenage tale about high school kids who form a rock band, this is a pleasant surprise. This simple honest account concerns misfits who sound terrible at first, but then gradually get it together.

D: Ron Howard                                             104 minutes

**CRASH**
**1/2 ABC

William Shatner, Eddie Albert, Adrienne Barbeau

Another of those plane-crash stories, this one based upon a real incident in which over 70 people survived. It's melodramatic, and often descends to soap-opera level because so many stories are told in the form of vignettes. However, the crash footage and the earnest depiction of the event in all its horror is a plus for those who enjoy "jeopardy" yarns.

D: Barry Shear                                            104 minutes

**CRISIS IN MID-AIR**
** CBS

George Peppard, Desi Arnaz, Jr., Karen Grassle

Back again in the crisis-ridden airport! This predictable drama is played in the aircraft and in the air traffic control center, and on the landing strip itself.

D: Walter Grauman                                         104 minutes

Talia Shire, Burt Young, Doug McKeon

Depressing, downbeat subject about a lower-middle-class family (which doesn't have a bright spot in their drab existence). Written by actor Burt Young, who also plays the laborer father, it focuses on the constant bickering of the married couple and the effect it has on their sensitive young son. Doug Mc-Keon gives the film's best performance as young Peter, but the focus of the story defeats everyone long before the final fadeout.

D: Adell Aldrich                                           104 minutes

Jane Seymour, Bert Convy

Corny, flashy melodrama about the Dallas Cowboys cheerleaders squad. Naturally, the girls—all 36 of them—are the big lure here, but Jane Seymour, as a journalist on assignment to write an exposé, carries the bulk of the acting chores. Bucky Dent, the baseball hero with the All-American look, has an incidental role as a boyfriend of one of the cheerleaders.

D: Bruce Bilson                                           104 minutes

Robert Forster, Adrienne Barbeau, Ray Milland

Another TV movie about the duplication of a human being. Labeled a thriller, there isn't much to prompt gooseflesh as Robert Forster agrees to assist in an experiment in which he is cloned.

D: Gus Trikonis                                           104 minutes

Richard Hatch, Bruce Davison

A sleeper for Rock 'n' Roll fans, this well-made film tells the story of a pair of California kids, Jan and Dean, who became famous with a string of hit surfing songs. Richard Hatch and Bruce Davison portray the real-life duo, with Hatch turning in a sensitive performance as cocky Jan, later crippled in an auto smashup at the height of their fame, struggling to retrain his damaged brain and body.

D: Richard Compton                                        104 minutes

Brenda Vaccaro, Arlen Dean Snyder, Ron Silver

Brenda Vaccaro tries to hit the bull's-eye with this pilot for a TV series, but once again, she's better than her material. Inspired by a French film of director Philipe DeBroca, Brenda plays a police detective sergeant who meets a professor and embarks on an offbeat romance while continuing her investigation of a multiple murder.

D: Dean Hargrove                                          104 minutes

Steve Forrest, Ned Romero

James Fenimore Cooper's intrepid hero Hawkeye, played by Steve Forrest, and his Indian blood brother, played by Ned Romero, steal through the woods, out to rescue cousin Wah-Tah-Wa from the Hurons. This clumsy version of an enduring American historical romance puts its emphasis on action rather than acting or dialogue.

D: Dick Friedenberg                                       78 minutes

**DESPERATE WOMEN**
*1/2 NBC

Susan St. James, Ronee Blakely, Ann Dusenberry, Dan Haggerty

Westerns seldom worked when played for laughs. This silly piece of business about three ladies abandoned in the desert is no exception. The girls ham it up as the scruffy females, while Dan Haggerty plays a gunman who comes to the rescue.

D: Earl Bellamy                                                            104 minutes

**DEVIL DOG: THE HOUND OF HELL**
* CBS

A Devil Dog is not always a piece of cake with white cream filling! There are shades of *The Omen* here when a family pet, an innocent enough looking puppy, turns out to be bewitched with the soul of the devil. Ridiculous!

D: Curtis Harrington                                                       104 minutes

**DONNER PASS: THE ROAD TO SURVIVAL**
*** NBC

Robert Fuller, Andrew Prine, John Anderson

Cannibalism comes to the home screen in this interesting version of an authentic Western tragedy. The unlucky Donner family survives hostile Indians, wild bears, stampedes, and bad weather, but starvation in the High Sierras turns humans into animals. How and why these pioneers broke the code of human behavior is the point of the drama, not the gory details, which are handled with restraint.

D: James L. Conway                                                         104 minutes

**DUMMY**
***1/2 CBS

LeVar Burton, Paul Sorvino

An astonishing account of a real-life drama, brilliantly performed by its leads, LeVar Burton and Paul Sorvino. Burton plays a 20-year-old black deaf mute charged, on circumstantial evidence, with the murder of a prostitute; Sorvino plays his attorney, a deaf man who lost his hearing after he had already learned to speak, read, and write. Their portrayal of the triumph of communication and trust between the defendant and lawyer is unfailingly moving.

D: Frank Perry                                                             104 minutes

**ELVIS!**
***1/2 ABC

Kurt Russell, Season Hubley, Shelley Winters

The first in what may become an unending line of films about Elvis Presley, the "King of Rock 'n' Roll." Kurt Russell is surprisingly adept at recreating Elvis in manner, appearance, speech, and performance. Elvis's saga traces him from meager beginnings to the triumphant 1971 comeback engagement in Las Vegas. Season Hubley is cast as Elvis's wife Priscilla; Shelley Winters and Bing Russell are his parents; and Pat Hingle plays Colonel Tom Parker, the manager who masterminded Elvis's phenomenally successful career.

D: John Parker                                                             104 minutes

**FAST FRIENDS**
**1/2 NBC

Edie Adams, Dick Shawn, Carrie Snodgrass, Susan Heldfond

A fairly provocative behind-the-scenes look at a network TV talk show, presided over by a not-so-nice host. This really isn't a roman à clef since writer-producer Sandra Harmon hasn't based her talk-show star on any one real-life personality. The story is played out through the initiation of a new assistant talent coordinator on the show, played by newcomer Susan Heldfond. Dick Shawn is perfectly cast as the host, and Edie Adams is quite good as a Judy Garland type of singer.

D: Steven H. Stren

## A FIRE IN THE SKY
**\*\*1/2** NBC

Richard Crenna, Elizabeth Ashley

Pretty fair disaster story: A comet is taking dead aim at Phoenix, Arizona, but since no one knows for sure, city officials procrastinate over arranging evacuation plans. When the panic button is finally pushed, the film takes off, with good special effects and crowd scenes in Phoenix, giving the drama real Hollywood gloss.

D: Jerry Jameson                                    156 minutes

## FIRST YOU CRY
**\*\*\*\*** CBS

Mary Tyler Moore, Richard Crenna, Anthony Perkins, Jennifer Warren

TV Newswoman Betty Rollin's candid book about her mastectomy and the readjustment period following the operation is turned into a poignant drama with Mary Tyler Moore giving an excellent performance as Ms. Rollin. The scene in which Betty is told she may have to have a mastectomy sets the stage for the tense and revealing portrait of a woman who feels that her life may be over. Mary honestly conveys the anxiety, depression, and torment of the situation, going from stoicism to tears to rage before beginning to build a new life for herself. One of the very best made-for-TV films.

D: George Schaefer                                    104 minutes

## FLATBED ANNIE AND SWEETPIE: LADY TRUCKERS **\*\*1/2** CBS

Annie Potts, Kim Darby, Harry Dean Stanton, Billy Carter

Women's lib meets *Smokey and the Bandit,* and they're off in a wild and woolly yarn about lady truckers trying to stay one step ahead of their creditors and an assortment of other bad guys. Potts and Darby are talented and almost redeem the silly story, otherwise notable for the brief appearance of Billy Carter, yes, *that* Billy Carter, in the role of a highway trooper. Now that even Hollywood TV film producers know what a swinish lout Billy Carter is, *Flatbed* marks the beginning, and likely the ending, of his movie career.

D: Robert Greenwald                                    104 minutes

LEFT: *Kurt Russell as* Elvis!

RIGHT: *Annie Potts with Billy Carter, making his film debut, in* Flatbed Annie & Sweetpie: Lady Truckers.

**FLYING HIGH**
**½\* CBS**

Jim Hutton, Kathryn Witt, Pat Klous, Connie Sellecca

This is the pilot (no pun intended) which sold the lamentable series of the same name about a trio of stewardesses. The inane dialogue and plotting make "Charlie's Angels" look like Pulitzer Prize material. The lasses are beautiful, and one of them can actually act; Jim Hutton, as a psychologist on the prowl, has some of the worst lines ever written.

D: Peter Hunt                                                    104 minutes

**FRIENDLY FIRE**
**\*\*\*\* ABC**

Carol Burnett, Ned Beatty, Sam Waterson

One of the finest made-for-TV films ever. To their lasting shame, during the 1960s and nearly all of the 1970s the television networks refused to broadcast any significant dramas dealing seriously with the Vietnam war (*Sticks and Bones* was one of the few exceptions to this rule). *Friendly Fire* is a deeply moving drama based on the actual story, adapted from C.D.B. Bryan's book, of an Iowa farm couple who turn against the war after learning that their son's death in Vietnam was caused by "friendly fire"—accidental shelling by American artillery. Carol Burnett gives her finest acting performance to date as the distraught mother fighting to extract the truth from the government about what happened to her son.

D: David Greene                                                  162 minutes

**THE GIFT OF LOVE**
**\*½ ABC**

Marie Osmond, Timothy Bottoms

Marie Osmond gets a chance to act in this dramatization based on the classic O. Henry story "The Gift of the Magi," and demonstrates that, lacking dramatic training, she'd best stick to singing.

D: Don Chaffey                                                   104 minutes

**THE GIRLS IN THE OFFICE \*\*½ ABC**

Susan St. James, Barbara Eden, Tony Roberts, David Wayne

The setting for this glossy glimpse of women trying to rise in the world of big business is a large department store. Susan St. James is quite effective as an ambitious worker who pays a big price to see her dreams realized. The rest of the cast is also pretty good; predictable, but not boring.

D: Ted Post                                                      104 minutes

**THE GRASS IS ALWAYS GREENER OVER THE SEPTIC TANK \*\*\* CBS**

Carol Burnett, Charles Grodin

At first glance, humorist Erma Bombeck's best seller about life in suburbia would seem to be a perfect vehicle for Carol Burnett, but it reads better than it plays in this adaptation which comes off as an updated version of *Please Don't Eat the Daisies*. Carol, as writer-mother-wife-and-bottle-washer Dorothy Benson, her ad agency exec husband (Charles Grodin), and their two kids leave the city to seek the good life in the suburbs, only to encounter one pitfall after another. Carol and Charles do their best. Has some nice moments.

D: Robert Day                                                    104 minutes

**HANGING BY A THREAD \*½ NBC**

Patty Duke Astin, Joyce Bulifant, Bert Convy, Donna Mills

Irwin Allen is at it again! The movie and TV master of disaster loves to throw a group together to fight fires, floods, flying insects, or worse, for what seems an

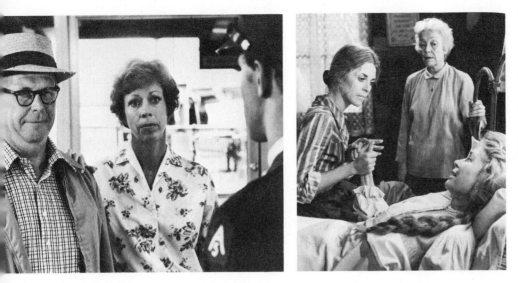

LEFT: *Ned Beatty and Carol Burnett in a real-life drama,* Friendly Fire.

RIGHT: *Lindsay Wagner brings modern medicine to backwoods folk Jane Wyman and Dorothy Mc-Guire in* The Incredible Journey of Doctor Meg Laurel.

eternity. This time, a disabled tram car dangling dangerously over a deep gorge supplies the treacherous setting for a lineup of guest victims. The subplots are many, as are the flashbacks revealing unhappy secrets of the trapped group. Strictly for those who like to sweat it out vicariously.

D: George Fenady                                                    208 minutes

Suzanne Somers, Bruce Boxleitner

Suzanne makes her starring TV-movie debut in this lightweight comedy-drama. Although every effort is made to help her bring it off well, she lacks the acting ability to project more than a cutout of the vulnerable young singer she portrays, drowning in the opportunistic world of show biz in Las Vegas. Bruce Boxleitner, on the other hand, is winning as the handsome lumberjack who pursues her with relentless glee. Their scenes together almost make up for the script's deficiencies.

D: Robert Scheerer                                                 104 minutes

**HAPPILY EVER AFTER**
**1/2 CBS

Grant Goodeve, Gregg Henry

Time-wasting opus about the National Drag Racing Championships, set in a small Southern town with more than its share of corrupt politicians. Strictly predictable racing car adventure.

D: George Armitage                                                 104 minutes

**HOT ROD**
* NBC

Peter Falk, Nicol Williamson, Tricia O'Neill

This intricately plotted, way-out baffler keeps Falk's deceptively fumbling Detective Columbo involved in a cunning game of wits with a more than worthy opponent—a mad psychologist dealing in mind control and well-fanged Dobermans trained to kill. One of the great actors of our time, Nicol Williamson, is well cast as the bizarre doctor, and his precise, clipped style contrasts beautifully with Falk's funky delivery.

D: James Frawley                                                   78 minutes

**HOW TO DIAL A MURDER**
**1/2 NBC

**HOW TO PICK UP GIRLS \*\*1/2 ABC**

Fred McCarien, Bess Armstrong, Desi Arnaz, Jr.

A fairly amusing romantic comedy in which relative newcomer Fred McCarien plays a shy guy learning to play the game and score with the ladies. McCarien is offbeat and appealing, and has a good supporting cast in Armstrong, Arnaz, and Deborah Raffin, who appears in an extended cameo role.

D: Bill Persky                                        104 minutes

**HUMAN FEELINGS \*\*1/2 NBC**

Nancy Walker, Billy Crystal

In this TV fantasy, God is not only a woman, but She is Nancy Walker! Miss Walker wants to wreak her vengeance on gawdy, bawdy Las Vegas and dispatches an emissary, angel Billy Crystal (seen on ABC's series "Soap") to handle the job. Naturally he falls in love with a sexy mortal and botches the mission. It's too cute, but the capable cast manages to keep the laughter perking sometimes.

D: Ernest Pintoff                                    78 minutes

**I KNOW WHY THE CAGED BIRD SINGS \*\*\* CBS**

Diahann Carroll, Ruby Dee, Esther Rolle, Madge Sinclair

Growing up black in the dusty Southern town of Stamps, Arkansas, during the thirties, was poetically explored by author Maya Angelou in her novel *I Know Why the Caged Bird Sings.* Though there's something lost in its transfer to the screen, enough of the flavor survives to make it worthwhile. The treatment may be fragmented and occasionally melodramatic, but Esther Rolle as the grandmother in Arkansas creates a memorable portrait of a courageous woman who maintains a sense of dignity for herself and her family, and Madge Sinclair sparkles in two brief scenes as a schoolteacher who encourages Maya to write.

D: Fielder Cook                                      104 minutes

**THE INCREDIBLE JOURNEY OF DR. MEG LAUREL \*\*1/2 CBS**

Lindsay Wagner, Jane Wyman

Lindsay Wagner stars in this sometimes interesting account of a determined young woman doctor who returns to her roots in Appalachia to try to help the backwoods inhabitants who are leery of modern medicine. Though three hours is much too long for this simple tale, once Lindsay's Meg Laurel gets to Appalachia and locks horns with the local healer, Granny Arrowroot (Jane Wyman), the drama comes to life. Lindsay does well in the leading role, but it's Jane who takes the acting honors.

D: Guy Green                                         156 minutes

**ISHI, THE LAST OF HIS TRIBE \*\*\* NBC**

Dennis Weaver, Elroy Phil Casados

An unusual Indian story unfolds starring Dennis Weaver and Apache Elroy Phil Casados. This is a sympathetic account of the last wild Indian, hounded by California gold miners, who finally gave himself up in 1911. Befriended by a Berkeley anthropologist (Weaver), Ishi tells his story through flashbacks from his residence in a San Francisco museum. We are witness here to the contrast between the Indian way of life and the white man's grasping style.

D: Robert Ellis Miller                               104 minutes

Dennis Weaver, Sheldon Leonard

Dennis Weaver's appearance as a retired lawyer manages to add a trace of sanity to a complicated plot about mobsters, call girls, and a law partner accused of beating a stewardess. In addition to the now-familiar Honolulu scenery, there's good old Sheldon Leonard making growling noises as the local hood.

D: Paul Krasny                                                                104 minutes

**THE ISLANDER**
*1/2 CBS

Elizabeth Montgomery, Bradford Dillman, Scott Hylands

Elizabeth Montgomery squares her jaw and comes out fighting as a widow battling for control of her late husband's boat-building firm. Based on a British TV series, the plot is fairly predictable: Most of the males in the story are rats, including the heroine's late philandering husband, but it's Liz's show.

D: Guy Green                                                                  104 minutes

**JENNIFER:
A WOMAN'S STORY**
** NBC

Peter Strauss, Richard Lawson, Roger E. Mosley, Miguel Pinero

Peter Strauss stars in this excellent film about a tense, wound-up prisoner serving a life term, who becomes obsessed with running the fastest mile possible. When his running comes to the attention of prison officials, they try to clear the way for him to qualify for the Olympic trials, and the story really takes off. Location filming at Folsom State Prison, with many of the bit parts and extras portrayed by actual prisoners, lends a startling note of authenticity. Strauss is quite convincing, and has a particularly memorable scene in which he breaks down while talking to the prison psychiatrist about his murder conviction. Credit for making this one of the better made-for-TV films must go to director Michael Mann who has given the film an incredible sense of place, and a big-budgeted theatrical look.

D: Michael Mann                                                             104 minutes

**THE JERICHO MILE**
***1/2 ABC

Raymond Burr, Stella Stevens

Raymond Burr is back with us playing—you guessed it—a criminal lawyer! Burr's Frank Jordan is an ex-con who served time for a crime he didn't commit,

**THE JORDAN
CHANCE** **1/2 CBS

LEFT: *Peter Strauss is a prisoner training for the Olympics in the contemporary drama* The Jericho Mile.

RIGHT: *Raymond Burr plays the familiar role of a lawyer in* The Jordan Chance.

and he studied law in the pen. Now outside, he specializes in defending those he feels have been given a raw deal by the courts. It's the old Burr formula, with a few new gimmicks added.

D: Jules Irving                                                        104 minutes

**KATIE: PORTRAIT OF A CENTERFOLD**
*1/2 NBC

Kim Basinger, Vivian Blaine, Dorothy Malone

Kim Basinger, a cutie from Georgia, plays Katie, a Texas lovely whose modeling career turns sour in Hollywood after an assignment as a centerfold girl for a men's magazine. Ms. Basinger has more than good looks, but she can't do much with the material here.

D: Robert Greenwald                                                    104 minutes

**KISS MEETS THE PHANTOM** ** NBC

Anthony Zerbe, KISS (Gene Simmons, Peter Criss, Ace Frehley, Paul Stanley)

The colorful superstar rock group makes its TV debut. KISS are a wild bunch: One spits fire, another shoots rays from his eyes, as they outwit an amusement park madman played by old reliable Anthony Zerbe. In addition to their weird optical effects, KISS offer a concert segment.

D: Gordon Hessler                                                      104 minutes

**LADY OF THE HOUSE** **1/2 NBC

Dyan Cannon, Armand Assante, Zohra Lampert

Dyan Cannon shines in this glossy, if laundered, version of the story of San Francisco's notorious madam, Sally Stanford, who becomes the mayor of the Marin County suburb of Sausalito. As Sally tells it, she was an honest woman until her divorce from a classy Bay City attorney (Assante); but after being framed on charges of running a bordello, she takes up the trade and prospers. This rags-to-riches-to-politics yarn follows some predictable avenues, but Ms. Cannon's energetic flair keeps the film from bogging down.

D: Ralph Nelson and Vincent Sherman                                    104 minutes

**LEGEND OF THE GOLDEN GUN** ** NBC

Jeff Osterhage, Hal Holbrook, Carl Franklin, Keir Dullea

Western about a farmer who turns into a deadly shot in order to seek revenge against Quantrill and his Raiders, who've murdered his family. Jeff Osterhage is the hero, John Colton, but the major attraction of the film is Hal Holbrook playing fast-draw John Hammer, the man who teaches Colton the tricks of the trade.

D: Alan J. Levy                                                        104 minutes

**LES MISERABLES** ***1/2 CBS

Richard Jordan, Anthony Perkins, John Gielgud, Celia Robson

Although this Victor Hugo classic has been filmed a number of times, this production may well become the definitive one. It's handsomely mounted, filmed for the most part in France, and boasts a script by John Gay that allows the characterizations to build in depth. Richard Jordan is superb as Jean Valjean, the impoverished man who is imprisoned for stealing a loaf of bread for his sister's starving family. Jordan has the stature, the bearing, and the talent to carry off the heroic role; Anthony Perkins is interesting as Inspector Javert, Valjean's nemesis. Jordan and this epic story will sweep you along.

D: Glenn Jordan                                                        156 minutes

Linda Lavin, Kristy McNichol

**LIKE MOM, LIKE ME**
** CBS

A sensitive, though slow-moving account of a mother and her teenage daughter who face life anew after their college professor husband/father runs off with a student. In lesser hands, the often soggy material would die, but Linda Lavin and the talented Kristy McNichol add a sense of reality.

D: Michael Pressman                                          104 minutes

Shaun Cassidy, Linda Purl, Hope Lange

**LIKE NORMAL PEOPLE**
*** ABC

This is the touching real-life story of Roger and Virginia Rae Meyers, a courageous retarded couple who fell in love and got married despite the odds against them. Similar to another TV film on the subject, *No Other Love,* the portrayals here are more realistic in this thoughtful and engrossing treatment. Linda Purl is astonishing in capturing the spirit as well as the mannerisms of the retarded young lady; Shaun Cassidy, surprise!, is quite valid as the retarded boy who fights for a normal life with the girl he loves. There are some overwritten scenes, but the performances of the stars shine through.

D: Harvey Hart                                          104 minutes

Glynnis O'Connor, Michael Learned, Anne Baxter

**LITTLE MO**
**1/2 NBC

Tough subject is given a good treatment. It's the story of Maureen Connolly, a girl from San Diego determined to become the best at something, who becomes the first woman to win the Grand Slam of tennis. Star Glynnis O'Connor certainly isn't Little Mo on the court, but the tennis sequences are still surprisingly good. Michael Learned plays Mo's single-minded tennis instructor, and Anne Baxter is effective as Mo's mom. Pretty good show.

D: Dan Haller                                          156 minutes

Mike Connors, Cloris Leachman, Stephanie Zimbalist

**LONG JOURNEY BACK**
*** ABC

An absorbing true story about a family's long, hard struggle to help a young high school girl recover from a school bus accident in which she lost a leg and suffered brain damage. Stephanie Zimbalist is very effective as the girl; Cloris Leachman and Mike Connors are also good as her parents. By the nature of the story the sentiment becomes thick at times, but for the most part it's a moving tribute to the tenacity and devotion of all concerned.

D: Mel Damski                                          104 minutes

**LOVE IS NOT ENOUGH**
**\*\*1/2 NBC**

Bernie Casey, Renee Brown, Stuart K. Robinson

This was the pilot for the short-lived TV series "Harris and Company" about a fine upstanding black family headed by a strong, caring father, a welcome departure from the standard sitcom formula built around cartoon characters played for laughs. A noble effort, led by Bernie Casey, who acts as every father ought to, black or white.

D: Ivan Dixon                                          104 minutes

**LOVE'S SAVAGE FURY**
**\* ABC**

Jennifer O'Neill, Perry King, Raymond Burr, Vernee Watson

Another rip-off of *Gone With the Wind*. Gorgeous Jennifer O'Neill is the focus of this Civil War saga, playing a Southern belle fallen on hard times. There's some nonsense about "hidden gold," while most of the action takes place in a Yankee prison camp. Pulp fiction, and you don't even have to turn the pages.

D: Joseph Hardy                                        104 minutes

**LOVEY, A CIRCLE OF CHILDREN, Part 2**
**\*\*\*\* CBS**

Jane Alexander, Ronny Cox

This extraordinary work, based on the experiences of Mary McCracken, a dedicated teacher of children with severe learning disabilities, continues where Part 1 left off. Jane Alexander, star of both dramatizations, is remarkable as the dynamic woman who finds solace, after the shattering divorce of her marriage of 23 years, in the challenge of reaching these seemingly unmanageable children. The wonders she works on a dirty, tantrum-bound child of eight she calls "Lovey" are enthralling.

D: Jud Taylor                                          104 minutes

**MANDRAKE**
**\*1/2 NBC**

Anthony Herrera, Ji-Tu Cumbuka, Gretchen Corbett, Robert Reed

From the classic comic strip comes the renowned Mandrake the Magician, conquering evil with his magical abilities. Anthony Herrera plays the title role with some style, and the enormous Ji-Tu Cumbuka looms appropriately large as his sidekick, Lothar, as Mandrake comes to the aid of a tycoon being blackmailed. For the kids.

D: Harry Falk                                          104 minutes

**THE MILLIONAIRE**
**\* CBS**

Robert Quarry, Martin Balsam, Eddie Albert

Remember "The Millionaire" from the early days of television? This is an updated version, with Michael Anthony, played by Robert Quarry, dispensing million-dollar tax-free checks to those in need; guest stars include Martin Balsam, Eddie Albert, The Hudson Brothers, and other familiar faces. It's just as tedious as the original.

D: Don Weiss                                           104 minutes

Rob Reiner, Penny Marshall

Rob Reiner cowrote and produced this comedy-romance, giving himself a sympathetic role and casting his real-life wife, Penny Marshall, in the female lead. Since some of the material seems clearly autobiographical, the love affair between Mandy and Alan takes on a special dimension as portrayed by the two stars, although the charming screenplay doesn't quite come together all the way. Reiner's lovesick writer is very believable, and Penny Marshall gets the best opportunity she's had to play a full-blown character with more than just funny bits and one-liners to deliver.

D: Jim Burrows                                104 minutes

**MORE THAN FRIENDS**
**1/2 ABC

Hal Holbrook, Katherine Ross, Barry Bostwick

The stars of this top-flight cast are excellent in this stylish mystery chock-full of clever plot twists. Holbrook brings a wonderful feeling of restraint to the piece as Arthur Sinclair, a successful mentalist whose wife Allison (Katherine Ross) is coolly plotting his death. Barry Bostwick is all emotion as a young actor the wife is using to bolster her scheme. It's fun to watch them all triple-cross one another.

D: Robert Day                                 104 minutes

**MURDER BY NATURAL CAUSES**
*** CBS

Sonny Bono, Lee Purcell, Lucille Benson

Sonny Bono tries the acting route in this pilot for a TV series, paired with sexy Lee Purcell playing a married couple who become involved in amateur detective work while on their honeymoon. The team come on like a spaced-out Nick and Nora Charles.

D: Leo Penn                                   104 minutes

**MURDER IN MUSIC CITY**
*1/2 NBC

Peter Falk, Louis Jourdan, France Nuyen

Peter Falk's shuffling sleuth, Lieutenant Columbo, has been pitted against some unusual murderers before, but this one literally takes the cake: He's a

**MURDER UNDER GLASS**
**1/2 NBC

LEFT: *Robert Quarry recreates the role of Michael Anthony from the early days of television in* The Millionaire.

RIGHT: *Louis Jourdan and Peter Falk cook up a mystery in* Murder under Glass.

famous food critic, of all things. Louis Jourdan is ideally cast as the celebrated critic with a taste for gourmet dishes and murder, while Falk as Columbo is effective as ever, pleasing his own palate while running a tasty investigation.

D: Jonathan Demme                                                      78 minutes

**MY HUSBAND IS MISSING**
** NBC

Sally Struthers, Tony Musante

Sally Struthers in a straight dramatic role plays a woman whose flyer-husband has been missing in action in Vietnam for more than six years, provoking her to travel to North Vietnam to attempt to find him, dead or alive. Tony Musante adds flavor as a cynical Canadian newspaperman who accompanies her, but *Missing* misses the mark.

D: Richard Michaels                                                    104 minutes

**THE NATIVITY**
**1/2 ABC

Madeline Stowe, John Shea, Jane Wyatt

This version of the story of the nativity is told from the unusual perspective of Joseph, following his courtship and betrothal to Mary, and his reaction to Mary's pregnancy and the virgin birth. Filmed in the desert terrain of Spain, the atmosphere of ancient times is convincing, and so is the cast led by Madeline Stowe as Mary and John Shea as Joseph.

D: Bernard Kowalski                                                    104 minutes

**THE NEW ADVENTURES OF HEIDI**
** NBC

Katy Kurtzman, Burl Ives, John Gavin

Based on Johanna Spyri's classic novel, and nowhere near as good as the magnificent 1968 TV version. This is a totally new contemporary musical about a girl named Heidi who lives with her grandfather in the Swiss Alps and befriends a spoiled rich little runaway whose mother is dead and whose father is too busy to care for her. The 10 unmemorable songs written for the film are pleasantly sung, particularly by Katy Kurtzman who makes this Heidi a lovely, sensitive little girl.

D: Ralph Senensky                                                      104 minutes

**THE NEW MAVERICK**
** ABC

James Garner, Charles Frank, Jack Kelly

The pilot which attempted to bring the latest member of the Maverick clan, Ben, back to the screen in a new series. James Garner is on hand as Brett, to introduce Ben, and he's still the whole show. Charles Frank is appealing as cousin Ben, the pace is leisurely, with more emphasis on characterization than on action.

D: Hy Averback                                                         104 minutes

**THE NIGHT RIDER**
* ABC

David Selby, Percy Rodriguez, Pernell Roberts

David Selby stars as a mild-mannered lawyer who turns into an avenging Zorrolike character once the sun goes down. It's set in the Old West, and the plot is as old as those old, old hills.

D: Hy Averback                                                         90 minutes

Richard Thomas, Julie Kavner

**NO OTHER LOVE**
**1/2 CBS

Moderately engrossing story about two slightly retarded young adults who fall in love and hope to get married. The pair, as played by Richard Thomas and Julie Kavner, don't appear disabled enough to warrant the conflicts generated when their marriage is proposed. Nevertheless, this is a commendable effort to present a delicate subject with sincerity.

D: Richard Pearce                    104 minutes

LeVar Burton, Paul Benjamin, Billy Martin

**ONE IN A MILLION:
THE RON LeFLORE
STORY**
*** CBS

LeVar Burton is quite appealing in this real-life story of baseball star Ron LeFlore. It chronicles the struggle of the young, poor, black Detroit teenager to escape from the violence, drug abuse, and apathy of the ghetto, his imprisonment for armed robbery, and the discovery in prison of his great athletic talent.

D: William A. Graham                    104 minutes

Dennis Weaver, Lisa Eilbacher

**THE ORDEAL OF
PATTY HEARST**
*** ABC

Well-done dramatization of the events leading up to the kidnapping of the heiress-turned-radical, and her eventual arrest by FBI agents. Lisa Eilbacher is well cast as Patty Hearst; Dennis Weaver is very good as the FBI special agent in charge of the case. The script tries to present a balanced depiction of the events, without being overly sympathetic to Ms. Hearst. The Symbionese Liberation Army hideout sequences are extremely graphic and pull no punches.

D: Paul Wendkos                    156 minutes

Yvette Mimieux

**OUTSIDE CHANCE**
*1/2 CBS

Loosely based on *Jackson County Jail,* an earlier theatrical film which excited some attention. In this sensationalized, and much less compelling TV version, Yvette Mimieux finds herself in a small-town jail after being terrorized on a cross country drive by two hitchhikers who steal her car and leave her unconscious by the roadside . . . and that's where her troubles just begin!

D: Michael Miller                                             104 minutes

**OVERBOARD**
** NBC

Cliff Robertson, Angie Dickinson

Cliff and Angie make an attractive couple in this supercharged film based on the best seller by Hank Searles. The pair embark on a dream vacation, sailing around the world on a yacht, but tragedy intervenes when the wife is washed overboard. Flashbacks spell out their life together in occasionally interesting fashion.

D: John Newland                                              104 minutes

**THE PIRATE**
*1/2 CBS

Franco Nero, Eli Wallach, Anne Archer, Christopher Lee

Harold Robbins's best seller, converted into a four-hour TV film starring Italian film favorite Franco Nero. But its an ordinary tale about an Arab prince, raised in the West, and married to a sexy American (Anne Archer).

D: Kenneth Annakin                                           208 minutes

**POLICE STORY: DAY OF TERROR, NIGHT OF FEAR**
* NBC

Warren Oates, Bruce Davison, Chad Everett

A rehash of the reliable, if familiar, bank-robbers-hostages premise, with Oates and Davison as a pair of misfits who bungle a bank job and barge into a travel agency, holding five people hostage. Chad Everett is good as the team's "mouth marine" who establishes phone contact with the fugitives and negotiates for their surrender.

D: E. Arthur Kean                                            104 minutes

**THE POWER WITHIN**
* ABC

Art Hindle, Edward Binns, Joe Rassulo

A silly story involving a man who acquires superhuman powers after being struck by lightning. Don't rush out during the next electrical storm to try this stunt.

D: John Llewellyn Moxey                                       90 minutes

**A QUESTION OF LOVE**
****ABC

Gena Rowlands, Jane Alexander, Ned Beatty, Clu Gulager

A remarkably sensitive, thoughtful, and superbly acted drama based on a real custody trial between a lesbian mother and her ex-husband. *A Question of Love* was one of the very best made-for-TV films of the decade. Its honest, restrained handling of the theme is in marked contrast to the sensationalized, exploitative way commercial TV so often deals with sexuality, including homosexuality. Rowlands and Alexander play lesbians who have combined their families and moved into a new house together. Rowlands is wonderful as the confused woman who puts her private life on the line, and Jane Alexander, in a slightly less important role as her lover, is equally poignant. The fine screenplay by co-producer William Blinn presents a balanced view of the case before the real court's decision is announced at the conclusion of this memorable drama.

D: Jerry Thorpe                                              104 minutes

Andrea McArdle, Piper Laurie, Martin Balsam, Jack Carter

Nostalgic film about the young Judy Garland. It's a corny, sentimental treat, packaged in the old Hollywood style, and showcasing Andrea McArdle, the young Broadway sensation from *Annie*. Andrea is a wonder in the musical segments, but she lacks assurance in the more dramatic scenes. The young star receives good support from Michael Parks as Roger Edens, Piper Laurie as her mother, Martin Balsam as Louis B. Mayer, and Don Murray as her troubled father.

D: Jackie Cooper                                                104 minutes

**RAINBOW**
*** NBC

Brian Dennehy, Forrest Tucker, Ken Howard

Pilot based on the story of Tennessee sheriff Buford Pusser, made famous in the "Walking Tall" films. Here Brian Dennehy is the angry sheriff, frustrated by "technicalities" of the law, that prevent him from putting a moonshiner out of business.

D: Lou Antonio                                                104 minutes

**A REAL AMERICAN HERO**
*1/2 CBS

Bob Denver, Alan Hale, Jr., Jim Backus, Natalie Schafer

It looks like a rerun that's been taken off the shelf and given a good dusting, reuniting the regular cast of idiot castaways, swept from their island by a tidal wave. When the gang are rescued, they receive a royal welcome in Honolulu, but fail completely in attempting to settle down back home. The scripts haven't improved over the years!

D: Les Martinson                                              104 minutes

**RESCUE FROM GILLIGAN'S ISLAND**
* NBC

Clarence Williams III, Peggy Lipton, Michael Cole, Sugar Ray Robinson

Dedicated to fans of the old series, which started the onslaught of shows about young undercover police officers. It's the same old plotting with the three deep in trouble at every turn.

D: George McCowan                                             104 minutes

**THE RETURN OF THE MOD SQUAD**
**1/2 ABC

Ricardo Montalban, Herve Villechaize

The pilot for the subsequent series . . . remember *Westworld* and *Future World?* In this variation a group of desperate people are shelling out exorbitant sums of money to live out their fantasies. The guests include Joseph Cotton, George Maharis, Adrienne Barbeau, and George Chakiris. Just dumb escapism!

D: George McCowan                                             104 minutes

**RETURN TO FANTASY ISLAND**
*1/2 ABC

Andy Griffith, Trish Stewart, Richard Jaeckel

Dull pilot for the series in which Andy Griffith plays an enterprising junkman who builds his own rocket from garbage to gather salvage on the moon (!). Can't be salvaged.

D: Lee Phillips                                                104 minutes

**SALVAGE I**
* ABC

**SAMURAI**
**\* ABC**

Joe Penny, James Shigeta, Beulah Quo

Joe Penny stars as a young district attorney who uses his martial arts skills to help solve his cases. Fernando Lamas, Ron Jacobs, and Danny Thomas confess to being executive producers of this misdemeanor.

D: Lee Katzin                                    90 minutes

**SANCTUARY OF**
**FEAR**
**\*\*\* NBC**

Barnard Hughes, Kay Lenz

The performance of Barnard Hughes as Father Brown, the detective-priest, is a treat. It's inconceivable that G.K. Chesterton, who created the character in a series of classic mystery novels, could have imagined a better portrayal of his hero. That said, it is a disappointment that the case here falls far short of the Chesterton model, as we are taken on a repetitive tour of a young girl's nightmarish experience of unexplained murders and disappearances. Kay Lenz provides an attractive presence as the unfortunate young lady.

D: John Moxey                                   104 minutes

**SECRETS OF THREE**
**HUNGRY WIVES**
**\*\* NBC**

Jessica Walter, James Franciscus, Eve Plumb

James Franciscus plays a playboy who preys on suburban housewives and their offspring in this sudsy whodunit. The harassed ladies all have good reason to murder the rat.

D: Gordon Hessler                               104 minutes

**THE SEEDING OF**
**SARAH BURNS**
**\*\* CBS**

Kay Lenz, Martin Balsam, Cliff DeYoung

Kay Lenz is fine as a young woman who volunteers to be part of an experiment in embryo transplantation (she carries the baby for a mother who can't risk childbirth complications). The early part of the drama is engrossing, but it soon settles into the obvious twist of the young substitute becoming too attached to the infant growing within her, and turns into soap operatics.

D: Sandor Stern                                 104 minutes

**SERGEANT**
**MATLOVICH VS. THE**
**U.S. AIR FORCE**
**\*\*1/2 NBC**

Brad Dorif, Marc Singer, Frank Converse, Barra Grant

Brad Dourif, an intense actor best known for his Academy Award nomination as the suicidal character in *One Flew Over the Cuckoo's Nest* does his best to bring the character of Sergeant Matlovich to life. Unfortunately, the script depicts the crusader who fights for the right to remain in the service despite his declared homosexuality as a one-dimensional figure, with little insight into the core of his deviation from the norm; however a strong case is made for his ability to function as an air force instructor. William Demarest is especially effective as an Air Force chaplain who counsels Matlovich. Flawed, but interesting on occasion.

D: Paul Leaf                                    104 minutes

**SILENT VICTORY:**
**THE KITTY O'NEILL**
**STORY \*\*\* CBS**

Stockard Channing, James Farentino, Colleen Dewhurst

Impressive drama about deaf stuntwoman Kitty O'Neill. Stockard Channing is first rate as the plucky Kitty, helped by her determined mother (Colleen Dewhurst) to achieve a normal life. Miss Channing's skill in depicting Kitty's speech difficulties, and her zest in overcoming them make this one of the more palatable inspirational sagas about the handicapped.

D: Lou Antonio                                                        104 minutes

Andrea Marcovicci, David Dukes

Occasionally affecting, wrenching wheelchair drama "suggested" by the book *But There Are Always Miracles,* by Jack Willis. Would have been better if the film had stuck more closely to the real story. Jack Willis happens to be one of the most gifted producers and documentary filmmakers working in American TV. The story tells of the severe injury he suffered while body surfing; David Dukes is particularly effective playing Willis struggling to walk again.

D: Jerrold Freedman                                                  104 minutes

### SOME KIND OF MIRACLE
**\*\*\* CBS**

Lauren Hutton, David Birney, Adrienne Barbeau

Here's a terror flick that's not as scary as it should be. The weak spot is fashion model Lauren Hutton, who appears as a TV news director being bugged by phone calls, notes, and presents from a nut who follows her every move. Ms. Hutton is swell to look at, but not up to conveying the hysteria and mounting panic the role calls for.

D: John Carpenter                                                    104 minutes

### SOMEONE IS WATCHING ME
**\*\* NBC**

James Farentino, Kathryn Harrold

Based on the real-life experiences of a couple who had to deal with their autistic son and refuse to accept the negative prognosis for his future.

D: Glenn Jordan                                                      104 minutes

### SON RISE: A MIRACLE OF LOVE
**\*\*1/2 NBC**

LEFT: *Kay Lenz is the surrogate mother, shown here with Cliff DeYoung and Martin Balsam in* The Seeding of Sarah Burns.

RIGHT: *Tom Bosley is the negligent foreman in* The Triangle Factory Fire Scandal.

**STEEL COWBOY**
** NBC

James Brolin, Rip Torn, Strother Martin, Jennifer Warren

Here's a trucker yarn with spurts of life to it: A trucker about to go broke hauls stolen cattle for a black-market bigwig, and manages to outsmart the opposition for a change. James Brolin and Rip Torn play the truckers, and Strother Martin is the sly black marketeer and a scene-stealer.

D: Harvey Laidman                                        104 minutes

**STRANGER IN OUR HOUSE** ** NBC

Linda Blair, Lee Purcell

*The Exorcist*'s Linda Blair is dealing with possession once again. This time her cousin takes over the entire family, who become terror stricken. Ms. Blair hasn't learned how to act in the intervening years since she spewed green bile all over the screen in the hit thriller, *The Exorcist,* but she really doesn't have to do much more than look horrified, as Lee Purcell does the lethal meanacing here.

D: Wes Craven                                            104 minutes

**STUNT SEVEN**
*½ CBS

Christopher Connelly, Christopher Lloyd, Bob Seagren

A novel kidnapping sequence in which a boat is lifted out of the water by a helicopter hoist sets the tone for this action adventure. Obviously a pilot for a proposed series, the gimmick here is in the formation of a vigilante group of seven Hollywood stuntmen who seek to rescue the glamorous movie star who's been snatched for a ransom of ten million dollars. Strictly for the action fans!

D: John Peyser                                           104 minutes

**SUDDENLY, LOVE**
**½ NBC

Cindy Williams, Paul Shenar, Joan Bennet, Lew Ayres

Cindy Williams, of "Laverne & Shirley" fame, proves she can handle a straight part in Ross Hunter's glossy love story. She's a Brooklyn girl, influenced by John F. Kennedy, determined to become an architect, and then married to a blue-blooded lawyer. This is a typical sudsy Hunter woman's tale, given a shot of adrenalin by Ms. Williams.

D: Stuart Margolin                                       104 minutes

**THE SURVIVAL OF DANA** **½ CBS

Melissa Sue Anderson, Robert Carradine, Talia Balsam

A drama that attempts to explain why kids from affluent families turn to mindless destruction. In an image switch Melissa Sue Anderson, of "Little House on the Prairie," plays the new girl in school who runs with the wrong crowd. Parents who drink, divorce, beat one another up, and generally neglect their offspring get the blame here. At times the parental sequences become hard to swallow, but the kids often achieve a realistic flavor unusual in made-for-TV films.

D: Jack Starrett                                         104 minutes

**TERROR OUT OF THE SKY** * CBS

Efrem Zimbalist, Jr., Tovah Feldshuh, Dan Haggerty

Who needs another yarn about killer bees on the loose? This one is worse than most because it takes itself so seriously. Efrem Zimbalist is head of the

National Bee Center, where some killer queen bees have infiltrated a hive and then have been shipped to beekeepers. Plodding, predictable, and juvenile.

D: Lee H. Katzin                                                    104 minutes


Peter Ustinov, Roddy McDowall, Kabir Bedi

Here's an easy-to-take European-produced version of the delightful Arabian Nights tale. Peter Ustinov keeps things moving as the wily caliph of Baghdad and Roddy McDowall is well cast as the thief, who gets about on a flying carpet when the traffic is heavy.

D: Clive Donner                                                    104 minutes

**THE THIEF OF BAGHDAD**
**1/2 NBC


Lou Gossett, Clu Gulager, Lonny Chapman

Lou Gossett is the only reason to see this pilot for a series about a minister who becomes the sheriff of a small Alabama town. You've seen this racial strife story before, but Gossett makes it worthwhile.

D: Jerrold Freedman                                                104 minutes

**THIS MAN STANDS ALONE**
**1/2 NBC


Louise Fletcher, Robert Reed, Wayne Rogers

Louise Fletcher stars in her first TV role since she won an Oscar as best actress in 1975 for *One Flew Over the Cuckoo's Nest*. She plays a woman who is encouraged by her husband to seek a sexual outlet elsewhere after he is incapacitated by an auto accident, and she settles on a golf pro (Wayne Rogers). Pure soap opera.

D: Delbert Mann                                                    104 minutes

**THOU SHALT NOT COMMIT ADULTERY**
** NBC


June Allyson, Ray Bolger, Rick Nelson, John Byner

This adaptation of a book by Stephanie Buffington, a real-life chaperone to winning couples from "The Dating Game," is spruced up with guest stars and silly subplots.

D: Bill Bixby                                                      104 minutes

**THREE ON A DATE**
* ABC


John Beck, Priscilla Barnes

Anyone need still another remake of the H. G. Wells classic about a time-traveling inventor who reaches a future civilization known as Elois?

D: Henning Schellerup                                              104 minutes

**THE TIME MACHINE**
*1/2 NBC


Lee Remick, George Peppard, Joe Bologna

The attractive stars here will hold your attention even when you feel that their story—about a happily married woman suddenly thrown into the company of a handsome, sophisticated, and divorced architect—may be a bit too contrived. Her decision to be honest with her husband concerning her affections leads to the most emotionally effective scenes in the drama simply because the husband's fury is the first thing that comes across as being real.

D: Delbert Mann                                                    104 minutes

**TORN BETWEEN TWO LOVERS**
**1/2 CBS

**TRANSPLANT**
**\*\*\* CBS**

Kevin Dobson, Granville Van Dusen, Ronny Cox, Melinda Dillon

This study of a heart attack victim is of interest mainly because of the relationship between the man—a highly charged individual who smokes like a chimney, drinks like a fish, and loves his family to a hysterical pitch—and his earthy, vigorous wife, who remains strong and supportive no matter how desperate the situation becomes. Fortunately, both these roles are extremely well played by Kevin Dobson and Melinda Dillon, and their presence carries the drama through all its tension, despair, and hope.

D: William A. Graham                                          104 minutes

**THE TRIANGLE FACTORY FIRE SCANDAL**
**\*\*1/2 NBC**

Tom Bosley, Tovah Feldshuh, Ted Wass, Stephanie Zimbalist

Based on a true incident in the sweatshop days of the garment industry during the early part of the century. When fire breaks out, the casualty list is enormous. Documentary specialist Mel Stuart directs with some snap and crackle, but the personal stories of various shop girls bog down the effort.

D: Mel Stuart                                                104 minutes

**THE ULTIMATE IMPOSTER**
**\*\* CBS**

Joseph Hacker, Keith Andes

Pilot for a superduper adventure series with a neat gimmick: a topnotch secret agent submits to a unique experiment so that he acquires the capacity to absorb knowledge fed from a computer, but which he can retain for only a limited time. Thus he can do almost anything—for a while. The excitement wears off as the plotting becomes more contrived.

D: Paul Stanley                                              104 minutes

**THE USERS**
**\*1/2 ABC**

Jaclyn Smith, Tony Curtis

Hollywood gossip columnist Joyce Haber's sex-ridden book about the great, near-great, and not-so-great of tinsel town is transformed into this overproduced, overdressed, and overundressed saga of opportunists in the movie col-

LEFT: *Jaclyn Smith is a former prostitute in* The Users.

RIGHT: *Len Cariou and Shirley Jones are foster parents in* Who'll Save Our Children?

ony. Jaclyn Smith, with more costume changes than Liberace in his Vegas act, does what she can as a former prostitute who climbs the social ladder until she is married to a multimillionaire businessman.

D: Joseph E. Hardy                                                    104 minutes


Michael Brandon, Priscilla Barnes, Barbara Feldon, Andrea Marcovicci

An exotic vacation turns into a horror story for four women, and, of course, the obligatory male. The female leads make an attractive group fleeing for their lives in a dense jungle on the outskirts of a posh tropical resort. Peppered liberally with women's libisms, you've seen it all before.

D: David Greene                                                       104 minutes

**VACATION IN HELL**
** ABC


Robert Urich, June Allyson, Tony Curtis, Red Buttons

The city of Las Vegas again provides a backdrop for tales of mystery and murder. In this pilot for the subsequent series, Robert Urich is the attractive ex-cop hired to find a runaway teenaged girl involved with corrupt forces in the glittering city of high rollers and desperate losers.

104 minutes

**VEGA$**
** ABC


Bess Armstrong, Tom Mason, Richard Masur

Another true story of a person's battle against cancer. But don't be put off from this genuine, engrossing testament to a courageous woman's indomitable spirit. Bess Armstrong gives a sensitive and passionate performance as Laurel Lee, who discovers she has Hodgkin's disease while carrying her third child and risks her life to have her baby.

D: Robert Day                                                         104 minutes

**WALKING THROUGH FIRE**
*** CBS


Shirley Jones, Len Cariou

Shirley Jones and Len Cariou star as a childless couple raising a pair of deserted youngsters in this carefully handled story directed by George Schaefer. It's a tale of adjustment, in which the couple, who grow to love the kids, must face the trauma of losing them. Their emotion is believable without going awash in sentimentality, and that's not easy under the circumstances.

D: George Schaefer                                                    104 minutes

**WHO'LL SAVE OUR CHILDREN?**
** CBS


Robert Conrad, Ross Martin, Paul Williams, Harry Morgan

Fans of the old TV series starring Conrad and Martin as a wily and unorthodox pair of 19th-century government secret agents will be happy to see their favorites back in a new adventure. Cloning is the crux of this wild and wooly case, and high style and campy fun prevail in this revamping of the former top-rated series.

D: Burt Kennedy                                                       104 minutes

**THE WILD WILD WEST REVISITED**
**1/2 CBS


Deborah Raffin, Clu Gulager, Diane Ladd, Nancy Marchand

Often interesting story about a woman with a dream she's determined to realize despite its incompatibility with her life: Willa, waitress at a hash-slinging

**WILLA**
*** CBS

joint, mother of two youngsters with a third on the way, deserted by her husband, and with an alcoholic mother, is going to become a trucker, come hell or high water! It's a little hard to be sympathetic with her dream, since it means leaving her kids with her drunken mom, and taking the newborn infant along on her trucking jobs. But Deborah Raffin's portrayal of Willa's drive keeps the interest alive.

D: Joan Darling and Claudio Guzman                104 minutes

**THE WINDS OF KITTY HAWK *** NBC**

Michael Moriarity, David Huffman

A loving tribute to the Wright Brothers' historic accomplishment. The talented Moriarity holds your attention playing the dogged dreamer Wilbur Wright, but the real stars of the show are the graceful gliders and facsimiles of the first motor-powered aircraft. The drama attempts to recreate the wonder of the Wrights achieving flight in their flimsy craft, and it succeeds—a feat in itself.

D: E. W. Swackhamer                104 minutes

**WOMEN AT WEST POINT **1/2 CBS**

Linda Purl, Andrew Stevens

A well-produced and interesting film dealing with the first women admitted to the U.S. Military Academy after 174 years of strictly male enrollment. Linda Purl, as a feisty young plebe, gives a thoroughly believable performance. Andrew Stevens is also good as an upperclassman who bends the nonfraternization rule and falls in love with plebe Purl.

D: Vincent Sherman                104 minutes

LEFT: *Linda Purl is the first woman enrolled at West Point with Andrew Stevens as an upperclassman in* Women at West Point.

RIGHT: *Suzanne Somers takes in more than just the sun in* Zuma Beach.

**YOU CAN'T GO HOME AGAIN **1/2 CBS**

Lee Grant, Chris Sarandon, Hurd Hatfield

Thomas Wolfe's thinly disguised autobiographical novel about writer George Webber and his emergence on the literary scene is clumsily abbreviated and adapted for TV, but it's only Chris Sarandon's sharply defined portrait of the hedonistic writer that makes it worthwhile. Sarandon captures the inner torment of a man blessed by rare genius but cursed by his excesses, and evokes an excellent feeling for the period in his look and manner. Lee Grant is helpful.

D: Ralph Nelson                104 minutes

Suzanne Somers

A routine comedy-drama in which Suzanne Somers portrays an "older woman" whose career is on the rocks, and who finds a new direction when she befriends a group of teenagers and helps them to work out their problems during a Labor Day weekend at the beach.

D: Lee H. Katzin                                        104 minutes

**ZUMA BEACH**
\*1/2 NBC

# THEATRICAL FILMS—NET-WORK DEBUTS

---

Robert Logan, Heather Rattray, George Flower, Mark Hall

An unusually well-done children's film. Two spunky orphans have plenty of adventures and hardships en route to their new home in Oregon in the Old West.

D\*: Stuart Raffill                                        89 minutes

**ACROSS THE GREAT DIVIDE** \*\*\*1/2 CBS
**(1976)**

Michael Douglas, Joe Don Baker, Lee Purcell

A good idea that almost works. Michael Douglas is a hip California college professor who starts questioning his life-style and takes some time off to get in touch with the "real world." His odyssey takes him to Missouri where he meets a variety of "just plain folks" who eventually let him down. The complex screenplay doesn't find its focus, but the performances are all good.

D: Robert Sheerer                                        100 minutes

**ADAM AT 6 A.M.**
\*\*1/2 NBC
**(1970)**

Lee Grant, Brenda Vaccaro, Joseph Cotten, Olivia de Havilland

More mindless diversion starring that triumph of technology, the Boeing 747. Disaster strikes when hijackers take over the plane and crash into the ocean. The plane is watertight; the script is not.

D: Jerry Jameson                                        113 minutes

**AIRPORT '77**
\*1/2 NBC
**(1977)**

LEFT: *Brenda Vaccaro and Jack Lemmon are in a desperate situation in* Airport '77.

CENTER: *Richard Drey-fuss appearing in the cult film* American Graffiti.

RIGHT: *Ron Howard and Cindy Williams are part of the gang in* American Graffiti.

\* D means Director.

**AMERICAN GRAFFITI**
**** NBC
(1973)

Ron Howard, Cindy Williams, Richard Dreyfuss

A remarkable film about the American car culture and what it was like to be a high school teenager in a small town in northern California in the fall of 1962. Gifted director George Lucas (who later gave us *Star Wars*) was himself a teenager in 1962, and has given us the best film that the nostalgia craze of the seventies has yet produced. The talented cast earns high marks all around.

D: George Lucas                                                110 minutes

**ANYTHING FOR LOVE**
*½ ABC
(1974)

Charles Grodin, Candice Bergen, Trevor Howard

This muddled, contrived caper film was originally released as *11 Harrow House*. Charles Grodin is a diamond salesman enlisted by a mad millionaire (Trevor Howard) to steal millions of dollars worth of diamonds. Candice Bergen is one of those flighty, bored heiresses who crave adventure with a capital A. A time waster.

D: Aram Avakian                                                95 minutes

**ASH WEDNESDAY**
**½ ABC
(1973)

Elizabeth Taylor, Henry Fonda, Helmut Berger

Miss Taylor does what she can with this picture about a woman who subjects herself to a series of face lifts, breast lifts, and foot lifts in order to bring back her wandering husband, Mr. Fonda. Liz is interesting to watch, first with fake wrinkles, and later as her then gorgeous self.

D: Larry Peerce                                                99 minutes

**AT LONG LAST LOVE**
* ABC
(1975)

Burt Reynolds, Cybill Shepherd, Madeline Kahn

It's disgraceful, it's deplorable, it's disastrous! Cole Porter would spin in his grave if he knew how his sophisticated songs were used in this inane musical clumsily directed, written, and produced by Peter Bogdanovich. Skip this one and look for the genuine item—an Astaire-Rogers film.

D: Peter Bogdanovich                                           115 minutes

LEFT: *Marsha Mason, Susan Swift, and John Beck appear in a story about reincarnation,* Audrey Rose.

RIGHT: *Walter Matthau and Tatum O'Neal face off in* The Bad News Bears.

Doug McClure, Peter Cushing

A sequel to the 1974 film *The Land That Time Forgot.* Occasionally entertaining blend of fantasy, humor, and chills, based on the 1923 novel by Edgar Rice Burroughs.

D: Kevin Connors                                            90 minutes

**AT THE EARTH'S CORE**
**\*\*1/2 ABC**
**(1976)**

Marsha Mason, Anthony Hopkins

My beloved Central Park West has been defamed by this unscary drivel about reincarnation. Another ripoff of *The Exorcist* gambit, and it fails, as another teenaged girl is seized by forces of evil.

D: Robert Wise                                            113 minutes

**AUDREY ROSE**
**\* NBC**
**(1977)**

Jan Michael Vincent, Glynnis O'Connor, Katherine Helmond

Story of a young man washed out of boot camp who returns to his home town claiming to be a war hero who has been to Guadalcanal. Idealized characters, vacuously played.

D: John Hancock                                            89 minutes

**BABY BLUE MARINE**
**\*1/2 ABC**
**(1976)**

Walter Matthau, Tatum O'Neal, Scott Baio, Vic Morrow

Sparkling comedy about the whipping into shape of a Little League team by an alcoholic coach. Morris Buttermaker (Matthau), a former minor-league coach currently making a living cleaning swimming pools, signs on to coach a team with lots of enthusiasm but little skill. His solution is to recruit the meanest spitball pitcher in the state, an 11-year-old girl; and a chain-smoking, motorcycle-riding 12-year-old slugger. The Bears' rise is inevitable, but the screenplay is endearing for its unsentimental approach.

D: Michael Ritchie                                            105 minutes

**THE BAD NEWS BEARS**
**\*\*\*\* ABC**
**(1976)**

George C. Scott, Joanna Cassidy, Sorrell Booke

How George C. Scott got involved in this yarn about a collection of losers who execute a bank heist (they actually uproot a small bank and tow it away) remains a mystery. He's boring as the mastermind behind the plot, and the supporting cast is no better.

D: Gower Champion                                            83 minutes

**THE BANK SHOT**
**\* CBS**
**(1974)**

Anthony Quinn, Frederic Forrest, Robert Forster

Originally released in theaters as *The Don Is Dead.* A *Godfather* imitation, but well acted. Anthony Quinn is perfect as the older Mafia boss, and Frederic Forrest scores as a modern-day member of a mob family who wants out but can't find the way to manage it.

D: Richard Fleischer                                            115 minutes

**BEAUTIFUL BUT DEADLY**
**\*\*1/2 ABC**
**(1973)**

**BLACK SUNDAY**
***1/2 CBS
**(1977)**

Robert Shaw, Bruce Dern, Marthe Keller, Fritz Weaver

One of many recent crisis-caper melodramas and better than most. Members of the Black September terrorist organization plan to blow up the championship Super Bowl football game while the president is in attendance. Builds to an exciting climax with a shootout between FBI-manned police helicopters and the terrorists who've stolen the Goodyear Blimp.

D: John Frankenheimer                    145 minutes

**BUFFALO BILL AND THE INDIANS**
***1/2 CBS
**(1976)**

Paul Newman, Joel Grey, Kevin McCarthy, Geraldine Chaplin

Robert Altman's eccentric, ambitious, flawed but invariably interesting bicentennial offering, a visually stunning celebration of his conviction that the business of America is, and has been for a long time, show business! Buffalo Bill is played with style and flourish by Paul Newman.

D: Robert Altman                    125 minutes

**BURN *** CBS**
**(1970)**

Marlon Brando, Evaristo Marquez

Ambitious film about an island in the Caribbean during the mid-19th century, made in Italy by director Gillo Pontecorvo, who directed the remarkable *Battle of Algiers*. Story concerns the troubled course of a slave revolt and a small island's battle for nationhood while brutalized and exploited by a succession of colonial powers. Brando plays a manipulative Britisher who betrays the islanders.

D: Gillo Pontecorvo                    91 minutes

**BURNT OFFERINGS**
* NBC
**(1976)**

Oliver Reed, Karen Black, Burgess Meredith, Eileen Heckart

Is it possible to create terror with an inanimate villain? Not if this trite, talky attempt at horror is an example. When Ms. Black and hubby Reed rent a summer house, they're faced with a number of surprises, none of which seem credible.

D: Dan Curtis                    106 minutes

Ben Gazzara, Susan Blakely, John Cassavetes

**CAPONE**
** CBS
(1975)

Just what we don't need—another movie about the rise and fall of Chicago mobster Al Capone. This time Ben Gazzara is the ruthless thug who climbs to the top of the hoodlum empire. Susan Blakely is featured as a flashy girl who hangs out with hoods, and Sylvester Stallone in his pre-*Rocky* days has a small supporting role as Frank Nitti, one of Capone's senior henchmen.

D: Steve Carver                                           101 minutes

Sissy Spacek, Piper Laurie

**CARRIE**
*** CBS
(1976)

Well-done thriller about a sheltered high school girl who discovers she has telekinetic powers. Sissy Spacek is excellent as the eccentric girl with the weirdo, fanatically religious mother (played to the hilt by Piper Laurie). Carrie gets to go to the high school prom with one of the most popular boys in school, but her dream-come-true turns into a nasty prank, causing her to cut loose her powers, bringing on havoc and destruction. The finale is pure "Grand Guignol" with all the stops pulled. Eerie and entertaining.

D: Brian DePalma                                          97 minutes

Franklyn Ajaye, George Carlin, Richard Pryor, Irwin Corey

**CAR WASH**
** NBC
(1976)

The activities of a workday at a Los Angeles car wash are woven into a fabric which is full of holes. The establishment is owned by a white man (depicted as an utter fool) and staffed mostly by blacks who are forever jiving each other and the audience. The whole thing plays like a group of slightly related sketches in an overlong TV sitcom, with the stress on "toilet jokes." The cast works too hard, especially Richard Pryor, who is lost as a wealthy phony preacher with an entourage of flunkies, including The Pointer Sisters. Streetwise but film-foolish.

D: Michael Schultz                                        97 minutes

LEFT: *Karen Black can't believe her eyes in* Burnt Offerings.

RIGHT: *Sissy Spacek is the girl with telekinetic powers in* Carrie.

**THE CASSANDRA CROSSING** ** NBC (1977)

Sophia Loren, Richard Harris, Burt Lancaster, Ava Gardner

An adventure yarn about beautiful people aboard a train possibly carrying a deadly virus, might make good summer reading, but as a film it fails. Sophia Loren, Burt Lancaster, Ava Gardner, Martin Sheen, Richard Harris, O. J. Simpson and others suffer through the long ride.

D: George Pan Cosmatos                                    125 minutes

**CHECKERED FLAG OR CRASH** * NBC (1977)

Joe Don Baker, Susan Sarandon, Larry Hagman

This routine car-racing story set in the Phillipines didn't get much of a theatrical release, playing mostly in drive-ins. The thrills and spills of the 1,000-mile race are the main lure for fans of this type of film.

D: Alan Gibson                                            104 minutes

**CLAUDINE** **½ ABC (1974)

Diahann Carroll, James Earl Jones

This comedy-drama about blacks on welfare in Harlem and their ups and downs is not as good as it should have been. Diahann Carroll, miscast as a Harlem mother of six kids, never drops her sophisticated veneer, and it finally defeats her despite the jargon-filled dialogue. James Earl Jones, as an appealing, jolly sanitation department worker who woos her, gives the film's best performance.

D: John Berry                                             95 minutes

**COACH** *½ CBS (1978)

Cathy Lee Crosby, Michael Biehn, Keenan Wynn

Sex and sports mix in this mild comedy involving a gorgeous woman coach of a high school basketball team. It appears she got the job through a computer error. The ridiculous plot may also be due to a computer breakdown.

D: Bud Townsend                                           100 minutes

**COME BACK CHARLESTON BLUE** ** CBS (1972)

Godfrey Cambridge, Raymond St. Jacques

Coffin Ed Johnson and Grave Digger Jones return in this sequel to *Cotton Comes to Harlem.* Unfortunately, the gritty frivolity that made *Cotton* a joy is missing in this opus that concerns the fight between the white and black gangs that hope to control the Harlem heroin trade. Some may find the hip lingo incomprehensible. All will notice the lack of continuity in the plot.

D: Mike Warren                                            100 minutes

**THE CONVERSATION** **** CBS (1974)

Gene Hackman, John Cazale, Allen Garfield, Cindy Williams

A shattering, brilliant, mystery-drama about surveillance and wiretapping in America, produced, written, and directed by Francis Ford Coppola. In it, a bugging expert played by Gene Hackman becomes uneasy about the contents of a tape he's made, and what the tape will be used for. There is murder at the end, but Coppola's theme is the much larger one of the erosion of our values and our civil liberties, and the ease with which new technologies can undermine our democratic heritage. Hackman is marvelous as the guilt-ridden bugger trying to keep his sanity.

D: Francis Ford Coppola                                   113 minutes

Julie Andrews, Jeremy Kemp, Lance Percival, Rock Hudson

Nearly twenty million dollars was invested in this glamorous dinosaur that quickly degenerates into self-parody. WW I, that musical-comedy natural, is the setting for what might have been a charming spoof of the Mata Hari legend. Miss Andrews, who projects the sex appeal of an angry nun, plays the English music hall star and secret German spy who must coax secrets from flyboy Hudson. Pure ennui.

D: Blake Edwards · · · · · · · · · · · · · · · · · · · · · · · · · · 136 minutes

**DARLING LILI**
1/2* ABC
**(1970)**

---

Christopher George, Leslie Nielsen, Michael Ansara

Story about the harmful effects on animals caused by the use of aerosol sprays, which turns them into mankillers! Christopher George and Michael Ansara play the fearless leaders of a wilderness tour. Despite the attempt to show concern about the environment, this film is pointless and repulsive.

D: William Girdler · · · · · · · · · · · · · · · · · · · · · · · · · · 95 minutes

**DAY OF THE ANIMALS** 1/2* CBS
**(1977)**

---

Faye Dunaway, Frank Langella, Barbara Parkins

Muddled thriller directed by France's Rene Clement. Faye Dunaway is a troubled wife and mother who appears to be suffering a mental breakdown, but there's more to it than meets the eye. It won't take long for you to guess what's up. Frank Langella plays Faye's preoccupied husband and both he and Faye are at least nice to look at.

D: Rene Clement · · · · · · · · · · · · · · · · · · · · · · · · · · 97 minutes

**THE DEADLY TRAP**
** CBS
**(1972)**

---

Julie Christie, Fritz Weaver

What if there was a computer that could think for itself? Would its first thought be to perpetuate itself by having offspring? With this premise, a supercomputer called "Proteus" tries to mate with the alluring wife of the scientist (Weaver) who created it. Miss Christie winds up with the unfortunate job of acting opposite the gadget-happy deep-voiced computer terminal that locks her in her home and woos her in a sadistic fashion.

D: Donald Cammell · · · · · · · · · · · · · · · · · · · · · · · · · · 94 minutes

**THE DEMON SEED**
*1/2 CBS
**(1977)**

**DRIVE-IN**
**1/2 ABC
(1976)

Lisa Lemole, Glenn Morshower, Gary Cavagnaro

Offbeat, original comedy-drama about the goings-on in a Texas drive-in movie theater. There are a bumbling pair of robbers, rival gangs, young girls on dates, and enough action for two or more films. There also are glimpses of the movie on the drive-in's screen, called *Disaster '76,* which is a funny parody of all disaster movies. Some of it is fun.

D: Rod Amateau                                                                    96 minutes

**THE EAGLE HAS LANDED**
**1/2 NBC
(1976)

Michael Caine, Donald Sutherland, Robert Duvall

The considerable talents of the cast are wasted in this improbable film about a group of kind-hearted Nazis who parachute into England in a bungled attempt to kidnap Winston Churchill. A superfluous love affair bogs down the story, but despite all the flaws, there is some suspense.

D: John Sturges                                                                   123 minutes

**FAT CITY**
**** ABC
(1972)

Stacy Keach, Jeff Bridges, Susan Tyrell

Director John Huston's deeply moving drama about a washed-up 31-year-old boxer (Keach) benefits greatly from the superb, lean, compassionate screenplay of Leonard Gardner, based upon his novel. This heartbreaking film is not essentially about boxing: It's about the lonely, empty life of the urban poor, and their limited expectations. There's a remarkable supporting performance by Susan Tyrell that earned her an Oscar nomination for her portrayal of a sherry-drinking alcoholic floozy.

D: John Huston                                                                    96 minutes

**FIGHTING MAD**
**1/2 CBS
(1976)

Peter Fonda, Lynn Lowry

This one did poorly when it played in the theaters, but it's actually a fairly nice little drama played for action. Peter Fonda is cast as a city-slicker-turned-farmer who locks horns with the big businessmen who are strip-mining in his domain. Not bad if you don't expect too much.

D: Jonathan Demme                                                                 104 minutes

**FINAL CHAPTER: WALKING TALL**
* ABC
(1977)

Bo Svenson, Margaret Blye, Forrest Tucker

The saga of real-life Tennessee sheriff Buford Pusser, who died under mysterious circumstances after crusading against vice and corruption in his part of the country, comes to an end in this third film about his exploits. It's bloody and boring, and Bo Svenson is a peculiar choice for Pusser since he never manages to overcome the script's inadequacies, of which there are many.

D: Jack Starrett                                                                  112 minutes

**FOR BETTER OR WORSE**
** CBS
(1974)

Gene Hackman, Liv Ullmann

Originally released under the title *Zandy's Bride,* Gene Hackman and Liv Ullmann costar in this frontier story about a rancher who answers a newspaper ad placed by an old maid. Interesting premise dissipates very quickly leaving a turgid melodrama behind.

D: Jan Troell                                                                     116 minutes

Liv Ullmann, Edward Albert, Gene Kelly, Binnie Barnes

The Broadway success about an older woman and a young lover plays like a glossy soap opera on the screen. However, if charm can suffice, this film is loaded with it. Liv Ullmann uses little of her ability playing the 40-year-old divorcee who falls for a 22-year-old while vacationing in Greece. Escapist fare!

D: Milton Katselas                                        110 minutes

**FORTY CARATS**
**1/2 ABC
(1973)

Peter Fox, Gregory Harrison, Scott Newman

Not a bad film about 1950s college fraternity hazing which ends in tragedy. Gregory Harrison and Nancy Morgan come off best, playing a straightforward couple who don't really like what's happening.

D: Thomas J. Tobin                                        104 minutes

**FRATERNITY ROW**
**1/2 CBS
(1977)

Jane Fonda, George Segal, Ed McMahon

Parts of this comedy about contemporary life are quite funny and zany, others are serious and contemptible. The writers and director seem never to have quite made up their minds whether they wanted to produce a satire or an apologia for some of the more repellant values of American middle-class life. Segal plays an unemployed executive who quite casually turns to armed robbery to maintain his luxurious life-style. Fonda and Segal help one get past the rough spots in this wacky, irritating film.

D: Ted Kotcheff                                          95 minutes

**FUN WITH DICK AND JANE**
*** ABC
(1977)

Jill Clayburgh, James Brolin, Red Buttons

A really terrible picture about the love affair of two great stars. It's not entirely the actors' fault—this is one of the worst scripts ever. It is inaccurate, shallow, slick, and totally lacking in real feeling.

D: Sidney J. Furie                                       131 minutes

**GABLE AND LOMBARD**
1/2* NBC
(1976)

LEFT: *Liv Ullmann and Edward Albert have an unlikely romance in* Forty Carats.

RIGHT: *George Segal and Jane Fonda try to pull off a big heist in* Fun with Dick and Jane.

**GONE WITH THE WIND**
**\*\*\*\* CBS**
**(1939)**

Clark Gable, Vivien Leigh, Leslie Howard, Olivia de Havilland

This landmark film won eight Oscars in 1939, and brought twenty million dollars for network broadcast rights in the 1978-79 season. The hardships of life in the South during the Civil War are masterfully depicted in this terrific spectacle, probably the most ambitious film Hollywood had ever attempted at the time. Vivien Leigh shows why she won her Oscar; Gable still makes the ladies' hearts flutter. This all-time box-office champ is part spectacle, part history, and all smashing entertainment.

D: Victor Fleming                                                          219 minutes

**GRAND THEFT AUTO**
**\*\*1/2 CBS**
**(1977)**

Ron Howard, Nancy Morgan

An amiable enough comedy with Ron Howard starring and making his directing debut. Ron is eloping with lovely heiress Nancy Morgan, and the whole city of Los Angeles seems to be in pursuit of the lovebirds on their way to Vegas to tie the knot. The car chase scenes are well staged, and Howard proves he knows his business.

D: Ron Howard                                                          89 minutes

**THE GUMBALL RALLY \*1/2 ABC**
**(1976)**

Michael Sarrazin, Norman Burton, Raul Julia

Stunts, car chases, and crackups are not enough for stunt coordinator/director Chuck Bail to salvage any interest in this dreary film. Thin plot centers around a no-holds-barred cross-country auto race. A few of the innumerable sight gags might tickle your funny bone.

D: Chuck Bail                                                          104 minutes

**HELL BOATS**
**\* CBS**
**(1970)**

James Franciscus, Elizabeth Shepherd

Predictable war drama. James Franciscus is a navy commander who has a plan to save the Mediterranean from the Nazis in WW II. Don't bother!

D: Paul Wendkos                                                          104 minutes

**HIGH BALLIN'**
**\* CBS**
**(1978)**

Peter Fonda, Jerry Reed, Helen Shaver

Another trucker opus that doesn't add anything to the previous films of the genre. This one stars Peter Fonda and country singer Jerry Reed. Time waster.

D: Peter Carter                                                          100 minutes

**HONDO**
**\*\*\*1/2 CBS**
**(1954)**

John Wayne, Geraldine Page, James Arness

One of Hollywood's best adult westerns. Strong in human relationships with a minimum of violence. Broadway actress Geraldine Page made her film debut in this underrated Western.

D: John Farrow                                                          120 minutes

**KILLER GRIZZLY**
**\* ABC**
**(1976)**

Christopher George, Andrew Prine, Richard Jaeckel

Originally called *Grizzly*. A cheap rip-off of *Jaws* with a 15-foot killer grizzly bear standing in for the shark. The bear preys on attractive female campers, of course, as it roams a national forest waiting to get blown to bits by a torpedo launcher. An insult to all ages.

D: William Girdler                                                92 minutes

Jeff Bridges, Charles Grodin, Jessica Lange

Dino De Laurentis's remake of the 1933 film classic falls way short of the original, even though twenty-five million dollars was spent on the mammoth project. The stars try their utmost to make an impression but find it difficult to compete with the 40-foot-tall ape who manages to look fairly realistic, albeit a little cross-eyed, as he stalks around New York City.

D: John Guillermin                                               134 minutes

**KING KONG**
** NBC
**(1976)**

LEFT: *Jessica Lange is in the grip of the great one,* King Kong.

RIGHT: *Dustin Hoffman becomes entangled in international espionage in* Marathon Man.

Sam Elliot, Ann Archer, Stephen Young

Aimless movie about an aging lifeguard who decides the time may have come for him to settle down and live a "real" life as a car salesman.

D: Daniel Petrie                                                 96 minutes

**LIFEGUARD**
*1/2 CBS
**(1976)**

Jodie Foster, Martin Sheen, Alexis Smith

A not-so-thrilling thriller about a teenaged murderer, Miss Foster, who poisons her evil mother and then does away with the landlady. Jodie gives an interesting performance.

D: Nicolas Gessner                                               94 minutes

**THE LITTLE GIRL WHO LIVES DOWN THE LANE**
** ABC
**(1977)**

Dustin Hoffman, Laurence Olivier, Roy Scheider, Marthe Keller

There is a lot of excitement in this thriller about double agents and elderly Nazis, but it's too heavily plotted and suffers finally from the constant doses of gratuitous violence. One is left with the feeling that these gifted artists and director John Schlesinger should have invested their time and money on something more substantial.

D: John Schlesinger                                              120 minutes

**MARATHON MAN**
*** CBS
**(1976)**

**THE MASTER GUNFIGHTER**
1/2* ABC
(1975)

Tom Laughlin, Ron O'Neal

Pretentious Western that is so boring you can actually fall asleep during the many killings. Tom Laughlin, who was "Billy Jack" in the cult-film series, stars as the master gunfighter (never knew they had rank). The acting is uniformly terrible.

D: Frank Laughlin                                                      121 minutes

**MIDWAY**
** NBC
(1976)

Charlton Heston, Henry Fonda, Glenn Ford, Cliff Robertson

The decisive air-sea battle which turned the odds in favor of the United States over Japan is painstakingly recreated with newsreel footage and lavishly staged battle scenes. An interesting account of the historical event, but the personal drama between battle sequences slows things up considerably.

D: Jack Smight                                                         132 minutes

**A MINUTE TO PRAY, A SECOND TO DIE**
1/2* ABC
(1967)

Alex Cord, Robert Ryan, Arthur Kennedy

Gunfighter takes on a town full of baddies . . . the worst. Cord, Ryan, and Kennedy should have their passports revoked for taking part in this Italian vision of the old West.

D: Franco Giraldi                                                      97 minutes

**THE MISSOURI BREAKS** **1/2 NBC
(1976)

Marlon Brando, Jack Nicholson, Harry Dean Stanton, Kathleen Lloyd

An enormously disappointing, muddled Western set in Montana during the 1880s. Marlon Brando sometimes sports an Irish brogue, sometimes not. Jack Nicholson gives the best performance in the film, but his and Brando's scenes together are curiously undramatic.

D: Arthur Penn                                                         126 minutes

**MOTHER, JUGS, AND SPEED**
*1/2 ABC
(1976)

Bill Cosby, Raquel Welch, Harvey Keitel

The easy camaraderie between three ambulance drivers is not enough to sustain the forced humor of this contrived, melodramatic farce. What could have been an urban version of M*A*S*H is marred by insensitive slapstick humor.

D: Peter Yates                                                         98 minutes

LEFT: *Charlton Heston embarks on an important World War II mission in* Midway.

RIGHT: *Jack Nicholson and Marlon Brando are less than great in* The Missouri Breaks.

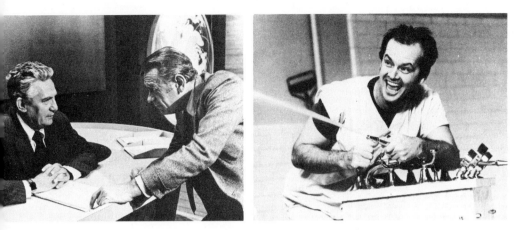

LEFT: *Peter Finch is the crazed network news anchorman, and William Holden is his producer in* Network.

RIGHT: *Jack Nicholson won an Oscar for his performance in* One Flew Over the Cuckoo's Nest.

Jackie Gleason, Terence Hill, Valerie Perrine, Slim Pickens

A light-hearted comedy about a young man from Italy (Hill) who inherits a business empire when his uncle in America dies. To claim his fortune, however, he must reach San Francisco in 20 days, which means eluding a villainous Jackie Gleason and a sumptuous Valerie Perrine, not to mention the slimy Slim Pickens. Occasionally enjoyable comedy-adventure.

D: Jonathan Kaplan                                    93 minutes

**MR. BILLION**
**1/2 CBS
(1977)

Henry Fonda, Terence Hill, Jean Martin

Interesting study of an aging gunfighter (Fonda) and the young cowboy (Hill) he teams with for one last shoot-'em-up before retiring. Fonda's portrait of the hero who must choose between becoming a dead legend or living in obscurity is well delineated.

D: Torino Valerii                                    115 minutes

**MY NAME IS NOBODY** *** NBC
(1974)

Faye Dunaway, William Holden, Peter Finch, Beatrice Straight, Robert Duvall

Paddy Chayefsky's searing, perceptive satire of network television deservedly won the Academy Award. It's a trenchant, grotesque comedy about a network news anchorman who's gone bananas, and the avaricious executives who decide to capitalize on his madness after initially firing him. The real theme of the film is accountability of network news, or the lack thereof. Astonishingly enough, this is the first major film in years to use TV as its principle backdrop.

D: Sidney Lumet                                    121 minutes

**NETWORK** **** CBS
(1976)

George Peppard, Roger Robinson, Abe Vigoda

Every cliché of the cop-movie genre has been retreaded here. Peppard is the righteous cop accused of corruption who tries to clear himself.

D: Richard Heffron                                    98 minutes

**NEWMAN'S LAW**
* ABC
(1974)

Jack Nicholson, Louise Fletcher, Brad Dourif, William Redfield

A stunning adaptation of Ken Kesey's novel that scored Oscars for best actor (Nicholson), best actress (Fletcher), best picture, and best director (Milos Forman). This story of conflict in a mental institution is a far cry from typical

**ONE FLEW OVER THE CUCKOO'S NEST** **** NBC
(1975)

Hollywood treatments. The acting is truly astonishing throughout, and makes you alternately laugh, weep, and despair, and there's not a false note in the film.

D: Milos Forman                                                    129 minutes

**ORCA** \* CBS (1977)

Richard Harris, Charlotte Rampling

Absurd adventure yarn which comes off as a mix of *Jaws* and *Moby Dick*. Richard Harris, employing an accent that fluctuates with every wave, has never been worse as the determined Captain Nolan out to get Orca, the killer whale. The special effects are good, but the story is ridiculous.

D: Michael Anderson                                                92 minutes

**THE OTHER SIDE OF THE MOUNTAIN** \*½ NBC (1975)

Marilyn Hassett, Beau Bridges

True-life story of Jill Kinmont, a skier who might have made it to the Olympics but for an accident which left her paralyzed. Heavy-handed tearjerker, but there's a good performance by Beau Bridges as a daredevil skier who falls in love with her.

D: Larry Peerce                                                    103 minutes

**THE PEOPLE THAT TIME FORGOT** \* NBC (1977)

Patrick Wayne, Doug McClure

Here we go again! Another lost civilization flick with prehistoric monsters, raging volcanoes, and primitive cavemen harassing Patrick Wayne, who is trying to rescue a marooned comrade, naval officer Doug McClure. Forget this one.

D: Kevin Conner                                                    90 minutes

**THE PINK PANTHER STRIKES AGAIN** \*\*\*\* ABC (1976)

Peter Sellers, Herbert Lom

Peter Sellers is so deliciously funny and inventive that this fourth farce about the addle-brained Inspector Clouseau is a welcome addition to the series. The plot, as always, is incidental to the wonderful puns and glorious sight gags. Sellers comes close to destroying your funnybone.

D: Blake Edwards                                                   103 minutes

LEFT: *Marilyn Hassett is a paralyzed former skiing champion in* The Other Side of the Mountain.

RIGHT: *Peter Sellers is the zany Inspector Clouseau in* The Pink Panther Strikes Again.

Jack Lemmon, Anne Bancroft

**THE PRISONER OF SECOND AVENUE** **\*\*1/2** NBC (1975)

Even Neil Simon's comic prose can fail sometimes, if it's played too broadly. Anne Bancroft, an actress of considerable talent, is miscast and just plain awful in the role of the wife of a man (Jack Lemmon) who loses his job at an ad agency after 22 years. Their readjustment consists of his having a nervous breakdown, and her yelling a great deal. Lemmon projects his own style of bewilderment, which works for the most part.

D: Melvin Frank                                    99 minutes

Robert Stephens, Colin Blakely

**THE PRIVATE LIFE OF SHERLOCK HOLMES** **\*\*\*** CBS (1970)

A great deal of wit and polish in this offbeat view of the great detective. Don't look for the usual clichés in this one—writer-director Billy Wilder has come up with a whole new look at the tweedy Mr. Holmes, including a strong suggestion that he preferred men to girls. Robert Stephens makes an excellent, if different, Sherlock Holmes, and Colin Blakely is entertaining as Dr. Watson.

D: Billy Wilder                                    125 minutes

Jeff Bridges, Elizabeth Ashley, Sam Waterston, Slim Pickens

**RANCHO DELUXE** **\*\*\*1/2** CBS (1974)

Thanks largely to a quirky, wry screenplay by novelist Thomas McGuane, this Western spoof works quite well most of the time. Bridges and Waterston play two nonchalant cattle rustlers who finally wind up in the pokey, but there's lots of fun along the way.

D: Frank Perry                                    93 minutes

Nick Nolte, Don Johnson

**RETURN TO MACON COUNTY** **\*\*1/2** NBC (1975)

Here's a picture that boasts Nick Nolte's first starring performance, but other than that it's quite routine. Nolte and Don Johnson, as a pair of itinerant racing bums, are really much better than their material. A few years earlier *Macon County Line* scored with the fans, and this was intended as a sequel of sorts with a different cast.

D: Richard Compton                                 104 minutes

**ROCKY**
**\*\*\*\* CBS**
**(1976)**

Sylvester Stallone, Talia Shire, Burgess Meredith

The Academy Award winner about a loutish lug who wants to become a boxing champ. In many ways it's surprising that the audience comes to care about the two-bit thumb-breaker working for the mob on the seamy side of Philadelphia. It may be thirties-make-believe, but Stallone, who also wrote the screenplay, and Talia Shire, as his painfully shy girlfriend, are splendid.

D: John G. Avildsen                                119 minutes

**ROLLERCOASTER**
**\*\* NBC**
**(1977)**

George Segal, Richard Widmark, Timothy Bottoms

Timothy Bottoms plays an extortionist who bombs rollercoaster rides in this predictable yarn which attempts to duplicate the Hitchcock style, but fails. George Segal, in the film's best performance, is an offbeat safety inspector hired to track the bomber down. The climax manages to generate what little suspense there is in this film.

D: James Goldstone                                119 minutes

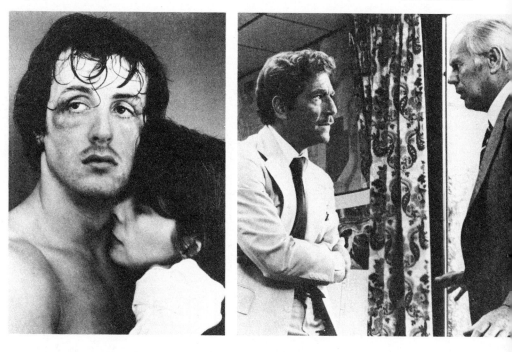

LEFT: *Sylvester Stallone and Talia Shire star in* Rocky, *one of the highest-rated films on television this season.*

RIGHT: *George Segal and Richard Widmark team up to stop an extortionist in the suspense drama* Rollercoaster.

**SCALAWAG**
**\*1/2 CBS**
**(1973)**

Kirk Douglas, Mark Lester, Neville Brand, Lesley Anne Down

A routine pirate film with all the clichés on board. Kirk Douglas stars as a bearded, peg-legged pirate, and also directed this opus, which is best appreciated by 10-year-olds who adore comic books.

D: Kirk Douglas                                    93 minutes

**SCOTT JOPLIN: KING**
**OF RAGTIME**
**\*\*\* NBC**
**(1976)**

Billy Dee Williams, Art Carney, Clifton Davis

A sad, touching story about the gifted American jazz composer. Billy Dee Williams plays Scott Joplin with cool dignity, and Art Carney delivers the goods as the only white publisher who believed in Scott's talent. Best of all, Joplin's ragtime music is heard throughout the film.

D: Jeremy Paul Kagan                               96 minutes

*Robin Williams as Mork and Pam Dawber as Mindy,
from the outstanding comedy success of the season,
"Mork & Mindy."*

LEFT: *Pint-sized Gary Coleman became a national favorite starring in the series "Diff'rent Strokes."*

OPPOSITE PAGE: *Pat Harrington, Jr., Valerie Bertinelli, Mackenzie Phillips, and (foreground) star Bonnie Franklin were the cast in the series "One Day at a Time."*

BELOW: *Doris Roberts (left), Robert Hays, and Donna Pescow, the stars of "Angie."*

The cast of "Alice": (left to right) Polly Holliday, Vic Tayback, star Linda Lavin, Beth Howland, and (foreground) Philip McKeon.

A group of eccentric misfits tried to revive a radio station in the series "WKRP in Cincinnati."

Leif Garrett and Kristy McNichol share a youthful romance in "Family."

Michael Landon starred as head of the Ingalls family in the popular series "Little House on the Prairie."

ABOVE: *John Houseman was the imperious professor and James Stephens his prize student in "The Paper Chase."*

OPPOSITE PAGE, LEFT: *Stockard Channing starred in the new series "Stockard Channing in Just Friends."*

OPPOSITE PAGE, RIGHT: *Ken Howard portrayed a high school basketball coach who solved problems both on and off the court in "The White Shadow."*

BELOW: *The 200 mph, coast-to-coast "Supertrain" stalled in mid-season despite supercostly production and scenic design.*

*Linda Carter was the female superhero in "The New Adventures of Wonder Woman."*

LEFT: *"The Incredible Hulk" in a dangerous mood, portrayed by Lou Ferrigno.*

ABOVE: *"Cliffhangers: Dracula," played by Michael Nouri, tried to mix terror with laughs, but failed to excite viewers.*

LEFT: *(left to right) Richard Hatch, Lorne Greene, and Dirk Benedict of "Battlestar Galactica."*

Jack Klugman starred as a crime-solving medical examiner in "Quincy."

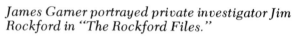

James Garner portrayed private investigator Jim Rockford in "The Rockford Files."

*(Left to right) Kate Jackson, Farrah Fawcett-Majors, Cheryl Ladd, Jaclyn Smith, and David Doyle, the stars of "Charlie's Angels."*

*Katharine Hepburn starred as the determined schoolmistress Miss Moffat in The Corn Is Green.*

*Shirley MacLaine performed with the famous Parisian variety revue in the special "Shirley MacLaine at the Lido."*

*Cicely Tyson portrayed Harriet Tubman, organizer of the Underground Railroad, which helped escaped slaves to freedom, in* A Woman Called Moses.

*Peter Ustinov starred as the Caliph in the TV-film
version of* The Thief of Baghdad.

*LeVar Burton contemplates the future from a prison cell in* One in a Million: The Ron LeFlore Story.

*Andrea McArdle portrayed the young Judy Garland, with Michael Parks as her singing teacher, in the TV film* Rainbow.

*Television viewers had a unique view of the historic first voyage across the Atlantic by three Americans in the hot-air balloon "Double Eagle II."*

BELOW: *Captain Jacques Cousteau investigated the origins of gigantic stone heads in "Blind Prophets of Easter Island," a segment of "The Cousteau Odyssey."*

BELOW: *One of the most tragic news stories covered by television was the Jonestown, Guyana, cult suicide-murders in which over 900 people died after drinking cyanide-laced Kool-Aid.*

Chris Sarandon, Christina Raines

**THE SENTINEL**
** NBC
**(1977)**

If you're looking for a cheap scare, here it is. Based on a best-selling novel, it's the story of a strange house in Brooklyn Heights which turns out to be the site of the gates of Hell. There's some nonsense about the denizen's of Hell finding a new "sentinel," and pretty Christina Raines, as a model living in the house, seems like the best candidate.

D: Michael Winner                                                              91 minutes

Warren Beatty, Julie Christie, Lee Grant, Jack Warden, Goldie Hawn

**SHAMPOO**
**** ABC
**(1975)**

Since Warren Beatty served as the producer, co-writer, and star of this funny, sardonic look at the contemporary sexual mores of Beverly Hills, he has to be given most of the credit for its success. Warren plays a sexy hairdresser named George who not only tends to the coiffures of his clientele, but to their other needs as well. Beatty is very agile making the rounds of his women—ex-mistress Julie Christie; rich matron Lee Grant; her teenaged daughter, Carrie Fisher; and his live-in love, Goldie Hawn—on Election Day, 1968. Beatty and his ladies, plus Jack Warden as a businessman who takes up with Ms. Christie, all shine.

D: Hal Ashby                                                              112 minutes

LEFT: *Warren Beatty is an amorous hairdresser in* Shampoo.

RIGHT: *John Wayne is an aging gunfighter and James Stewart a physician in* The Shootist.

**THE SHOOTIST**
*** CBS
(1976)

John Wayne, James Stewart, Ron Howard

A western about an old gunman dying of cancer who decides to go out a-blazin' and take a few mean varmints with him. It's episodic and uneven but provides the best role John Wayne has had in some time, and he makes the most of it.

D: Don Siegel                                                          100 minutes

**SKY RIDERS**
**1/2 CBS
(1976)

James Coburn, Susannah York, Robert Culp

Well above—several thousand feet above, as a matter of fact—the level of most melodramas, thanks entirely to some exciting, well-photographed scenes of hang-gliding. Here the sport is deftly employed to rescue some hostages held in an abandoned monastery on a high peak in Greece.

D: Douglas Hickox                                                      90 minutes

**A SMALL TOWN IN TEXAS**
* ABC
(1976)

Bo Hopkins, Timothy Bottoms, Susan George

Dim-witted movie about another crooked red-neck sheriff (Bo Hopkins) chasing a couple of innocent youths. Timothy Bottoms returns from jail after serving time on a drug bust to find Hopkins pursuing his girl (Susan George).

D: Jack Starrett                                                       95 minutes

**THE SPIKES GANG**
** CBS
(1974)

Lee Marvin, Ron Howard, Gary Grimes, Charlie Martin Smith

Lee Marvin stars in this mediocre western filmed in Spain, about an elderly outlaw who takes three young farm boys "under his wing" and tries, unsuccessfully, to tutor them in the fine art of robbing banks. The cast do their best with the rambling screenplay, but this undistinguished addition to a long line of coming-of-age films turns into a violence-filled opus.

D: Richard Fleischer                                                   96 minutes

**S*P*Y*S** *1/2 ABC
(1974)

Elliot Gould, Donald Sutherland

Misguided attempt to pair that marvelous team from M*A*S*H together again for more comedy. Gould and Sutherland are CIA agents whom their boss has decided are expendable. They are, and so is S*P*Y*S.

D: Irvin Kershner                                                      87 minutes

**STARSHIP INVASIONS**
1/2* NBC
(1978)

Robert Vaughan, Christopher Lee

This rip-off of *Star Wars* and "Star Trek," without the finesse of either, is a theatrical film that made it to TV in what seems like record time. Cast does its best with a below-par script about a UFO expert who befriends a peaceful group of aliens to stop a villainous power from—you guessed it!—taking over the earth.

D: Ed Hunt                                                             89 minutes

**STAY HUNGRY**
**1/2 NBC (1976)

Jeff Bridges, Sally Field, Arnold Schwarzenegger

Promising premise of a young, privileged boy intent on his independence, and the spunky working girl he lives with, fizzles out due to unmanageable plot strands. Bridges is good as the boy who occupies a Taralike mansion, and Miss Field's first mature role shows her to good advantage.

D: Bob Rafelson                                            103 minutes

Paul Newman, Robert Redford, Robert Shaw

**THE STING**
**** ABC
(1973)

A marvelously entertaining caper about two deft con artists (Newman and Redford) operating in and around Chicago circa 1936. Director George Roy Hill gives the film a fast pace and glittering style; Marvin Hamlisch provides a score of rollicking Scott Joplin rags. One of the best wrap-up scenes in many years, as Newman and Redford swindle Shaw out of a big bundle in one of the most inventive schemes ever depicted on the screen. A joy from beginning to end.

D: George Roy Hill                                         129 minutes

Olivia Hussey, Keir Dullea, John Saxon, Margot Kidder

**STRANGER IN THE HOUSE**
* NBC
(1974)

Muddled murder mystery. A crazed killer makes obscene phone calls to his victims in a college sorority house before he does them in. Best thing about this film is Margot Kidder as a hard-drinking sorority sister whose language was cleaned up for the TV version. Originally called *Black Christmas* and released as *Silent Night, Evil Night,* a stinker whatever its title.

D: Bob Clark                                               104 minutes

Robert Shaw, James Earl Jones, Peter Boyle, Genevieve Bujold

**SWASHBUCKLER**
* NBC
(1976)

Inept, embarrassing pirate film, circa 1718 in Jamaica. Plush production values and tongue-in-cheek tone don't hide the lack of plot or direction. Shaw grins enthusiastically throughout, Boyle overacts wildly as the villain, and Bujold has a part so silly it can't be salvaged.

D: James Goldstone                                         101 minutes

LEFT: *Paul Newman and Robert Redford plan for better days ahead in* The Sting.

RIGHT: *Janet Margolin and Woody Allen embark on a life of crime in* Take the Money and Run.

**THE TAKE** *½ ABC
(1974)

Billy Dee Williams, Eddie Albert, Frankie Avalon

Corrupt cops and double-crosses abound in this trashy police story with Billy Dee Williams cast as a cop who works out a system by which he plays both sides of the law for profit. Eddie Albert is the police chief, and Frankie Avalon overacts in a bit as a crook who can't stand up to Williams's threats.

D: Robert Hartford Davis                                    93 minutes

**TAKE A HARD RIDE** *½ CBS
(1975)

Jim Brown, Lee Van Cleef, Fred Williamson

He-man star Jim Brown is a cowboy traveling to Mexico to return a large sum of money to his late employer's widow. Along the way he encounters a bounty hunter (Van Cleef), a dishonest gambler (Williamson), and a mute Indian (Jim Kelly), who display their own brands of macho posturing. Mucho violent.

D: Anthony M. Dawson                                    103 minutes

**TAKE THE MONEY AND RUN** **** ABC
(1969)

Woody Allen, Janet Margolin, Lonny Chapman, Mark Gordon

Allen's marvelous version of an ancient Biblical theme: The meek shall inherit the earth. Woody plays a timid, fumbling gangster, who winds up inheriting more jail time than jewels. The plot really doesn't matter in this gloriously funny farce; what counts are the inspired sight gags and one-liners. Take time to see this laughfest.

D: Woody Allen                                    85 minutes

**TENTACLES** ½* NBC
(1977)

John Huston, Henry Fonda, Shelley Winters, Bo Hopkins

Trying to lure the *Jaws* audience, this poor-man's imitation has a giant octopus as the menace. However, the real culprits are the producers and writers of this lame-brained excursion into violence for its own sake.

D: Oliver Hellman                                    102 minutes

LEFT: *Charlton Heston is a police commander with his work cut out for him in* Two-Minute Warning.

RIGHT: *Evel Knievel plays himself in* Viva Knievel.

Maurice Evans, John Carradine, Ray Milland, Elsa Lanchester

Silly mystery thriller. The plot centers around a wax museum, and some bizarre people connected with it, filled with figures of infamous murderers who have a strange way of coming to life at opportune moments.

D: George Fenady                                        93 minutes

**TERROR IN THE WAX MUSEUM**
** ABC
**(1973)**

Candice Bergen, James Caan, Peter Boyle

A "romantic" view of a working girl's life and loves during the early 1970s. Candice Bergen gives a subdued, thoroughly appealing performance as a young woman searching for answers in her formless life. James Caan also scores a bullseye as a divorced man whose relationships seldom amount to more than one-night stands.

D: Herbert Ross                                        104 minutes

**T.R. BASKIN**
**1/2 CBS
**(1971)**

Charlton Heston, Gena Rowlands, David Janssen, John Cassavetes

Originally a mindless piece of disagreeable claptrap about a mad sniper in a jammed football stadium. However, for TV an entire subplot was added and spliced into the existing footage through extensive editing. What resulted was an even more confusing yarn: the sniper, never seen full-face in the original, emerges here as a member of a gang of art thieves, using the sniping incident as a diversion. Clumsy and muddled.

D: Larry Peerce                                        156 minutes

**TWO MINUTE WARNING**
* NBC
**(1976)**

Barbra Streisand, David Selby, Ariane Heller

A funny, wry, genuinely touching story about a young New York housewife; one of the very first films to deal with the women's rights movement. Benefits greatly from one of Streisand's most observant, restrained performances, in this her sixth film. Nicely handled, except for a clumsy ending, by director Irvin Kershner.

D: Irvin Kershner                                       97 minutes

**UP THE SANDBOX**
***1/2 ABC
**(1972)**

Evel Knievel, Gene Kelly, Red Buttons, Lauren Hutton

A mindless piece of drivel starring one-time superstuntman Evel Knievel, in a yarn involving crooks trying to ace him out of his hard-earned champion daredevil status. There are stunts to thrill those who go for that kind of thing, but the whole affair is a crashing bore. Gene Kelly almost ruins the memory of his former movie career with a performance so bad it makes Hutton, Buttons, and even Evel himself seem like descendants of the Barrymores.

D: Gordon Douglas                                       104 minutes

**VIVA KNIEVEL**
* NBC
**(1977)**

Burt Reynolds, Ned Beatty, Jennifer Billingsley

A few sparkling moments in this fast-paced melodrama about murder, revenge, and moonshine in the New South. Reynolds is a convict who's released in order to help the feds to nail sadistic sheriff Ned Beatty.

D: Joseph Sargent                                       101 minutes

**WHITE LIGHTNING**
**1/2 CBS
**(1973)**

**WHO IS KILLING THE STUNTMEN?**
** NBC
(1977)

Robert Forster, Fiona Lewis, Joanna Lewis

Routine action film deals with a movie company being plagued by "accidental deaths" of stuntmen. The background adds interest, but it all amounts to little. Robert Forster is well cast as a Hollywood stuntman who sets out to get to the bottom of the mystery.

D: Mark L. Lester                                                                104 minutes

**YOU LIGHT UP MY LIFE**
*** ABC
(1977)

Didi Conn, Joe Silver, Michael Zaslow

The song's the thing. If you haven't already overdosed on the popular Oscar-winning song, you may enjoy this sometimes affecting sentimental yarn about a plain Jane who finds love in a one-night stand with a sexy film director, and then meets him again when she goes to an audition. Miss Conn is much better than the material. Her solid performance gives the film much of its appeal.

D: Joseph Brooks                                                                 90 minutes

# DAYTIME
# PROGRAMS

# RUB-A-DUB DAYS

by John N. Goudas*

**D**AYTIME TV rolls along with its blend of soap operas, game shows, and reruns of popular sitcoms, and the picture changes little from year to year. However, an interesting aspect of this past season was that the daytime-ratings story reflected prime time. ABC was the leader once again, outdistancing the competition, with CBS coming up second, and NBC dragging tail end. NBC was the only network to cancel a soap, "For Richer, For Poorer," and it expanded one of its hour-long daytime dramas, "Another World," to 90 minutes. It appears the expansion of "Another World" hasn't set a trend. CBS and ABC aren't planning to convert any of their current soaps to 90-minute marathons. The NBC experiment was looked upon as a failure by the two competing networks and they could be right. "Another World" wasn't leading its time period in the ratings as an hour show, so the move to 90 minutes was implemented with the hope of building an audience that would stay for the whole hour and a half. It did not work out that way; "Another World" still didn't lead its time period. In any event, NBC has been toying with the idea of turning "Days of Our Lives" into a 90-minute entry.

Interestingly enough, the hour format seems to work quite well for soaps. There are still many half-hour soaps on the air, but CBS plans to expand its current highest-rated daytime drama, "The Young and the Restless," from a half-hour to an hour in the near future.

As for the plots of the soaps, they still dealt with those staples—illegitimate children, long-lost lovers popping up from nowhere, and an assortment of illnesses including hysterical blindness (a particularly popular item). However, as fans of the "stories" (as they are more commonly known out there in the hinterlands) have probably detected, there has been an acceleration of the pacing of the plot lines. It used to be that you could go on a two-week vacation and come back assured that you could tune in and pick up the thread of Vanessa's plight without too much trouble. That has changed, more than ever during this past season. As one CBS soap-opera exec observed, "The storytelling is the main thing, and now you can't dawdle too long with it or the viewer will lose interest."

Another important development was the use of "headline" stories adapted to fit the soap. For instance, "Guiding Light" dealt with a wife accusing her husband of rape (remember the Greta and John Rideout case?). Of course, in the soap, Roger was shot by his wife Holly, which took the real-life-inspired incident a step further. There were also story lines dealing with religious cults, mastectomies, and homosexuality in prisons.

Perhaps the biggest single factor that altered the look of soaps was location shooting. In the past the traditional home, office, courtroom, and hospital sets were all the soap viewer ever saw; but now the daytime dramas suddenly took the viewer on a honeymoon in the Caribbean (complete with swimming sequences). This practice wasn't initiated this season, but it became more prevalent and many of the soaps plan on doing more of the same, even though it adds quite a bit to the budget.

On the more serious side, soap operas are being used by therapists in the treatment of near-catatonics in a psychiatric hospital in Connecti-

PRECEDING PAGE: *Ron Tomme and Audrey Peters have played the roles of Bruce and Vanessa Sterling since 1959 in "Love of Life."*

*"You should watch this. You might learn something."*
(Drawing by Modell; © 1978 The New Yorker Magazine, Inc.)

cut. The patients related to the problems of some of the characters on the show and opened up a little after viewing the soaps on a consistent basis. Colleges are also "legitimizing" soaps. There are courses in universities which examine the sociological impact of daytime serials.

Afternoon viewing is dominated by the soaps, but the early daytime hours are turned over to the razzle-dazzle of the game shows, which have been labeled by some as "a monumental tribute to greed." The prizes are the lure for contestants to jump up and down and scream and shout and generally make fools of themselves. CBS introduced a new one this season titled "Whew!," which has nothing to do with the game played, but refers to the breakneck speed with which the competing contestants do their thing. NBC's new game show was something originally called "Hollywood Secrets" which became "All Star Secrets." One of the "stars" who served on the Celebrity Panel during the year was Michele Triola Marvin, who helped coin the word "palimony" in her precedent-setting case against her lover of many years, Lee Marvin. What possible secrets could she still have after the highly publicized trial? At least she didn't qualify for ABC's "Family Feud," which incidentally is the highest-rated game show on TV.

Daytime programming is very lucrative for the networks. They make big bucks from the lineup of soaps, games, and comedy reruns. The profit is enormous compared to the expenditures, so the programmers know enough not to tamper with a successful formula. The only deviation from the schedule is the occasional preemption for an "Afterschool Special" or a "Special Treat." Many of these presentations, from June 1978 through May 1979 last season, were of extraordinarily high quality. (See section on Children's TV.)

The dedicated daytime viewer is evidently still interested in getting the morning started with the slam-bang noisy game shows in which hosts shout, contestants scream, lights blink, and buzzers go off, almost simultaneously. Once the adrenalin is flowing, the viewer opts for the traumatic trials and tense tribulations of the soaps, before getting down to the more serious business of deciding whether to have stuffing or potatoes for supper.

# DAYTIME SERIES

**ALL MY CHILDREN**
(ABC)
60 minutes
*Premiere date:*
*January 5, 1970*

STARS: Julia Barr as Brooke English, Mark LaMura as Mark Dalton, Susan Lucci as Erica Kane Cudahy, Richard Van Vleet as Chuck Tyler, Ruth Warrick as Phoebe Tyler
CREATED BY: Agnes Nixon    PRODUCER: Bud Kloss
DIRECTORS: Jack Coffey, Del Hughes, Henry Kaplan
WRITERS: Agnes Nixon, Wisner Washam, Jack Wood, Mary K. Wells, Ken Harvey, Cathy Chicos, and William Delligan

**ANOTHER WORLD**
(NBC)
90 minutes
*Premiere date:*
*May 4, 1964*

STARS: Beverlee McKinsey as Iris Carrington, Beverly Penberthy as Pat Randolph, Douglass Watson as Mackenzie Cory, Victoria Wyndham as Rachel Cory
EXECUTIVE PRODUCER: Paul Rauch
PRODUCERS: Mary S. Bonner, Joseph Willmore
DIRECTORS: Ira Cirker, Melvin Bernhardt, Paul Lammers
WRITERS: Harding Lemay, David Robinson

**AS THE WORLD TURNS** (CBS)
60 minutes
*Premiere date:*
*April 2, 1956*

STARS: Larry Bryggman as Dr. John Dixon, Dennis Cooney as Jay Stallings, Eileen Fulton as Lisa Shea Coleman, Don MacLaughlin as Chris Hughes, Marie Masters as Dr. Susan Stewart, Helen Wagner as Nancy Hughes
EXECUTIVE PRODUCER: Joe Rothenberger    PRODUCER: Arthur Richards
WRITERS: Robert Sodenberg, Edith Sommer, Ralph Ellis, Eugenie Hunt, Ted Apstein, Gillian Spencer

**DAYS OF OUR LIVES**
(NBC)
60 minutes
*Premiere date:*
*November 8, 1965*

STARS: Macdonald Carey as Dr. Tom Horton, John Clarke as Mickey Horton, Bill Hayes as Doug Williams, Susan Seaforth Hayes as Julie, Frances Reid as Alice Horton, Suzanne Rogers as Maggie Simmons Hanson
EXECUTIVE PRODUCERS: Betty Corday, H. Wesley Kenney
PRODUCER: Jack Herzberg    DIRECTORS: Joe Behar, Frank Pacelli, Al Rabin
STORY BY: William J. Bell
WRITERS: Ann Marcus, Michael Robert David, Raymond Goldstone, Joyce Perry, Elizabeth Harrower, Roccina Chatfield, Laura Olsher

**THE DOCTORS** (NBC)
30 minutes
*Premiere date:*
*April 1, 1963*

STARS: Peggy Cass as Sweeney, Lydia Bruce as Dr. Maggie Powers, Shawn Campbell as Billy Allison, Jennifer Houlton as Greta Powers, James Pritchett as Dr. Matt Powers
PRODUCER: Chuck Weiss
DIRECTORS: Gary Bowen, Ivan Cury    WRITER: Linda Grover

STARS: Denny Albee as Steve Guthrie, Tony Craig as Draper Scott, Joel Crothers as Dr. Miles Cavanaugh, Terry Davis as April Scott, Sharon Gabet as Raven Jamison
ORIGINATED BY: Irving Vendig   PRODUCER: Erwin W. Nicholson
DIRECTORS: John Sedwick, Richard Pepperman
WRITERS: Henry Slesar, Steve Lehrman

**THE EDGE OF NIGHT**
(ABC)
30 minutes
*Premiere date:*
*April 2, 1956*

STARS: Richard Backus as Jason Saxton, Cynthia Bostick as Connie Ferguson, David Knapp as Desmond Hamilton, Julia MacKenzie as Laurie B. Hamilton
CREATED BY: Harding Lemay   EXECUTIVE PRODUCER: Paul Rauch
DIRECTORS: Jack Hofsiss, Barnet Kellman   WRITER: Tom King

**FOR RICHER,**
**FOR POORER** (NBC)
30 minutes
*Premiere date:*
*December 6, 1977*

STARS: Denise Alexander as Dr. Leslie Faulkner, Rachel Ames as Audrey Hobart, Richard Dean Anderson as Dr. Jeff Webber, John Beradino as Dr. Steve Hardy, Emily McLaughlin as Jessie Brewer
CREATED BY: Frank and Doris Hursley   PRODUCER: Gloria Monty
DIRECTORS: Phil Sogard, Marlena Laird, Alan Pultz
WRITERS: Douglas Marland, Robert Dwyer, Frank Salisbury, Nancy Franklin, Andrea Russo

**GENERAL HOSPITAL**
(ABC)
60 minutes
*Premiere date:*
*April 1, 1963*

STARS: Charita Bauer as Bertha Bauer, Christopher Bernau as Alan Spaulding, Mart Hulswit as Dr. Ed Bauer, Lenore Kasdorf as Rita Stapleton, Don Stewart as Michael Bauer, Michael Zaslow as Roger Thorpe
EXECUTIVE PRODUCER: Allen M. Potter   PRODUCER: Leslie Kwartin
WRITERS: Jerome and Bridget Dobson, Virginia McDonnell, Nancy Ford, Jen Rouverol, Bob and Phyllis White

**THE GUIDING LIGHT**
(CBS)
30 minutes
*Premiere date:*
*June 30, 1952*

*The cast of "Ryan's Hope": (clockwise from center) Bernard Barrow as Johnny, Sarah Felder as Siobhan, John Blazo as Pat, Daniel Hugh-Kelly as Frank, Kathleen Tolan as Mary, and Helen Gallagher as Maeve.*

**LOVE OF LIFE** (CBS)
30 minutes
*Premiere date:*
*September 24, 1951*

STARS: Lloyd Battista as Ray Slater, Chandler Hill Harben as Ben Harper, Audrey Peters as Vanessa Dale Sterling, Birgitta Tolksdorf as Arlene Lovett Slater, Ron Tomme as Bruce Sterling
PRODUCER: Jean Arley   DIRECTOR: Larry Auerbach
WRITER: Gabrielle Upton

**ONE LIFE TO LIVE**
(ABC)
60 minutes
*Premiere date:*
*July 15, 1968*

STARS: Jacqueline Courtney as Pat Ashley, Al Freeman, Jr., as Ed Hall, Lee Patterson as Joe Riley, Erika Slezak as Viki Riley, Robin Strasser as Dorian Lord
CREATED BY: Agnes Nixon   PRODUCER: Joseph Stuart
DIRECTORS: Norman Hall, Peter Miner, David Pressman
WRITERS: Gordon Russell, Sam Hall, Peggy O'Shea, Lanie Bertram, Marisa Gioffre, Don Wallace

STARS: Bernard Barrow as Johnny Ryan, John Blazo as Pat Ryan, Randall Edwards as Delia Reid Ryan Coleridge, Sarah Felder as Siobhan Ryan, Helen Gallagher as Maeve Ryan, Nicolette Goulet as Mary Ryan Fenelli, Daniel Hugh-Kelly as Frank Ryan
CREATED BY: Clair Labine, Paul Avila Mayer
PRODUCER: Ellen Barrett
DIRECTORS: Jerry Evans, Lela Swift
WRITERS: Claire Labine, Paul Avila Mayer, Mary Munisteri, Judith Pinsker, Jeffrey Lane

**RYAN'S HOPE** (ABC)
30 minutes
*Premiere date:
July 7, 1975*

STARS: Marie Cheatham as Stephanie Wyatt, Val Dufour as John Wyatt, Larry Haines as Stu Bergman, Sherry Mathis as Liza Kaslo, Mary Stuart as Joanne Vincente
EXECUTIVE PRODUCER: Mary-Ellis Bunim
DIRECTORS: Ned Stark, Bob Schwarz
WRITERS: Henry Slesar, Chuck and Patti Dizenzo, Sam Reese

**SEARCH FOR TOMORROW** (CBS)
30 minutes
*Premiere date:
September 3, 1951*

LEFT: *Larry Haines plays Stu Bergman on "Search for Tomorrow."*

RIGHT: *Mary Stuart, in the role of Joanne Vincente, was an original cast member of one of television's longest-running daytime dramas, "Search for Tomorrow."*

LEFT: *Victoria Mallory is concert pianist Leslie Brooks and Tom Ligon is her friend Lucas Prentiss in "The Young and the Restless."*

RIGHT: *David Hasselhoff plays Dr. Snapper Foster in "The Young and the Restless."*

**THE YOUNG AND THE RESTLESS** (CBS)
30 minutes
*Premiere date:*
*March 26, 1973*

STARS: Jaime Lyn Bauer as Lorie Brooks Prentiss, David Hasselhoff as Snapper Foster, Tom Ligon as Lucas Prentiss, Victoria Mallory as Leslie Brooks, John McCook as Lance Prentiss

EXECUTIVE PRODUCER: John Conboy    PRODUCER: Patricia Wenig

DIRECTORS: Richard Dunlap, Bill Glenn    WRITER: William J. Bell

# 4

# BROADCAST
# NEWS

# ALL THE NEWS THAT'S FIT TO GLITTER

by Edwin Diamond *

NETWORK television news began its season with a disconcerting threat to its future; it ended the season with the brighter promise of things to come. In between it managed to cover some extraordinarily difficult stories with energy and intelligence. On balance, then, it was a good year, if not a great year, for television news.

The threat had to do with what I have come to think of as "disco news." Discerning viewers have been watching the arrival of disco news on a number of local newscasts around the country with growing shock and disbelief. These alleged news programs featured shorter news items, more items, with a faster pace, and less serious, "soft news" themes. The on-air talent must be younger, snappier, better-looking, "with-it" people. The programs must have music, lights, beat, and production. Like disco music, disco news celebrated mindlessness. It isn't what you say, it's how you look.

ABC, CBS, and NBC networks were, of course, much too responsible—and too sensitive to criticism—to play to an outright disco beat; but the form was intruding. Straightforward news had to defend itself against glitter values.

Toward the end of the season, veteran newscaster Howard K. Smith announced his resignation from ABC News, where he had served with distinction since 1961. Smith had been doing a three-times weekly commentary on ABC's "World News Tonight." When management told him it planned to cut down on commentary—in order "to lighten the show," Smith reports—he decided to leave.

CBS News was still the most serious television news organization and the acknowledged news leader. Yet there wasn't a steady place for the thoughtful Bill Moyers and his real-life "CBS Reports."

At NBC News, the length of interview segments on its 7:00-9:00 A.M. "Today Show" were cut back considerably. In the interests of that sought-after quality called pace, senators talking about SALT II or energy policy had to do so with more finger-popping dispatch. To liven up its morning news even more, the "Today Show" brought on Phil Donahue, the talk show personality and daytime TV heartthrob.

In the battle for morning-news ratings, the "Today Show" felt pressure from ABC's featurized "Good Morning America," hosted by the amiable David Hartman. During one week last spring, "Good Morning" slipped past the "Today Show" for the first time.

CBS remained committed to one hour of hard-hitting news (7:00-8:00 A.M.). A new set, a new anchor, even a new name ("Morning" preceded by each day of the week) didn't change its low ratings.

An encouraging development on the morning news scene was the introduction of a 90-minute program on CBS called "Sunday Morning" (9:00-10:30 A.M.), hosted by correspondent Charles Kuralt. The entry quickly increased the number of CBS affiliates carrying the network feed at that hour and turned into a rewarding and civilized magazine show. It introduced the insightful comments of author Jeff Greenfield talking about television itself, and frequently closed the program with several minutes of cinematography without narration.

PRECEDING PAGE: "ABC News Close-Up: Youth Terror: The View from Behind the Gun," Wednesday, June 28 (10:00-11:00 P.M., ET).

*Edwin Diamond is a commentator for the Post-Newsweek Television Stations in Washington, D.C., and Senior Lecturer in the Political Science Department at M.I.T. in Boston.

*"The President today fired James Schlesinger, Griffin Bell, Michael Blumenthal, Alfred Kahn, Jody Powell, Stuart Eizanstat . . . Ha, ha, ha! We were only fooling."*
(Drawing by Dana Fradon; © 1979 The New Yorker Magazine, Inc.)

Like Studio 54, the New York City disco that wouldn't let people in if they didn't look kinky enough, television news already began to check out hairstyles and chin lines. In Boston this past season, a weatherman and a reporter were dropped from the CBS affiliate station because they looked "too old" and "too wrinkled" on camera. Even ABC's. Barbara Walters, a recognized superstar on her own network, worried that the day was approaching when she'd be barred from the studio; television, she feared, may be willing to present 60-ish "Uncle Walter" Cronkite on the news, but not a 50-ish "Aunt Barbara."

Still, the intrusion of disco at the network-news level was kept, mercifully, to the edges. At ABC's "World News Tonight," where the beat seemed most likely to catch on with the ascension of Roone Arledge, a group of professionals continued to put out a first-rate hard-news program. For years ABC News had been last in the three-network news ratings. With nothing to lose, it was more willing to experiment. Instead of one anchor person CBS-style (Cronkite), or NBC's two anchors (John Chancellor and David Brinkley), ABC News decided to deploy three anchors (Frank Reynolds, Max Robinson, and Peter Jennings). ABC News also tried for more stories and for more people-oriented stories, often choosing lead pieces on the gut-issue domestic economy while its rivals at CBS and NBC were playing international political stories. But the new ABC format with its three news desks controlled by an invisible fourth producer's desk in New York actually has become more rigid and scripted than the others. By the end of the season, however, ABC's evening news was gaining ground on number two NBC, thanks in part to the strong ABC network entertainment schedule.*

Over at PBS, the "MacNeil-Lehrer Report," which devoted its full half-hour broadcast to one subject, steadily gained a loyal audience. Last season "MacNeil-Lehrer" claimed about 2.5 million viewers per day.

*It passed NBC's Nightly News in ratings for the first time during the week of April 16-20, 1979.

The promise for television news was that it will go forward to a more sensible, more substantial news format, rather than step down to disco sound-and-light shows. Television viewers were becoming a better-educated, more worldly audience; this audience needed much more than show biz and headline service from television news. Television, in fact, has only just begun to catch up to its mature audience. Television producers have remained frozen in their conviction that the audience has the attention span—and mental apparatus—of an amoeba. The notion that viewers must be continually attracted with bright objects, visual dazzle, and loud noise never made sense for millions of intelligent, older adults who grew up on books and radio. It was equally nonsensical when applied to a younger generation who grew up in the era of paperbacks and television. People in their 30s have been watching TV for almost three decades. They knew all its conventions.

The convention in most need of change was the 30-minute newscast (actually, 23 minutes when commerical time and other clutter is subtracted). In the 1950's and early 1960's network television news followed a strict 15-minute format of news flashes; John Cameron Swayze used to say, "let's go hopscotching the world for headlines . . ."

The man who helped bring network television out of this deadly ritual was CBS News president Richard Salant. He led CBS to the present half-hour program format in September 1963. This past season, Salant reached the mandatory CBS retirement age of 65 (mandatory, that is, for everyone but Board Chairman and founding father William S. Paley). Now Salant has gone over to NBC, where as vice chairman he announced that one of his major goals will be to move NBC to one hour of nightly news, preferably in prime time from 8:00-9:00 P.M. As Salant told the *New York Times,* "One of the great problems in TV news is lack of air time. That's why we're superficial and shallow. We let a lot of things go by the boards simply because there isn't enough air time." NBC News's shift to an hour could mark the beginning of the end of covering the cosmos in 23 minutes—what Columbia University sociologist Herbert Gans has called the network news style of "highlights of highlights."

Good in the abstract, Salant's proposal had a number of attractive features special to NBC. NBC's entertainment schedule was considered to be the poorest of the three networks. A typical half-hour entertainment program cost the networks some $250,000 per episode; according to Salant, the same half-hour period could be added to the news for just an extra $5,000 a night, saving the network over $1 million each week. Also, with news, producers don't have to worry about running out of new material or thinking up new ideas. The news doesn't go into reruns in February.

The arguments against news in prime time were as familiar as the laugh lines of an ABC situation comedy. News was not supposed to attract the same high ratings as entertainment. The TV audience was thought to want to escape from the troubles of the world (ex-NBC programmer Paul Klein used to argue that on an entertainment series, if someone has syphillis, he recovers; on news and public affairs programs, if someone has syphillis, *you* are likely to catch it . . .). How would news compete with the Fonz or one of Charlie's Angels in a wet tee shirt?

One answer seemed to be that CBS's prime-time news magazine show, "60 Minutes," consistently ranked in the top-ten television programs. Also, other programs besides jigglevision cop shows and teeny-bopper comedy did well in prime time. For example, Barbara Walters's interview specials ranked high; so did the various awards ceremonies—New York's theatrical Tonys, as well as Hollywood's motion picture Oscars. "Monday Night Football" and baseball's playoff games won high ratings too.

If NBC leads the networks to a one-hour newscast in the next few years—one NBC executive producer commented, "Salant isn't over here to play chess"—it will have to be a different kind of evening news. An hour-long prime-time news just can't make each story twice as long. It can develop certain important stories for four or five minutes, as opposed to two minutes now; but it must develop new interests. Why not sports on the network news and reviews and previews of the arts—

*"Morning" anchormen Bob Schieffer (left) and Charles Kuralt. Schieffer is at the anchor desk for the weekday editions of the broadcast, Monday through Friday (7:00-8:00 A.M., ET); Kuralt takes over on "CBS News Sunday Morning" (9:00-10:30 A.M., ET).*

movies, theater, dance, concerts, music, sculpture? And why not live studio interviews with newsmakers and satellite hook-ups bringing together adversaries such as Governor Jerry Brown and former energy boss James Schlesinger to argue the cause of gasoline shortages? Certainly, too, there ought to be room for the commentaries of a Howard K. Smith, Bill Moyers, or any of a dozen other broadcast journalists. All this would make for fresh, lively, and informative prime-time news.

While broadcast journalism was making news about itself this past season, it also performed its proper journalistic function. The major domestic running stories were inflation and the economy. While economic reporting still remained the vast wasteland of American journalism, print as well as broadcast, the situation was rapidly changing for the better. Each network had at last developed economic news specialists who didn't seem intimidated by a story about the discount rate or the market for gold, or even by a Phillips curve. Graphics and videofonts (machines that make text appear on the TV screen) were at last being used to help explain the dynamics of economic stories. Television no longer approached the daunting subject of economics with its hands and tongue tied, though economics journalism on television was still a long way from instructing with the ease of a Paul Samuelson at a classroom blackboard. Unfortunately, too much economics reporting on television still consisted of a reporter at a supermarket checkout counter telling the price of ground round. The viewers knew *what* things cost; they wanted to know why.

Of the major breaking stories, three in particular challenged television: the Middle East peace negotiations, the Jonestown mass murder-suicides, and the Three Mile Island nuclear accident.

President Carter's decision to act as both participant and mediator in the negotiations involving Egypt and Israel brought American television right into the picture. American public opinion, we know, can influence the direction of American foreign policy. And America's perceived national interests, in turn, can influence public opinion. During the Middle East negotiations, American public opinion was courted by three interested parties—Egypt's Sadat, Israel's Begin, and America's Carter. Each engaged in television diplomacy to win support. To a certain extent, Walter Cronkite, John Chancellor, and Barbara Walters became accomplices of the television diplomats. Like home-grown American politicians, Begin and Sadat learned how to use the press— granting exclusive interviews, creating visual events (like Sadat's trip to Jerusalem), arranging photo opportunities, and otherwise delivering dramatic images and "good television." In fact, however, "good television" can make for poor information when not accompanied by the drab explanations necessary to tell the news. One antidote for television diplomacy, or for that matter, one corrective for *any* official manipulation of television, would be for network news to turn its cameras around and examine its own role in the reporting of public events.

Jonestown also became something of a television story; first, because two television newsmen were killed on the scene; second, because the story provided the range of action that television news can handle so well on many occasions. Not only were network television crews rushed to the Guyana site, but television was also able to produce

VITAMIN C TABLETS

RID:5:G:D

IRON PILLS

THE NEWS IN CAPSULE FORM

LIQUID PROTEIN

(Drawing by Levin; © 1979 The New Yorker Magazine, Inc.)

breaking news coverage from the State Department in Washington, from the remnants of the Reverend Jim Jones's People's Temple in San Francisco, and from other points around the country (for example, from Jones's old home town in Indiana). The result was an immediate, authoritative account of the Jonestown cult and of the tragic, doomed men and women who put their trust in the messiah who went mad. Along with print journalists, television correspondents rushed to their bookshelves for literary references to Eugene O'Neill's *Emperor Jones* and to Joseph Conrad's *Heart of Darkness*. In this case the imagery was apt; the darkness of the bush does lie just a few feet away in all of us, and television helped bring that message home.

A different sort of darkness had to be confronted at the damaged reactor in Pennsylvania and television news performed less successfully. The Three Mile Island accident proved to be a triple test of competence. It tested the ability of an industry to build and operate safe, efficient nuclear plants; it tested the ability of government agencies to regulate these plants in the public interest; and it tested the ability of the press, particularly television, to cover complex stories in a clear, coherent, nonpanicky voice. With the benefit of 20/20 hindsight, it's possible to see that industry, government, and the press didn't measure up. The three institutions that should be helping the public—and the public's representatives at the local, state, and national levels—determine the future of nuclear power in the United States needed help themselves.

Television news necessarily depended upon information supplied by the operators of the plant—Metropolitan Edison—and by state and federal authorities. As officials lost their self-assurance, television reflected this. When these officials began contradicting one another, the news began to sound contradictory and confusing. Since the people running things were badly informed, bad information was passed on to the press and by the press to the public.

Television news has the power to transmit auras. In the case of Three Mile Island, TV first gave the feeling of an alert, next it gave the sense of official reassurance, and finally, it transmitted the danger of a lethal hydrogen explosion. Television news began to falter when it tried analysis: explanations went by too fast; not enough time or care went into graphics; scripts read like tabloid news, either too urgent (*lethal, massive, dreaded, nightmarish*) or too bland (*mishap, malfunction*). Television was also much too diffident about looking into causes. It didn't put authority's feet to the fire. With the immediate crisis over, television news walked away from the story.

Despite all these shortcomings, it's still possible to conclude, as one opponent of nuclear power did, that television provided more valuable education in nuclear energy in those two weeks in March and April 1979, than it had in the previous 25 years of the "Atomic Age."

It was a mixed compliment and one that can serve as a verdict on the year in television news.

# MAJOR TV NEWS STORIES JUNE 1978— MAY 1979

*1978*

**JUNE 6** California voters pass Proposition 13, a measure limiting property taxes and cutting government spending.

**JUNE 12** The Supreme Court refuses to block a planned march by Nazis through the predominantly Jewish community of Skokie, Illinois, a suburb of Chicago.

**JUNE 16** President Carter signs the ratification of the Panama Canal treaty with General Omar Torrijos in Panama.

**JUNE 28** The Supreme Court upholds Allan Bakke's claim that he was denied admission to the University of California Medical School because of the school's minority-admission plan. The high court agreed that Bakke was the victim of reverse discrimination.

**JULY 13** The trials of two Soviet dissidents, Anatoly Scharansky and Alexander Ginzburg, bring charges that the Soviet Union is crushing human rights. Both are found guilty and sentenced to long prison terms.

**JULY 21** Tentative agreement is reached on a new postal contract. The settlement calls for a 19$\frac{1}{2}$ percent increase in wages and benefits over the next three years.

**JULY 21** The Association of American Railroads announces tentative settlement with four unions. The new contract contains wage and cost of living increases of as much as 35 percent.

**JULY 26** The first test tube baby, Louise Brown, is born in Olham, England.

Pope Paul VI dies at his summer home in Castel Gandolfo, Italy. **AUGUST 7**

Federal health officials announce a breakthrough in the detection of bacterium **AUGUST 11** causing Legionnaires disease. The mysterious illness was first diagnosed in 1976.

Three Americans make the first transatlantic balloon crossing in their craft, the **AUGUST 17** *Double Eagle II.* They land in a wheat field 60 miles west of Paris.

Sixty-five-year-old Albino Luciani, cardinal of Rome, is elected pope of the **AUGUST 26** Roman Catholic Church. He takes the name of John Paul I.

Meetings between Egyptian President Anwar Sadat, Israeli Prime Minister **SEPTEMBER 5–18** Menachem Begin, and President Carter at Camp David, Maryland, result in the signing of the Camp David peace accords. The leaders agree to a framework for a peace treaty.

President Carter signs legislation providing $6.8 billion in supplemental ap- **SEPTEMBER 8** propriation for fiscal 1978. The largest item: a $3.2-billion appropriation to cover pay raises for federal employees.

Strikes in 13 states cancel or curtail school instruction for over 600,000 **SEPTEMBER 8** students.

One hundred fifty people are killed when a Pacific Southwest Airlines jet and a **SEPTEMBER 25** single engine training plane collide midair over San Diego.

The Senate approves the natural gas compromise bill almost 18 months after **SEPTEMBER 27** President Carter sent it to Congress. The bill calls for deregulation of natural gas produced within the state.

Pope John Paul I dies in his Vatican Palace in Rome. He had served as pope for **SEPTEMBER 28** 34 days.

Israeli cabinet approves Camp David summit agreements with Egypt, includ- **SEPTEMBER 28** ing the removal of Jewish settlements from the Sinai. This clears the way for Egyptian-Israeli negotiations and sets into motion the machinery for the peace talks.

Senate approves the extension of the deadline to ratify the Equal Rights **OCTOBER 6** Amendment. The House had approved it earlier. The new deadline: June 30, 1982.

President Carter signs the Civil Reform Act, the first major revision of the Civil **OCTOBER 13** Service system since it was established in 1883.

The Humphrey-Hawkins full employment bill, in watered-down version, **OCTOBER 15** clears Congress. The compromise bill calls for reducing the unemployment rate to 4 percent by 1983.

Karol Wojtyla, archbishop of Krakow, Poland, is elected pope of the Roman **OCTOBER 16** Catholic Church after the death of John Paul I. He is the first non-Italian pope in 456 years. His new name—John Paul II.

*Three heads of state join hands in the signing of a Mideast Peace Treaty on the White House lawn. President Sadat of Egypt, U.S. President Carter, and Prime Minister Begin of Israel.*

**OCTOBER 20**  Firestone Tire and Rubber Company agrees to recall ten million steel belted radial tires. It's the largest recall in history.

**OCTOBER 24**  President Carter unveils his new anti-inflation program. Basic guidelines call for ceilings of 7 percent on pay increases and $5^3/4$ percent on price increases.

**NOVEMBER 7**  Midterm U.S. elections. Democrats retain more than 60 percent of their seats in the House of Representatives. Republicans make net gains of three Senate seats, twelve House seats, and six Governorships.
Restrictions on taxing or spending are passed in 14 states.

**NOVEMBER 8**  President Carter signs a bill providing $54 billion in subsidies for highways and mass transit over four years. The new law combines federal financial assistance aid for highways with mass transportation for the first time.

**NOVEMBER 9**  President Carter signs the National Energy Act of 1978. It contains the controversial natural gas deregulation provision. The new regulation would require most electric utilities and industrial companies to use coal or nuclear power as primary energy sources for new installations.

**NOVEMBER 18**  U.S. Congressman Leo Ryan (D-Ca.) and four other Americans including an NBC correspondent and cameraman, are gunned down in Jonestown, Guyana, by members of the People's Temple, a California-based religious cult.
Shortly afterwards, about nine hundred people commit suicide, some voluntarily, most under force.

**NOVEMBER 21**  The Israeli cabinet approves United States sponsored draft of an Israeli-Egyptian peace treaty that links the accord with self-determination for Palestinians on the West Bank and Gaza strip.

**NOVEMBER 28**  Consumer Price Index marks a milestone in consumer price trends. Index for the month stands at 200 percent of 1967 base average. This means that consumer prices in October are more than double their average in 1967.

**DECEMBER 4**  San Francisco Board of Supervisors elect acting mayor Dianne Feinstein to succeed assassinated Mayor George Moscone.

Former Israeli Prime Minister Golda Meir dies of cancer in Jerusalem.    **DECEMBER 8**

President Carter revises his wage and price guidelines. He relaxes rules on wage increases and restricting company profits.    **DECEMBER 13**

Cleveland, Ohio, becomes the first United States city to default since the Depression.    **DECEMBER 18**

Jury's verdict is not guilty in the wife-rape trial of John and Greta Rideout in Salem, Oregon.    **DECEMBER 28**

## 1979

Formal diplomatic relations are estabished between the United States and the People's Republic of China.    **JANUARY 1**

Ohio State's Controlling Board approves an out-of-court settlement of the Kent State University civil liability suit. The board agrees to pay $600,000 to the parents of the four students who were killed in the 1970 shootings.    **JANUARY 4**

Cambodian rebels and Vietnamese soldiers join forces and capture the Cambodian capital of Pnom Penh. The government of Pol Pot is overthrown.    **JANUARY 7**

The worst storm in recent memory hits the Midwest. Snowfall measures 20 inches in many places. At least one hundred people die during the storm. Chicago hardest hit. O'Hare International Airport closes for a record 42 hours.    **JANUARY 12**

The Shah of Iran and his family leave Iran . . . ostensibly for a long vacation. Most observers feel it's a permanent exile.    **JANUARY 16**

Former vice president and governor of New York Nelson Rockefeller dies from a heart attack in New York City. He was 70.    **JANUARY 27**

Chinese Vice Premier Teng Hsiao-Ping arrives in Washington for a nine-day American tour.    **JANUARY 29**

Ayatollah Khomeini returns to Iran after 15 years in exile. His aim is to establish an Iranian Republic based on the laws of Islam.    **FEBRUARY 1**

Armed revolutionary followers of Khomeini overthrow the government of Premier Shahpur Baktiar, the Shah's hand-picked successor.    **FEBRUARY 9, 10, 11**

China invades Vietnam on charges that Vietnam instigated attacks on their joint border.    **FEBRUARY 17**

In a major political upset, Jane Byrne defeats incumbent Mayor Michael Bilandic in Chicago. Byrne goes on to win the general election with the largest majority since 1901.    **FEBRUARY 27**

Egypt and Israel formally end a 31-year state of war with the signing of a peace treaty in Washington, D.C.    **MARCH 26**

A series of breakdowns in the cooling system of Three Mile Island's nuclear power plant's reactor results in the worst nuclear accident in U.S. history. Officials worry about a possible core meltdown and the threat of a hydrogen    **MARCH 28** gas bubble exploding. Three Mile Island is located 10 miles south of Harrisburg, Pa.

**MARCH 30, 31** Iranians overwhelmingly approve the formation of an Islamic Republic in a nationwide referendum.

**APRIL 2, 3** The hydrogen gas bubble is eliminated at the Three Mile Island nuclear power plant outside Harrisburg, Pennsylvania.

**APRIL 4** Former Pakistani Prime Minister Zulfikar Ali Bhutto is hanged at the district jail in Rawalpindi. He was convicted on charges that he conspired to murder a political opponent.

**APRIL 5** President Carter announces the gradual decontrol of domestic oil prices. He also proposes a tax on corporate windfall profits from the decontrol.

**APRIL 11** An invasion force of five thousand Tanzanian soldiers raid Kampala, Uganda. Tanzania announces the formation of a provisional government to replace President Idi Amin's eight-year rule.

**APRIL 15** Iran says it will raise oil prices by 13 percent over the 9 percent hike that OPEC (Organization of Petroleum Exporting Countries) announced in March.

**APRIL 18** The Supreme Court rules that journalists can't use the first amendment to avoid answering questions about their "state of mind" when they become targets of libel suits by public figures. (*Herbert* vs *Lando, CBS*)

**APRIL 24** Bishop Abel Muzorewa becomes Rhodesia's first black political leader in the first universal suffrage election in the country's history.

**MAY 1** Long gas lines, first in California, then spreading to other states, attest to an increasingly acute nationwide gasoline shortage.

**MAY 3** Margaret Thatcher, a conservative, becomes Britain's first woman prime minister. She defeats Labor Party leader James Callaghan.

**MAY 7** The U.S. and Soviet Union announce the completion of the SALT II Treaty limiting the use of strategic arms.

**MAY 25** An American Airlines DC-10 crashes shortly after take-off from Chicago's O'Hare Airport; 272 people die in the worst crash in U.S. history.

"What a shame! How we'll miss those long Sunday drives with the whole family."

One Sunday night in early winter, an encouraging thing happened in American living rooms. More people watched CBS News's "60 Minutes" than any other television program during that December week. When a news and public affairs program beats out entertainment programs in the audience ratings, that's big news, and the event was given the proper media attention. The triumph of "60 Minutes" was also good news because the idea that the television viewer preferred any laugh-track entertainment show to even the most important news program was firmly engraved in the minds of all respected network executives. Later during the season, "60 Minutes" slipped back in the ratings a bit; but overall it managed to stay in the top 10 more often than not during the past season. At ABC and NBC, the lesson of "60 Minutes" had to be studied with particular care. "60 Minutes" is a so-called magazine show —three or four major pieces on varied national-affairs subjects, once-over-lightly commentaries, and letters to the editor. ABC News's "20/20" and NBC News's "Weekend," also magazine-style shows, could not come anywhere near "60 Minutes," as measured by audience acceptance ("Weekend" once stood seventy-seventh out of the seventy-nine programs ranked nationally).

The elements in the success of "60 Minutes" were not hard to find, any more than the reasons for the failures to date of "20/20" and "Weekend." "60 Minutes" had been around for over 10 years; CBS gave the program time to develop its own style and to find its own audience. Equally important, this gift of time allowed the audience to find it. Intelligently, too, CBS scheduled the program on Sunday nights opposite NBC's "World of Disney" and ABC's "The Osmond Family Hour," both young people's programs. ABC and NBC thus competed for the same home audience, while CBS, by offering adult fare, permitted "60 Minutes" to win over anyone who had moved on from bubble-gum concerns.

"60 Minutes" also achieved its success in part because it was not a hard- or straight-news program; it boasted some genuine television stars. Dan Rather, Mike Wallace, Morely Safer, and Harry Reasoner (who joined the program this past season) built a following based on their fine reporting work; but they were also recognized personalities. Don Hewitt, the executive producer who presided over "60 Minutes," said that he believed millions turned to the program in order to see what "those boys are up to next . . ." But with all due respect to the manic genius of Hewitt, the root cause of the success of "60 Minutes" lay in something more than the continuing adventures of Mike and Dan and Morley and Harry. "60 Minutes," quite simply, was well-researched, well-reported, well-produced, and well-thought-out. It had an ample budget (befitting a program that can command $150,000 per commercial minute) and lots of talented people behind the camera. Around CBS News, the program was sometimes called "60 Producers," to signify the care, support, and talent that went into the program.

The contrast at "20/20" and "Weekend" was painful. NBC never

gave "Weekend" the time or attention to find its proper voice and viewers.

With preemptions and a too-modest advertising budget, it was as if the audience was being dared to find out when the program went on. "Weekend" won awards for excellence, but after four years of struggle NBC changed producers, talent, even its name—everything that might remind anyone of its lost "Weekend." In June 1979 the revamped program, called "Prime Time Sunday" (10:00-11:00 P.M., EST), went back on the air with Tom Snyder as host, show biz mannerisms and all. About the best that could be said about the choice of Snyder was that it kept him away from the still-serious precincts of the "NBC Nightly News."

At ABC, similar surgery was performed on "20/20" to make it more competitive. "20/20" had a confused, show-business beginning. In fact the initial show was so bad that no one at ABC would claim responsibility for it. More recently, with the mellowed Hugh Downs as host, "20/20" appeared to be going the route of laid-back features, rather than news documentaries. "20/20" became so soft it threatened to curdle. At the end of the season, however, ABC appeared willing to assure the new program a regular weekly schedule and the last shows of the season were, in fact, demonstrably better. For 1979-80, the program hired Richard Wald and Karen Lerner, two serious journalists from NBC; they could make "20/20" competitive *and* good.

Across the board, ABC documentaries showed improvement. ABC's "Close-Up" series, with Pamela Hill as executive producer, attempted to bring reality back to television documentaries in the form of real-life stories. A highly acclaimed ABC News "Close-Up" was "Youth Terror: The View From Behind the Gun," written, directed, and produced by Helen Whitney. It powerfully told the story of street gangs and violence in the Williamsburg section of Brooklyn. It showed the rage and anger of these young people through their own words and actions. There was no narration or editing to soften the language. A group called the Black Producers Association alleged that some scenes were staged; ABC denied the charges and the FCC later ruled that the allegations were unfounded. "Close-Up" ended the season with a two-hour documentary entitled "The Shooting of Big Man," based on an actual trial in our criminal justice "non system."

While CBS led in the field of magazine shows, it *was* vulnerable. "60 Minutes" tended to take on comfortable, middle-class issues, the kinds of stories that appealed to its comfortable, middle-class audience. More generally, CBS's acknowledged dominance in documentaries was being threatened. "CBS Reports," having lost the valued Bill Moyers, found no real replacement for him in the tradition that Edward R. Murrow and Fred W. Friendly started in the 1950s. A series of Charles Kuralt "On the Road" pieces—done in *Reader's Digest* "Most-Unforgettable-character" style—were strung together to make a one-hour "CBS Reports." While Kuralt has a loyal audience which thinks he can do no wrong, the material symbolized how mannerisms can turn into ruts.

But networks can also fall *out* of bad habits as well as into them. Perhaps the best news from any of the networks this past season was the word that NBC has begun to extricate itself from its notorious Ford-Kissinger entanglement.

Shortly before leaving office, both Gerald Ford and Henry Kissinger signed multi-year contracts with NBC. Kissinger's contract called for him to be an "adviser-consultant" to NBC News; he would be on-call and available to appear on one news special a year, and would also do no more than eight interviews on international developments. For this work he would be paid around $1 million. Gerald Ford, his wife, and his family also agreed to provide certain on-air services for NBC. The Ford family was to be paid something like $1.5 million.

The name usually given such deals is "checkbook journalism." In exchange for money, a news source agrees to sell his or her "exclusive" story. The Ford and Kissinger arrangements had some strings attached: both men reserved the right not to talk about certain subjects (Ford, for example, wouldn't allow NBC to ask him about the apparent deal that led him to the White House in exchange for the pardon of Richard Nixon). To no one's surprise, NBC tripped over these strings.

Mercifully, last season Gerald Ford and NBC negotiated to end the Fords' contract (Ford was making the sounds of a 1980 candidate and appearances would have caused equal-time problems). The Kissinger connection continued to be an embarrassment for NBC; when the author of a highly critical—and highly praised—account of Kissinger's role in the bombing of Cambodia was shut out of appearances on the "Today Show," many people thought it might be due to Kissinger's contract with NBC.

Bill Moyers's switch to a regular series on public television should have been the occasion for more good news in the field of specials and documentaries. But "Bill Moyers Journal," while appearing weekly, was a surprisingly mixed series. It was most successful when Moyers appeared doing what he does best—interviewing intelligent, exciting people who have something to say: people such as UN Ambassador

Andrew Young, A. Leon Higginbotham, Jr., of the U.S. Court of Appeals, poet Robert Bly, or activist-minister William Sloan Coffin. There was also a solid documentary on a "quiet boy" who killed his family in New Jersey. But other "Journal" programs just weren't up to Moyers's own high standards, perhaps because a weekly schedule stretched his—and public television's—resources too much.

The rest of the regular documentary series on public television also appeared to be struggling. The "Nova" series was devoted to amiably harmless science travelogues. It was hurt by a labor-management dispute at its parent station, WGBH in Boston, and production for several episodes was delayed. A WGBH-based series, "World," suffered through painful behind-camera funding problems and production battles. "World" had the noble intention of showing the world to Americans as non-Americans see it. In practice it was a mind-numbing exercise more often than not. For example, one program on Red China, with its droning narration, succeeded in making a fascinating country look dull. On the other hand, a program on Europe which was coproduced with European crews, called "F-16: The Sale of the Century," proved an excellent account of how NATO countries buy new fighter planes.

Toward the end of this generally lackluster year in specials and documentaries, two independent productions provided excitement and the promise of full realization of the potential of reality television. One was the documentary "Scared Straight," commissioned for showing by station KTLA in Los Angeles and eventually broadcast on nearly one hundred stations around the country. "Scared Straight" showed what happened when a group of "trouble-prone" teenagers were brought together with some hard-core lifers from the Rahway State prison in New Jersey. The idea was to scare the teenagers—with stories of prison brutality, pain, rage, and rape—into a straight life. The program won an Academy Award for its producers and started an argument about just

*"Don't make me hurt you!" threatens a convicted murderer in the one-hour special "Scared Straight!," about a unique prison program designed to scare the crime out of hard-core juvenile delinquents.*

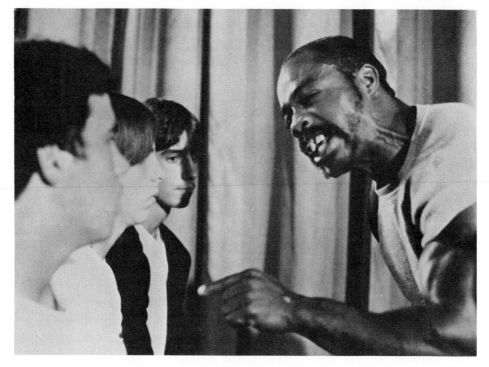

how successful the unorthodox counseling program had been in achieving long-term gains among the young participants. As critics pointed out: How fair was it to expect a two-hour counseling session, no matter how vividly conducted by "authentic" convicts, to solve all the emotional and social problems that led to delinquency in the first place? But for a television program to get this subject debated in the first place qualified for some sort of prize.

There was no debating the long-term effects of perhaps the brightest moment in the field of specials and documentaries last season. On May 6, 1979 over 100,000 people gathered to protest nuclear power development on the steps of the U.S. Capitol in Washington. On hand to cover the rally was a group of young, independent documentary makers organized as Public Interest Video. Within one week of the announcement of the planned demonstration, Public Interest Video managed to put together an "instant network" of stations to carry its live, three-hour coverage. For less than $2,000 the group was able to get channel time on the Westar satellite and beamed the program to 23 stations who were willing to pick it up. The program had rough spots, but the principle had been established: We don't need Walter Cronkite, John Chancellor, Max Robinson, or their establishment counterparts at public broadcasting to tell us "and that's the way it is. . . ." Other groups can, with imagination and enterprise, achieve access to national networks. Other groups, besides those certified "professional" or "network," can offer wider choices to the home audience. As if to demonstrate the even-handed potential of satellite access television, Public Interest Video went from Washington to Cincinnati to provide coverage of a pro-life rally in late June.

Other people, moved by public spirit and/or entrepreneurial instincts, began to look into the possibilities of news and public affairs specialty services via satellite. Ted Turner, the owner of the Atlanta Braves baseball team and of an Atlanta independent television station, already used a satellite to beam his station signal to outlets around the country. Turner announced plans for a news service from Washington to supply cable television stations. Still other groups planned alternative coverage of the 1980 national political conventions, via satellite. For 30 years now, ABC, CBS, and NBC—and, on occasion, public television—were the sole stages upon which these high spectacles unfolded. This season the monopoly started breaking up. That alone made the 1978-79 season very special.

## MAJOR TV NEWS SPECIALS JUNE 1978— MAY 1979

*1978*

President Carter signs the Panama Canal Treaty in Panama. (ABC-live.)    **JUNE 16**

Pope Paul VI dies in Rome. (ABC, CBS, NBC-live, film, and tape of funeral,    **AUGUST 6**
procession of cardinals, and selection process for new pope.)

**AUGUST 26**     John Paul I is elected pope. (ABC, CBS, NBC-live, film, tape.)

**SEPTEMBER 5**     President Anwar Sadat of Egypt, Prime Minister Menachem Begin of Israel, and President Carter arrive at Camp David, Maryland, to discuss framework for Mideast Peace Treaty. (ABC, CBS, NBC-live, film, tape.)

**SEPTEMBER 17**     Signing of Mideast peace documents between Israel and Egypt at the White House. (ABC, CBS, NBC-live.)

**SEPTEMBER 18**     President Carter's address to joint session of Congress where he outlines documents signed by Israel and Egypt. (ABC, CBS, NBC-live.)

**SEPTEMBER 25**     Bulletins on plane crash over San Diego (ABC, CBS, NBC-live.)

**OCTOBER 4**     The funeral of Pope John Paul I at St. Peter's Square in Rome. (ABC, CBS, NBC-live, tape.)

**OCTOBER 16**     Cardinal Wojtyla is chosen to be the new pope of the Roman Catholic Church. (ABC, CBS, NBC-live, tape. Coverage includes the first papal blessing by Pope John Paul II.)

**NOVEMBER 7**     Election 1978. (ABC, CBS, NBC. Live coverage of congressional, senatorial, and gubernatorial races.)

**NOVEMBER 22**     People's Temple cult and Jonestown, Guyana, massacre. (NBC News included film of ambush taken by NBC cameraman Bob Brown before he was shot. Also, interviews by NBC Correspondent Don Harris with former cult members and with Reverend Jim Jones before Harris was shot. Special reports from ABC and CBS too.)

**DECEMBER 15**     President Carter announces the establishment of diplomatic relations between China and the U.S., beginning January 1, 1979. (ABC, CBS, NBC-live.)

*This photo was taken by NBC cameraman Bob Brown moments before he and three other Americans were gunned down by members of the People's Temple in Jonestown, Guyana. NBC News correspondent Don Harris is second from left.*

President Carter issues his State of the Union message, 1979. He stressed efficient government rather than calling for any new proposals and asked Congress to build a new foundation for the future by controlling inflation and approving a new strategic arms treaty with the Soviet Union. (ABC, CBS, NBC-live.) **JANUARY 23**

Bulletin on death of former vice president Nelson A. Rockefeller, who dies of a heart attack in New York City. (ABC, CBS, NBC-live.) **JANUARY 27**

President Carter officially welcomes Chinese Vice Premier Deng to the United States. (ABC, CBS, NBC-live, tape.) **JANUARY 29**

The solar eclipse. (ABC-live, tape.) **FEBRUARY 26**

President Carter's trip to the Mideast. (ABC, CBS, NBC-live, tape. Includes live coverage of arrival in Israel and in Egypt.) **MARCH 5**

President Carter comes home from the Mideast. (ABC, CBS, NBC-live.) **MARCH 13**

Israeli cabinet approves last two key issues that will lead to a signed peace treaty. (ABC, CBS, NBC-live.) **MARCH 14**

A Mideast peace. The signing in Washington, D.C. (ABC, CBS, NBC-live.) **MARCH 26**

Nuclear accident at Three Mile Island power plant near Harrisburg, Pennsylvania. (ABC, CBS, NBC-live, tape.) **MARCH 30, 31**

President Carter's National Energy Policy Address. (ABC, CBS, NBC-live.) **APRIL 5**

SALT II: the arms debate and decision. (ABC, CBS, NBC-live, film, tape.) **MAY 9**

# DOCUMENT-ARIES
# JUNE 1978—
# May 1979

## NBC
*1978*
NBC Reports **JUNE 16**
"Mad as Hell: The Taxpayer's Revolt"
The rising tax revolt is spreading across the country, resulting from the successful passage of Proposition 13 in California.

NBC Reports **JUNE 28**
"Escape from Madness"
Report on the treatment of several forms of mental illness using drugs and psychosocial rehabilitation techniques.

NBC Reports **JULY 20**
"I Want It All Now"
Documentary on the unusual lifestyles and values of people who live in Marin County, California, one of the country's 10 wealthiest communities. The report

examines the abuse of drugs and alcohol, the search for "self," and the effect on children in the fast-paced lifestyle.

*1979*

**JANUARY 2**  NBC News Special Report
"The American Family: An Endangered Species"
Three-hour program on the American family focusing on different changes that have occurred in the traditional family unit in recent years. Fourteen family portraits are presented—each depicting a different lifestyle.

**JANUARY 5**  NBC News Special Report
"A Conversation with Betty Ford"
An exclusive interview with the former First Lady, reflecting on her years in the White House.

**JANUARY 11**  NBC News Special Report
"China: A Class By Itself"
An inside look at how China, through education and exposure in the West, hopes to become a modern, industrialized power by the year 2000.

**JANUARY 13**  NBC News Special Report
"Dr. Martin Luther King, Jr., Remembered"
Filmed highlights in the life of Dr. King, who would have been 50 years old on January 15.

**APRIL 29**  NBC News Special Report
"College Sports, Inc."
A look at the big bucks involved in college sports.

## CBS

*1978*

**JUNE 7**  CBS News Special
"What's Happened to Cambodia?"
An in-depth look at Cambodia before and after the takeover by the Khmer Rouge.

**JUNE 15**  CBS News Special
"The Angry Taxpayer"
Results and analysis of Proposition 13 in California.

**JUNE 20**  CBS Reports
"You Can Beat City Hall"
One man's campaign to reform Laredo, Texas.
"The Taiwan Dilemma," a look at the problems facing Nationalist China.

**JULY 5**  CBS Reports
"Into the Mouths of Babes"
Controversy over using infant formula in underdeveloped countries.
"Going, Going, Gone"
Report on increasing number of Southern Blacks losing their land.

**JULY 14**  CBS News Special
"The Business of Newspapers"

A look at the daily American newspaper and how newspaper economics affect editorial policies and coverage.

CBS Reports
"The Fire Next Door Update"
A report on arson, the fastest growing crime in America, and how it's affecting the South Bronx.

JULY 26

CBS News Special
"Is Anyone Out There Learning?"
An in-depth look into the public education system in America today.

AUGUST 22, 23, 24

CBS News Special
"1968"
An assessment of 1968, the year which saw a turning point in the Vietnam War, two assassinations, protests, and social change.

AUGUST 25

CBS Reports
"The Battle for South Africa"
A look at the escalating terrorist war being waged by the Black underground against the White South African government.

SEPTEMBER 1

CBS Reports
"A Turning Page in History"
Exclusive interview with President Carter on new relations with China.

DECEMBER 18

CBS Reports
"What About the Children?"
Examination of children after their parents divorce.

DECEMBER 23

CBS Reports
"Anyplace but Here"
Controversies and problems of mental health services.

DECEMBER 26

*1979*

CBS Reports
A Conversation with Eric Sevareid and Walter Cronkite.

JANUARY 6

CBS Reports
"The Boat People"
Plight of homeless Vietnamese refugees stranded along the coasts of Malaysia and southeast Asia.

JANUARY 16

CBS Reports
"Inside the Union"
A look at today's labor movement.

MARCH 6

CBS Reports
"How Much for the Handicapped?"
A look at the conflict between conscience and cost for making public facilities available for the handicapped.

APRIL 3

CBS Reports
"Boston Goes to China"
The Boston Symphony tours China.

APRIL 27

## ABC

**JUNE 29**
ABC News Close-Up
"Youth Terror: The View From Behind the Gun"
The documentary focuses on real-life delinquent youth—their backgrounds, frustrations, words, and deeds—without narrative, statistics, or commentary.

**JULY 14**
ABC News Close-Up
"Asbestos: The Way to Dusty Death"
An investigation into asbestos, the biggest industrial killer in history. The film reveals original investigative material that the U.S. Navy and other federal agencies knew long ago about the hazards of asbestos, but on which they failed to act.

**AUGUST 3**
ABC News Close-Up
"Arson: Fire for Hire!"
An investigation of arson—who sets the fires, who profits, and who loses.

**AUGUST 17**
ABC News Close-Up
"The Police Tapes"
A camera team lives, works, and rides with policemen in one of the nation's most difficult urban areas, the South Bronx.

**OCTOBER 30**
ABC News Close-Up
"Terror in the Promised Land"
Palestinian men and women who turn to violence and terrorism to achieve political ends.

**DECEMBER 5**
ABC News Close-Up
"Mysterious World of the Supernatural: Fact, Fraud, or Faith?"
The world of the supernatural, and current preoccupation with psychic phenomena, focusing on psychic healing and past lives.

**DECEMBER 27**
ABC News Close-Up
"The Politics of Torture"
An examination into President Carter's human-rights policy—its successes and failures, its contradictions, and its effects on U.S. allies.

*1979*

**JANUARY 30**
ABC News Close-Up
"Mission: Mind Control"
The alleged use of mind-altering drugs by the Central Intelligence Agency on mental patients and C.I.A. employees.

**MARCH 29**
ABC News Close-Up
"The Killing Ground"
An examination of the disposal of hazardous wastes.

**APRIL 21**
ABC News Close-Up
"Man Under Seige—Life with the Modern Woman"
The changes that have taken place for the American man since the start of the women's liberation movement.

# PBS

*1978*

"Youth Unemployment: A Question of Survival"                                      **JUNE 4**
The crisis of unemployed youth in American society and the relationship
between unemployment and education, economics, and racial discrimination.

"Welfare"                                                                          **JUNE 5**
Study of the clients and administration of a New York City welfare center.

"Solzhenitsyn at Harvard"                                                          **JUNE 8**
Alexander Solzhenitsyn's commencement address at Harvard University and a
post-speech analysis.

"The Rosenberg-Sobell Case Revisited"                                             **JUNE 19**
Observance of the twenty-fifth anniversary of the executions of Julius and
Ethel Rosenberg who were convicted of selling secrets to the Soviet Union.

"The Unwanted"                                                                     **JUNE 20**
The plight of illegal Mexican aliens.

"Canal Zone"                                                                       **JUNE 26**
The daily lives of American residents of the Panama Canal Zone played out
against the drama of the 1977 treaty negotiations between the U.S. and
Panama.

"College Can Be Killing"                                                           **JUNE 27**
College suicide and the ways universities deal with student stress, anxiety, and
potential suicide.

"The Williamson Disaster"                                                          **JULY 5**
The aftermath of the West Virginia flood disaster in April 1977, focusing on the
conflict over the Department of Housing and Urban Development's allegedly
ill-directed deployment of housing for the community.

"Guale"                                                                            **JULY 18**
The history of the chain of barrier islands protecting Georgia's coast from the
sea.

"Of Race and Blood"                                                                **JULY 25**
The story behind Nazi art and the part it played in the Nazi machine.

"The Edelin Conviction"                                                            **AUGUST 1**
A reenactment of the trial of Dr. Kenneth Edelin, Boston gynecologist, convicted of manslaughter in performing a legal abortion.

"The People vs. Inez Garcia"                                                       **AUGUST 8**
Re-creation of the California murder trial of Inez Garcia, who allegedly killed
a man after he raped her.

"TV on Trial"                                                                      **AUGUST 15**
The highlights of the Florida murder trial of 15-year-old Ronney Zamora who
claimed that TV violence caused him to kill his 82-year-old neighbor.

| | |
|---|---|
| AUGUST 17 | "Southie!"<br>The Irish-American community of South Boston, Massachusetts, and its impact on the city as a whole. |
| AUGUST 28 | "A Day to Remember"<br>Documentary commemorating the fifteenth anniversary, of Martin Luther King's freedom march on Washington, D.C., and his "I Have a Dream" speech. |
| SEPTEMBER 3 | "Otto: Zoo Gorilla"<br>Otto, a West-African gorilla, adjusts to life at the Chicago Lincoln Park Zoo. |
| SEPTEMBER 3 | "You're Not a Hero Until You're Sung"<br>The American hero in myth and media. |
| SEPTEMBER 5 | "Antonio: A Portrait of the Woman"<br>A profile of Antonio Brico, first woman to conduct the Berlin Philharmonic. |
| SEPTEMBER 19 | "Union Maids"<br>The story of three women in the rank-and-file labor movement in the '30s. |
| SEPTEMBER 29 | "A Conversation with Earl Warren"<br>Taped interview with the late former Supreme Court Justice on his early political career and controversial decisions on the Warren Commission and the Warren Court. |
| OCTOBER 3 | "Opium: The White Powder Opera (Part III)"<br>Third in a trilogy on the narcotics trade in Hong Kong. |
| OCTOBER 10 | "Word Is out"<br>The lives and experiences of homosexuals in America today. |
| OCTOBER 14, 15 | "The Champions"<br>The public and private lives of the two most powerful men in Canada—elected leader of the Province of Quebec Rene Levesque and Prime Minister Elliot Trudeau. |
| OCTOBER 17 | "Sinai Field Mission"<br>Life for American workers on the surveillance base in the buffer zone of the Sinai desert between Egypt and Israel. |
| OCTOBER 19 | "Boston's Marathon Man"<br>Documentary on Bill Rodgers, record-holder and two-time winner of the Boston Marathon. |
| OCTOBER 22 | "California Reich"<br>Documentary on the organized Neo-Nazi movement in America today, focusing on three communities in California. |
| OCTOBER 29 | "Bad Boys"<br>A documentary examining juvenile crime, the conditions causing it, and the inadequacies of the juvenile justice system. |
| NOVEMBER 2 | "Supreme Court"<br>The history of the Supreme Court from its founding to today. |

"Portrait of a Nurse"　　　　　　　　　　　　　　　　　　　　　　**NOVEMBER 8**
Portrait of Jean Steel, R.N., and the expanding role of the nurse-practitioner.

"Arms for South Africa—The American Connection"　　　　　　　**NOVEMBER 9**
Investigative documentary on the American involvement in illegal arms shipments to South Africa.

"Race War in Rhodesia"　　　　　　　　　　　　　　　　　　　　**NOVEMBER 15**
Documentary about the rising tensions in Rhodesia, considered the second most dangerous area in the world after the Middle East.

"The New Klan"　　　　　　　　　　　　　　　　　　　　　　　**NOVEMBER 19**
An inside look at the secret organization of the Ku Klux Klan and the new Klan's present day emphasis on open political activity.

"Wild Horses, Broken Wings"　　　　　　　　　　　　　　　　　**NOVEMBER 22**
One woman's unique approach to rearing her 15 foster children.

"Forgotten Frontier"　　　　　　　　　　　　　　　　　　　　　**DECEMBER 5**
The missionary heritage of the Southwest, surveying the missions of the Sonoran Spanish borderlands.

"Nuclear War: The Unthinkable"　　　　　　　　　　　　　　　　**DECEMBER 7**
Day-long conference on nuclear war.

"Golda Meir"　　　　　　　　　　　　　　　　　　　　　　　　**DECEMBER 8**
Portrait of the former prime minister of Israel who died on December 8, 1978.

"Mairead Corrigan: On the Road for Peace"　　　　　　　　　　　**DECEMBER 12**
A portrait of Mairead Corrigan of Ireland, who was awarded the Nobel Peace Prize in 1977 (along with her friend Betty Williams) for efforts to obtain peace in Northern Ireland.

"The Wages of Congress"　　　　　　　　　　　　　　　　　　　**DECEMBER 27**
A look into the salaries, benefits, and lifestyles on Capitol Hill.

*1979*

"One Superlative Song"　　　　　　　　　　　　　　　　　　　　**JANUARY 1**
Children with special health problems at summer camp.

"Alton Ochsner at Eighty"　　　　　　　　　　　　　　　　　　　**JANUARY 4**
Documentary on one of the first doctors to connect smoking and lung cancer.

"Robert Flaherty's Man of Aran: How the Myth Was Made"　　　　**JANUARY 6**
Film maker George Stoney examines the effect of "Man of Aran" on the island and its people 35 years after making the film.

"Raised in Anger"　　　　　　　　　　　　　　　　　　　　　　**JANUARY 11**
The reasons behind child abuse and how abusive parents can find help.

"Jacques Lipchitz"　　　　　　　　　　　　　　　　　　　　　　**JANUARY 11**
Biography of the sculptor.

| JANUARY 17 | "The Talking Walls of Pompeii"<br>The lifestyle of the people of Pompeii—their art, religion, sports, and theatre. |
|---|---|
| JANUARY 17 | "Thieves of time"<br>The destruction of America's archeological resources by "pot hunters" in search of Indian artifacts to sell for personal collections. |
| JANUARY 18, 25/<br>FEBRUARY 1 | "Palestine"<br>The emergence of the Jewish State from 1918 to 1948. |
| JANUARY 21 | "Rizzo"<br>The explosive world of Philadelphia politics and the rise and reign of Mayor Frank Rizzo. |
| JANUARY 22 | "Mr. Speaker: A Portrait of Tip O'Neill"<br>House Speaker Tip O'Neill carries out his official and personal duties. |
| JANUARY 23 | "North Star: Mark di Suvero"<br>American sculptor Mark di Suvero, his work, family, life, and philosophy. |
| JANUARY 25 | "John Cage"<br>Composer-philosopher John Cage's influence on avant-garde music. |
| JANUARY 28, 29, 30 | "The Energy War"<br>Legislative battle over President Carter's proposal to put controls on the natural gas industry. |
| JANUARY 29 | "Treasures of Tutankhamun"<br>A look at the vast array of treasures from the tomb of Egypt's boy-king. |
| JANUARY 31 | "Bikes! Bikes! Bikes!"<br>History of the country's fastest growing form of transportation—the bicycle. |
| JANUARY 31 | "Interview with Teng Hsiao-Ping"<br>Jim Lehrer interviews China's vice premier during his American visit. |
| FEBRUARY 4 | "To Mrs. Brown: A Daughter"<br>Documentary of the birth of the first test tube baby. |
| FEBRUARY 7 | "Roots, Rock, Reggae"<br>The development of reggae music in Jamaica. |
| FEBRUARY 11 | "Dragons of Paradise"<br>Life portrait of the American alligator. |
| FEBRUARY 15 | "All for One"<br>The Lamaze method of childbirth. |
| FEBRUARY 24 | "Mehta and His Music: A Tour and a Triumph"<br>The LA Philharmonic and conductor Zubin Mehta's 1977 Mediterranean cruise-concert tour. |
| FEBRUARY 25 | "Paul Jacobs and the Nuclear Gang"<br>The real and potential hazards of low-level radiation. |

"Governor Brown and the Tax Revolt"  **FEBRUARY 28**
California Governor Jerry Brown's presidential bid with a movement for a new federal constitutional convention and a balanced federal budget.

"Fluorocarbons: The Unfinished Agenda"  **MARCH 1**
The environmental risks of fluorocarbons.

"Echoes of Silver"  **MARCH 9**
The rise and fall of Colorado silver magnate H.A.W. Tabor.

"The Islander"  **MARCH 16**
Artist Walter Anderson and his relationship with his island and its life.

"Up in Rosebud County"  **MARCH 20**
Effects of the coal boom, strip mining, and power production on social patterns in Montana.

"Grand Jury: An Institution under Fire"  **MARCH 20**
History and workings of the grand jury system in the U.S., and abuses of present-day grand juries.

"I Was Born at Home"  **MARCH 22**
Growing trend of allowing midwives to deliver babies in the home.

"The Making of 'The Scarlet Letter' "  **MARCH 23**
The excitement, tension, and pressure of the making of WGBH's "The Scarlet Letter."

"Methadone: An American Way of Dealing"  **MARCH 27**
Problems inherent in methadone maintenance are explored.

"The Three Mile Island Mishap: An Update"  **MARCH 29**
Update on the radiation leak in the Three Mile Island nuclear power plant and the health threat to Pennsylvanians.

"Diplomatic Style of Andrew Young"  **MARCH 30**
The Young approach to diplomacy and its results.

"They Said It Wouldn't Happen: A WHYY Report With Chuck Stone"  **MARCH 30**
Three Mile Island incident.

"Newsmakers"  **APRIL 3**
Media coverage of the world's first significant nuclear accident.

"Who Killed Martin Luther King?"  **APRIL 7**
Examination of the recent House Assassination Committee findings on the death of Martin Luther King, Jr.

"Mystery Murals of Baja California"  **APRIL 8**
The search for giant rock paintings by ancient Indian civilizations.

"Library of Congress"  **APRIL 10**
The library's facilities and its relationship with Congress.

"Hamper McBee: Raw Mush"  **APRIL 10**
Life and experiences of a Tennessee moonshiner.

| APRIL 10 | "Boston Marathon '79"<br>Wrap-up of the Boston Marathon. |
|---|---|
| APRIL 17 | "The 81st Blow"<br>The oppression of European Jews during World War II. |
| APRIL 18 | "The Great Midwest Hot Air Balloon Rally"<br>The Midwest hot-air balloon rally at the Wisconsin Dells. |
| APRIL 18 | "Who Remembers Mama?"<br>Economic and emotional devastation of middle-aged women when they lose their homemaker role through divorce. |
| APRIL 21 | "California's Public Worker: A Time of Crisis"<br>The tensions between taxpayers and public employees prior to the passage of Proposition 13. |
| APRIL 23 | "Generation on the Wind"<br>Planning and construction of the world's largest and most powerful windmill. |
| APRIL 24 | "An Americanism: Joe McCarthy"<br>The life and times of Senator Joseph McCarthy. |
| APRIL 28 | "An Act of Congress"<br>Legislative power in action as law is being made. |
| MAY 3 | "Inflation: The Sky Is the Limit"<br>The key issues in the war against inflation. |
| MAY 6 | "Close to Home"<br>A small Michigan town caught in the crosscurrents of a teacher's strike, a school board election, and Proposition 13 fever. |
| MAY 8 | "Alexander's Bachtime Band"<br>Performance/documentary of young string musicians from all over the country who play in Carnegie Hall concerts. |
| MAY 8 | "L.A., L.A., Making It in L.A."<br>Performers and musicians striving for stardom and success in Los Angeles. |
| MAY 9 | "Once a Daughter"<br>Exploration of the mother-daughter relationship. |
| MAY 16 | "George Segal"<br>Portrait of a sculptor. |
| MAY 17 | "Gravity Is My Enemy"<br>Story of a quadriplegic artist who holds his brush in his mouth to paint. |
| MAY 20 | "Rites of Spring"<br>The annual seal-pup hunt in Newfoundland. |
| MAY 22 | "Lewis Mumford"<br>Mumford's philosophy on modern architecture. |

"Cat"                                                               MAY 24
A professional woman boxer successfully changes New York's prohibition
against professional women fighters.

"Border Traffic"                                                    MAY 29
The 1200-mile boundary dividing Texas and Mexico and its role in illegal drug
smuggling into the U.S.

"Esiampa Flamenca"                                                  MAY 30
Documentary about the American Flamenco dancer, Maria Benitez, and her
dance company.

"Tattooed Tears"                                                    MAY 31
Cinema-verité documentary on the youth training school in Chino, California,
operated by the California Youth Authority.

# NEWS MAGAZINES

## WEEKEND (NBC)

*1978*

The growing popularity of basketball in Bologna, Italy, the basketball capital   JUNE 3
of the world; a profile of Ervin Nyiregyhazi, a child prodigy in Hungary who
dropped out of sight for 50 years and was recently rediscovered; the over-
crowded conditions at Yosemite National Park (R); auto junkyards as a source
for used car parts.

A report on Louise Brown, the world's first test tube baby, born in England on   SEPTEMBER 10
June 25, 1978; a bookselling outfit in Nashville, Tennessee, which hires college students to peddle books; a freelance action news team in New York City
which follows late-night violence and sells footage to television stations.

Sports-oriented universities promote their star players through public relations   OCTOBER 12
hype; government bureaucracies make it almost impossible for the nursing
home industry to survive; real-estate values soar in Washington, D.C., despite
economic slow-downs.

President Idi Amin of Uganda's double; discovery of crude oil reserves in   DECEMBER 2
Canada; full-service gas stations falling to new self-service stations; artificial
insemination; Pete Rose becomes the highest paid baseball player.

Voters defeat casino gambling in Miami Beach, Florida; casino gambling in   DECEMBER 9
Atlantic City doesn't benefit the residents; "downsizing" in packaging; Chi-
cano art in San Jose, California.

Real estate in Beverly Hills, California; Japanese and Americans compete in   DECEMBER 16
the making of silicon electro chips in Santa Clara Valley, California; violence
in 24-hour supermarkets.

British Parliament's House of Lords; life with traveling tent circuses; "cus-   DECEMBER 23
tomized vans"; adult toy stores.

**DECEMBER 30**   Residents in Chesapeake, Virginia, fight an ordinance regarding their water supply; goose-hunting on the Maryland shore; women's ice hockey; selling what comes naturally—Perrier water.

*1979*

**JANUARY 7**   Employee theft; the Taj Mahal contrasted with the squalor of the city it's located in; a ventriloquist who performs on New York City streets.

**JANUARY 14**   Criminal gangs in Japan; the sport of flying pigeons from rooftops; disco dancing on roller skates.

**FEBRUARY 11**   Profile of divorce lawyer Marvin Mitchelson who defended Michele Triola Marvin in her case against actor Lee Marvin, whom she lived with but never married.

**FEBRUARY 18**   Toxic effects of crop dusting on human and animal life in Scottsdale, Arizona.

**FEBRUARY 25**   Language difficulties for Arab students in American universities; how two colleges handle foreign students.

**MARCH 11**   Status of the Israeli cabinet debate over the Egyptian-Israeli peace agreement; profile of the chief lobbyist who wants a constitutional amendment that requires a balanced federal budget; big corporations recruit graduates with masters degrees in business administration.

**MARCH 18**   A 24-year old drug addict who kicked a 10-year habit; crowded conditions in Japan are resulting in more abortions; a popular teeny-bopper magazine called *Tiger-Beat*.

**MARCH 25**   Sweatshops in New York City where undocumented aliens work; union manufacturers comment on the existence of sweatshops; story of a Cuban teacher who was thrown into prison because he denounced Communism after helping Castro overthrow the Batista government; wholesale smuggling from Laredo, Texas, into Mexico.

**APRIL 1**   A report on "clinical ecology"—the study of environmental agents and their effect on human health; Mexico and its newly discovered oil reserves; a look inside a modern-day salt mine.

**APRIL 8**   A profile of a former Marine and college professor who teaches people how to use handguns in his backyard; a look inside Taiwan; a report on unscrupulous publishers ripping off amateur songwriters.

**APRIL 15**   New technique to help children with Downs Syndrome; Haitians trying to flee their country's poverty; religious shelters in Jacksonville, Florida.

**APRIL 23**   A report on the family of Karen Ann Quinlan and how it is coping with her comatose condition; teenage runaways in Fort Lauderdale, Florida; an interview with former President Gerald Ford.

# 60 Minutes (CBS)

*1978*

| | |
|---|---|
| Profiles of India's Prime Minister Desai; lyricist "Yip" Harburg (R). | **JUNE 4** |
| An Alaskan land deal; illegal activities in the meat industry (R); the dangers of dog litter (R). | **JUNE 11** |
| A medical recall program; illegal activities in the meat industry (R). | **JUNE 18** |
| The Reverend Robert Schuller; Chicago corruption; "dream" vacations. | **JUNE 25** |
| Illegal cigarette operations; the big business of discos (R). | **JULY 2** |
| The Arab influx in Great Britain; a look at naval hospitals; an update on a con game (R). | **JULY 9** |
| Phobias and clinics that deal with them; kidnapping, Italian style; experiments to communicate with apes. | **JULY 16** |
| East German sports; a nurse who treats terminally ill patients; the popularity of backgammon (R). | **JULY 23** |
| Couples who can't find a place to live because they have kids; valium addiction; Hiroshima and Nagasaki after the bombing. | **JULY 30** |
| The mysterious disappearance of pleasure yachts; life for the wives of homosexuals; space colonies of the future. | **AUGUST 6** |
| "Ghost Surgery" by residents; discos (R); profile of Western novels' author Louis L'Amour (R). | **AUGUST 13** |
| Angel dust; the Catholic Church in Communist Poland; a profile of portrait photographer Josef Karsh. | **AUGUST 20** |
| Car theft; phony degrees; a woman who survived Auschwitz because she was a musician. | **AUGUST 27** |
| Federal student-loan programs in trouble; corruption in Rock Springs, Wyoming; civil defense in Sherman, Connecticut. | **SEPTEMBER 3** |
| A cancer-cure program at a health spa; Israelis disagree on the future of the West Bank; male therapists who exploit their female patients. | **SEPTEMBER 10** |
| Corporal punishment in Texas; violence in Rome; an update on three heart patients on the Pritikin diet of monitored eating and exercise. | **OCTOBER 22** |
| The fraud in the moving industry; a lawyer who teaches his clients to look innocent; community anticrime patrols. | **OCTOBER 29** |
| A low-cost fire department; an international arms merchant; the status of the Japanese woman. | **NOVEMBER 5** |

| | |
|---|---|
| NOVEMBER 12 | Life with an autistic child; trouble in Iran; a study of Franklin Mint commemoratives. |
| NOVEMBER 19 | Modern-day preachers who use the airwaves to spread the gospel; foreign investors buying up American land; a profile of film director Roman Polanski. |
| NOVEMBER 26 | The problems facing unmarried couples who live together; profile of Boston Pops conductor Arthur Fiedler; an inside look at Calcutta, India. |
| DECEMBER 3 | An insurgency movement within the Teamsters; an update on Pearl Harbor; an investigation of fraud charges in the fast-food franchise business. |
| DECEMBER 10 | Mexican-American gangs in Los Angeles; practicing doctors who may be alcoholics, drug addicts, or potential suicides; one of the latest self-help movements, "Fat Pride." |
| DECEMBER 17 | A new antimissile ray and charges that the Russians are ahead in developing it; coming showdown in Nicaragua between President Somoza and his widespread opposition. |
| DECEMBER 25 | The Chinese in Singapore; a look at the face of Christ as done by artists through the centuries; the international perfume industry. |
| DECEMBER 31 | Penn State's football coach, Joe Paterno; Ted Morgan, the former French count who thinks the U.S. is the greatest; a look at the people who work the sugar cane fields of Louisiana. |

*1979*

| | |
|---|---|
| JANUARY 7 | The promotion of music and talent in Nashville; mainstreaming handicapped children into normal classes; publishers who will print any book—for the right price. |
| JANUARY 14 | An interview with Katharine Hepburn; use of deadly force by police; a look at government paper work. |
| JANUARY 21 | A visit to oil-rich Abu Dhabi; an around-the-world yacht race; the Nazi movement in Germany 34 years after Hitler. |
| JANUARY 28 | Heavy drug traffic in South Florida; a profile of jazz musician Count Basie; a look at how the poor pay more for industrial insurance. |
| FEBRUARY 4 | Brown lung disease; government witnesses involved in relocation programs; home-town welfare in Bordentown, New Jersey. |
| FEBRUARY 11 | A look at Mexican oil; a visit to the Maldive Islands; the worldwide rat problem. |
| FEBRUARY 18 | A profile of dancer Mikhail Baryshnikov; investigation of charges of an oil industry swindle; a report on "Off-the-Road" vehicles. |
| FEBRUARY 25 | Videotape piracy; a profile of baseball star Pete Rose; ways to minimize your chances of getting mugged. |
| MARCH 4 | Runaway kids exploited by the sex industry; America's forgotten secret army in Indochina; a profile of a Texas pool hustler. |

A visit backstage with the Muppets; a profile of Roger Baldwin, founder of the American Civil Liberties Union; the search for Nazi war criminal Joseph Mengele. **MARCH 11**

An interview with Yasir Arafat, head of the Palestinian Liberation Organization; classroom combat in Brooklyn; "See It Now" program, one week after the Ed Murrow broadcast on Senator Joseph McCarthy (R). **MARCH 18**

A man sues the government for allegedly using him for LSD experiments without his permission; an update on the West Bank in Israel; a profile of Supreme Court Chief Justice Warren Burger. **MARCH 25**

An interview with Judge John Sirica; a tax law in Ireland that keeps writers and artists at home; a profile of British actress Vanessa Redgrave. **APRIL 1**

An energy device that saves up to 30% on electric bills; people who deliberately overpay their income taxes; a look at the General Accounting Office. **APRIL 8**

The fiscal practices of the Worldwide Church of God; a profile of Congressman Jack Kemp (R-NY), who advocates greater prosperity with lower taxes; a solution to blockbusting in Chicago. **APRIL 15**

Interviews with Joshua Nkomo and Robert Mugabe, who oppose voting for the Black majority government in Rhodesia; a profile of Atlanta Braves owner Ted Turner; a look at the chiropractic profession. **APRIL 22**

An interview with Johnny Carson; Britain's racist right-wing political party; the heavy drug traffic in South Florida (R). **APRIL 29**

BROADCAST NEWS: MAGAZINES **163**

**MAY 6**  Profile of tennis player Arthur Ashe; a look at the former leader of Britain's Liberal Party, Jeremy Thorpe (R); binge credit buying.

**MAY 13**  Doping horses before a race; a profile of Boston Pops conductor Arthur Fiedler (R); auto repair fraud (R).

**MAY 20**  A talk with Alfred Kahn, chairman of the Council on Wages and Price Stability; the island of Malta becomes an independent nation; white construction firms using minorities as fronts to get government grants.

**MAY 27**  Neighborhood patrols that some consider vigilante groups (R); the plight of the disabled whose needs for public assistance are cut off before they can help themselves; a visit to the island of Furudu in the Indian Ocean.

## 20/20 (ABC)

*1978*

**JUNE 6**  The inhumane treatment of jackrabbits in the training of greyhounds; a profile of comedian Flip Wilson; the chances of nuclear terror in the United States; Ted Kennedy (D-Mass.) recalls his brother Robert on the tenth anniversary of his death; a profile of California's Governor Jerry Brown.

**JUNE 13**  The growing use of Caesarian section as the American way of birth; street people in major American cities; the ease with which individuals can arm themselves with nuclear devices; the new movie *Jaws 2*.

**JUNE 20**  The dangers of gas tanks exploding in certain Ford-made cars; profile of Mick Jagger and the Rolling Stones; wonder drugs used in livestock feed may be causing new diseases in human beings.

**JUNE 27**  A profile of heavyweight boxer Leon Spinks; follow-up of earlier report on hazards in Ford cars; profile of Roger Baldwin, founder of the American Civil Liberties Union.

**JULY 4**  Report on how Americans are being contaminated by low-level radiation; a former prisoner of war tells how he survived seven-and-a-half years in a North Vietnamese prisoner of war camp; a $36-million art sale at Sotheby's in London.

**JULY 10**  The role of an FBI informant during the civil rights struggles of the 1960's; Heisman Trophy winner Earl Campbell's relationship with his mother; the use of heroin in the army's elite Berlin Brigade; a profile of Hollywood producer Alan Carr.

**JULY 18**  Part II on the dangers of low-level radiation; an interview with Soviet dissident Anatoly Scharansky before his arrest; the latest craze—discomania.

**JULY 25**  Agent Orange, a chemical used to kill the enemy in Vietnam, may now be killing Vietnam vets; a profile of southern talent agent, Candy Rice; the treasures of King Tut; a profile of Cincinnati Reds third-baseman Pete Rose as he tries for a National League batting record.

**AUGUST 1**  Clevelanders try to recall their boy mayor—Dennis Kucinich; an outbreak of roller-coaster mania; Part II of the dangers of defoliant Agent Orange; a profile of Harry Oppenheimer, leading white opponent of South Africa's apartheid policy.

Profile of race-car driver Mario Andretti; the effects of gas regulation on the average American; a day in the life of long-distance swimmer Diana Nyad; a profile of *Saturday Review* founder Norman Cousins.

**AUGUST 8**

Some Marine recruiters break the law to fill their ranks; remembering Elvis Presley has become big business; the creation of art objects from cars.

**AUGUST 15**

The Civil Rights Commission is beginning a major investigation into police brutality; American Catholics explain the importance of who is elected pope; ex-Yankee pitcher Jim Bouton wants to play again in the major leagues.

**AUGUST 22**

Secrets of the art of belly dancing; endangered species at the zoo; infrared telescopes probe the mysteries of the universe; confidential medical records can be tampered with.

**AUGUST 29**

Former British Liberal Party leader, Jeremy Thorpe, at the center of a scandal involving homosexuality and murder; producer Chuck Barris and his tacky but profitable productions; the resurgence of the Ku Klux Klan in Mississippi; Jim Bouton starts for the Atlanta Braves.

**SEPTEMBER 10**

Inside look at Hawaii's marijuana industry; profile of hockey star Bobby Orr; an analysis of the dispute over generic drugs.

**NOVEMBER 30**

Exploitative medical practices, including an attempt by a doctor to give a nonpregnant woman an abortion; a look at a 50-year-old gospel musical group; an examination of complaints by combat veterans at the Veteran's Administration Hospital in Albuquerque, New Mexico.

**DECEMBER 18**

*1979*

An investigation of alleged abuses in the Pentagon's purchasing practices; mismanagement and cruelty involved in a $35-million federal program to round up horses; a profile of John Gacy, who is under investigation for murder of 29 young boys in Chicago; the human side of developments as Americans flee the turmoil in Iran.

**JANUARY 8**

A look at the people in charge of Howard Hughes's multi-billion-dollar empire; a report on a mystery man who is buying up billions of dollars worth of underground water rights in Colorado; Mardi Gras festivities in New Orleans.

**FEBRUARY 27**

Insufficient social services and inadequate legal monitoring present problems in western coal fields; fifteen years after the death of Kitty Genovese, witnesses still don't want to get involved; rebuilding the Evansville, Indiana, basketball team after the entire team was killed in a plane crash; graft and waste connected with a billion-dollar sewer project in Suffolk County, New York.

**MARCH 21**

The real-life drama at the Three Mile Island nuclear power plant in Harrisburg, Pennsylvania, and the movie melodrama, *The China Syndrome;* a look at the miserable conditions in certain Chicago nursing homes; a profile of Chicago's mayor Jane Byrne; an interview with actress Lauren Bacall.

**APRIL 24**

# SPORTS
# ON TV

by Peter Coutros*

"TELEVISION invites you to detach your emotions," said one sociologist.

That assessment may be true of soap-opera buffs and all those other millions who seek escape in talk shows and late-night movies, but it is hardly applicable to the sports fan who thrills vicariously to the exploits of his heroes through their exposure on the tube.

Involvement is the key here, the bait that lured so many new partisans last year. Of all the categories in which ratings are recorded, sports viewing produced the most significant increase, with a jump of slightly more than 3 percent.

If it moves and wears a number, call it a sport—and you can bet a whole lot of people will sit there and watch it.

Here was Billy Martin, blubbering for all to see on network television. Here was the camera, reaching beyond Martin's dark "shades," beyond the tears streaking his face, probing the man's innermost sensitivities and laying them bare on the 19-inch diagonal screen.

Here was Larry Bird letting fly at the basket and here was the camera, catching Bird on the wing. Here was Muhammad Ali being left almost for dead by a reckless whippersnapper named Leon Spinks, and here was Ali, less than a year later, risen from the moribund. TV was there, for the death and the resurrection—in living color.

Without so much as bestirring himself from his sofa—other than to replenish his six-pack supply—the golf aficionado could fancy himself as being at the tee, in the fairway, and on the green with the hero of his choice, and still keep an eye on all those other guys.

Strategically placed cameras (their cables laid underground) put the fan at home cheek-by-jowl with Jack Nicklaus, Tom Watson, or any of the dozens of others whose names had become household words and whose income ballooned, thanks to television.

The ubiquitous cameras put the fight fan in a ringside pew and those same cameras put the football fan on the 50-yard line. The baseball fan was out there on the mound with the pitcher, in the batter's box with the hitter, and in the dugout with the manager nervously chewing his tobacco wad.

A far cry, all this, from the inception of televised sports at Ebbets Field in the first game of a double-header between the Cincinnati Reds and the Brooklyn Dodgers in 1939. The proceedings were televised via two cameras, one outside each foul line. "The players were distinguishable but it was not possible to pick out the ball," wrote one reviewer.

But the electronic baby has come a long way and television sports fans are not only afforded closeup views of the action with instant replays and slow-motion reprises from all conceivable angles, but they also have access to locker rooms, training quarters, and other areas usually limited to those wearing press cards on their lapels.

When the New York Yankees squared off with the Boston Red Sox to determine the championship of the American League's Eastern division, the event drew the attention of a network (ABC), as well as the local WPIX station, which beamed the game back to New York City.

*Peter Coutros is a television sports commentator for the *New York Daily News.*

PRECEDING PAGE: *Los Angeles, California, Oct. 17—New York Yankee Reggie Jackson follows the flight of the ball as he hits a two-run home run in the seventh inning of Tuesday night's final World Series game. The Yankees beat the Dodgers 7-2 to win the World Series.*

*"The night, they say, was made for love."*
(Drawing by Frascino; © 1979 The New Yorker Magazine, Inc.)

The game turned on a homerun which barely made it to the left field screen in Boston. It was hit by Yankee shortstop, Bucky Dent, and was played and replayed so many times as to become indelible in the mind's eye.

Subsequently, the Yanks went on into the World Series where they defeated the Los Angeles Dodgers. Within minutes after the final out, television fans were transported past the surging crowds on the field, through cramped passages, and past security guards into a roomful of milling players, reporters, and camera crews. Above the din which made it impossible for many in the room to hear anything, TV fans clearly heard Reggie Jackson, Thurman Munson, and other Yankees express their elation.

Yankee fans could exult with their idols in their moment of triumph and never suffer the dampening effects of all that champagne being squirted at each other by jubilant jocks.

Many of these same fans shared the frustration of Phil Rizzuto in a game earlier in the year. The incident is worth recounting for the insight it offers into the announcers who deliver the tidings, those who make the medium the message.

Rizzuto had played shortstop for the Yankees, and when his playing days were done he moved into the broadcast booth. He exudes congeniality and is intimately familiar with the game's nuances. He is also a self-confessed, unabashed fan.

In a game midway through the 1978 season, the Yanks were engaged in a nail-biter against the Oakland team. Late in the game Oakland's Mike Edwards scored a run by narrowly beating Jackson's throw to home.

Watching the replay on a monitor, Rizzuto observed that Edwards had missed the plate as he slid. For the next few minutes, Rizzuto fretted audibly, wondering how the information could be relayed to manager Billy Martin so that he might appeal the play to the home-plate umpire.

Fortunately for the integrity of the game, Rizzuto was not able to reach Martin. "I can't help it, I'm so much of a Yankee fan," Rizzuto conceded to a critic who looked askance at his attempt to tamper with the game's outcome.

Rizzuto's friend, Martin, caught the camera's eye about a month later as he arrived at a New York airport after taking leave of his troops in the middle of a road trip. In an emotional outburst he had labeled Reggie Jackson and club-owner George Steinbrenner, liars. Immediately after that, he packed his bags and headed home.

As he stepped off the plane, Martin found himself confronted by a TV crew from CBS. The crew held its ground resolutely, like a catcher guarding the plate against a sliding baserunner.

The red-eyed camera zoomed in on Martin. For a while his oversized sunglasses obscured his eyes and the hurt in them. But then, as the sweat poured forth, the glasses slid down his nose and we saw the haunted expression in his eyes. His jaw went slack, melting like butter left in the sun.

Billy Martin would have to spend many hours on the analyst's couch to reveal as much of himself as the camera told us about him on that very warm day. But then he was no newcomer to the cameras. A year earlier they caught him in action—very determined action—as he vent his spleen on Reggie Jackson and had to be forcibly restrained from attacking the Yankee outfielder in the dugout.

On the first Saturday in May 1978, while a high school band tootled "My Old Kentucky Home" and clutching $5 refreshments, trackside fans almost congealed into a gloppy mass, the magic medium of television transferred the Churchill Downs oval into our living rooms. We watched the race as though through the lens of an expensive set of binoculars. Then we saw it all over again and then once more, this time via the isolated camera focused on the winner, Affirmed, through the whole mile-and-a-quarter distance.

The scene shifted to Baltimore two weeks later and, without packing a bag or buying a ticket, we thrilled to Affirmed's victory (those who weren't rooting for any of the other horses, especially). Finally, there was Belmont and the Triple Crown; when Affirmed swept to victory to claim the turf tiara, millions of viewers in such remote areas as San Diego and Saskatchewan were privy to the coronation.

Starring in this extravaganza, of course, was a handsome three-year-old colt, its gleaming coat etched with sinewy striations. That the adventures of a four-legged animal should captivate millions tells us something of the eclecticism of TV sports fans.

They have sat there by the millions, glued to the screen to stare at behemoths with bulging bellies pull trolley cars, carry refrigerators up

steep hills, or hoist platforms loaded with pretty girls. The ABC network hit upon the idea of inviting big-name athletes to engage in a competition called "The Superstars," in which they vie for money prizes. The gimmick here is that each athlete must participate in a variety of sports, but never in his own specialty. For instance, Jimmy Connors would not take part in tennis if he were invited to "Superstars," a track star would have to eschew the running events, and so forth.

Not satisfied to televise productions staged by established sports entrepreneurs, the networks undertook to furnish their own shows with their own stars. Hence ABC packaged Sugar Ray Leonard, a flashy welterweight with intimations of Muhammad Ali and Sugar Ray Robinson dancing in his head, and offered him to viewers in what virtually amounted to a monthly Sugar Ray Leonard series.

His opponents were mostly of an undistinguished stripe, hardly calculated to upset the star of the show. To show how sweet they were on Sugar Ray, the network brass paid him $200,000 for each outing, which usually amounted to little more than a good sparring session.

The CBS network countered by signing Howard Davis, who, like Sugar Ray Leonard, was a gold-medal winner in the Montreal Olympics. Davis had to settle for $100,000 a performance, but was also given a steady diet of popovers to fatten up his reputation as a ring menace.

Neither Leonard nor Davis—nor anyone else for that matter—could do for television ratings what Muhammad Ali was able to do. His skills

demonstrably eroded—he could no longer sting like a bee or float like a butterfly at the age of 36—Ali surrendered his title to a helter-skelter challenger named Leon Spinks early in 1978. Along with Spinks, CBS was a winner, too, reaping big Nielsen numbers with its telecast of the bout.

Unable to come to terms with CBS for the rematch, promoter Bob Arum peddled the television rights for the sequel to ABC. In New Orleans in September, a remarkably well-conditioned Ali boxed, bothered, and befuddled Spinks into submission to become the first man in the history of the game to lay claim to the heavyweight crown three times.

Along with the crowd of more than 70,000 jammed into the New Orleans Superdome to watch the fight, many millions—lured by the prospect that this might be Ali's last hurrah—caught the action via the tube to give ABC another shove upward in the ratings war.

With rare exception, sports profited mightily as a television product. NBC tried hockey, only to discover what others had learned before, that the game is not a viable TV entity. Too fast to follow, suggested one critic; another felt there wasn't enough scoring; yet another cited all the whistle-blowing which interrupted the flow of action.

The game on ice was left to local TV stations. In New York, WOR showed many Ranger and Islander matches. Despite the successful seasons enjoyed by both clubs, the station did not experience any substantial climb in the Nielsens.

In the matter of basketball as a television attraction, there was

*Las Vegas, Nevada, Feb. 16—Leon Spinks connects with a right hook to Muhammad Ali during the late rounds of their championship fight. The twenty-four-year-old Spinks won the bout in a fifteen-round decision.*

ambivalence among the viewers at home. The college brand of Dr. Naismith's creation brought in high ratings, the professional version of the game did not.

One man long associated with pro basketball ascribed its TV shortcomings to the fact that neither the New York Knickerbockers nor the Los Angeles Lakers generated the sort of excitement necessary to draw large television audiences. When two teams representing two of the biggest media markets in the country came up as empty as the Knicks and Lakers did, the man explained, the game of hoops is in trouble on the tube. CBS learned this the hard way.

On the other hand, NBC tuned in on college ball and fared much better. With the country's best teams competing in the NCAA tourney at season's end, NBC hit the jackpot when the championship game pitted Indiana State against Michigan State.

The Sycamores of Indiana State featured the passing, shooting, and all-round hard-court excellence of Larry Bird, while the Michigan State Spartans' ace-in-the-bucket was Earvin Johnson, the one they called Magic for his sleight-of-hand with the round ball.

On a Monday night late in March 1979 the Spartans' defense grounded the Bird as Magic wove his spell to lead Michigan State to a 75-64 victory which snapped Indiana State's win skein at 33.

While the game itself featured a pair of Midwest powers, the telecast was characterized by an unmistakably New York sound, thanks to Al McGuire. Knowledgable assertive, almost always irreverent, the former St. John's and Knickerbocker alumnus added that last fillip which made the NCAA finals a smash hit on the home screen.

Like pro basketball and hockey, baseball has gone to the playoffs' route to provide the best teams the game has to offer to play in the final confrontation. The National Pastime and its fans got lucky when the New York Yankees and Los Angeles Dodgers, the best each league had to offer, were able to beat off the challenges of pretenders to emerge as World Series foes.

After the first two games, the Yankees were laboring under a deficit of two losses. Then third-baseman Graig (CQ) Nettles turned in what most observers termed the best fielding they'd ever seen at that position, to stymie the surging Dodgers and provide the momentum which carried the Yankees to another world championship.

Still, all of the pinstripers' heroics could not dim the luster of Pete Rose's achievement. Rose, known as Charlie Hustle around the league, set a new mark for hitting in consecutive games when he passed Tommy Holmes's old record of 37 straight games set in 1945. He fell short, however, of erasing Joe DiMaggio's major-league mark of 56.

Aware of the public's abiding interest in Rose's streak, NBC kept interrupting one of its regularly scheduled "Games of the Week" to switch to the Cincinnati game every time Rose came to bat. His feat endeared him to the fans and made him a tremendously salable commodity on Madison Avenue, where all those TV commercials are conjured up.

With commercials featuring his pixie countenance, Pete Rose became as visible to fans at home in the off-season as he was between April and October.

Like baseball, pro football was fortunate in that the two teams which survived the playoffs to reach the title game in Super Bowl XIII were Pittsburgh and Dallas. The Steelers were a surer bet to get to the Orange Bowl—where the game was played—but there was no gainsaying the Cowboys' right to be there, either.

Overcoming an early Dallas lead achieved on the strength of a Cowboy steal of the ball from Terry Bradshaw, the Steelers opened a sizable lead and midway through the final quarter appeared to be a lock. Then Roger Staubach connected twice with receivers in the end zone to bring his team to within four points of Pittsburgh, at 35-31, before the final gun killed Dallas's last hope of winning.

One of the more surprising aspects of televised sports in the last two years has been the emergence of tennis as something more than just a game played by proper people amid proper surroundings before terribly proper audiences.

Eschewing the hitherto widely accepted niceties of the sport, young Turks named Jimmy Connors, Ilie Nastase, and John McEnroe began giving vent to their emotions. Where only the pinging sound of ball meeting racket broke the somnolent silence of the game previously, now there could be heard the screeching and hollering of the sport's superstars as they quarrelled with officials and quibbled with fans.

If the game appeared to be becoming more democratic, its more successful practitioners were rapidly ascending into the realms of royalty with all those bundles of cash proffered by television networks.

Golf, too, reaped the harvest of huge monetary rewards; sponsors shelled out millions for the privilege of being allowed to bring one tournament after another into America's living rooms, where the multitudes could enjoy the sport without trudging over miles and miles of undulating fairways to keep abreast of their particular hero. Not altogether incidental to the sponsors' plans was the prospect of reaching all those potential customers for their products.

Thanks to Nancy Lopez, who utilized her putter with the same startling effect magicians get from a wand, women picked up considerable ground as TV sports entities. Lopez disproved that golf was a sport solely for the country-club set. From origins which might be charitably described as middle class, the curvaceous Lopez flowered into a talent of consequence by winning a string of LPGA tourneys as she set a new earnings mark for female rookie golfers. Her smile, alone, was worth a small ransom.

Undeniably a major factor in the proliferation of televised sports is the vast custom-tailored market provided by the tube. Income derived from advertisers enabled the networks to up the ante for pro football from $61 million in 1976 to more than $145 million two years later, with the end not yet in sight.

In 1980, NBC will be investing hundreds of millions of dollars to televise the Olympics from Moscow. If these illustrious international games can do for NBC what the Montreal Olympics did for ABC, the huge outlay will have been worth every penny.

Psychologists have offered a variety of theories to explain America's preoccupation with sports. There is considerable disagreement among them. Their dissonance can hardly be heard above the tinkle and clatter of all that gold being mined by the networks putting all that fun and games before a ravenous insatiable public.

# 6

# CHILDREN'S
# TV

# INNOCENTS "ABROADCAST": THE POWER OF PERSUASION

by Maureen Harmonay*

T HE real center of power behind children's television during 1978-79 was not in New York or LA but in Washington, D.C. The Federal Trade Commission (FTC), spurred by two petitions from public-interest groups working on behalf of children and nutrition, threatened to seriously curtail certain classes of advertising on children's programming. The Federal Communications Commission (FCC), meanwhile, was looking into whether the amount of advertising on children's shows should be cut back. The stakes were high: $600 million in broadcast revenue. Clearly, this was no ordinary year in the annals of "kidvid."

On February 28, 1978, by a unanimous vote, the FTC initiated an unprecedented rulemaking proceeding designed to restrict advertising on children's television. The agency's action came in response to separate requests from Action for Children's Television (ACT), a national consumer advocacy organization headquartered in Newtonville, Massachusetts, and the Washington, D.C.-based Center for Science in the Public Interest, both of which had asked the FTC to ban television advertising of highly sugared foods directed at children. The FTC staff responded with a 364-page report recommending: 1) a ban on all televised advertising directed to children under eight, who are "too young to understand the selling purpose of, or evaluate, the advertising"; 2) a ban on children's commercials for sugared products, "the consumption of which poses the most serious dental health risks"; and 3) advertiser-funded nutritional and health messages to balance ads for sugared products.

Although exhaustive, the FTC staff report raised as many questions as it answered:

How would "children's programs" be defined? The FCC defined kids' shows as those originally designed for children 12 and under, but it was thought that the FTC might wish to adopt a broader standard involving the "percentage of children in the audience," because afternoon reruns of sitcoms and adventure series on independent stations, though not made for children, attract sizable numbers of young viewers.

Was there empirical evidence that advertising for sugared foods was directly related to tooth decay? Although dental disease is at epidemic proportions in this country, it had never been firmly established that the number of commercials a child saw for candies, gum, and presweetened breakfast cereals was in direct ratio to the number of cavities in his or her mouth.

At what age could children be expected to develop an understanding of the difference between programming and advertising, and when did they begin to realize that a commercial was trying to sell them something?

It was hoped that some of these issues would come into sharper focus during a series of public hearings that the FTC would hold in early 1979. But even this initial investigatory period would be jeopardized before the clamor of 1978 subsided.

With the exception of cigarette advertising, never before had broad-

PRECEDING PAGE: *Barkley, a giant Muppet puppy joins the kids for a romp in the park.*

*Maureen Harmonay is a writer and editor based in Newton, Massachusetts. She has written numerous articles and edited two books on children's television.

casters and advertisers been held accountable by the federal government for their potential harm to the health and well-being of young children. The industry's response was immediate and unmitigated. Within weeks of the FTC's vote to adopt a rulemaking, *Broadcasting* magazine reported that commercial-broadcaster-related trade associations had begun to marshall a "$2-million war chest" to stem the governmental process of rulemaking. This economic clout paid off—at least in the short run.

With the fervor of drowning rats, well-funded broadcast lobbyists climbed all over Capitol Hill during House and Senate deliberations on the FTC budget for the fiscal year 1979. Desirous, perhaps, of garnering political support for his ultimately short-lived presidential candidacy nearly a year later, Senator Lowell Weicker (R-Ct.), a ranking member of the Senate Appropriations Committee, became in the spring of 1978 a champion of the commercial broadcasters' interests. He fiercely attacked the FTC's children's rulemaking, publicly calling the agency a "national nanny," a description borrowed from a *Washington Post* editorial. Senator Weicker and his like-minded colleagues were partially successful: Congress appropriated sufficient funding for the commission to continue its investigation into children's ads, but with a proviso that no actual regulations could be promulgated at least through June 1979. Industry lobbists may have won the battle but lost the war: A vote on the FTC staff proposals would not even be scheduled until mid-1980.

Not satisfied with this peremptory victory, a coalition of trade associations decided to let FTC Chairman Michael Pertschuk know that they weren't fooling around. Soon after his appointment as chairman in 1977, Mr. Pertschuk, long known as a consumer advocate, vowed that his agency would become "the largest public-interest law firm" in the country. Even before the commission voted to look into children's TV advertising, Chairman Pertschuk had been outspoken in his criticism of broadcast practices directed to young viewers. As early as July 1977 he had expressed the view that "advertising directed to children may be unfair without being deceptive," cautioning that children are a vulnerable population that may require special forms of protection.

By his candor did Mr. Pertschuk perish. On November 3, 1978, Washington, D.C., district court judge Gerhard Gesell disqualified the FTC chairman from any further participation in his agency's children's-advertising proceeding. Ruling on a suit filed by the American Association of Advertising Agencies, the Association of National Advertisers, the Toy Manufacturers of America, and the Kellogg Co., Judge Gesell agreed with the plaintiffs that Mr. Pertschuk "had conclusively prejudged" the issues relating to the case. If an appeal is unsuccessful, Judge Gesell's decision may haunt the federal regulatory agencies like a specter of silence during future debates of controversial issues.

Pertschuk's disqualification, though a symbolic victory for anti-regulation forces, did not disrupt the proposed hearings. With FTC administrative law judge Morton Needelman presiding, they began as scheduled on January 15, 1979, in a courtroom in San Francisco. Before they would end—some 6 weeks and 220 witnesses later—the FTC had begun to inch toward a more precise understanding of the problems and possible solutions to the children's-advertising question. And although consumer groups and industry lobbyists remained as polarized as ever, a few members of both factions offered what they thought were constructive compromises. There were a few, too, who denied the existence of *any* problems and wondered what all the fuss was about.

Among the latter was Seymour Banks, vice president of Leo Burnett, the large advertising agency that for years has handled the Kellogg account. After delivering his testimony to a packed audience in San Francisco, Mr. Banks confided to a *Washington Post* reporter that "children, like everyone else, must learn the marketplace. You learn by making judgments," he explained. So, "even if a child is deceived by an ad at age four, what harm is done? He will grow out of it. . . . Even if," Mr. Banks continued, in what is now an infamous interview whose very mention warms consumerists' hearts, "even if, as many psychologists claim, a child perceives children in television advertising as friends, and not as actors selling them something, what's the harm? All a parent has to say is, 'shut up or I'll belt you!' "

A somewhat more humane stance was taken by child psychologists such as Prof. Robert Liebert, of the State University of New York at Stony Brook, who asserted that "it is horrible to think of children as targets, as the advertising industry does." And by Dr. Aimee Dorr, of the University of Southern California's Annenberg School of Communications, who testified that "the evidence is reasonably strong that the majority of children younger than seven do not understand the selling purpose of commercials. Given this evidence," she said, "I believe the commission ought to conclude that advertising to children of these ages is unfair." (Dr. Dorr is widely recognized as one of the most knowledgable scholars studying the effects of television on children.)

While most broadcasters and advertisers who would be directly affected by an FTC curtailment of children's advertising did not exactly agree that commercials aimed at kids were unfair, one or two (two, to be exact) proposed a form of remedial action.

The industry had come under double-barreled pressure. Not only the FTC, but also its sister agency the FCC, had pointed a finger at broadcast licensees and said, in effect, "show me." Also acting in response to a petition from Action for Children's Television, the FCC in July 1978, quietly and without much fanfare, reopened the children's docket, which had been resting undisturbed since 1974 when the commission had issued its last definitive document, the *Children's Television Report and Policy Statement.* It was this policy statement that had effectively ended the practice of host-selling on kids' programs; called for a "clear separation" between programs and commercials; and mandated industry-wide compliance with the National Association of Broadcasters' (NAB) code standard of no more than 9½ minutes of advertising on any hour of Saturday or Sunday morning children's television.

Since 1976, when the 1974 guidelines went into effect, the FCC has maintained a court-sanctioned "hands-off" policy; now it was asking stations to demonstrate their compliance with the spirit and the letter of the law. Commercial broadcasters well understood the agency's hidden message: If a policy statement wasn't enough of a warning that licensees were expected to "serve the unique needs of the child audience," then maybe *rules* were in order.

In an effort to convince both the FCC and the FTC of their sincerity, a few savvy broadcasters initiated voluntary efforts at reform—the first since 1974 when, then as now, the bleak prospect of more government regulation inspired the industry with uncharacteristic zeal. First to grab the spotlight during the hearings in January 1979 was Kenneth Mason, president of Quaker Oats, makers of Cap'n Crunch and Life cereals, as well as Fisher-Price toys. His not-so-modest proposal was that the three commercial networks pool their resources to create a special "public-interest time period" from 9 A.M. to noon on Saturdays, during which ABC, CBS, and NBC "would jointly prepare and simulcast the finest children's programs they could make." Mr. Mason also suggested that under his system commercials would be clustered at suitable intervals and that they, too, would be simulcast on the three networks. He asserted that the intent of his proposal was to "upgrade dramatically the networks' Saturday-morning programming for children without losing audiences and without increasing production costs." While the idea was publicly commended by FCC Chairman Charles Ferris, it was solidly trounced by ABC, CBS, and NBC, who insisted that it was unworkable, unrealistic, and a good way to enrich the coffers of independent stations, which presumably would not participate in the plan.

Next on stage amid the first-week theatrics in the FTC's San Francisco drama was ABC president James Duffy, who announced that his network would voluntarily reduce commercial time on weekend children's programs over a two-year period beginning January 1980. The rollbacks would give ABC 7½ minutes of advertising per hour, two minutes less than it is currently permitted under the existing NAB code. The extra time would be allotted to program promotions, public-service announcements, and health and nutrition messages—strikingly similar to what the FTC staff had recommended.

Industry reaction to the ABC cutback was less than enthusiastic. CBS network president James Rosenfield was perhaps the most vociferous in his objections, warning that, "It . . . merely starts us on a road toward the ultimate elimination of advertising to children, which is contrary to the best interests of all concerned." While Rosenfield continually averred that "CBS has no plans to change its advertising standards," his implacability may have been misguided. It is inconceivable that ABC would risk a significant loss of advertising revenue unless it hoped to gain something in return. The network's message to the FTC was, "Listen, we're willing to meet you halfway. We'll admit that too many commercials may cause some problems for some kids. In lieu of government fiat, won't you accept this as a reasonable solution?" So it remains to be seen whether ABC was crazy—like a fox.

Meanwhile, even the usually immovable National Association of Broadcasters was being affected by the irresistible force of public opinion. An independent ABC News/Harris poll released on March 14, 1979, revealed that, "a sizable majority of the American people would ban from television: advertising of sugary foods directed at children (and) all ads aimed at children under eight." The pollsters explained that "those who favor a ban claim that manufacturers are taking unfair advantage of young people who are not able to distinguish between products that are good or harmful for them. They also charge that these ads can turn children against their parents and undermine parental authority." It began to look like the opposition forces were in a heap of trouble.

Motivated, perhaps, by a public relations panic, the NAB decided it was time to do something—anything—to salvage its carefully cultivated reputation as one of the good guys. In April, therefore, TV code Board Chairman Robert Rich announced that the NAB had decided to require code subscribers to insert five- to ten-second audio-video messages—bumpers—between programs and commercials aired during children's weekend viewing hours. Mr. Rich explained that "the purpose of the separator devices—'We will return after these messages' . . . 'Now back to the program'—is to help or to reinforce a child's ability to differentiate between program and nonprogram material." By amending its code to require bumpers during kids' shows as of September 1979, the NAB had exercised its seldom-used prerogative to change its mind. Only five months before, in formal comments on the FTC staff proposals, the organization had flatly denied that a child's ability to discern "The Pink Panther Show" from the Tony-the-Tiger commercial was in any way clouded, asserting that "significant numbers of young people can distinguish programs from advertisements."

When they weren't embroiled in the brouhaha over proposed federal regulation of the programs kids watch, the commercial broadcasters were hard at work hoping kids would keep on keeping it on—the television set, that is. They needn't have worried. The latest available Nielsen statistics for 1978 show that two- to five-year-old children were glued to the set for more than 31 hours in any given week, with their older brothers and sisters (6 to 11 years old) putting in weekly totals of 27 hours.

But the Nielsens brought both good news and bad news to some broadcasters. Other figures showed that during the first quarter of 1979, CBS was the easy winner of the intramural ratings war on Saturday morning, with ABC and NBC, respectively, trailing a point or more behind. Among CBS's perennial trump cards was "Fat Albert," a Bill Cosby-inspired and hosted cartoon program that earned kudos from educators, parents, and others who appreciated its sensitive and realistic treatment of young Blacks and the young in general. In May 1978 the program received a deserved and prestigious accolade in the form of an "Achievement in Children's Television Award" from Action for Children's Television, which commended the show for its "humane sense of humor." CBS's proud moment was to be short-lived, however, for barely a week later, Filmation's Norm Prescott and Lou Scheimer, producers of "Fat Albert," blasted the network in a *Variety* interview for not putting its money where its mouth was. "The kids of this country are being cheated," they charged, revealing one of CBS's well kept secrets. It seems that although "Fat Albert" had been on the air for seven seasons, no new episodes of the series had been ordered from Filmation since 1976. Scheimer and Prescott, while not exactly impartial, did have a point. "The network," they said, "talks out of both sides of its mouth because it uses 'Fat Albert' to go to Washington to convince the politicians and the action groups of the terrific job they're doing." CBS must have taken the criticism to heart, because when "Fat Albert" returns in the fall of 1979, it will be with some never-before-broadcast episodes, including one that will deal with the question of busing.

Among the network's other noteworthy children's programs was the early Saturday afternoon feature "30 Minutes," a teenage version of CBS's successful prime-time news magazine. Consistently informative and often entertaining, segments on "30 Minutes" examined the pitfalls of being a teenage parent and the problems of young runaways, interspersed with an occasional lighthearted profile of up-and-coming rock stars. A regular on-the-air column, "Who's Right?", provided a forum for attorney Patricia McGuire to discuss salient issues relating to young people and the law. Ms. McGuire responded to such queries as whether a high school principal had the right to go through students' lockers without permission, and whether an employer could pay a younger person less than an older one for doing the same job.

As for ABC, its number-one status in prime time wasn't quite matched by its standings during the children's hours. But not for lack of trying. The bright spots on its Saturday-morning schedule were the "Weekend Specials," half-hour live-action or animated dramas based for the most part on popular novels and short stories for kids. During the 1978-79 season, these included *The Winged Colt*, a three-part miniseries based on the book by Betsy Byars, whose work has also been adapted for "Afterschool Specials"; *The Contest Kid*, patterned on Barbara Brooks Wallace's novel, *The Contest Kid and the Big Prize;* and *The Seven Wishes of Joanna Peabody,* featuring *Gone-With-the-Wind* star Butterfly McQueen as the fairy godmother of a girl in Harlem.

But, as ABC vice president Squire Rushnell testified before the FTC, this type of high-quality programming is expensive, running about $225,000 for a single half-hour production. Rushnell, like so many other broadcasters, warned that any severe advertising restrictions could jeopardize children's television as we know it. Perhaps this would not be as terrible as it sounds, given all three networks' propensity toward near-ancient reruns of "Scooby Doo," "The Flintstones," and "Bugs Bunny." (Even these have doubled in price since 1974, with new half-hour episodes costing in the range of $130,000.) As ABC has recognized, however, even aging programming packages in standard formats can be spruced up with lively short segments, such as "Schoolhouse Rock." The creation of advertiser David McCall of McCaffrey and McCall, these cartoon vignettes have for years decorated ABC's children's schedule with quickie courses in history, grammar, multiplication ("three is a magic number"), and, new last season, science. Rotated in repertory with vintage "Schoolhouse Rock" segments, "Science Rock" episodes included features on the human digestive system, or "Body Machine," and "Them Not-So-Dry Bones," a look at the "Skeleton Locked Inside" us.

In an effort, perhaps, to minimize soaring production costs and maximize audience appeal, ABC this year experimented with a hybrid format to fill Sunday-morning air time. Combining the drawing power of an attractive male host and the entertainment value of a "Merv Griffin Show," the network spawned "Kids are People Too." But when the 90-minute series premiered in September 1978 with former "Wonderama" host Bob McAllister at the helm, the chemistry just wasn't right. The network soon jettisoned him for a younger, more contemporary personality, Michael Young, who had presided over Warner Qube's "Columbus Goes Bananaz" in Ohio. It made a difference. Young was credited, in part, with boosting ABC's pull with the two- to eleven-year-old audience by 27 percent over the 1977-78 season. When he returned in the fall of 1979, doing double duty as host of both "Kids are People Too" and the "Weekend Specials," it was hoped that his charismatic appeal would achieve the same magical results for the latter series.

The loser in Saturday morning's race for ratings was NBC. Desperate, the network looked to the United Nations—in a manner of speaking—for help. As virtually no one needed to be reminded, 1979 was the International Year of the Child. It was as good an excuse as any for the network to spew forth reams of rhetoric about its "commitment to children," announcing new programs that would not even begin, ironically, until the Year of the Child was approaching old age.

In the fall of 1978, before IYC had become fashionable, one would have thought that the enrichment of Saturday's children was the furthest thing from NBC's collective mind. When children's programming executive Michael Brockman (since relegated to second-class status under former CBS rival Jerry Golod) announced the network's new schedule, his press release language was clearly designed to soothe anxiety-ridden affiliates—not child development specialists. "The new lineup," he said, "is filled with a highly promotable galaxy of proven 'stars,' designed to appeal to the broadest possible audience of young viewers. . . . The elements of this schedule are representative of the exciting things that are happening at NBC, things that are making NBC a stronger competitive force on Saturday morning." It should be noted that some of these "exciting things" included an array of shows devoid of any genuine creativity—the network called it "Saturday Morning Fever"—that included Hanna-Barbera's "Yogi's Space Race" and "The Godzilla Power Hour" (about which ACT president Peggy Charren jokingly quipped to an industry convention, "I assumed it was a show on energy"). Maybe Ms. Charren had something. NBC certainly didn't. About every two months the network announced that it was revising the lineup, until the Year of the Child conveniently happened along.

At that point NBC brought out the big guns: one salvo involved network president Robert Mulholland. Accepting the "Man of the Year" award from the Advertising Club of Baltimore in February 1979, Mr. Mulholland told his audience that he and his colleagues would be "increasing our efforts for young viewers, because this is the year that the United Nations has designated as the International Year of the Child. It's a time of worldwide discussion and action on the needs and welfare of children, and NBC is doing its part with a commitment across the board in entertainment, news, and sports." From the tone of Mr. Mulholland's remarks—and those of all broadcasters paying lip service to IYC—one had to wonder whether these marvelous programming promises would turn into pumpkins at the stroke of 1980, when all bets would be called off and all new shows would revert back to reruns.

At any rate, NBC's plans for the fall of 1979 were as follows: a series of 75-second Saturday morning sports briefs on "physical fitness, health, and the right kind of food for growing youngsters"; "capsule news reports of major events of the week"; and an hour-long entertainment show, "Hot Hero Sandwich," to be produced by the team of Bruce and Carole Hart, whose credits include original scripts for "Sesame Street" and production (with Marlo Thomas) of "Free to Be . . . You and Me," a widely acclaimed special broadcast on ABC.

The International Year of the Child brought other news about the networks, not all of it good. In a *Television Radio Age* article (March 26, 1979) devoted exclusively to children's television, FCC commissioner Joseph Fogarty wrote that "by any standard of intelligence, creativity, and caring, the bulk of commercial television is an insult to our children. . . . I wish I could say," he went on, "that there are substantial improvements on the horizon. . . . However, recent events are not particularly encouraging. On the same day that NBC announced that 1979 was to be 'The Year of the Child,' the network also announced the return of 'The Flintstones.' While Fred Flintstone and Barney Rubble are no doubt beloved and fondly remembered in many TV households, I trust that their reincarnation on NBC is not to be the hallmark of the network's commitment to young Americans."

These were strong words coming from an FCC commissioner, but Mr. Fogarty was not alone in his concern. April brought the release of Dr. George Gerbner's "Violence Profile Number 10," the latest in an annual analysis of the previous year's dramatic content on network television. The results were dismaying. Defining violence as "unambiguous" and "physical"—hurting or killing a person or the credible threat of hurting or killing"—Dr. Gerbner found that there was more of it during 1978 children's programming than in nearly any previous year. Equally disturbing was the fact that *new* children's programs were found to be more violent than series that had returned from previous seasons—an ominous sign.

Perhaps more significant, even, than the body counts on the kids' shows were the effects they were having on young viewers. Schoolchildren who watch a lot of television, explained Gerbner, "are more likely to believe that the police frequently use force and that the average policeman will often [draw] his gun as well as shoot fleeing subjects." Further, noted the researcher, "children and adolescents who watch more television are more likely to mistrust people and believe that they 'mostly just look out for themselves.'" While Gerbner's findings and methodology are certainly open to criticism—is it really fair, for example, to compare a rape or a murder on prime-time drama with a cartoon character who harmlessly falls off a cliff?—they are worth attention as trends that bear watching.

While the networks' Saturday-morning programming got mixed reviews, their weekday-afternoon efforts could be pointed to with pride. The afterschool hours had been virtually ignored as a profitable prospect for children until ABC mined their potential with the "Afterschool Specials" in 1972. By 1978, the idea of providing drama of prime-time quality for daytime-viewing children, considered radical and risky when first proposed by ABC's Squire Rushnell, had gained cautious acceptance in the wake of the success of the "Afterschool Specials."

If children's programming was supposed to be all sweetness and light, the "Afterschool Specials" didn't qualify. They consistently and honestly grappled with problems that television usually considered too hot to handle. Sex, for example. Love. Death. "My Mom's Having a Baby," in which the nine-year-old protagonist's mother was seen actually giving birth, caused quite an uproar when it was originally broadcast in 1977, with some parents outraged at the lack of a "parental discretion" advisory (on a children's program!). The show went on to reap prestigious awards. It drew the highest rating of any previous "Special" and captured the largest audience of any daytime dramatic special in the history of television, attracting some 25 million viewers.

Among ABC's presentations this year was an afterschool valentine in the form of "Make-Believe Marriage," which followed ten high school seniors through "a crash course in the realities of married life," including, for some of them, "divorce." In "The Terrible Secret," a guilt-ridden teenage girl concealed her identity as the driver in a hit-and-run accident that badly injured a 12-year-old boy. Though ostensibly designed for children, both programs provided astonishingly grown-up lessons in the consequences of shirking responsibility.

At NBC the emphasis this year was on a different kind of learning: the kind you get from books. The network's "Special Treat" series, also aired on weekday afternoons, initiated a new feature—"When You Turn Off the Set, Turn on a Book"—to encourage viewers to read the print sources from which the programs have been adapted. At the conclusion of "Rodeo Red and the Runaway," for example, about Stacy, a runaway girl who is befriended by Emma, a strong-willed prairie woman, there is the following segment:

MARTA KOBER: "Hi. I'm Marta Kober and you just saw me as Stacy. Stacy and Emma are based on two characters in a book entitled *Shelter from the Wind* by Marion Dane Bauer. The book, which is probably available at your library, is very different from the story in our 'Special Treat,' but it explores some of the same feelings about love and hate and you might enjoy it. So, consider reading it . . . and when you turn off your set, turn on a book!"

Another unique educational endeavor on NBC involved "Reading, Writing and Reefer," a program about the use of marijuana by high school and junior high students, originally aired as part of "NBC Reports" in prime time. Response to the program was so great, with the network receiving thousands of requests for tapes and transcripts, that NBC decided not only to rebroadcast the show as a "Special Treat," but to waive licensing rights so that educational institutions with prior written permission could tape it off-air. Through this unprecedented arrangement, NBC reimbursed Films, Inc., the usual distributor of its documentaries for nonbroadcast use, for the revenue it could have earned from rentals. More than 2200 educators took the network up on its offer when "Reading, Writing and Reefer" was aired on April 17, 1979.

CBS's major afterschool contribution this year was "Joey and Redhawk," remarkable not for its content—the conflicts and camaraderie between two boys: one a Ute Indian, the other from a middle-class Ohio family—but for its format—a one-week-only, Monday-Friday, late-afternoon miniseries. Black Rock has since dubbed the concept "Afternoon Playhouse," and will repeat it during the 1979-80 season, with an encore showing of "Joey and Redhawk" plus two other miniseries yet to be announced. In addition to its ongoing efforts—the monthly magazine, "Razzmatazz" and irregularly scheduled "Festival of Lively Arts for Young People" specials—CBS planned three puppet programs about mainstreaming disabled children, under the umbrella title "Kids on the Block," and "CBS Library," one-hour trilogies of book-inspired dramas.

1978-79 was a year of anniversaries in children's television: Captain Kangaroo and Mr. Rogers celebrated their twenty-fifth year as benevolent models for preschool youngsters. "Children's Television Workshop" and "Sesame Street" celebrated their tenth birthdays.

Mickey Mouse turned 50. Though his memory lived on, his show fared less well, accused by its promoters of being a casualty of the shaky future of children's TV advertising. Although syndicator Stan Moger had firm commitments of $2 million in advertising for another season, each contract, it seemed, contained a clause voiding the advertiser's obligation if the government found it incumbent to ban ads for sugared foods. Alas, "The New Mickey Mouse Club" died a quiet death in January 1979. Mr. Moger attributed the show's demise to "advertisers' extraordinary uptightness over what the Federal Trade Commission and Federal Communications Commission plan to do about advertising to kids."

This uncertainty remains. But while broadcasters flaunt the specter of independent stations going out of business and Saturday-morning television going down the tubes if the regulatory agencies have their way, it is unlikely that the truth is anywhere as near gloomy as the broadcast lobbyists have predicted. More probable is a compromise between sugar and the status quo (we may not have Tony the Tiger to kick around anymore and Cookie Jarvis may be banished from the airwaves).

Even with these restrictions, however, it seems certain that Saturday-morning programming will survive. Yet to be confronted in some future year are new technologies and distribution systems, "superstations," and cable—all of which may have as great an effect on the future of children's television as any rule the Federal Trade Commission may choose to enact.

**7**

# TV
# TECHNOLOGY

The past year was one in which television technology took a major leap forward and inaugurated revolutionary developments which could result in significant changes throughout the 1980s in the form and format of television itself.

Broadcast equipment continued its metamorphosis toward the more portable and versatile, with lightweight electronic newsgathering tape equipment continuing the preceding year's gradual replacement of film cameras, resulting in economies, greater speed, and in many cases improved quality.

The use of video tape was moving beyond news and the "live-on-tape" studio productions, which had been its main use in recent years. Video tape was now being extended to the production of regular television series, once virtually the exclusive province of film. The initials EFP (electronic field production) joined ENG (electronic news gathering) to represent the use of exclusively television techniques in video production.

One significant development, widely heralded in broadcasting circles but virtually unrecognized elsewhere, was the development of a new standard for studio video tape recording—the first change since the original four-headed video tape recorder was introduced by Ampex in 1956. The new system uses one-inch, instead of two-inch, videotape and has a "helical-scan" system, as opposed to the transverse scanning (perpendicular to the orientation of the tape) used in the previous standard equipment. The Society of Motion Picture and Television Engineers conducted the official standardizing, compromising between systems proposed by Ampex and Sony. The new standard machines cost less than the old "quad" recorders and use about one-third as much tape. This simplifies storage as well as lowers production costs—while producing pictures which many broadcast engineers feel are significantly better. It will be many years before the workhorse quad machines are phased out, but virtually all broadcasters are buying the new machines when they replace old ones or add to their recording capabilities.

Digital television equipment, which uses computers for special effects and picture control, previously unknown in television broadcasting, was now making its first inroads into the field through special-effects generators, tape editors, and other peripheral equipment. During the season several companies both here and abroad demonstrated early prototype models of digital video tape recorders, clearly labeling them as "laboratory projects" in order not to hurt sales of existing equipment. Digital recorders have the remarkable ability to reproduce a picture with no noticeable loss of quality, no matter how many "generations" of tape are copied from one to another. Although practical digital VTRs may be a decade off, as some manufacturers insist, there was a substantial minority view that a new type of recorder will produce breathtakingly real pictures for network use by 1985.

There has probably been more excitement created by satellite communication this season then by any other development in broadcasting technology. RCA, Western Union, and Hughes have their own satellites

*David Lachenbruch is the editorial director of *Television Digest,* an industry newsletter. He is a contributor to *TV Guide* and other consumer magazines in the area of technology.

# MASTER CONTROL FROM THE BEDROOM TO SPACE

**by David Lachenbruch***

PRECEDING PAGE: *Earth station of the type providing programming to cable TV systems or broadcast stations. RCA is proposing to build and maintain "receive-only" installations free of charge for television broadcasters who receive syndicated programming from RCA's Satcom satellites.*

*"I have faith that someday, somehow, Ed will turn up. In
the meantime, I'm taping 'Bionic Woman' for him."*
(Drawing by Stevenson; © 1977 The New Yorker Magazine, Inc.)

aloft for relaying television programming. The Public Broadcasting
System used satellite transmission exclusively for network programming among its television stations. PBS was building earth stations to
receive satellite-beamed radio as well. In the spring of 1979, NBC announced a major project to determine whether it would switch much of
its intercity transmission from AT&T's land lines to satellites. RCA
Satellite Communications (Satcom) probably made the biggest stir of
all when in March 1979 it offered to build, operate, and maintain receiving earth stations without charge for all of the nation's 725 commercial
TV stations. This way, the stations could receive syndicated programs
directly by satellite, in place of the traditional "bicycling" of films and
tapes by mail and express. RCA's third satellite was scheduled for
launch in December 1979, and it planned to offer up to four full-time
channels for the program syndication service.

RCA has also had substantial success using its satellites to relay
programming to cable TV systems. In fact, virtually all intercity
"networking" of cable programming—particularly pay cable and the
so-called "superstations"—was done by satellite this season.

The subject of direct satellite-to-home broadcasting cropped up
with ever-increasing frequency. In the near future, the idea will become
more and more a thorn in the side of local broadcasters. At least theoret-
ically, four direct-broadcasting satellite channels could replace all local
stations for network broadcasts. Local stations pointed out that such an
arrangement would eliminate all local expression from the air, and
could be the broadcasting equivalent of wiping out local newspapers
and substituting three or four national ones instead. But whether it's
good or bad, it was increasingly becoming a strong technical possibil-

ity. Most European countries (where broadcasting is more government related than in the United States) were developing major projects for testing and demonstrating direct satellite broadcasting into the home. Japan has completed its experimental phase and plans to move now to regular satellite broadcasting into sparsely populated and mountainous areas inadequately served by ground-based stations. In the Western hemisphere, Canada was experimenting with direct satellite-to-TV-set broadcasting for the same purpose.

One indirect benefit of using satellites has been the sharp improvement in TV sound, along with making possible a simpler and cheaper system for using FM stations to provide stereo sound with TV broadcasts. Although PBS had pioneered simulcast stereo many years earlier, it wasn't until it started broadcasting by satellite that it could send along the stereo sound channels *with* the picture. The satellite eliminated the need to rent high-quality audio lines from the telephone company and use elaborate phasing equipment to synchronize the sound with the picture at the receiving end. Today, the stereo sound can be directed from the receiving earth station to the FM outlet involved in simulcasting without the need for special lines or complex phasing gear. Perhaps more important than the potential for stereo simulcasting was the sharp improvement of the standard *monophonic* sound accompanying the PBS telecasts. When conventional land lines were used in the past for network television broadcasts cross-country, the sound was carried by a separate telephone line, which limited the frequency response to a mere 5 kilohertz—about the same as that of a standard AM radio broadcast. When PBS started using satellites, it "folded" the sound in with the picture channel, giving a full 15-kilohertz high-fidelity audio channel, taking full advantage of the hi-fi capabilities of TV sound transmission.

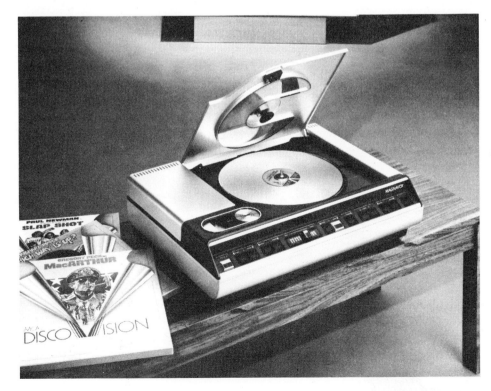

*In the past twelve months the widely anticipated video disc became a reality for the home. The Magnavision player by Magnavox and DiscoVision records by MCA went on sale in some market areas, with nationwide availability scheduled for 1980.*

*Although home video cassette recorders were first marketed for recording programs off the air, new battery-powered models with accessory color cameras provided a popular substitute for home movies. Shown is the AKAI portable VCR with color camera.*

Whether AT&T was inspired by PBS's accomplishment, or was concerned that networks might abandon its terrestrial program-distribution system, AT&T's Long Lines Department quickly added a "diplexing" system which sent the sound along with the picture via its earth-bound channels, delivering to local affiliates a network program with true high-fidelity sound.

The development of hi-fi television sound networking, first by PBS satellite and later by commercial land lines, began to create a demand for television sets to accommodate this new sound. Although the high-quality sound had been available in 1978, most existing television sets were designed for a far more limited audio channel. In fact, many of them deliberately clipped off some of the audio to avoid distortion and to maintain intelligibility. The television set manufacturers in the spring of 1979 began adding models capable of true high-fidelity sound —that in some cases simulated stereo—adding a "new dimension" to television reception. It adds to the cost of TV sets, too, and the results of this experiment haven't yet been tabulated in the marketplace.

Even before the television manufacturers were able to capitalize on the new sound, several makers of hi-fi equipment introduced television audio tuners for home stereo systems, to permit the reception of television's sound channel over quality audio gear, as an accompaniment to the television picture (viewed on a TV set with the sound turned down).

AT&T's new land-based sound system was also designed to carry two or more sound channels with a single TV picture, if desired, and the telephone company already has announced it will make multisound available to stations upon request. This could provide either stereophonic sound or dual soundtracks—in two languages, for example. The FCC has inaugurated a proceeding looking toward future standards for regular stereo-sound broadcasting with TV—the audio signal to be carried along with the picture over the air—as opposed to simulcasting on an FM station. At the same time, an all-industry committee formed under the aegis of the Electronic Industries Association has been studying proposed standards for various multichannel sound systems for television and will make recommendations to the FCC after extensive field-testing.

While television station and cross-country network transmissions improved, so, too, did television receivers. The progress has been gradual, but the improvements have become increasingly dramatic in recent years. Most of the recent advances have been designed to make tuning and color adjustment automatic while increasing the life of the set and the quality of the picture. Many of these improvements involved the increasing use of the microprocessor unit (MPU), which is actually a minicomputer on a fingernail-sized chip of semiconductor material.

One of the major accomplishments of the MPU in television tuning has been the ability to tune to the exact frequency of an incoming television station without the necessity of any fine tuning at all—so that even the so-called automatic fine-tuning systems were being eliminated. By spring 1979 the overwhelming majority of color TV sets had eliminated the clanking mechanical tuner, substituting all-electronic tuning systems which used either a single knob (for UHF and VHF), pushbuttons, or touchtone-style keyboards for selecting the proper channel. The latter two approaches were called "random access," because they permitted the viewer to tune directly to any channel from any other at random without going through the channels in between, as one would have to do using a conventional rotary tuner.

With the almost universal adoption of all-electronic tuning, remote control was spreading rapidly. In the past, remote control involved the use of expensive and cumbersome electric motors to turn knobs and shafts. The electronic tuner eliminates all moving parts and makes remote control truly practical and simple. For the calendar year 1979 it was estimated that fully 20 percent of all color TV sets would be sold with wireless remote control.

*"How about some sex and violence for poor ol' Granny?"*
(Drawing by Geo. Price; © 1977 The New Yorker Magazine, Inc.)

Every brand of color TV now was equipped with some form of automatic color system, generally divided into two types: VIR and autocolor. The first made use of the vertical interval reference (VIR) signal transmitted by networks and some stations along with the picture, designed as a digital guide to correct color. Although it was originally intended for the transmitter engineer to adjust his equipment for uniform color, some TV receivers were equipped with decoders to adapt this signal for keeping the color accurate in the home set. The other type of automatic color adjustment, autocolor, was designed more for consistency than for accuracy. Most autocolor systems kept fleshtones within the proper range (no more pink or purple faces) and kept color, brightness, and contrast constant. There was still considerable dispute among manufacturers as to which system was best. Some, to play it safe, included both systems in the same sets—autocolor taking over when there was no VIR signal.

The season just ended was one in which it was becoming obvious that television itself was just one of many developing video services—that the family TV set was becoming an all-purpose display device which can be programmed by a plurality of inputs. This seemingly was a tough pill for broadcasters to swallow; indeed, the networks were ignoring the potential competition—at least publicly—while privately hedging their bets by experimenting with the new video media.

The past season probably represented a major launching for various new graphic transmission services which are generally grouped under the generic names "teletext" and "viewdata." Both systems were capable of displaying a vast amount of constantly changing material on the home TV screen at the push of a button. Already in use in Europe, these services were being tested in the United States by various companies and groups. Teletext systems could be broadcast or carried on cable TV and use the vertical interval (between television pictures) to transmit digital information which may be converted into images at the press of a decoder button. Teletext could carry such material as constantly updated weather forecasts, road traffic conditions, TV logs, theater attractions and starting times, stock market reports, news, and sports scores. The viewer whose TV set was equipped with a decoder could call up any of this information on command by "punching up" the proper page number. Viewdata systems generally employed telephone lines to carry information to and from the TV set and gave the home (or office) viewer access to material from a centralized computer. A viewdata system, such as the one that has been tested by Great Britain's General Post Office, could offer literally hundreds of thousands of "pages" of information, while teletext usually was limited to a hundred pages or so. An industry-wide engineering group was studying various viewdata and teletext programs for recommendation to the FCC.

A very simple form of teletext has already been approved by the FCC and will go into use within the next year. This was "closed captioning" for the deaf. With the cooperation of ABC, NBC, and PBS, captions will appear on the TV screens of those who buy special television decoders or new sets equipped with built-in decoders. A nonprofit captioning institute will prepare captions for selected programs on those three networks. CBS has chosen not to participate in the program

"Eddie's family has a machine that watches TV for them."

*Newest RCA Satcom satellite, which is capable of distributing up to forty-eight television programs simultaneously through twenty-four "transponders." It is powered by silicon solar cells on two panels continuously pointed toward the sun.*

because it feels that decoding should be one function of a more elaborate teletext system and that the use of a decoding system will delay or prevent the introduction of more versatile teletext systems in this country.

If teletext and viewdata presented *potential* new uses of the television screen. there were several *actual* uses which already were competing with broadcast and cable TV for the viewer's time and attention. Video games were becoming more and more sophisticated, and in many cases were being upgraded into computers through the addition of typewriterlike keyboards and special cartridges or cassettes. Nearly a million programmable games—those with computer functions—have been sold in the last season, along with perhaps four or five million simpler "Pong"-type games.

The home computer was becoming a formidable product in its own right. Many so-called home computers were not true consumer products, but small-business or hobbyist instruments. Nevertheless, there was no question that there would soon be computers for the average consumer—and most of them would probably use the family television screen to display information. Some of these "computers" obviously were coming in through the back door—video games upgraded into computers. But others were being sold as home computers per se, with perhaps some game cartridges available for amusement. Either way you looked at it—computers becoming games or games becoming computers—this was a new category of video device, which competed with broadcasting for home time and attention.

Another contestant for the use of the home television screen was the video cassette recorder, or VCR. By the end of May 1979 nearly 800,000 were estimated to be in use in American homes, and total sales for 1979 were forecast at between 550,000 and 600,000. The home VCR was a triple-threat device: Its principle and most widely advertised use was as a time-shift machine, for recording broadcast or cable television programs for later viewing. Most home VCRs were equipped with timers for unattended recording—some could be set to record several programs up to a week in advance, turning on and off and changing channels automatically. When used with home color or monochrome cameras, the VCRs became electronic instant home-movie machines, making sound and vision tapes which were playable through the TV set. Battery-operated portable VCRs could be taken out of the home. In addition to their use with cameras, home VCRs could be used to show photographic home movie films and slides, as several companies were specializing in making transfers from film to video cassette for easy storage and showing on the TV set. The third use for the home VCR was the playing of prerecorded video cassettes. Here, motion pictures—either sold or rented—were the big favorites.

The latest home video device came on the market in a small way at the end of 1978: This was the video disc player, a color-picture-and-sound version of the phonograph. The first video disc system to reach the United States market was the Philips-MCA optical type, developed jointly by the electronics firm of Philips of the Netherlands and MCA Inc., the American movie, TV production, record, and talent company. Philips' American subsidiary Magnavox marketed the first player, while MCA's DiscoVision supplied the discs. Each twelve-inch disc was capable of playing—through a television set and stereo sound system if desired—up to two hours of prerecorded programming, one hour on each side. The video disc was an instant success in its first market, Atlanta, Georgia. By the end of May, a second market—Seattle—was added, and the system's proponents hope to be in nationwide distribution some time in 1980. The Magnavision players sold for $695 each at time of introduction (but an increase seemed likely) with records selling for up to $15.95 for recent movies.

Another video disc system was promised by RCA, which was expected to market it on a nationwide basis late in 1980 or early in 1981. RCA claimed its system would be simpler than the optical type and was aiming at a four-hundred-dollar price for the player, with discs scheduled for sale at about the same price as the DiscoVision records.

Both video disc systems provided excellent pictures and could employ stereophonic soundtracks. Other, mutually incompatible, video disc systems have been demonstrated by Matsushita Electric, Japan Victor Company, and Sony Corporation. Most American television set manufacturers and many program producers considered the video disc system the beginning of a major new mass-market entertainment medium, and, as such, to be far more significant than the video cassette recorder in terms of sales.

The season which ran from June 1978 through May 1979 saw the introduction of new technology which improved the transmission and reception of television programming. At the same time, it was a season which brought into focus many potential new home entertainment and communication services which eventually could provide greater diversity and programming choices for the viewer.

# TV
## AND BUSINESS

# BROADCAST NUMBERS GAME

by Anthony
Hoffman*

THE fierce battle among the networks for ratings is not merely a matter of pride or achievement. Ratings mean dollars to the television industry. Since ratings are the basis on which advertisers buy time, the dollars received from the sale of commercial time vary in proportion to ratings. In prime time, which has the largest audiences of any part of the day, even a difference of one rating point can mean a difference in annual sales of many millions of dollars. For example, in the fall season of 1978 the three networks charged approximately $6,100 per rating point for each minute sold. ABC maintained a 20.2 rating average versus an 18.2 for CBS. This difference of two-rating-points multiplied by $6,100 per rating point across 1,800 minutes of advertising for the fall season generated $22 million more in ad revenues for ABC than for CBS.

In addition, ABC derived a substantial bonus merely for being number one. Since a rating point represents 1 percent of the total American homes with television, its value *should* be the same regardless of which network delivered the audience. In practice, however, the competition to get commercial minutes on the number-one network is so intense that the leader can actually charge 5 percent to 10 percent more per rating point. Indeed, in 1978-79 it was ABC in the lead, so it earned the bonus. In the fall season of 1978, ABC was able to charge $6,680 per rating point for each minute sold, while NBC and CBS realized only $6,100. The bonus of $580-per-rating-point applied to the 1,800 minutes sold produced $21 million in extra revenue for being number-one in prime time. This was on top of the additional money derived from the greater value of the larger audience itself. These numbers are for prime time, but a similar effect is discernible in other dayparts, although the dollar figures are smaller.

Prime time represents about half of the revenues of the three networks and the dollar profits from that daypart are larger than any other; but measured by the percent margin on revenues, prime time is actually one of the least profitable dayparts due to the high costs of prime time programs. These costs have been boosted by three elements: (1) the current highly competitive environment in the industry; (2) the frequent cancellation of series; and (3) the overuse of specials. For many years the competitive environment in network television was very stable; ABC had no money and thus ran a perennial third; NBC was content to be in second place; and CBS, with the most talented programming executives and the biggest budgets, was the unopposed leader. When ABC turned the tables on the others in the fall of 1976, neither CBS nor NBC had enough new program concepts being tested and developed to allow wholesale replacement of failing series. The short-term solution to this problem was to acquire a large inventory of theatrical motion pictures to create high ratings in the nonseries periods. This had the effect of drastically increasing the prices paid for the use of top theatrical features. Although multimillion dollar deals for the use of a given picture were unusual a couple of years ago, purchases that did not amount to at least a couple of million were rare in 1978, with the top prices being paid for *Gone With the Wind* ($35 million),

PRECEDING PAGE: *Fred Silverman, President and Chief Executive Officer, National Broadcasting Company.*

*Anthony Hoffman is a vice-president of Bache, Halsey, Stuart, Shields, Inc., where he is a media and entertainment analyst.

*Jaws* ($25 million), and *Close Encounters* ($19 million). To be sure, these prices represent payments over a couple of years for multiple uses of these films and the annual package at any one network does not consist entirely of high-priced blockbusters. There is no question, however, that the average price per play has gone from about $500,000 four years ago to about $1.2 million this season. There are 14 network commercial minutes in a two-hour movie, and the average minute rate paid in the fall of 1978 was about $120,000 per minute. This would generate about $1.7 million in billings which would be reduced to $1.4 million after agency commissions and discounts. Thus each two-hour movie offers a profit potential of about $100,000 to $200,000 per hour. This forms an interesting contrast with the profit range typical of series.

The top-rated series in 1978-79 was ABC's "Three's Company," which cost advertisers about $210,000 per minute. Three minutes of advertising were sold per show by the network, which produced approximately $535,000 in revenues per show to ABC. Against these revenues ABC paid approximately $205,000 per show to the producer. So before any application of the show's share of general network overhead, "Three's Company" generated a gross profit of $330,000 per show in the fall season. Similar economics apply to the original episodes used in the winter. The economics change somewhat when the show goes into reruns after March. The price per minute drops to about 88 percent of the fall rate, thus generating total revenue of about $470,000 per show. But the only costs incurred by the network in the reuse of that episode is the payment of residuals to talent and the producers—normally around 20 percent of the production cost of the original episode. Thus the total cost for a rerun of "Three's Company" this season would be approximately $41,000. As a result each rerun of this series would produce a gross profit of $429,000, almost $100,000 more than the original.

This sounds fantastic, but unfortunately the large profits on a big winner like "Three's Company" are not indicative of the norm. On some hit shows the talent has negotiated special deals, guaranteeing them large cash payments for each show produced. The two lead actresses of "Laverne & Shirley" are reputed to be getting $75,000 per original episode. Since the studio passes most of this cost on to the network, "Laverne" cost ABC about $260,000 per episode last fall compared to the $215,000 for "Company." The longer a series runs as a hit, the more likely it is to involve special payments to talent. The long-running "All in the Family," the most expensive half-hour series this season, cost CBS about $290,000 per episode for this very reason.

Although everyone complains about rising costs, it is the level of advertising revenues that really determines the profitability of a network show. And, as we have seen on an overall basis, revenues depend on ratings. This point can be vividly demonstrated by contrasting the numbers for a failing series with the above numbers for successes. Take, for example, 1978's lowest-rated series, "Who's Watching the Kids," which was canceled after only nine episodes had been aired. "Kids" was only capable of realizing about $68,000 per minute or a total of $204,000 per show, barely enough to cover the production cost of $185,000, thus generating a loss after the application of a share of the administrative costs of the network. Theoretically, if these episodes were rerun, the cost would drop to $37,000, while revenues would decline to $180,000, creating a profit of $143,000 per show. Unfortunately, the episodes of relatively unsuccessful series are not rerun because the poor audience level pulls down the ratings of the shows which follow on that night, as well as hurting the weekly average.

Thus cancellation of a large portion of the regular prime-time schedule can have dramatic effects on costs. During the 1978-79 season, as in the previous season, the percentage of original episodes was abnormally high due to the failure of a large number of shows on NBC and CBS—thus eliminating reruns of successes. As the competitive environment brought the relative performance of the three networks closer together, the number of shows needing to be replaced declined, providing NBC and CBS with some relief on the cost side of the profit equation in prime time.

So far the discussion has centered on prime time, the most important daypart by far, but not the only one. To put the network business in perspective, it is instructive to review the following breakdown for the season.

## DAYTIME: MONDAY–FRIDAY

The second largest source of network revenue, weekday daytime, had very different economics than prime time. The cost of producing a *full week* (five) episodes of a half-hour daytime serial was about the same as *one half hour* of a prime-time series. The "soaps" were always shot on tape, often using facilities provided by the network, and the talent consisted of relative unknowns who were not able to command large fees for their appearances. The NAB code (a voluntary guideline

**Network Billings by Daypart**

| Daypart | Days of Week | Types of Shows | Revenues (Millions) | % of Total |
|---------|-------------|----------------|---------------------|-----------|
| Prime time | Mon.-Sun. | Series, miniseries, specials, movies | $1,952.6 | 47.6 |
| Daytime | Mon.-Fri. | Serials, game shows, comedy reruns | 833.7 | 20.3 |
| Sports | Mon.-Fri. | Sports, documentary | 618.5 | 15.1 |
| News | Mon.-Sun. | News reports | 286.7 | 7.0 |
| Late night | Mon.-Sun. | "Tonight," "Tomorrow," reruns of action series and movies | 213.9 | 5.2 |
| Kids' shows | Mon.-Fri. (CBS) Sat.-Sun. (All) | Cartoon and live action | 142.1 | 3.5 |
| Early morning | Mon.-Fri. | "Today," "Good Morning America," "CBS Morning News" | 53.3 | 1.3 |
| Other (political, etc.) | | | 4.3 | 0.1 |
| | | Total | $4,105.1 | 100.0 |

SOURCE: Broadcast Advertisers Reports, Inc.

of the National Association of Broadcasters) allowed more commercial minutes in daytime than in prime time and the networks generally sold six minutes per half hour. The average daytime show got ratings about one-third as large as a prime time show and because of the larger inventory of commercial time available, the cost per thousand households was lower. Thus a top daytime serial like "All My Children" brought in an average of $42,000 per minute (after commissions) in 1978, or around $1.25 million per week against production costs of around $250,000, indicating profit potential of about $1 million per week. At the other end of the spectrum, a relatively low-rated game show like "Hollywood Squares" might bring in only $220,000 per week. Although generally costing less than a serial to produce (game shows averaged about $200,000 per week), the profit was smaller.

Unlike prime time, there were on daytime programming almost no reruns. Thus with the exception of a couple of shows which offered reruns of old prime-time series, all daytime products were used only once. Nevertheless the three networks' daytime schedule, although accounting for only 20 percent of the total revenues, accounted for a substantially larger share of the profits. In the case of ABC and CBS during 1978-79, daytime profits as a percent of the total were probably in the 40 percent area; at NBC the percentage was a good deal higher due to heavy losses in prime time. Thus a series which is canceled after a few weeks greatly increases the ratio of original episodes to reruns in that particular time period but, as we have already seen, reruns offer the greatest profit potential.

Generally in the course of one season, a successful series used 24 original episodes (each repeated once) and was preempted (replaced by sports or specials) on four nights. Under successful conditions, the full 52-week complement would be 24 originals, 4 specials, and 24 reruns. Normally series cancellations were made at the end of the fall season (after 12 uses although more recently cancellations have been made after as few as 6), requiring that a new series with original episodes replace it. On the assumption that the failing series was also preempted twice in the initial 14 weeks, there would remain 38 weeks of the 52-week season to be filled. If 4 preemptions occurred in the last 38 weeks, 17 original episodes would be required (with 17 reruns) to fill the remaining 38 weeks. So the total for the season, when one series was canceled and replaced by a second show, would be 30 original episodes, 4 specials, and 18 repeats. If we assume that specials cost the same as the original episodes and many specials cost considerably more, and used a price of $200,000 per half hour for both, the total difference in cost over a 52-week season becomes meaningful:

| | Original Episodes | | Specials | | Reruns | | Total Cost |
|---|---|---|---|---|---|---|---|
| | No. | Cost | No. | Cost | No. | Cost | |
| Successful series | 24 | $4,800,000 | 4 | $800,000 | 24 | $960,000 | $6,560,000 |
| Failure after 9 uses | 30 | $6,000,000 | 4 | $800,000 | 18 | $680,000 | $7,480,000 |
| | | | | | Difference | | $ 920,000 |

## SPORTS

Analysis of sports as a daypart is impossible since it is a collection of individual events with widely varying revenues and costs. But one regularly scheduled sports event, "Monday Night Football," does allow profitability analysis. The average game ran 2 hours and 55 minutes allowing a total commercial load of 25 minutes. During the first 2 hours of each game, the network was limited to 7 commercial minutes per hour. But in the period which occurred after prime time, the allowable network commercial load rose to 12 minutes per hour. The average billed rate in the fall of 1978 was $85,000 per 30 second commercial; thus the average evening football game would bring in net revenues of about $3.6 million. Against this must be applied each game's share of the rights payments to the National Football League ($232 million over 4 years). With 20 games per season and payments of $58 million per year, the rights cost ABC $2.9 million per game. The addition of production costs of about $1.5 million per game raised the total costs to $4.4 million or $800,000 more than revenues. Why did they operate at a loss? The answer lies in what happens in years 2-4 of the contract.

Assuming productions costs grow 10 percent annually and total revenues grow 20 percent annually, the package becomes profitable in year 3.

**ABC NFL Football**

Per-Game Profitability Analysis (in Millions)

| | Year 1 | Year 2 | Year 3 | Year 4 | Total |
|---|---|---|---|---|---|
| Costs–Rights | $2.90 | $2.90 | $2.90 | $2.90 | |
| Production | 1.50 | 1.65 | 1.82 | 2.00 | |
| Total | $4.40 | $4.55 | $4.72 | $4.90 | |
| Revenues | 3.60 | 4.32 | 5.18 | 6.22 | |
| Profit (Loss) | $(0.80) | $(0.23) | $0.46 | $1.32 | $0.75 |

In the aggregate, sports represents a modest profit for all three networks, although it returns a relatively small percentage of sales generated.

## NEWS

For a variety of reasons, the three networks' news operations, based on *their* bookkeeping systems, consistently lost money. The main reason for this, many insiders believe, was to substantiate the networks' contention to the FCC and other regulatory authorities that the profits from entertainment programs subsidized the expenditures made in broadcasting the news. Thus for many years, networks set their news budgets predictably higher than expected revenues. In recent years the ability to provide live coverage of worldwide events via satellite forced all three to dramatically increase the number of remote units around the globe with a corresponding increase in operating costs. In view of this, the networks would like to increase the length of their evening news broadcasts to one hour, thereby deriving greater revenues to offset their largely fixed investment. Until such a move is accomplished (over the strong objections of the local stations with which the networks are affiliated), the three networks will continue to lose around $50 million annually.

## LATE NIGHT

The late-night time period has for years been dominated by NBC's "Tonight Show," due in large measure to the popularity of its host, Johnny Carson. In recent years, Carson has derived an ever-increasing salary, although serving as host on an ever-decreasing percentage of the broadcasts. Recently a dispute arose between Carson and NBC president Fred Silverman about the number of shows in which Carson would appear during the balance of his contract. At one point Carson was reported to have resigned, although subsequently he indicated his willingness to continue. At issue here was a very important profit center for NBC, whose performance in other dayparts leaves a considerable amount to be desired. On an annual basis during 1978, the "Tonight Show" brought in billings of about $61 million, or a net of about $1 million per week after discounts and commissions. Like daytime programs, the weekly production costs of an entire week of this 90-minute show is about the same as one 90-minute block of prime time ($300,-000). Add to this the payment of about $50,000 per week for Johnny Carson and other smaller payments for other regulars, and the total weekly program expense probably totals $400,000. The result of these mathematics is an annual profit of about $31 million before overhead items. Generally when Johnny does not host, the show's ratings drop by about 30 percent. If Johnny were to resign, experts have estimated a drop of about that magnitude. A linear reduction of 30 percent in revenues, even including the elimination of the $2.5 million paid annually to Johnny would cut the show's profits by about 42 percent, to around $18 million. Conversely if Johnny were to host nearly all of the shows, a 20 percent or so increase in revenues might result, producing $10 million more in profits. It was little wonder that Fred Silverman tried hard to get Johnny to step up his appearances, but it was equally obvious why the whole RCA-NBC organization went into cardiac arrest when he threatened to quit.

## KIDS' SHOWS

The three networks devoted a considerable number of hours every week to shows designed to entertain young audiences. But this effort was anything but philanthropic, since the profits derived from these shows represented a rather high percentage of sales. The majority of the kids' shows ran on Saturday morning, although CBS and ABC also had partial schedules on Sunday and CBS offered "Captain Kangaroo" every weekday morning. Historically the shows themselves have been largely animated cartoons although, in recent years, live-action shows became quite popular. But popularity is relative. In the case of the weekend morning fare, a rating level 2/3 as high as for the average adult afternoon program was considered good.

Over the years, the FCC and FTC have made numerous changes in the regulations concerning advertising for children. A ban on commercials for vitamin and other pharmaceutical products was implemented some years ago, as was a reduction in the allowable commercial load (now the lowest of any daypart). Throughout all of these changes, there were two factors which have preserved the high profits in kids' shows. First, the advertisers of products such as cereals, toys, candy, and gum have had no other part of the network day in which they could buy an audience made up almost entirely of kids. Second, the weekly production cost of a children's series was very small. The perception among those in television that animated programs were expensive (per minute of film) was correct. But the heavy reuse of the material in this daypart lowered the cost. Generally the networks tried to run each episode of a given series six times. Compared with live programs, the residuals for reuse were miniscule. Although some criticized this as exploiting the short memory span of the very young, actually the reverse was true;

kids enjoyed the repeat episodes as much as or even more than ones they had not seen before.

A top-rated 90-minute Saturday morning show like "Bugs Bunny/ Road Runner" brought CBS about $4.5 million in net revenues in 1978-79. This translated into about $90,000 per show. This total was applied to costs of about $50,000 per week. (Actual production costs of original episodes was much higher, but the high number of reruns kept the average low.) So over the course of a year that one series could contribute about $2 million in direct profit. Other less successful shows would make much lower contributions, but it was very unusual for a children's show on ABC or CBS to lose money.

## EARLY MORNING

One of the most interesting competitive battles between the networks over the last few seasons has been waged in the smallest daypart. NBC's stranglehold on this two-hour time period with its "Today" show has been challenged by ABC's "Good Morning America." (CBS elected to throw a news broadcast against the first hour of these two shows and then turned the last hour over to "Captain Kangaroo.") During 1978 the production costs of both "Today" and "GMA" were in the same general area, about $350,000 per week (or $18 million per year). But the difference in revenues meant a profit for one network and an almost equivalent loss for the other. The "Today" net revenues of about $23 million allowed NBC a $5 million profit, while the $12 million revenues for "GMA" produced a $6 million loss for ABC. Toward the end of the season "GMA" began achieving ratings almost equal to "Today," so 1979-80 may well see ABC's first profits in this daypart.

## TOTAL PROFITS

If profit projections for each show in the entire network schedule were prepared along the lines of the above analysis, the totals for each network would greatly exceed the actual profits reported annually to the FCC. This is because the analysis of each daypart ignores some of the other costs of doing business. One of the largest components of cost not considered above is the money paid to affiliated stations for carrying the networks' shows. During 1978-79, $303 million or 9.3 percent of the three networks' combined revenues was paid out to affiliates. In addition, the networks paid AT&T (and other carriers) about $90 million to carry signals to these affiliates as well as to bring programming from remote locations to the networks' central operations. And finally there was the general network and corporate overhead to cover the cost of network and corporate personnel, facilities, and materials (most programs are produced outside and thus very little of the network operating costs was included in direct program costs). Between the three networks there was over $300 million in "overhead" expenses to be deducted from the direct program profits.

After all these calculations have been made, the financial results of the three companies as reported to the FCC were as follows:

**Television Network Income Statements—FCC Basis**
(in millions)

| | 1978 | 1977 | 1976 | 1975 | 1974 | 1973 | 1972 |
|---|---|---|---|---|---|---|---|
| **ABC—** | | | | | | | |
| Revenues* | $1,110 | $918 | $708 | $510 | $478 | $436 | $405 |
| Expenses | 923 | 753 | 625 | 481 | 429 | 399 | 382 |
| Profits | $187 | $165 | $83 | $29 | $49 | $37 | $23 |
| Margin | 16.8% | 18.0% | 11.7% | 5.7% | 10.3% | 8.5% | 5.7% |
| **CBS—** | | | | | | | |
| Revenues | $952 | $843 | $725 | $596 | $563 | $497 | $459 |
| Expenses | 816 | 704 | 596 | 490 | 453 | 409 | 399 |
| Profits | $136 | $139 | $129 | $106 | $110 | $88 | $60 |
| Margin | 14.3% | 16.5% | 17.8% | 17.8% | 19.5% | 17.7% | 13.1% |
| **NBC—** | | | | | | | |
| Revenues | $903 | $820 | $684 | $568 | $505 | $471 | $407 |
| Expenses | 852 | 718 | 601 | 464 | 439 | 411 | 379 |
| Profits | $58 | $102 | $83 | $74 | $66 | $60 | $28 |
| Margin | 5.6% | 12.4% | 12.1% | 13.0% | 13.1% | 12.7% | 6.9% |
| **Industry—** | | | | | | | |
| Revenues | $2,965 | $2,581 | $2,118 | $1,674 | $1,546 | $1,405 | $1,271 |
| Expenses | 2,591 | 2,175 | 1,822 | 1,465 | 1,321 | 1,220 | 1,160 |
| Profits | $374 | $406 | $296 | $209 | $225 | $185 | $111 |
| Margin | 12.6% | 15.7% | 14.10% | 12.5% | 14.6% | 13.2% | 8.7% |

SOURCE: *TV Digest*
*As defined by the FCC: Time billings plus other sales less compensation to affiliates and commissions.

## AFFILIATE SWITCHES

Each network operates in partnership with its affiliated stations. Under ideal conditions, each network would have an affiliate in each of the country's 217 television markets. Unfortunately there were not enough frequencies available in many small markets to allow all three networks to have an affiliate. Generally the most successful network had the most affiliates and therefore covered the largest possible population. ABC's surge to number one produced a corresponding desire to switch to ABC on the part of many NBC and CBS affiliates in these one- and two-station markets. The other networks resorted to higher-than-usual payments to these stations to persuade them to stay. Although the press has expended a great deal of coverage on the switches of network affiliation, as a practical matter no one change can have a discernible effect on the ratings and, in total, it would be unlikely that all of the change would add more than 3 percent to ABC's ratings.

## THE IMPORTANCE OF FRED SILVERMAN

A shock wave, registering about 9.5 on the Richter Scale, hit the industry in early 1978 when it was announced that Fred Silverman, network program chief at ABC, would be moving to third-place NBC with the title of president. Only two years before Fred had left CBS to join third-place ABC just before its dramatic rise to first place in the prime-time sweepstakes. Fred's salary ($1 million per year) plus the scope of his new responsibilities at NBC (TV network, owned TV stations, radio stations, and network) were somewhat mind-boggling in view of his relatively narrow experience (television program development) in his 2 years at ABC and 15 years at CBS. It took but a few days for the trade press to begin dissecting the legend of "Freddie the Great." ABC personnel were quick to point to the programming successes that Fred had not been involved in. Others in the industry predicted a short tour for Fred as NBC president, in expectation that nothing positive could happen to NBC's prime-time schedule for several seasons.

In reality, a number of factors contributed to ABC's dramatic turnaround in the fall of 1976. By far the most important of them was the unique synergy between ABC's historic emphasis on programs designed to secure a youthful audience and a change implemented that fall in the network program policies which created the "family viewing hour." Originally proposed by then CBS President Arthur Taylor, the family-viewing-hour code purged the portion of the prime-time schedule before 9:00 P.M. New York time (8:00 P.M. central and mountain time zones) of programs with "mature" or violent themes. Ironically this scheduling restriction proved far more beneficial to ABC than CBS. Most of CBS's ratings strength was in comedy, but most involved themes allegedly unsuitable for viewing before 9:00 P.M., while ABC's quest for the young had led to the development of comedies with a definite juvenile appeal ("Happy Days," "Laverne & Shirley," "Welcome Back, Kotter," and "Barney Miller"). Thus ABC was able to dominate the 8:00-9:00 P.M. period with innocuous comedies and then hit hard at 9:00 P.M. with violent dramatic shows and movies. CBS, with no tested program concepts which went after the juvenile audience, was left at the post.

Thus those who attributed ABC's meteoric rise to factors other than Fred Silverman were closest to the truth. Nevertheless, Fred is the medium's most gifted programmer, and NBC could eventually benefit immensely from the association, although a dramatic reversal of NBC's uncompetitive position appeared unlikely before the fall of 1980.

## THE SALES PROCESS

The three television networks sell their commercial time to advertisers well in advance of the actual air date. In fact they generally announce their schedules in April for the coming new shows of the season (beginning in September). Once the shows are announced, the advertisers and their ad agencies develop elaborate forecasts of the ratings to be generated by every show. Armed with these projections, they then begin to negotiate with the networks for advertising time for the full 52-week broadcast season. Usually by the end of May, several large clients have completed their "buys," and by the end of June, 50 percent to 70 percent of the total prime-time schedule is usually sold. But the 1978 "up-front" selling season was quite different due to the impending arrival of Fred Silverman in July. (ABC held Fred to the full term of his contract, which expired in July, 1978, and legally prevented him from communicating with NBC until after that date.) The industry expected Fred to radically revise the NBC schedule once on the scene, and so the "up-front" sales progress was slow.

In fact, once aboard NBC, Fred did rather little to the schedule, canceling one show and moving a couple to new time periods, none of which particularly pleased the buyers. But the unusual delay in actual commitments and the uncertainty over NBC changes allowed lots of time for the buyers to haggle over prices, resulting in the smallest increment (over the prior year) in several years. The industry had become accustomed to rapid escalation in prices for prime-time commercial minutes; prices rose 28 percent in 1976 and 18 percent in 1977, but only 12 percent in 1978. As the year progressed, it became apparent that the networks sold out at too low a level. Sales of commercial time placed directly on TV stations (called spot time) rose more than 20 percent. The loss of advertising dollars by the networks was particularly painful because they derived no cost reduction from the lost sales, so the lost revenues meant a corresponding reduction in profits. Indeed network profits were down nearly 8 percent in calendar 1978.

# WHO OWNS THE NETWORKS?

by Peter L. Brosnan*

A bill designed to replace the Communications Act of 1934 raised a storm of criticism from both the public and the broadcasters themselves. The aim of the Communications Act of 1978 was to narrow regulation of broadcasting and allow "market forces" to govern the industry. It would also replace the Federal Communications Commission with a new policy unit of the executive branch to be called the National Telecommunications Agency.

Critics of the FCC have often charged that on important issues it has tended to side with broadcasters at the expense of the public. They feared that the new agency will do even less to safeguard public interest, while maintaining the status quo of the three-network monopoly. Broadcasters, for their part, feared that state and local governments will step in to fill the void left by the narrower scope of the new bill with their own rules and regulations, thus creating a nightmare of varying, hence conflicting, local requirements. Both sides have raised valid points that deserve much discussion before the bill becomes law, but one issue was not addressed by either the bill or its critics, and it is the issue that may prove most important in the context of the First Amendment.

*Peter Brosnan is writing his graduate thesis at the University of Southern California on the corporate history of broadcasting networks. This essay was adapted from an article which appeared in *The Nation*, November 25, 1978.

Ownership of American news media in general, and broadcast media in particular, became for the most part concentrated in the hands of a few large corporate conglomerates. Among the largest of these were the three networks, but it was less often noted that their ownership has, in turn, become concentrated in a relatively small number of financial institutions, especially banks, which often controlled the majority of voting stock. The full extent to which these institutions dominated the broadcasting industry was difficult to determine, because various loopholes in federal laws made possible a complex system of front accounts and disguised ownership. However, a potential for conflict of interest and outright control of the media existed. Several private and Congressional studies have called attention to the possibility, but it was understandable that they have been given little publicity. No action resulted.

Media critic Ben H. Bagdikian has written: "One of the greatest exposés of all time was *The New York Times* destruction of Boss Tweed's gang, accomplished after the publisher, George Jones, in 1871, turned down an offer of $5 million to suppress the stories. This was pretty crude. Today a syndicate of lawyers and brokers could use the money to buy an offending news medium, not just knock out one series of articles." The danger Bagdikian described bears an unsettling resemblance to the situation in the TV industry of the '70s. Concentrated ownership may be tolerable in manufacturing or transportation, but concentrated ownership of communications media threatens the free exchange of information and opinion vital to a democratic society. When that ownership is in the hands of banks, with heavily vested interests, there is a good reason for alarm.

Current FCC procedure required the networks, along with all other FCC licensees, to file an annual ownership report with the commission. It must list every owner of more than 1 percent of the outstanding stock in the corporation, that is, the network, and must be available for public inspection. Aside from a few large individual owners, most of the listed stockholders were financial institutions. On the surface, the reports seemed to present accurate summaries of network ownership, but that was not the case.

By using cumulative investment accounts, known as nominees, banks and other large stockholders could hide the full extent of their holdings. A nominee is basically a technique of convenience, a discretionary agreement with an underlying owner by which the trustee (the bank) votes the stocks assigned to the trust, thereby exercising control since it holds the shares in trust agreement. A nominee owning less than 1 percent of the stock in a network need not have reported its holdings to the FCC. Thus, by spreading their holdings over a number of such accounts, banks could conceal the full extent of their interest in the corporation from the FCC and the public.

A 1973 Senate report on disclosure of corporate ownership, issued by senators Edmund Muskie and Lee Metcalf, concluded: "The holdings of institutional investors, especially banks, are often hidden from view of regulators and the public through use of multiple nominees. . . . The consequence . . . is *a massive coverup of the extent to which holdings of stock have become concentrated in the hands of very few institutional investors, especially banks*" [italics added]. On the subject of media stocks, the report noted: "The potential implications of concentrated ownership by a group of financial institutions in the broadcasting and publishing industries are so great as to merit special attention. These problems would be potentially more intense if the same group of financial intermediaries held a significant proportion of the outstanding voting stock of two or more large competing companies." Several institutions did indeed hold stock in more than one network, and at least five (Chase Manhattan, Prudential, Chemical Bank, Citibank, and Bankers Trust, which among them hold 15 percent of ABC, 12 percent of CBS, and 8 percent of RCA/NBC) owned shares in all three.

In addition to holding stock, many of these same institutions were agents or trustees for the debentures, or debts, of the networks. This arrangement placed a great deal of power in the hands of a few institutions, since in order to assume control, it was not necessary to own an outright majority of stock. When the shares in a company were widely held, control of a relatively small block of stock by a single institution, or by a few who are like-minded, assured disproportionately large influence within the company. The House Banking and Currency Subcommittee and the Securities and Exchange Act of 1932 (as amended in 1970) considered 5 percent (in some cases as little as 1 percent or 2 percent) to be sufficient for great influence, if not outright control.

This fact was recognized long ago by the FCC, which originally limited a bank's ownership to no more than 1 percent of the stock in a given broadcasting company. In 1972, however, the FCC raised the limit to 5 percent. It did so because so many banks were violating the 1 percent rule that, to comply with it, nineteen of them would have been forced to divest themselves of nearly $1 billion in stock. In other words, since the banks would not obey the law, the law had to be changed. Actually, FCC rules now permitted banks to own far more than 5 percent, provided they submit a "disclaimer of intent to control," a meaningless legal formality. They had, in effect, been given carte blanche to control the nation's broadcasting companies.

The banks, of course, denied any interest in controlling network policy, but the question was whether, as a society, we need or should permit the risk of such abuse. Those who argued that no action need be taken until there was abundant evidence of abuse fooled themselves. As former FCC Commissioner Nicholas Johnson pointed out: "Abuse is very hard to show, and there is no institution in our society that regularly examines the functioning of the mass media to determine whether these abuses occur. . . . Legitimate editorial judgment to include, alter, or omit information is almost impossible to distinguish from similar decisions motivated by corporate economic self-interest."

Print journalism long acknowledged its responsibility to place public interest ahead of maximum profit. That the networks had no such policy was apparent to any observer of the ongoing ratings wars, current programming, or profit figures. Simply by assuming ever greater profits from the networks, stockholding banks exerted a demonstrable influence over programming. As "bottom-line" consciousness increased, and the business school graduates with their demographics and pocket-calculator mentalities gained more and more say on the choice of material, certain types of programs just didn't get on the air.

Documentaries, or responsible, in-depth news reports, for example, usually earned poor ratings and, if controversial, risked loss of sponsors or audiences. Dollar sagacity, then, dictated their omission from seasonal schedules. Thus, in a very real way, bottom-line responsibility to stockholders became a form of censorship.

A look at 1977 ownership figures for the three major networks revealed the extent of the financial community's interest in, and potential influence over, these companies.

*RCA/NBC.* Since the National Broadcasting Company was a wholly owned subsidiary of RCA Corp., ownership reports filed for individual NBC stations reflected the ownership figures of the parent company. According to the 1977 report for KNBC-TV, only four holders of record (Chase Manhattan, St. Louis Union Trust, Merrill Lynch, and one individual) owned more than 1 percent of the stock of RCA. Together, they controlled nearly 10 percent of the stock outstanding. This, to be sure, placed a controlling interest in the hands of a relative few, but it was a tip-of-the-iceberg figure for RCA, whose ownership information has proved misleading in the past.

In 1972, for example, RCA told the FCC that only six stockholders owned more than 1 percent of its stock, holding a total of 13.7 percent of stock outstanding. That same year, the Muskie/Metcalf investigative group obtained from RCA a list of its "Thirty Top Stockholders." It included a number of nominee accounts, each of which held less than 1 percent of stock. From this list emerged a picture of RCA ownership considerably different from what the corporation had reported to the FCC, a picture which exposed the glaring deficiencies in the FCC's ownership reporting procedures.

Not listed, for example, was First National Bank of Chicago, which held a full 2 percent of RCA stock spread over three nominee accounts, each having less than 1 percent. Similarly, First National City Bank divided its 1.1 percent of RCA stock between two nominees. Chase Manhattan, through its nominee Egger & Co., held an additional unreported 0.5 percent, and Chemical Bank, with 250,000 shares, also avoided disclosure.

In total, the "Thirty Top Stockholders" list showed that nearly 25 percent of RCA was controlled by nine banks and a handful of insurance companies and individuals. And this, too, was only a partial figure, based as it was on a list of only thirty stockholders in a corporation with more than 250,000 stockholders. A further study, made in 1973 by The Network Project, a Columbia University research group, concluded that "30 percent of RCA voting stock is controlled by eleven banks and a handful of investment and insurance companies, whose ownership is spread over a large number of (nominee) accounts."

*ABC.* The history of the American Broadcasting Company was somewhat different from that of its sister networks, a fact reflected in stockholder figures. RCA and CBS started up in the 1920s and were for many years tightly held companies. ABC was created in 1944 when the Justice Department forced RCA to divest itself of one of its two networks, the Red and the Blue. E. J. Noble, the Life-Savers tycoon, bought the Blue network for $8 million, and it became ABC. Four years later, the company made a public offering of 500,000 shares of stock, which sold out at $9 a share in four hours. In following years, ABC became an attractive investment and was soon far more dominated by financial institutions than CBS or RCA.

In 1978-79, with almost 18 million shares of stock held by more than 16,000 shareholders, nearly 80 percent of ABC was held by a relative handful of banking interests.

*CBS.* The stock of Columbia Broadcasting System was generally assumed to be widely held, with nearly 28 million shares in the hands of 38,000 shareholders. However, according to the 1977 ownership report, eight banks, four funds, and three members of the board of directors owned nearly 35 percent—an unchallengeable controlling interest. Further figures from *Vicker's Guides* to bank trusts, insurance companies, and investment companies showed that about two hundred financial institutions—roughly 0.5 percent of CBS shareholders—controlled 62.66 percent of CBS stock. Again, as with RCA, this should be considered a partial figure since further amounts were likely held in nominee accounts of less than 1 percent.

In 1973 the Muskie/Metcalf group found that 14 percent of CBS was controlled by Chase Manhattan Bank, which was, of course, the cornerstone of the Rockefeller financial group, with David Rockefeller as chairman and president. ("Does CBS Have a Friend at Chase Manhattan?" *Variety* asked in a headline when the report was issued.) According to the latest ownership report, Chase now owned less than 1 percent, although there was reportedly much more in small nominee accounts. *Vicker's Guide* reported that Chase had 1.19 percent of CBS in its trust department. It is worth noting that Chase and the other Rockefeller institutions were among the largest holders of network stock, with substantial interests in all three networks.

What made this interesting, if not ominous, was the publication of *Crisis of Democracy,* a report on the "governability of democracies" to David Rockefeller's Trilateral Commission. In a section, "Restoring a Balance Between Government and Media," the report complained that "the press has taken an increasingly critical role toward government and public officials." To remedy the situation "*significant measures are required* to restore an appropriate balance between the press, the government, and other institutions in society . . . there are obviously important [First Amendment] rights to be protected, but the broader interests of society and government are also at stake" [italics added]. The report then called for legislation to "regulate" the press, such as assuring government "the right and ability to withhold information at the source. . . . The courts should consider moving promptly to reinstate the law of libel as a necessary and appropriate check upon the abuses of power by the press. Journalists should develop their own standards . . . the alternative could well be regulation by the government." Or regulation by the stockholders?

To be sure, broadcasting was not the only industry in which the market forces of the past 20 years have encouraged a heavy concentration of ownership; it existed as well in manufacturing, transportation, and utilities. But as Joe Saltzman, veteran broadcaster and producer, now head of the broadcasting department at the School of Journalism, University of Southern California, said: "The concentration of such power is frightening in any American business and it is critical in the broadcasting industry."

Until now there unfortunately has been little research in this area and little pressure for new laws for regulation of ownership. One course of action might be to return to the original 1 percent ownership limit for banks. Should such disinvestiture prove impractical, an alternative might be to separate ownership and control, that is, to prohibit financial institutions from voting their stocks. That remedy has already been proposed by Robert Soldofsky, a professor at the University of Michigan's School of Business. The debate over the Communications Act of 1978 could provide the perfect forum for an open and overdue discussion of these issues. The opportunity may not come again.

# TV AND THE
# PUBLIC INTEREST

# WHOSE INTEREST? WHAT PUBLIC?

### by Scott Robb*

THE popular conception has been that television in the United States has been largely a two-city enterprise—Hollywood and New York. The vast majority of programs which found their way onto network schedules were produced on Hollywood soundstages. The network scheduling decisions, as well as the multibillion-dollar advertising commitments which supported the programs, were made in office suites between Madison and Sixth avenues in midtown Manhattan. This, of course, was not the full story.

The television industry has been in large part a creature of the public policy which owed its existence to the issuance of federal licenses permitting local stations to transmit television signals within their communities. Thus the business of broadcasting has involved far more than rating points, costs-per-thousand, sitcoms, newsbreaks, and the like. A key element of the service aspects of the industry has been firmly rooted in law, regulation, policy, and rule, all derived from the so-called public interest. While Hollywood produced and New York bought, Washington watched.

It is true that television could not operate without producers, agencies, and sponsors. However, it is just as true that the industry has not operated without lawmakers, bureaucrats, and judges, all seeking to set out a coherent policy governing the operation of television. Such has been the case since the earliest days of broadcasting.

The scorecard of regulations was large and expanding. Congress legislated the necessary policy and the White House enacted it. From there, the Federal Communications Commission (FCC) administered and, in case of dispute, it fell to the courts to set down a decision. Throughout this process, the ultimate product of broadcasters—which is programming—became a commodity protected under the Constitution's free-speech guarantees. Therefore, whatever the public interest might seem to dictate to the Congress, Commission, or courts, the broadcasters, both commercial and public, must be accorded full First Amendment rights.

The television industry has been actually governed by a broad framework of federal statutes, Commission regulations, and court decisions which loosely defined standards of conduct expected of broadcast licensees. The continued evolution of the industry, brought about in large part by ever-changing technology, has created increased interest in the application of regulatory policies. Television licensees, for example, must be concerned with the manner in which the newly emerging video forms (cable, pay cable, subscription television, multipoint distribution systems [MDS]) comply with existing federal policy. An altered Commission rule, or new policy, a revised court interpretation, and a myriad of similar factors formulated and often reformed the competitive structure of the television industry.

The 1978-79 season saw yet another upswing in activity related to the setting of new and revised regulatory policy. The expansion of newly developing video forms combined with the introduction of tech-

PRECEDING PAGE: *The Carnegie Commission at a press conference on January 29, 1979 (standing: Chairman McGill; front row, left: Alan Pifer, president of the Carnegie Corporation).*

*Scott H. Robb is a communications attorney who practices law in New York City. He is a senior partner in the firm of Robb and Kuhns and is the author of *Television/Radio Age Communications Course Book.*

nical innovations, such as the communications satellite, have focused increased attention on public-interest policy considerations.

What follows is an outline of some of the vital regulatory issues of the past season. Some of the items won their way into the headlines of the daily press, but many others went unnoticed. However, all will in one way or another have an impact on the type, quality, and even quantity of the television service presently available throughout the country.

## A NEW ACT TO FOLLOW: CONGRESS REWRITES COMMUNICATIONS LAW

The broadcasting industry (including all interstate communications facilities from telegraph to satellites) has been regulated under a statute first signed into law in 1934. Thus the United States television industry has been governed by a law which does not contain a single reference to the video medium. As things have developed, the courts and the FCC have had little trouble in extending the basic precepts of the law to new communications media such as television, cable TV, and pay TV.

Over the past season, however, there has been growing interest on Capitol Hill in backing plans to bring the basic communications statute up to date. From the first word of the possible new law, much opposition has been voiced by industry representatives fearing the loss of comfortable and protective legislation. The leading argument by industry lobbyists has cited the track record of the United States Constitution which they noted has been around from the first days of the Republic with only minor change. A number of legislators in both houses who did see an immediate need for updating the nation's communications legal framework during the first half of 1979 offered a series of detailed proposals to change the existing rules.

While there was significant interest in Congress favoring the adoption of a new telecommunications law, there developed a difference of opinion as to how extensive the rewritten language should be. On the House side, Congressman Lionel Van Deerlin (D-Cal.), who chaired the House Communications Subcommittee, has actively pushed for a top-to-bottom rewrite of the entire Communications Act for the past two years. On March 29, 1979, Van Deerlin, along with congressmen James Collins (R-Tex.) and James Broyhill (R-N.C.) introduced a bill (H.R. 3333) which proposed an extensive overhauling of the existing law. Among the changes would be the immediate removal of federal regulation of the radio industry, and a gradual "deregulation" of the television industry over a 10-year period. Both of these changes reflected the concept that the competition among stations in the marketplace—rather than government agency rules and regulations—should be sufficient to shape the workings of the broadcast industry.

As a trade-off for the removal of the existing regulatory framework which broadcasters now face, the bill would impose a so-called spectrum-use fee (or type of tax) to be paid out of broadcasting revenues to the federal government. The broadcasting industry would be called

"*And now Bob Ferguson, with an analysis of our reporting staff's 'state of mind' during the preparation of tonight's news.*"
(Drawing by Dana Fradon; © 1979 The New Yorker Magazine, Inc.)

upon to pay a share of earnings (in addition to normal business taxes) in return for the privilege to use the public airwaves for commercial purposes. Needless to say, this aspect of the proposal met with much opposition from the industry. Still another provision of the House bill would remove regulations from the cable television industry and restructure (and rename) the FCC. One other proposal would permit public broadcasting stations to sell a limited amount of advertising time to help support their operations.

The general view in the Senate was that what was needed was not a full-scale rewriting of the existing legislation, but rather a more limited measure to update the current law. Senator Ernest Hollings (D-S.C.), chairman of the Communications Subcommittee, and Howard Cannon (D-Nev.) submitted a bill (S.611) which proposed a number of restricted changes in the existing communications law. The goal of radio and television deregulation was proposed under the bill, as was the adoption of a spectrum-use fee. An even more limited proposal was introduced by senators Barry Goldwater (R-Ariz.) and Harrison Schmitt (R-N.M.), who suggested the adoption of a limited-use tax to be paid by broadcasters.

Both the House and Senate Communications Subcommittees began the long legislative process (draft legislation, committee hearings, reports, committee bills) to bring the nation's communications law into step with the 1980s. It was expected that this activity would remain a high priority in the next year. While the sponsoring congressmen and committees were committed to moving the legislation with dispatch, the 1980 elections would no doubt alter the best-formulated plans.

## NEW RULES FOR THE SAME:
## FCC STUDIES THE NETWORKS

When Congress first passed laws to regulate the broadcasting industry in the late 1920s, an effort was made to bring the networks under the direct supervision of the federal government. This initial effort fell victim to the network's lobbying power, setting a precedent which continues to this day. Thus while the individual broadcast stations—both radio and television—that served the nation had to secure federal licenses in order to operate, the three commercial networks which provided so much of the programming, including the network news shows, needed no such permits.

Over the years many attempts have been made to alter the regulatory framework to give the FCC a substantial supervisory role over the networks. The concern was voiced that the growing power and influence of the network organizations endangered the independence of the individual stations. The facts clearly underscored the danger of network domination.

The typical television station maintaining network affiliation received more than 70 percent of its program material from the network. Under this arrangement, the station received a majority of its programming and a share of the network advertising revenues for clearing the programming. In addition, the local station was also able to sell advertising messages during station breaks, within the network programs, at high prices, reflecting the audiences drawn to the station by network programming.

The business arrangement had its advantages for both the network and the station. The network needed ready access to television audiences throughout the nation to sell to national advertisers. In return for delivering audiences, the stations received an extensive programming service, a share of national advertising revenues, and a means of attracting local advertisers to support the station.

However, the system did have its defects. One industry figure voicing opposition to the dangers of network power was Donald McGannon, chairman of Group W, the broadcast division of Westinghouse Corporation. Over the years, McGannon's efforts brought changes in the operations of the network companies. For example, largely as a result of his extensive campaigning, the FCC adopted a rule limiting the number of hours of network programming which can be carried by affiliated stations during prime time. The rule, called the "Prime Time Access Rule," restricted network schedules to three hours each night. While the rule had the positive effect of opening a new market for program producers to fill the void left by the network companies, the resulting programming efforts have been far from inspiring. Nearly every viewer grew familiar with the early evening programming selection of game shows and animal anthologies which owed their existence to the Prime Time Access Rule.

McGannon continued his antinetwork efforts as he sought to have the FCC review the commercial practices and programming production activities of the networks. While the McGannon petition has been on the FCC agenda for the past three years, real activity on the part of the Commission staff was seen during the past 12 months. The objective of this investigation was to gain an understanding of the inner workings of the three networks which controlled the United States television industry.

A special staff has been recruited to find out how networks buy and produce programs, sell and schedule advertising, and secure and compensate their affiliated stations. It clearly represented the most comprehensive study of the network machinery ever conducted by the federal government.

While the scope and general thrust of the special inquiry has been defined by the Commission, the possible results cannot be known. A number of observers have cautioned that a new set of federal rules directly regulating network practices could fundamentally alter the shape of the American television industry. Time and again, the staff directors of the inquiry have noted that there was no such restructuring objective. However, it was clear that this extensive proceeding would have an impact upon a number of the business practices of the network organizations.

Questions were raised concerning the manner in which the networks compensated the affiliated stations for advertising carried on network programs. In addition, problems were cited relating to the expansion of the network schedules (which now stretch from sunrise until 1:00 or 2:00 A.M.), and the need for affiliates to review programs prior to broadcast. And of course, the entire process of acquisition of network programs was also being dissected by federal investigators.

Thus, while the FCC's network inquiry was not launched with the objective of altering the shape and face of network television, substantial changes were coming and will continue to come—some, no doubt, as a result of the FCC's inquiry.

## AN OFFER THAT MIGHT BE REFUSED: FTC'S CHILDREN'S ADVERTISING INQUIRY

Controversy still continued over the use of commercials to support programs directed to young audiences. A proceeding was underway at the Federal Trade Commission (FTC) to study various factors related to the airing of commercials directed at children. Among the proposed trade regulation rules was an outright ban on all television ads directed at children too young to realize that they were the targets of a sales message. (The FTC staff was left to determine what children might come within this ban.) Further, an outright ban was sought on all ads for "highly sugared" products where the commercials were directed to children under the age of 12. An additional proposal would require all advertisers of highly sugared products to support public service ads designed to encourage good eating habits in children.

The thrust of the FTC proceeding reflected the concern that children constitute a special audience in need of protection against the influences of television advertising. Several health questions were also involved. Studies showed that diets containing large quantities of sugar and sugar products could be detrimental to a child's general health condition and could cause serious dental problems. The FTC staff proposed that the advertising of highly sugared products should be limited.

A coalition of advertising agencies, food processing companies, candy companies, toy manufacturers, psychologists, nutritionists, and

*"So what if the First Amendment does go? We still have
twenty-five more."*
(Drawing by Dana Fradon; © 1979 The New Yorker Magazine, Inc.)

of course television networks and local stations was organized to attack nearly every aspect of the FTC proposal. The common "industry" position charged violation of constitutional free-speech guarantees. It rejected the theory that restricted advertising would reduce the consumption of sugared products and questions the hypothesis that children were unable to distinguish between commercials and program material.

Industry officials were joined by certain interest groups in opposing the FTC action. The American Civil Liberties Union, for one, went on record in opposition to the full range of FTC proposals. The ACLU concluded that the proposed rules seeking to limit the content of advertising were a violation of First Amendment free speech protections under the Constitution. Most public interest groups, however, disagreed with the ACLU position.

During the season, the FTC held a number of fact-finding hearings to assess the need and impact of its proposed rule. These hearings produced a mountain of data on the question of children's television advertising.

As the fact-finding continued, the affected industries began to respond with various proposals for changes in prevailing policies. For example, ABC announced plans to reduce the amount of advertising carried on its Saturday morning children's programs by nearly 25 percent over the next two years. In addition, ABC introduced a plan to insert five-second "separators" between Saturday morning program material and commercials. The adoption of this policy followed the development of study data showing that certain young viewers could not distinguish between television programs and commercials.

Both NBC and CBS rejected ABC's plan to reduce commercial time in Saturday morning programs. CBS said there was no evidence that the presentation of advertising has harmed young viewers. Furthermore, the network worried that the voluntary cutbacks of advertising time, for whatever reason, might lead to similar demands for advertising limitations in other parts of the network schedule.

The result of industry testimony was growing speculation that any final FTC action would fall far short of the proposed general ban on children's advertising. One popular theory held that the agency's probable action would take the form of a policy directive requiring industry-financed public service messages dealing with nutrition. It was widely thought that such a move would avoid a Constitutional test in court.

There have also been opposition voices on Capitol Hill. Senator Lowell Weicker (R-Conn.), a member of the Senate Appropriations Subcommittee which administered the FTC budget, repeatedly opposed an advertising ban. Weicker felt that the rule would violate First Amendment rights of advertisers. Representative Mark Andrews (R-N.D.), whose responsibilities parallel those of Senator Weicker's on the House side, also went on record in opposing the FTC proceeding.

As a result of the increasingly complex nature of the FTC's children's advertising inquiry, the ultimate decision will most likely be voted on by the full membership of the Commission in careful coordination with Congress.

## THE FUTURE ACCORDING TO CARNEGIE II:
## THE RESTRUCTURING OF PUBLIC BROADCASTING

Fourteen years ago, the Carnegie Corporation founded a special study to determine the future course of noncommercial broadcasting in the United States. The study produced the Carnegie Commission Report which charted a new organizational form for public television. Among its innovations was the establishment of the Corporation for Public Broadcasting (CPB) to coordinate the funding and expansion of public broadcasting facilities, and the founding of the Public Broadcasting System to function as the central programming organization for local stations.

Changing needs and the growing complexity of public broadcasting led to the establishment of a second study commission (Carnegie II) in 1977 under the chairmanship of William J. McGill, president of Columbia University. Over a two-year period, the Commission undertook a complete review of the functioning of the noncommercial broadcasting system. The objective was to study its programming, facilities, funding, and other operational requirements, and to analyze future needs as affected by such factors as the shifting to satellite distribution of programming. The result was the drafting of a blueprint outlining the proposed future of public television. The report was released in late January 1979.

Among the recommendations was the establishment of a new, nonprofit Public Telecommunications Trust to replace CPB and to function as the principal policy planning and evaluation agency in public broadcasting. The trustees drawn from presidential appointments would administer the spending of all federal funds earmarked for public television. In addition, the group proposed the creation of a Program Services Endowment to coordinate the underwriting of television and radio productions, programming services, and related research.

The Commission also addressed the issue of funding, which is the key problem facing public broadcasting. The study proposed a marked increase in the federal funding of public broadcasting to reach the $1 billion level by 1985. Under the plan, public broadcasting stations would receive one dollar in federal funds for every $1.50 raised locally. The Program Endowment would receive one-half of the total federal funds provided to the stations, and the Public Telecommunications Trust would receive funding through direct appropriations from Congress. Support funding for the increased spending levels would in part be provided by the establishment of a spectrum-use fee to be paid by broadcasters and other parties utilizing the public airwaves.

In addition, Carnegie II members focused on the continuing conflict between the goals of local public broadcasting stations, and the objectives of the national programming organizations. Much attention has been given to balance funding grants to support local and national programming projects. Panel members took the position that the availability of satellite interconnection facilities will in part reduce the allocation conflicts as new national and regional station groups develop. The extensive CPB satellite interconnection system now in place permits simultaneous distribution of programs to variable configurations of stations. It was thought that the flexibility and low cost of satellite distribution will have a direct impact on the type and number of programs offered within the system.

The Carnegie Commission submitted its recommendations in a four-hundred-page report. The recommendations were expected to shape the debate in Congress over the need to revamp the Communications Act of 1934. In addition, the administration stated that it would carefully consider the need for proposing specific legislative recommendations to achieve the objectives of the Carnegie II Report.

Whatever the course chosen, it appeared that the conclusions of the Carnegie Commission would provide a useful guide to future policy discussions and planning.


## THE WIRED NATION, ONE STEP CLOSER: THE DEREGULATION OF CABLE TV

Since the early 1950s the cable television industry tried to secure a foothold in the country's multibillion-dollar media industry. From the outset, television station owners and the networks sought to restrict the operations of the cable industry. FCC regulations largely operated to the advantage of the television industry in confronting the cable operators with mountains of federal paperwork, permits, consents, and other red tape. Furthermore, most cable systems had to contend with local regulatory agencies from town franchising committees to state utilities commissions.

Through this maze of rules and regulations, the cable industry continued to expand, though often at a reduced timetable. In early 1979, however, a glimmer of light was seen as the FCC announced its intention to eliminate two cumbersome regulations which the cable industry has long regarded as substantial obstacles to its expansion.

One regulation was the FCC's "syndicated exclusivity" rule that allowed local television stations within a 35-mile radius of a cable system a virtual monopoly on the use of syndicated reruns of television programs. The rule gave the TV station the rights to a syndicated program such as "The Odd Couple" or "The Brady Bunch" and enabled the station to force the local cable system to black out the signal of any other station which carried the same program, even if the first station was not presenting the program at the same time as the competing station.

The rationale behind the exclusivity rule was the belief that the market value of syndicated programs and station advertising prices would be reduced if the blackout rule was not enforced. But recent studies by the FCC staff have led to a general reevaluation of the competitive factors in the cable industry. The study revealed that the danger of adverse economic impact of cable TV on the operations of local TV stations was strictly limited. As such, the Commission concluded that there was no need to enforce program exclusivity rules in an effort to protect the programming marketplace. As a result, the Commission proposed the abolition of the exclusivity rule.

Another long-observed rule has limited the number of additional channels on the cable systems which emanated from so-called distant markets. The FCC enforced rules which strictly limited cable systems to importing one or two signals from stations not readily available over the air in local markets. Again, the signal-importation-limiting rule reflected an attempt by the Commission to assure that the local television stations carried on cable systems were protected from significant competition from other imported signals.

The FCC has proposed the abolition of the distant-signal rule. Here again, market studies led the FCC to conclude that the lifting of the signal restrictions would have only a limited impact on the operations of local TV stations. As a result, it concluded that cable systems should be freed of the distant-signal-limitation rule to encourage the expansion of cable service.

An additional boost to cable deregulation came from the United States Supreme Court. The high court ruled in *Midwest Video Corporation v. FCC* that the basic framework of FCC regulations compelling cable systems to operate certain channels for public and private use was illegal.

For the past 10 years, the cable industry operated under an extensive set of federal regulations which, among other things, required cable companies to maintain studio facilities so that individuals and groups—public and private—might be given the opportunity to originate programs to be carried on the systems. These so-called "public-access" rules were challenged by an Arkansas cable system on the grounds that the systems were required to become "common carriers" similar to telephone and telegraph, open to use by anyone. The Court ruled in a six-three decision that since cable systems had to be regarded as ancillary to broadcasting, the FCC was prohibited from requiring the cable operators from observing common carrier-type regulations.

Even with the removal of these rules, the Court decision would have only a limited effect on the operations of local cable systems. The fact remained that many state and local governments have established cable TV regulations similar to those set forth by the FCC. These local regulations have not been affected by the Supreme Court's ruling. As a result, it was expected that cable studio facilities would remain available for use by local groups on a leased basis as well as by government departments and educational institutions. Indeed, a number of leading cable companies confirmed that they will continue their efforts to encourage local people to make use of the so-called public-access programming channels.

One other cable regulation problem which developed over the past season involved the expansion of a new programming concept known as "superstations." The idea was the creation of the flamboyant sportsman-entrepreneur, Ted Turner. As the owner or WTCG-TV, a UHF independent station in Atlanta, Georgia, Turner devised a plan whereby the station's signal would be provided to cable systems throught the country via satellite transmission. The Atlanta station was on the air 24 hours a day, programming sports broadcasts, TV reruns, and movies. With such a program schedule, WTCG became an attractive prospect for fulltime or parttime use as a distant signal on cable systems. The WTCG station was actively marketed, especially through the South and Southwest, with the result that at season's end Turner could claim access to upwards of 3 million potential viewers outside of Atlanta via some 800 cable systems.

The success of the Turner project led to the selection of other stations such as WOR-TV in New York, KTVU in San Francisco, and WGN in Chicago as superstations. As such, their signals were transmitted to cable systems throughout the country. However, many commercial broadcasters opposed the concept of superstations.

The basic problem related to the effects of extending the reach of the local television station far beyond its normal market. Programs carried on local stations were often acquired from syndication companies at prices that reflected the size of the market and strength of the purchasing station. When signals were transmitted via satellite to hundreds of cable systems, the impact on these syndication arrangements could be substantial. For example, the importation of a TV signal on one program may have reduced the value of another sale of that program in a distant city.

The motion picture interests and professional sports leagues were particularly concerned with the impact of superstations on the value of syndication films and off-network reruns. In fact, the motion picture producers petitioned the FCC to adopt a rule prohibiting superstations. But the Commission refused to restrict the distribution of TV signals to cable systems via satellite. Of course, it can be expected that the expanded use of these signals will follow the removal of the existing distant signal limitation rules as proposed by the FCC.

The controversy over superstation signals was expected to continue, especially as satellite transmission facilities expanded. One possible solution would require cable systems to secure the permission or "retransmission consent" of the superstation before adding the signal to its system. This measure or some other will probably be sought by the Commission or, given the complex copyright questions involved, it may become necessary for Congress to legislate an answer.

## DECISIONS, DECISIONS: TELEVISION AND THE COURTS

The federal courts regularly maintained an active interest in the broadcasting business. This past season saw the judiciary deal with a number of decisions which directly affected the manner in which television broadcasters did their jobs.

The most important decision of the past twelve months was handed down by the United States Supreme Court in the case of *Herbert v. CBS, Inc.* Many TV and print commentators termed the decision a dangerous setback for journalists required to defend their reporting in libel cases.

The court action grew out of a segment carried in the highly rated CBS news magazine program "60 Minutes," which presented a report on the controversial Vietnam service record of army Lieutenant Colonel Anthony Herbert. CBS considered the report to be fair and informative. Lieutenant Herbert, however, charged that the network had maliciously defamed him so as to discredit his report of atrocities in Vietnam.

In seeking to establish his claim of libel against the network, Herbert faced a considerable burden of proof. Since the army officer had achieved a degree of public notoriety prior to the CBS broadcast, he was regarded as a so-called "public figure" under the law. When celebrities and other public figures charged reporters with libel, past decisions established that the courts were required to find that the reporter-defendant had broadcast or published a defamatory falsehood not merely through negligence, but with "actual malice." A charge of actual malice could be proven by showing that the untrue information was reported with full knowledge or reckless disregard of its falsehood.

The "actual malice" standard was established by courts in an effort to give reporters some measure of insulation against the danger of being faced with legal actions related to the exercise of their First Amendment rights. The courts have consistently maintained an interest in preserving the essence of editorial freedom for reporters, especially in the area of libel where there was the danger of using the legal process to harass and hinder the free flow of news and information.

In the Herbert case, CBS submitted hundreds of pages of reporters' notes, transcripts, program drafts, and video tapes of used and unused interview material, all related to the information known by the "60 Minutes" staff and in the effort to establish when and how the facts had become known. After a year of pretrial proceedings, the network's attorneys attempted to draw a distinction between the submission of documentary evidence and questioning concerning subjective news judgments (for example, why reporters had followed one line of evidence and not another, why one witness was featured over another, why some interview material had been cut, and other material left intact, as well as a number of other similarly subjective areas of investigation). The network also sought to avoid testifying concerning conferences between the executive producer of "60 Minutes," Don Hewitt, and correspondent Mike Wallace, the reporter assigned to the story. In all these instances, the network's attorneys felt that the information being sought went beyond proper fact-finding, and challenged the freedoms guaranteed to the reporters and editors.

In a 6-3 decision, the Supreme Court found that no such line of demarcation could be drawn. The court found no problem with authorizing the plaintiff in a libel suit to elicit evidence concerning the thoughts and motivations of reporters in assembling stories.

The reaction from the press was predictably one of outrage. Most journalists regarded the decision as a dangerous precedent for basic protections of freedom of expression that they felt were needed to insulate news gathering and editing from outside scrutiny.

The immediate result of the Herbert decision will be the resumption of the pretrial discovery of proceedings with the plaintiff's attorneys given full authority to investigate the substance of the editorial decisions involved in the reporting of the "60 Minutes" segment. The plaintiff's goal will be to establish that Mike Wallace did in fact intentionally (or recklessly) include false information concerning Lieutenant Herbert.

Some commentators have argued that the decision will have little practical effect as it would always remain difficult to assess individual intent and motivation. Yet others cautioned that the decision has given increased leverage to the plaintiff in a libel suit, thereby subjecting reporters to the possibility of increased court actions (along with mounting legal bills and the general inconvenience brought on by the legal process). Such practical results, should they come to pass, could create one additional burden on the exercise of press freedoms.

While delving into the mind of the broadcast journalist was deemed approriate by the United States Supreme Court, a California court rejected a theory that would have delved into the minds of some juvenile delinquents. The case grew out of an assault on a young girl by three other youngsters. The plaintiff's attorney charged that the attack had been inspired by a made-for-television movie titled *Born Innocent* on NBC. The film included an assault on a young girl in prison in a manner which resembled the facts in the law suit.

NBC based its defense on its First Amendment right of free speech. There was a narrow exception to the Constitutional protection of free speech which denied the right of free speech where the speech was intended to incite or produce imminent lawless action. The plaintiff obviously could not prove that the defendants—NBC and its San Francisco TV affiliate, KRON-TV—had included the scene with the express intention to incite the criminal behavior that took place.

Establishing the knowledge of the probable intent and outcome was an absolute requirement in such a case. The plaintiff sought to establish that the scene had been broadcast through negligence, since under the argument, the network could have determined that the scene in question might inspire criminal acts.

The court refused to accept this extended negligence theory. The judge concluded that even the presence of negligent conduct on the part of NBC and its San Francisco affiliate, were it to be established, would not be sufficient to deprive the network of its basic First Amendment rights.

Over the past year, California courts have been faced with another First Amendment challenge, involving the rights of the networks to present news programs which they produce. The basis of the action was a long-standing network policy under which the networks generally have prevented outside organizations from presenting news programs over the network.

The policy grew out of cautious legal advice and practical necessity. Since the networks were responsible for the material which they provided to the affiliated stations, they constantly tried to avoid programming that may lead to legal complications. Since the presentation of news was particularly vulnerable to various legal problems (from fairness doctrine challenges to libel suits), the networks have sought to carry only those news programs they produced "in-house."

In addition, all the networks maintained extensive news divisions with staff producers, writers, directors, and other talent. For the good of staff morale and simple cost efficiencies, the networks have sought to utilize their vast news division facilities to produce all necessary news and public affairs programs.

A group of independent producers challenged this exclusion policy. The plaintiff producers charged that as producers of news and public affairs programs, they were denied any practical way of reaching the nation's millions of viewers since the network companies refused to purchase their programs. The networks argued that the producers could obtain access to the stations by dealing through the syndication process. Further, they contended that the exclusion policy was necessary to assure maintenance of legal and production standards for such programming.

The producers' law suit did raise important questions. However, with the increasing availability of satellite program distribution facilities, the exclusive nature of the network interconnection with stations will become a lesser factor in the program supply process.

One other California action involving the makeup of network schedules was still being pursued by the Department of Justice against ABC and CBS. The antitrust action dated back to the Nixon administration when federal antitrust attorneys first sought to limit the control of the networks over supplying prime-time television programming.

Justice settled the NBC case a couple of years back with the network agreeing to limit the number of programs that it can produce for its prime-time schedule. ABC and CBS continued to challenge the premise of the suit on grounds that the First Amendment fully protected their rights to produce programs for presentation over their facilities.

The case has been slowly making its way through the court process with years of appeals awaiting the outcome of the initial decision. In the meantime, NBC has been sitting on the sidelines saving sizeable legal fees waiting for the final decision. (The NBC settlement would not take effect until the termination of the proceeding and the securing of a similar order against the other networks.)

Also wending its way through the federal courts in California was the so-called family-viewing-hour case. This action stemmed from a policy established a few years back by the television industry which called for the airing of so-called all-family entertainment programming during the first hour of the network prime-time schedules each evening. The name given to the scheduling concept was "family viewing," and its adoption came after Capitol Hill and the FCC questioned whether the content of television programming was becoming more objectionable, especially when viewed in terms of its effects on younger viewers.

After the adoption of the industry guideline, a number of Hollywood producers brought suit charging that government pressure had been improperly brought against the networks to establish the new policy. Such action was said to violate the broadcasters' First Amendment rights. For their part, the producers contended that their rights were being affected since they could no longer supply programs of a particular type to the networks for presentation during a large segment of their schedules.

A federal district court in California ruled in favor of the producers. It concluded that evidence did show that the FCC had been instrumental in getting the broadcasting industry to adopt the voluntary family-viewing policy.

ABC and CBS and the FCC have appealed the decision to the Ninth Circuit Court of Appeals. (NBC has filed a limited appeal.) Pending the outcome of the appeal, the National Association of Broadcasters has altered its Television Code, eliminating the family hour, but placing on the stations the responsibility of prohibiting material found to be "obscene, profane, or indecent."

One additional federal court action which concerned the production of television programming was the so-called Betamax Suit. Shortly after the first appearance of video cassette recorders (first introduced in the United States by the Sony Corporation of Japan), two television production companies brought suit against the rights of VCR owners to tape programs off the air.

MCA-Universal, a major TV and movie production company, and Walt Disney Productions contended that the producers' copyrights protected them against any private recording of their material. Extensive evidence was produced at the trial earlier in 1979, showing that owners of video cassette equipment exchanged recorded tapes through organized clubs and informal transactions. Such widespread taping of copyrighted material would lead, in the view of the producers, to a serious eroding of the market for their material.

There were many practical and legal problems raised by the case. The question of copyright liability for private recording and viewing had to be resolved. Furthermore, the salient question involved the practical problem of enforcing a court decree which would prohibit or limit offair taping. These critical problems have led many observers to conclude that the only answer rests with Congress, not with the Courts. A definition of copyright liability and the possible levying of a user charge or tax on recorders and tapes to be shared by copyright owners was a possible route which could be set out in legislation. It was argued that this would provide a practical approach to the expanding private use of copyrighted material. However, it was not expected that any such action will be taken until the court has had an opportunity to rule on the pending suit.

## TELEVISION 1980: A LOOK AHEAD

As noted at the outset of the chapter, the impact of regulatory policy has become an increasingly critical factor in determining the market structure of television and the newly expanding video media.

No longer was the legislative process restricted to a few select players: key committee members and lobbyists. The democratization of Congressional rules and the changing younger composition of members had brought forward for the first time in over 40 years a new interest in developing policies in the communications area. In the case of industry, the proliferation of new companies from television group owners to cable multiple system owners has eroded the power of network lobbyists and other establishment licensees. The result was the continued prospect for change reflecting trade offs among multiple interests and, in the end, a new definition of public-interest policies.

The status quo is not under attack. Rather, it was becoming outmoded by the continued change on the media horizon. The introduction of the communications satellite, for example, held the promise of radically changing the three-network market structure of television. No longer would the networks alone provide the only practical means for interconnecting two hundred or more TV stations. Satellites offered instantaneous, coast-to-coast interconnection at a fraction of the current telecommunication charges. As the satellite systems were put into place, the FCC quite appropriately launched a full-scale review of network operations and practices. These factors no doubt would combine, reformulate, and perhaps even restructure the long-established three-network system.

In addition to reviewing the operations of television networks, the Commission has also begun an overall review of the practicality of establishing new television channels and generally upgrading the technical capabilities of UHF service throughout the country. This attention to increased numbers of stations held the real prospect for expanded television service, a promise unfulfilled since the early "golden" days of television.

And then, of course, there was the continued expansion of cable television. Even before the removal of various cumbersome regulations, the cable industry enjoyed a fast-paced growth rate, reaching over 20 percent of the nation's 91 million television homes. This growth rate held even greater promise for continued expansion as cable was able to divert increased cash flow revenues to underwrite new programming sources. Possibilities ranged from pay cable movie channels to all-children-entertainment channels, "pay-cable" video game services,

24-hour news and picture service, special sports channels, and two-way talk-back services.

On balance, the public interest would be well served by the continued technical evolution of television and its related video media, and the parallel adaptation of law and policy to accommodate the changed conditions.

# OTHER
# VOICES

# TV ISN'T LIFE, BUT THEN WHAT IS?

## by James Wolcott*

FRIDAY, May 18. Nicholas Yanni—who covers TV for *Cue* and the *Soho Weekly News*—has been known to hole up in a screening room with a 16-part miniseries, armed with nothing except a note-pad, a thermos, and a tennis ball cylinder filled with processed potato chips. Weeks later, he staggers out, blinking, yawning, his fingernails as lethally long as Fu Manchu's. I wish I had that sort of commitment, but after two hours or so in the screening room, my astral self departs and my body is left behind, blissfully insensible. Only when the Betamax clicks off are soul and body (grudgingly) reunited. Besides, most shows are unendurable without a few interruptions: phone calls, rude raps at the door, the sound of a cat scratching "Open the bathroom door, schmuck, I'm locked in."

A cattle stampede or a meteor shower would have been more than welcome during ABC's two-hour TV movie, *Return of Mod Squad*, which reintroduced those forlorn flower-power detectives Julie, Linc, and Pete. As the movie opened, a crazed assassin began firing at their former boss and father protector, Captain Greer (Tige Andrews). So out of retirement came the Mods to track down the would-be killer. The years had been both kind and cruel. Julie (Peggy Lipton) hadn't lost her hippie-princess dreaminess—she swayed with every breeze, and her brown eyes glowed like chocolate Lifesavers—but Pete (Michael Cole) was banged-up and badly scarred. As for Linc (Clarence Williams III): He still stalked criminals with his shoulders hunched forward, and his thick gleaming Afro seemed to have been wired to pick up UHF, VHF, the BBC, and radio beeps from distant galaxies. Hyperattentively aware, Linc did a 360-degree scan of Evil in the neighborhood without even turning his head, sidestepping trouble like Astaire skipping around a puddle.

However, *Return of Mod Squad* was less a thriller than a lachry-mose sniffler about the end of innocence, idealism, honorable poverty, and honorable causes—about, in short, the end of the '60s. As with the recent film *The Big Fix*, in which Richard Dreyfuss played a counter-cultural dick, *Return* was full of self-pity masquerading as sorrow over lost possibilities. Pete, in his nifty three-piece suits, agonized over selling out, and (as Wilfred Sheed wrote in another context) it was as if he wanted us to say, "It's okay—you can keep the money." Later, Pete asked Julie if she remembered the peace movement and ZPG, making those causes sound like something that happened before the invention of movable type. What's funny is that the Mods mourned the recent TV past as if it were a time of gentle feelings and brave passions. In fact, on the old "Mod Squad," Linc, Julie, and Pete had to chase down drug pushers, wife beaters, child beaters, child molesters, bent Vietnam vets, rapists, looters, hit-and-run drivers, thieving junkies, trigger-happy cops, and Charlie Manson sickos before soulfully moping off into the sunset. What a strange past to be nostalgic about.

Later: Curled up with the '69 movie *Last Summer*. Director Frank Perry should have gone into porno—the best scenes are the shampoo group grope and the movie-theatre group grope, which offer lather,

*James Wolcott is a writer for the *Village Voice*. This essay originally appeared in that newspaper on June 4, 1979.

palpitations, and glimpses of Barbara Hershey's lust-moistened eyes. Slept dreamfully.

Saturday. Uneventful evening. Dick Cavett tried to tap dance on "The Merv Griffin Show": His brain said, "Hit it," but his body said, "Who are you trying to fool?" The high point of "Saturday Night Live" was Bill Murray crooning his cocktail-lounge version of "Beast of Burden" to an unimpressed Pearl Bailey (Garret Morris in drag). Belushi was also funny playing a cockroach lured into a Roach Brothel; he looked like a Dickensian pickpocket, and the roach-prostitutes fanned themselves like bored Southern belles. Guest host Maureen Stapleton buzzed through the show looking tense and perplexed, as if she hadn't fully recovered from *Interiors*.

Sunday. After the nuns untied me and washed the blood off the walls, I puttered away the afternoon watching acrobats and Sisyphean runners. On ABC's "Wide World of Sports," arrow-limbed, supple-spined Russian and Rumanian girl gymnasts executed chin stands, back-roll extensions, triple forward somersaults, aerial corkscrew spins, and somersault-corkscrew combinations that fused athletic rigor with Baryshnikovian exurberance. Gymnast after gymnast offered a flurry of astonishments, particularly Nadia Comaneci, who ended her floor exercises with a few jauntily jazzy kicks, a la Twyla Tharp. Enthralling stuff.

From there I clicked to NBC's "Sportsworld," where a half-dozen or so wire-muscled young men wearing running shorts and Sam Peckinpah bandannas carried red gas cans up a rocky slope. At first I thought they were participating in some strange jock-protest against high fuel prices. "We will carry these cans from Maine to Montana to bring the country to its senses," etc. Instead, they were competing in a paramilitary exercise that took self-mortification to the shadow-line of suicide. As commentator Bruce Jenner chortled off-camera, these poor buggers climbed back down the hill, filled their cans at the river (each can held 45 pounds of water), then reascended and emptied the cans into a larger tank. To win the contest, the men had to fill the tank nearly to the brim —a task that required several grueling trips. The competitors wheezed and panted like Dustin Hoffman on the run in *Marathon Man,* but the sight of stragglers limping in the dust made one think of Paul Newman digging his own grave in *Cool Hand Luke.* The runners' mood wasn't lightened by Jenner's insipid chatter. When one man—veins throbbing, rib-cage aching—reached the top and poured his load into the tank, Jenner was pickled with amusement. "Ha-ha-ha, that's why he's first up the hill—his cans are practically empty!" Finally Chuck Lyda (who he? asks the ghost of Harold Ross) triumphantly filled his tank; the others soon filled theirs; and Jenner, in a red windbreaker, hopped into view to congratulate the winners. Instead of doing the sane, decent thing—i.e., lashing Jenner to the nearest tree and letting crows peck on his head— the men stood around looking sick and wasted, like gladiators locked out of the vomitorium.

Afterwards I paged through P.G. Wodehouse, listened to the ultra-articulate Brian Eno chat and spin records on WPIX, and —perversely, inexplicably—watched a pair of presidential contenders go through their tired motions. On Channel 13, saintly Bill Moyers sullied himself with Ronald Reagan, who hasn't minted a new phrase or image or metaphor since the fall of Troy. In a recent *Esquire* column, Richard Reeves described Reagan's vision of America as "hindsight filmed in Technicolor." That judgment seems generous: Reagan's America seems to be a black-and-white MGM Eden where Judge Hardy sagely raps his gavel as boys in straw hats go fishin' with sapling rods. Reagan was at his most animated praising a new invention: an aluminum stein handle that can be clamped on to canned beverages. Eyes beaming with delight and envy, Reagan described how the handle worked, musing, "And (the inventor) is going to make a million dollars." If aluminum stein handles are the only thing that turn the Ray-Gun on, he really is finished.

So is Jerry Brown, I suspect. On Channel 5's "David Susskind Show," the sullied Susskind did battle with the saintly Zen-Jesuit space cadet. Susskind was surprisingly tough and thorough, but he still found himself wrestling with air. (I'd quote some of Brown's answers but they evaporated from my notebook.) Most dismaying was Brown's haughty humorlessness. Susskind repeated Carter's joke about Brown's candidacy being California's contribution to the Year of the Child, and an unamused Brown said Easterners often made such remarks at the expense of the West, that Carter's crack was a "fair commentary," and that he had nothing further to say on the subject. The camera then cut to Susskind, who was covered with frost. Compared to Jerry Brown, Reagan is a tatterdemalion rogue out of Tobias Smollett; indeed, I don't recall ever seeing Brown laugh unself-consciously during an interview or debate. Does he have a sense of humor? He seems to regard himself and his candidacy with a visionary seriousness that makes unwelcome intruders out of laughter and irony.

But I suppose the time to really worry is when California's Lieutenant Governor Mike Curb gets the presidential itch—he's clean-cut, dumb, and Republican.

Monday. Spent most of the evening with a Wodehouse novel: ". . . I'm all for rational enjoyment and so forth (says Bertie Wooster), but I think a chappie makes himself conspicuous when he throws soft-boiled eggs at the electric fan." My sentiments exactly. Hours later, on NBC's "Tomorrow," Tom Snyder interviewed the up-and-coming young controversialist, R. Emmett Tyrrell, Jr. Tyrrell, author of *Public Nuisances* and editor of a brash right-wing mag called *The American Spectator,* is often compared to H.L. Mencken, and here he impudently sucked on a thick, green, smelly Menckenesque cigar. He didn't do it convincingly: he looked like a tyro practicing his puffs in front of Dad's mirror. In print, Tyrrell tries to unleash the Menckenesque artillery, but all you hear are a few feeble pops. Compared to the true masters of Destructive Criticism, he's little more than a small-town heckler: he doesn't have the acute, analytical intelligence of a Dwight Macdonald or Marvin Mudrick, or the bombastic energy of a Mencken; he simply—crudely—labels his enemies boobs, morons, lunatics, louts. And he chooses easy, stale targets. Writing for an audience that snickers at the mere mention of Bella Abzug's name, Tyrrell seldom strays from the obvious lefties—Betty Friedan, Ralph Nader, George McGovern, et al. So of course his book comes christened with praise by William Simon, Robert Nisbet, and (the kiss of death) Ben Wattenberg.

With Snyder, Tyrrell trickled from subject to subject without provoking laughter or indignation. He made the sensible point that the publisher of the racist and scummy *Hustler* should never have been compared to a Russian dissident shivering in the Siberian cold; but others have said the same thing, and far more forcefully. Jr. then regretted that Hubert Humphrey didn't become a truly great senator—a disingenuous remark, because if Humphrey had become a great senator he would have continued championing the sort of liberal-reformist legislation Tyrrell so heartily deplores. Snyder, unseduced by Tyrrell's thick-cigar posturing, asked him if he were an iconoclast simply to be an iconoclast, and Tyrrell said no, that the country needed to be ridded of its nuisances, mumble harumph mumble. He wasn't even candid enough to admit that icon-smashing is fun. What's dismaying about the emergence of R. Emmett Tyrrell, Jr., is that it threatens to give Destructive Criticism a bad name.

Tuesday. Saw a screening of *Nancy Drew, Detective* (Channel 13, June 2). One good line: "Aw, quit disturbin' the molecules."

Later, clicked from *A Man Called Intrepid* to *Blind Ambition* to "The Helen Reddy Special." I sadistically looked forward to the Reddy show. A few years ago I saw Reddy perform in Las Vegas; she tried to mount the sort of brassy, high-voltage laser-and-neon spectacle Ann-Margret is famous for. Unfortunately Reddy didn't have A-M's kitschy glamour, and her singing lacks warmth, color, sensuousness. And when she tried to do comedy—well, it was too much for me. After an hour or so, an elderly woman kindly reported, "You can come out from under the table, Sonny—the show's over." Despite that frightful experience, I was keen on seeing Reddy's medley with guest star Jane Fonda; I tried to imagine what songs they would chirp together. "Under My Thumb"? Not likely. "Bring on the Nubiles"? Even less likely. Perhaps a new version of "Some Girls": "White boys just want to snack all night/I don't have that much Spam"? No.

It was all humdrum anticlimax, of course. Fonda and Reddy simply rattled off a string of songs written by women—among them "Ode to Billy Joe," "Seventeen," and "The Battle Hymn of the Republic" (they changed the ending to "*Her* truth is marching on"). Fonda, who looked as if she had spent the month sipping nectar with the gods in the groves of Valhalla, was also trapped in a number of jokeless and unflattering comedy sketches with costar Elliott Gould. The executive producer for the special was Reddy's shrewd-bullet husband Jeff Wald, who bathed his wife in soft angelic light—to no avail. Standing next to the gleamingly fit Fonda, Reddy looked wan and undernourished, and her singing never rose above metallic proficiency. She may be strong, she may be invincible, she may be Woman, but she still ain't capable of carrying her own show without making people dive under tables.

Rushed up to a rock club where a British punk unit bashed away like a bad imitation of X-Ray Spex and young men threw soft-boiled eggs at the electric fans. Anatole Broyard strutted in and cried, "Hey everybody—let's twist!" Fled home, turned on an old Jack Benny movie; Jeeves shimmered in with a soothing whiskey and soda; darkness; silence; bliss.

# US MAIL

## by David Mould*

"EVERY television program has a purpose—to put another one off the air."

A cynical view, perhaps, but in a season with an unprecedented mortality rate among TV series, it has more than a ring of truth. And the man who said it—writer Bill Stratton—has cause to be frustrated with the industry. Last year, four of the projects on which he worked met an early and, in his view, undeserved, death before they got on the air.

But Stratton is no maverick, railing at the life-and-death hold of the networks over series old and new. He has an established reputation, having written for series like "Hawaii Five-O," "The Rockford Files," "Cannon," and "Harry O." And while some ideas may end up on the shelf—or in the waste basket—the regular work (and the residuals) keep coming in.

Stratton hasn't gotten where he is—a large house in the Ojai Valley, north of LA, and a rented beach house where he writes—without a keen appreciation of what goes into a successful action-adventure series. And he admits that most writing follows some well-established guidelines.

"Every series is based on a blend of personalities and action. You can have a great plot—but if it isn't the kind of thing James Garner or Jack Lord would do, you might as well forget it. In every story you look for a slightly different way to present a character. But it must be credible—something Rockford would do, something which provides a good stage for his talents."

Some series place more emphasis on action than others. In its early days, "Hawaii Five-O" was conceived as a mystery story in an exotic setting—"a mixture of Agatha Christie and James Bond," according to Stratton.

"At that time, it was a real challenge to write for the series. You had to come up with an original idea, not just a series of shoot-outs and car chases. The stories had a human dimension—and some pathos."

So, "Five-O" dealt with complicated swindles, intricate crimes, and the personal dilemma faced by law officers. Stratton fashioned one story around a serious environmental problem on the islands—the pollution of the sea.

Even so, he found himself under pressure to introduce more "incidents" into his scripts—and "incidents" usually meant killings.

"They started to call me a pacifist crime-writer because I wasn't killing off enough people. I didn't think that death was essential to my stories; my characters got wounded and then recovered. But they kept adding killings."

He recalls one exchange with "Five-O's" executive producer, when he presented a script in which no one died. "It's good, but you'll prob-

*David Mould is a contributor to *Broadcast* magazine, which is based in London, England. This essay originally appeared in that magazine on April 23, 1979.

ably have to kill someone," he was told. "Is that absolutely necessary?" he asked. "It could be counterproductive if you don't" came the reply.

Stratton still believes that excessive violence is not an essential element. "Occasionally, I'd send in a story without a killing and see what happened. If it went through I'd call and say: 'you just let through a story where no one got killed. Gotcha.'"

"Five-O" is not the show it was, in his view. It's not just that the current stories place more emphasis on incidents than on character and human relationships; they also lean heavily on cliches in words and action.

"I've met a lot of cops, and I think I know how they talk—which is not the way the words come out on the screen. Even when a story was based on a true event, they would alter the script to fit the character. That's not what Steve (or Danny) would say here, they'd tell me. And a cliche would go in instead."

Stratton hasn't written for "Five-O" for some time and has no regrets because he feels that the series has lapsed into well-tried formulas. He finds Rockford a more interesting personality, although as a writer he still has to keep to a framework for plot and character.

"When you walk in, the first thing they ask you is, 'Have you got a premise?' A different idea which will fit the characters—a story with a good twist he can exploit. The acid test is—will it play and work?"

A key element in many stories is what Stratton calls the "time-lock." "There's a race against time—to stop the murder, to catch the runaway, to find the bomb. That's what gives a story its tension, its suspense."

Stratton is skeptical of claims that better-quality programs attract good audiences. The fault lies not only with overcautious network executives fretting over the loss of a rating point—but with the audience itself.

"It is said the American public gets what it deserves. I used to resist that idea, but I'm coming round to it. When you see a good play wind up low in the ratings, you begin to despair. A recent study of the activity of the human brain classified television watching as just a little above sleeping. It's hard to get people to sit still for something which requires them to think."

Stratton has spent most of his working life in the industry. Before he moved to the West Coast 13 years ago, he wrote and directed commercials for an advertising agency and he has learned to greet disappointment stoically.

"Last year I worked on two good projects—a television version of *Paper Moon* and a series called 'The Contender,' about a lumber-yard worker who fights when he gets mad, but is a gentle character. Neither got on the air. There's so much jockeying and in-fighting between the networks, the advertisers, and the producers, that many good ideas never make it. It's disheartening, but you keep on working."

Stratton does not believe that the growth of cable television in major markets will lessen the dominance of the networks. More shows may be syndicated independently, but he doesn't believe that the standards will measurably improve. "You can't rely on the American public to make a rational choice for quality programming," he says.

# HOW'D YOU LIKE TO PICK THE NATION'S PROGRAMS?

## by Ron Miller*

NEARLY everyone would love to be a network programmer for at least one week. Imagine the thrill of being able to arrange the TV diet of an entire nation! Besides, they pay those guys so well.

If I had the chance, I'd want to make a good impression so they'd ask me back for a whole season. In the meantime, I'd try to put all the things on the air I've always wanted to see.

Here's a small sample of the shows, special events, and other strokes of genius I'd try to put on during my week as network programmer:

A "surprise" visit by all four Beatles to ABC's "American Bandstand." Can't you just see the look on Dick Clark's face as John, Paul, George, and Ringo tell him they don't know how to lip-synch a record so they'll have to go on live?

Harry Reems, John Holmes, Linda Lovelace, and Marilyn Chambers racing against the clock on "Celebrity Challenge of the Sexes."

A visit by J. D. Salinger to "The Dick Cavett Show," in which he explains why he has constantly refused to sell the movie rights to *Catcher in the Rye* to Jerry Lewis.

The debut of a new daytime talk show hosted by Greta Garbo and called, of course, "Garbo Talks"

A guest-star appearance by Fred Astaire on a dramatic series in which he does not play an amiable con man.

A new game show called "Punch Out," in which different Hollywood macho men attempt to knock a battery off Robert Conrad's shoulder in order to earn all-expense-paid trips to international spas.

A new version of "The Mary Tyler Moore Show" with Mary cast as a comedienne who has just fractured her leg while having her tonsils removed, thereby prohibiting her from singing and dancing.

An expensive new miniseries called *Roots—The Alternate Generations,* which traces what might have happened if Kunta Kinte had jumped ship and made his way into the Bermuda Triangle.

A special "Ingrates Awards" show in which famous people like Marlon Brando, George C. Scott, Katharine Hepburn, and William Saroyan are forced at gunpoint to accept Oscars, Pulitzer Prizes, and other awards they've refused to show up to accept in the past.

A made-for-TV movie called *Silent Defeat,* in which a beautiful blind girl valiantly struggles to win a spot on the U.S. Olympic Gymnastics team, but can't find the arena and never gets to compete.

A special edition of "60 Minutes" in which Gore Vidal, William F. Buckley, and Norman Mailer debate with each other under a giant bell jar with only a 60-minute supply of oxygen.

A new sitcom called "Lollipop Fever," based on Nabokov's *Lolita* and starring Brooke Shields with a different middle-aged male guest star each week.

A Barbara Walters special in which all of her guests are speech therapists.

A live edition of "Great Performances" with Eugene Ormandy and the

*Ron Miller is the television editor of the *San Jose Mercury News.* This essay originally appeared in that newspaper on April 10, 1979.

Philadelphia Orchestra performing "A Salute to the Great Soap Opera Organists."

Truman Capote as a guest on "The Dating Game."

A new miniseries called "Backstairs at Black Rock," based upon the memoirs of all the yes-men who have worked for William S. Paley since he formed CBS.

A new series called "Greatest Heroes of the Zend Avesta," which attempts to do for Zoroastrianism what Fred Silverman has been doing for (or to) Christianity with his Bible programs.

"The Alexander Portnoy Show," a new variation of the old Arthur Godfrey Talent Scouts program in which screen tests of starlets are judged by teenage boys with acne.

"Rossi," a spinoff of "Lou Grant," with reporter Joe Rossi (Robert Walden) leaving the *Trib* to become an anchorman on a TV station called WJM in Minneapolis.

What do you mean it never would work? Can you imagine the ratings for such a lineup? You network presidents out there know where you can reach me. I'll be waiting by the phone.

## TELEVISION, IQ, AND SCHOOL ACHIEVEMENT

by Michael Morgan and Larry Gross*

ONE of the more frequently heard concerns about the effects of television is that it may be harmful to school achievement. There are, however, two sides to the issue. Some have urged us to acknowledge and appreciate the enormous variety of information that television provides to young people—more information than most people of earlier times had access to in their whole lives. By bringing the world into all of our living rooms, television may have expanded our children's sense of history, culture, art, and science and given them far greater knowledge of the world and its people. Television may even stimulate students to read about what they have seen on the screen.

On the other hand, many point to a frightening decline in basic, traditional academic skills. Television has been blamed for the much-publicized decline in SAT scores. Watching television is said to hypnotize bleary-eyed students, preventing them from reading, and interfering with homework; it is not unusual to hear television accused of "destroying the language."

Readers of this article may recall similar worries about the dangerous effects of movies and comic books on students' school performance. And it goes back even farther; in fact, exactly one hundred years ago, a Miss M.A. Bean warned teachers at a conference in Boston that reading fiction (a practice generally encouraged by parents and teachers today) "is not going to produce a generation of thinkers or workers but rather of thoughtless dreamers."

Television, however, is different from all other popular media. Its pervasiveness and the sheer number of hours young people devote to it make it an unparalleled phenomenon. Students today were watching

*Michael Morgan is a Ph.D. candidate and Larry Gross is an Associate Professor at the Annenberg School of Communications, University of Pennsylvania.

television before they could read or probably even speak. It is the dominant carrier of popular culture and public information for most people, especially children and adolescents. Television continuously presents coherent and stable images of life and society and cultivates distinct notions among its viewers about the way the world works.

Our research has been tracing patterns of television content and studying their effects on children, adolescents, and adults for over a decade. It is called "Cultural Indicators," and is directed by George Gerbner and Larry Gross at the Annenberg School of Communications, University of Pennsylvania.

In the course of a three-year longitudinal study of television's influence on adolescents' views and assumptions about social reality, we uncovered some striking negative relationships between television viewing and both IQ and standardized achievement test scores. That is, the more television students watch, the worse they score; and the less they watch, the higher they score. (These students were in the sixth through ninth grades at a public school in New Jersey.)

About a dozen or so earlier studies had also found that heavy viewers of television have lower achievement scores, including statewide assessment programs in Pennsylvania and Rhode Island. Similarly, other researchers have found that heavy viewers have lower IQ's. However, no previous research ever investigated whether these apparent relationships are in fact the result of some other factor. For example, students of higher social class watch less television and have higher IQ's. It is quite possible that if the "effects" of social class were removed from the relationship (i.e., "held constant"), the relationship would disappear. This, however, is not the case at all. Our data show that the association of TV viewing to both IQ and achievement does not change when social class is held constant.

More importantly, no other studies have looked at what happens to the association between viewing and achievement with IQ held constant. Given that low-IQ students watch more TV (and have lower achievement scores) and that high-IQ students watch less TV(and do better on achievement), there may be no relationship between TV and achievement with IQ held constant. In other words, if IQ scores represent "ability," then television viewing may have no impact on actual performance when ability is taken into consideration.

According to our data, holding IQ constant does indeed eliminate the relationships viewing has with many areas of achievement, especially math scores. Yet two significant connections remain: Even when the effects of ability are removed, heavy viewers score worse on tests of reading comprehension and language usage. Therefore we can say that television viewing does not have a uniform influence on all areas of achievement, but that reading comprehension and language usage stand out as skills which may be impeded by watching a lot of television.

There is one further important qualification. The relationship between viewing and comprehension in reading is not the same for everybody. The pattern is different for low-, medium-, and high-IQ students. Students with high IQ's who watch a lot of television score quite poorly on achievement, relative to others with high IQ's. However, among students with low IQ's, the heavy viewers do *better* on reading comprehension than the light viewers. This is especially true for girls.

Perhaps for low-IQ students, watching television provides stimulation and may actually help improve achievement. Low-IQ students who do not watch much TV may be particularly disinterested and unmotivated. The important thing is that by looking at students of different IQ's separately, we see that heavy viewing is actually an indicator of *middle* achievement scores.

The moral is that television may affect different students in different areas of achievement in different ways. Our analysis hardly suggests that television improves the academic performance of most children; at the same time, we have no evidence to support the most dramatic claims of television's disastrous effects on achievement.

Television may serve to reinforce a reading problem in at least two ways. First, heavy viewing may cut down the amount of time students spend reading. Also, we find that heavy viewers very often say they read and do homework while they are watching. Comprehension skills could logically suffer in the presence of such a strong distraction.

In sum, we find that a student's amount of daily television viewing will predict his or her scores on reading comprehension and language usage better than many other variables. It is unlikely, however, that television can single-handedly cause poor performance. The effects of television viewing can only take shape in the context of many complicated personal, family, and social factors.

# TV RATINGS— THERE JUST MIGHT BE A BETTER WAY

by Carolyn E. Setlow*

THE Nielsen Ratings, "the numbers" upon which the entire commercial television industry pivots, might some day have competition in determining programming popularity. Instead of an estimated "headcount" of the number of people viewing a particular TV program, a new form of measurement—qualitative ratings—is being advocated by influential individuals within the government, the broadcasting industry, and the nonprofit sector. This new measuring procedure, which would be used to supplement rather than supplant the Nielsens, would report not just how many people are watching a program but how much—or how little—those viewers actually like it. This proposed system could use polls to measure whether the viewer found the program engaging, enriching, and enlightening, or simply an empty diversion.

According to its advocates, qualitative ratings would benefit the viewing public by allowing them greater input into television programming, thus increasing the quality and diversity of programming fare. As Margita White, a former Federal Communications commissioner and a strong supporter of qualitative ratings, said, "The (present) rating system—by encouraging imitation rather than innovation, by overemphasizing 'the numbers' at the expense of quality and encouraging bland programming to the lowest common denominator—may be the single

*Carolyn E. Setlow, who studied qualitative ratings as an independent consultant to the John and Mary R. Markle Foundation, is director of corporate planning for Newsweek., Inc. This essay originally appeared in *The New York Times,* December 31, 1978.

major obstacle to better-quality programming." If Nielsen or some other polling service were to survey viewers' attitudes, these advocates maintain, commercial broadcasters might realize that public tastes demand broader and more diversified fare than the "cookie-cutter" parade of situation comedies and police dramas.

Chairman of the National Association of Broadcasters, Donald Thurston, whose group represents commercial stations across the country, believes that a quality measurement (or "Q-factor," as he has dubbed it) would serve not only the public but the best interests of the broadcasting industry as well. "A very serious problem for broadcasters is the limited supply of programming," he said. "If a show came in with good but not great ratings, but the Q-factor showed that it left viewers with wonderful feelings, it might have a chance to stay on the air."

In late 1977, General Foods supplied the National Citizens Committee for Broadcasting, the Washington-based public-interest group headed at the time by former FCC commissioner Nicholas Johnson, with a grant of $7,500 to conduct a pilot study of qualitative ratings. A small sample of television viewers outside the capital recorded in diaries their attitudes toward the prime-time programs they had watched during a test week. The results, while not projectable to the population at large, nonetheless indicated that there were considerable discrepancies in the perceived quality of programs with otherwise identical Nielsen ratings.

Although further financial support has not been forthcoming from General Foods, Samuel Simon, the executive director of the NCCB, is hopeful of obtaining $150,000 from other sources so that the pilot study can be expanded to a national sample, perhaps by the end of the 1979 fall TV season.

Models for qualitative ratings already exist in Great Britain and France. The BBC, Britain's public television system, is obliged by its charter to supplement its audience headcounts with surveys of public reactions to programs, or "Reaction Indices." British commercial television is required by the Independent Broadcast Authority Act of 1973 to conduct a continuous appreciation survey, from which "Appreciation Indices" are gleaned. On a regular basis, panels of viewers receive questionnaires in the mail that ask them to rate the programs they have recently viewed.

Similarly, programs on French television are periodically judged by an "index de qualité." The cost of these polls of television viewers is covered by fees levied on the sale of new television sets. Both the size of the audience and the reactions of viewers as to the quality of programs determine the way public funds (from both the fee and advertising revenues) are distributed to the producers of French television programming.

Taking a leading role in developing qualitative ratings in this country is the Corporation for Public Broadcasting. Cortland Anderson, acting president of CPB, recently explained the organization's interest in developing a supplement to headcounts: "The public broadcaster's mandate is to provide an 'alternative' source of programming, that is, to satisfy viewer needs left unfulfilled by commercial programming. A qualitative rating system would provide us with a way to measure our success in meeting this goal."

CPB has contracted with Roger D. Percy and Co., a Seattle-based research firm, to experiment with a new mechanism called VoxBox. Percy's system currently permits 200 in-home viewers to register their on-the-spot response to programs by pushing buttons on a remote-controlled box wired to Percy's central computer.

The commercial broadcasting industry, with the exception of the NAB's Thurston, has so far not thrown its support behind qualitative measurements. Indeed, network executives recently interviewed generally defended the status quo. A CBS programming vice president summed up the typical network viewpoint: "The Nielsen ratings are the measure of the quality of programs. A large-audience show is by definition good."

Yet, the A.C. Nielsen Company makes no claims that its ratings reflect programming quality. Indeed, in its brochure "Everything You've Always Wanted to Know About TV Ratings but Were Maybe Too Skeptical to Ask," the company states: "As far as we're concerned, there is no such thing as a TV rating. . . . The word 'rating' is a misnomer, because it implies a measurement of program quality—and this we never do. NEVER!"

Industry resistance to qualitative ratings appears to be threefold. First, with no measure of the perceived quality of programs, network executives can continue to argue that "if the public watches us, they like us." A more accurately representative public scorecard might divulge public dissatisfaction.

Second, advertisers, the networks, and local stations have agreed on a common currency in which they trade—rating points. If they had to factor in "quality" ratings, the process of buying and selling commercial time would become even more complicated than it is now.

Finally and perhaps most importantly, network executives as well as local station managers fear that new audience-reaction data could be used by advertising agencies to drive down the price of television advertising time. If a quality measurement showed that a program had a large but uncommitted or inattentive audience, agencies could readily use this information as a bargaining chip in negotiations for commercial time.

The advertising community seems more indifferent than opposed to qualitative ratings. Many heavy television advertisers believe that the content or type of program (the so-called "ad environment") neither enhances nor detracts from the sale of their products. As Richard C. Butler, the media director for Lever Brothers, recently explained: "While we carefully screen our programs to be sure that their content will not offend our consumers, I have no feeling that my commercial in Mary Tyler Moore works better than one in Kojak. The average consumer sees my commercial over and over again. How can it have a positive effect in one show and a negative effect in another?" Harry Way, the media director for the Colgate-Palmolive Company, echoed this view: "In print media, I am careful about the positioning of an ad, but I never thought there was much rub-off between editorial environment and ad effectiveness in television."

In the absence of clearcut indications that viewer satisfaction with programs translates directly into sales of their products, it would seem unlikely that advertisers will take the lead in launching qualitative ratings. Fred Friendly, advisor on communications to the Ford Foundation, has suggested, however, that although support may come not from the heavy mass-market advertisers like Proctor & Gamble or General Foods, it may come from advertisers who are trying to reach a more affluent and better-educated audience. Advertisers like Xerox or IBM, ever anxious to enhance their corporate image, might be the first to endorse and use such an audience measurement.

In the absence of advertiser support, it will probably take some outside business threat to convert the networks to the use of qualitative ratings. Margita White feels such threats are imminent in the form of increased pressure from public-interest groups, more federal regulation or legislation, and growing competition from new entertainment technology (cable, satellite distribution, video cassettes and discs).

Even the staunchest opponents of change at the networks admit that they could not ignore the results of qualitative ratings should they become a reality. "If such ratings existed and there were a demonstrable difference between Nielsen and public attitudes," admitted one top network research executive, "we'd have to find out why." His counterpart at a rival network agreed: "If someone devised a 'quality' rating scale, broadcasters would have to use it. The networks can't fly in the face of public opinion."

# THE CABLE TELEVISION BREAKOUT & ITS IMPLICATIONS FOR THE FUTURE OF COMMERCIAL BROADCASTING

by Sidney W. Dean, Jr.*

Q.
Has the "Cable Television Revolution" finally arrived?


A.
Unquestionably, the cable television industry has broken out of the principal technical, financial, and political handicaps which, over the past 15 years, have prevented it from building a national system for transmitting and marketing video and other communications services which are competitive with television broadcasting.

Hitherto hemmed in by the relentless pressure of broadcasters on Congress and regulators, cable is now breaking out of the political constraints of its early years. Its 16 million households in 1979 may become 20 million by 1982 and 30 million by 1990. Territories already franchised include half of the urban population of the United States. The most dramatic recognition of this new political reality was the decision of President Carter in May of 1979 to give the cable television industry the first opportunity to present a live, two-way video conference between himself in the White House and, in this instance, the delegates to the cable industry's convention in Las Vegas. The conference was simultaneously fed by satellite to over 1000 cable systems with 6 million homes.

*Sidney W. Dean, Jr., is a businessman and consultant in marketing and communications.

How will the Cable TV breakout affect the revenues and audiences of **Q.**
commercial TV broadcasting?

Negligibly over the next 8-12 years, both from the standpoint of adver- **A.**
tising revenue and of broadcast program audiences. Advertising revenue is the governing factor since it funds mass-audience programming. National advertisers, network and spot, will be unwilling and
unwise to replace predictable circulations of mass entertainment programs with lower-impact, irregularly distributed cable programs which
must compete in each home. It is predictable that cable's slow advertising growth will first come from local retail services.

It is probable that by 1990, more people will spend more time with
broadcast television programs delivered by cable than delivered over
the air, but it will not materially affect advertisers' expenditures for the
programs. The new benefits that cable carriers will bring both to communications users and producers will be new types of popular cultural
and educational programming.

What will supply the revenues to support a national cable system? **Q.**

Four sources are identifiable in current trends and policy studies: **A.**
1) *Advertising revenues,* now at $6 billion a year for commercial
   television, are the exclusive source of income to broadcasters. Cable advertising revenue is now running at an annual level of
   $100-$200 million.
2) *Public payments to receive television broadcasting,* the amortiza-
   tion of receivers, is estimated at over $10 billion a year. Public
   subscription payments for basic cable system connection, exclusive of pay-cable and optional outlays, is now running at $1.5
   billion a year.
3) *Public payments to cable systems for subscription "pay-cable"
   programs* will shortly reach $1/2 billion. Drawing from several
   independent studies, there is a revenue potential of $50-$100 billion per year in direct public payments for the full range of communications services which national, multi-channel broadband
   carriers can market.
4) *Public payments to the telephone industry,* which have the legal
   right to develop all broadband services except the relay of broadcast signals could account for half of "pay-cable" revenues. The
   telephone industry operates more miles of coaxial cable and other
   broadband carrier media than the cable industry. It can be assumed that telephone systems will give top priority to the huge
   concentrated business and institutional information, transaction,
   and message markets. The expansion of consumer expenditures
   for pay-cable may trigger telephone entry into what could be a $20
   billion a year national consumer market within 10 years.

Where does, and will, cable television secure growth capital? **Q.**

A. The financial performance of cable television systems cannot be gauged by conventional net profits after taxes. Their tax-exempt depreciation, allowed reserves, investment tax credits, and other tax-free receipts help create a cash flow to the operator which can approximate 40 percent of gross revenues while showing small, if any, taxable net earnings. Total industry revenues of $1.5 billion can generate $500 million in capital for new investment. With this assurance and the protection of long-term franchises, banks, syndicates, and insurance companies may lend twice this amount in senior loans, with the possibility that junior lenders may put up a third as much. Thus, a $1 million cash flow from a stable operation can be leveraged up to $3-$4 million for new investments. Communities already franchised and generating adequate cash flow will receive few if any investments for new or slow pay-out services. The funds they generate will leave town for new franchising or fast pay-out services. To the writer's knowledge, few if any governments have required cable franchises to invest a given share of their cash flow from the market back into services to the market. Unless the municipal government pays the costs, there is no programming for delivery of government services, nor for general citizen access.

Q. What is cable television's current regulatory status?

A. Congress has enacted no legislation to define the structure and operations of cable television. The FCC finally attempted to regulate cable as "a hybrid of broadcasting and common carrier," but the courts have now denied FCC jurisdiction over any aspect of cable other than broadcast signal carriage unless authorized by Congress. The disposition of the three pending Communications Act rewrites and FCC, now seems to favor withdrawing all federal regulation, though passage of any one of them is unlikely.

There are two unchallenged regulatory jurisdictions. The 50 states have sovereignty over the use of their public rights-of-way and services affecting the public interest. Twelve states have established cable regulatory agencies or placed cable under their public utility commissions. Since practically all states have delegated to their local governments the power to grant franchises or licenses for use of local rights-of-way, the basic terms of cable franchises have been negotiated locally by 10,000 local governments. State and local governments, with a dozen exceptions, lack the knowledge and resources to deal with fast-evolving, complex, broadband technology, which interfaces practically every activity in society. Cable franchises with capital values of $1000-$2000 per household in the area are being awarded for 15-20 years (in practice, indefinitely renewable). The local franchising process often receives not much more consideration than is given to the award of a fast-food concession in a public park.

Q. Lacking stable regulatory status, what has been the growth strategy of cable television operators?

The current state of public policy for cable television can best be de- **A.** scribed as a decentralized vacuum which is highly favorable to cable entrepreneurs. Their strategic decision has been to act upon the popular assumption, strengthened by the FCC's ambiguous classification of cable as a "hybrid of broadcasting and common carrier," that a cable system can exercise broadcasters' privilege to solely determine what they carry.

Cable systems look to the future of their revenues, profits, and powers from complete control of whatever content they choose to carry (on their own terms).

Ted Turner, who has negotiated his satellite-distributed Atlanta Superstation to over 1000 cable systems, bluntly summed up his experience to the 1979 NCTA convention: "Cable can be a worse monopoly than the telephone companies."

What can go wrong with this scenario for cable de-regulation? **Q.**

The public, through its three tiers of government, may not find it possi- **A.** ble to overlook four compelling realities and their consequences.
1. A cable television system is the only video carrier system generally available to the public, to business, and institutions in its franchised area. It is a total multi-channel monopoly.
2. Cable television systems could profitably lease, at attractive rates, television and other high capacity channels to independent suppliers of communications services.
3. The capital available to the television industry over the next 10-15 years will be inadequate to develop these diverse services.
4. Cable carriers' legal strategy is valid for only the "broadcasting" half of the FCC's hybrid definition; it is incompatible with the "common carrier" portion. Nearly every major public policy study has recommended that cable carrier systems be separated from control and engagement in communications content, including:
   —the Geller study for the House Sub-Committee on Communications
   —the President's Cabinet Study
   —the Office of Telecommunications Policy (U.S.)
   —the Communications Committee, Science and Technology Section of the American Bar Association

A final question supplies its own answer. Cable television is the pioneer **Q.** multi-channel television carrier service for the general public. Its fight for life has been arduous, buffeted by the enmities of established technologies and the vacillations of policy makers.

Cable television deserves to succeed to the extent it will free but not abridge, develop but not exploit our freedoms to communicate. The question both for ourselves and the cable carrier industry is this:

"WILL CABLE BRING US THE ULTIMATE DIVERSITY OR THE ULTIMATE MEDIA MONOPOLY?"

# THE YEAR IN TELEVISION RESEARCH

by W. Russell Neuman*

WE will attempt in the scope of a few pages to highlight some of the more interesting books and research findings which have recently been released. Literally thousands of research studies and scores of books concerning television and its potential impact are published annually, so we will make no attempt at a comprehensive overview. A much smaller number of studies, however, are especially comprehensive, controversial, or original and receive considerable attention from concerned viewers, the industry, and the press, and it is this latter group on which we will focus. As it turns out, television researchers, commentators, and critics have been unusually prolific in recent months, so we will have to limit our review to several of the especially active issue areas.

## A MAJOR NEW COMPENDIUM OF TELEVISION RESEARCH

One of the notable events of the year in television research was the publication this fall of the long-awaited review of research by George Comstock and his associates entitled *Television and Human Behavior* (Columbia University Press, 1978, $9.95). This massive volume (581 pages) was painstakingly assembled over a five-year period and moves far beyond the more specialized bibliographic reviews published by Comstock under the same title for the Rand Corporation in 1975. Written with unusual clarity and directness, and with a minimum of technical terminology, it is likely to be of interest to the general reader with a curiosity about the effects of television and a central reference work for researchers and professionals in the field.

Major sections of the book deal with the character of entertainment programming including the portrayal of racial groups, social classes, and sex roles, as well as patterns of news coverage, and trends in the level of violence in prime time and in childrens' programming. One chapter goes into considerable detail about the size and character of the typical television audience and the trends in public attitudes toward this influential medium. There are chapters on the impact of extensive television viewing on other activities in the home, the persuasive effects of television (including an intriguing comparison of the advertising of products and political candidates), and a theoretical overview of the psychology of behavioral effects. The primary focus and central chapter of the book (it is about twice as long as the others) reviews research on children and television with a special emphasis on the issue of television violence and aggressive behavior.

The book bulges with numbers, graphs, and charts compiled and abstracted from some of the 2500 original sources reviewed in this massive undertaking. We find, for example, that in the fall of 1976, 72 percent of leading characters in randomly sampled prime time action programs committed violent acts, a rate up dramatically from the previous year (p. 73); the average home with television had the set turned

*W. Russell Neuman is an assistant professor of Sociology and Mass Communications at Yale University.

on for 6.82 hours every day, up an hour since 1963 (p. 87); only 40 percent of parents of small children set any limits on the amount of time the children are allowed to view (p. 189); 60 percent of the Saturday morning childrens' programming with human characters presents no black or minority characters (p. 291); and over-the-counter drug manufacturers spent $265 million on television advertising in 1973 (p. 463). But the book is much more than a compendium of statistics. The contributors, each an expert in a research subfield, carefully reviewed the reliability of the data and the appropriateness of research designs and, with unusual and refreshing candor, identified which conclusions might fairly be drawn from individual studies. The result is a balanced appraisal of the diverse, often conflicting research studies in this complex field. They describe one study, for example, which revealed that a two-week, $1-million advertising campaign conducted for the Northwest Mutual Life Insurance Company during the 1972 summer Olympic telecasts raised that company's standing in public recognition of insurance company names from thirty-fourth to third. It is a striking finding. But in further discussion the authors put it in context, noting carefully that brand recognition and actual consumer behavior are very different kinds of variables. They report, "there are no publicly available studies which unambiguously relate changes in behavior to exposure to television advertising" (p. 379). This latter finding is even more striking given that advertisers spend over $3 billion yearly in the belief that consumer behavior is indeed influenced by their televised commercial messages. The book also includes helpful discussions of the ongoing debate about appropriate measurement of violence trends (pp. 64-70) and the public reliance on television for news (pp. 135-140). Fortunately, all of this is done without getting unnecessarily bogged down in methodological details.

The final chapter reviews agendas for further research and a sophisticated appraisal of the realpolitik of communications policy. Noting that he is not convinced that the current system of television is the best system possible, Comstock observes:

The system is likely to continue much as it is for the reasons of sociology and politics. A society does not dismantle its major institutions in the absence of public displeasure, and usually that displeasure must reach the level of fury for such transformations to occur. And there is no evidence of great public dissatisfaction with television, and certainly there is no sign that any dissatisfaction that exists is accompanied by any widespread belief in the desirability of radical reform. Furthermore, the present system has created in the broadcasters who benefit from it a very powerful set of vested interests which will oppose any change [p. 484].

Comstock's analysis of the major actors in communications policy decision-making and the characteristic role played by research in these complex adversarial processes ought to be required reading for all who enter the fray.

Comstock and his colleagues have organized a veritable mother lode of research findings which no doubt will be mined for years to come; much of it will ultimately find its way into robust polemics both pro and con. Research findings such as those reported here are frequently distorted, abused, misread, and taken out of context. Perhaps it will happen less often as a result of this comprehensive and extremely fair-minded review of the field.

## QUALITATIVE RATINGS

There is an exciting movement involving members of the television-research community which focuses on new methods of assessing how viewers react to the ongoing flow of programming. The interest is not in one shot laboratory experiments to be reported years later in scholarly journals, but in a continuous ratings-like index of how viewers feel and what they think about what they see. The Nielsen and ARB ratings services provide relatively precise answers to a very concrete question—how many households have sets tuned to which channel? But ratings do not answer the question of why one particular program outscores others in the nightly competition. Ratings are mute on whether the favored program was seen as particularly enjoyable or interesting, or whether it simply was consensually seen as the least worst on at that time. Because such questions are important, each of the networks employs a large staff of analysts who pour over the ratings and speculate on why the audience flows as it does from one channel to another. This interest in a new and expanded multidimensional ratings system among researchers suggests that the traditional system of attempting to divine audience tastes from the Nielsens is prone to distortion. Former FCC commissioner Margita White, for example, has argued that the current ratings system by its nature encourages imitation rather than innovation.

One of the more ambitious efforts to explore "qualitative ratings" (so dubbed to differentiate them from the quantitatively-focused Nielsen approach) has been conducted by the National Citizens Committee for Broadcasting. In November 1977 it provided specially designed viewing diaries to 200 Washington, D.C., area households for one week. It focused on the level of perceived enjoyment and perceived importance of the programs viewed. The sample design and sample size are insufficient for drawing conclusions about the preferences of the national television audience, but the data demonstrate the promise of the concept. "Happy Days," for example, rated third in the ratings portion of the test, but twenty-seventh in the Quality Index. In contrast, PBS's *I, Claudius* ranked forty-sixth in the ratings, but first in the Quality Index.

Some more technologically sophisticated versions of qualitative ratings have been explored in Columbus, Ohio, as part of the Qube two-way cable system set up several years ago by Warner Communications and the R.D. Percy Company of Seattle, Washington. The Percy group has installed electronic "VoxBoxes" in 200 randomly sampled households in the Seattle area with various buttons which indicate that the viewer finds the program "informative," "funny," or "poor." The boxes are connected by dedicated phone lines to their main computer, which tracks the in-home audience reactions to television programming as it is broadcast. The most negative button on the VoxBox is labeled "Zap." It not only registers on the computer but blanks out both video and audio for as long as it is depressed.

It turns out that qualitative ratings have been used in both diary and computer systems for years in Europe with a less than radical impact on programming. But further research hopefully will generate a more subtle measurement tool capable of both enriching and expanding audience feedback in the programming process.

## THE FRONTAL ATTACK ON TELEVISION

The last several years have produced a bumper crop of books critical of television. One of the most prominent of them focuses on television and children, Marie Winn's *The Plug-In Drug* (Bantam, 1977, $2.25). Cornell sociologist Rose K. Goldsen published *The Show and Tell Machine: How Television Works and Works You Over* (Dell, 1977, $4.95). Her primary concerns are the portrayal of social roles on TV and the pervasive commercialism. Jerry Mander, a former (reformed?) advertising executive, has an even more explicit title: *Four Arguments for the Elimination of Television* (Morris, 1978, $4.95). Finally, McGovern's campaign manager, journalist and now National Public Radio executive Frank Mankiewicz and his associate Joel Swerdlow contribute, *Remote Control: Television and the Manipulation of American Life* (Times Books, 1978, $15). Each of these books has been written for audiences which want to be told how terrible television is. The dust jackets insure there is no ambiguity. On Winn's cover: "You're right to be worried. Now, Marie Winn provides positive, documented proof of the damaging effects television can have on your children's developing brain . . . Unless you are willing to let TV undo most of the good things you do for your children, you should help them kick the TV habit now." On Mander's: "The case against TV has never been made more effectively. It should be read by all addicts and anyone contemplating participation in the decertification of the mind to which TV leads."

Actually the books are more informative and less strident than the dust jackets would lead one to believe. They are well-written, thought-provoking, and likely to engage even those who have no strong feelings for or against television. None is scientific or scholarly by the usual definition, but each is dependent on behavioral research for support of its major themes. Each attempts to present a cogent and interestingly persuasive case by weaving together selected scientific findings, anecdotes, and personal insights. They are popularizers of science. Unfortunately, the scientific community itself pays very little attention to the way the products of its labors are used and misused in the popular literature, especially in cases when the personal convictions of the authors lean toward evangelism. In all likelihood the careers of most of these authors will involve an ongoing struggle with the beast, freelance Davids battling the Goliath. Goldsen, for example, produced a weekly radio series in Ithaca entitled Blowing the Whistle on Broadcasting for a number of years and Winn has been very active on the public-speaking circuit.

For evangelists they exhibit surprising care with footnotes and frequently acknowledge contrary evidence or, more often, the lack of conclusive proof for various points they make. The exception is the Mankiewicz-Swerdlow volume. More pretentious and less cautious in interpreting research, they claim to have put together "the first survey of virtually *all* the scientific studies on the question of television violence" (emphasis theirs, p. 10). Unfortunately, as a result of this laborious undertaking, they were a little pressed for time and did not manage to include citations of *any* research articles in either footnotes or a bibliography (emphasis mine).

In most of these books the language is lawyerlike, not shrill or strident but subtly persuasive. Winn, for example, often introduces an idea with, "it does not seem unreasonable to suggest" (p. 114). Later she admits, "There is no proof that television viewing is seriously related to declining verbal abilities, to the appearance of a new lifestyle, to the alarming trends such as drug use and drug abuse among increasing numbers of young people." But she feels compelled to note, "When all the elements of the puzzle are brought together and examined, television seems seriously implicated from the outcome of the first generation that grew up under its influence . . ." (p. 116). Fair enough. Actually, even the most conservative of television executives would not disagree with some of the statements made. Goldsen, for example, argues that there is little chance for a change in the general themes and character of television programming because of the economic structure of the television industry. "The job of those who man the network bureaucracies and the advertising and public-relations agencies feeding into them, is to attract attention and keep as many heads as possible turned toward the screen. If they were to abandon policies that effectively accomplish the task, even pursue them less diligently, they would be remiss in their responsibility to the corporate enterprises whose executives make policy decisions . . . It is the business of the midway, spruced up a bit and headquartered in fancy offices in New York and Hollywood." True enough. But although executives might attest to the accuracy of her assessment, they simply do not see it as a social problem. Goldsen shudders at the thought.

Our twin concerns in this review are first to explore the use and misuse of scientific research in the popular literature and, second, to try to identify some of the more challenging issues raised which might ultimately prove amenable to further scientific inquiry. One of the most fascinating aspects of the use of research in these volumes is the striking ambivalence toward science itself. The fact of the matter is that most research indicates no significant effects, positive or negative, from television. At various points most of these authors derogate science for its inability to demonstrate what seems to be the obvious, yet they all lean heavily on selected scientific studies to illustrate and lend authority to their arguments when the evidence seems to point in the right direction. Curiously, Mander argues that scientists spend too much time demonstrating the obvious. A major research institute, he cannot resist noting, spent more than $50,000 to discover that the best bait for mice is cheese. Yet a few pages later, he questions whether science can demonstrate anything. Is the ozone layer safe despite spray aerosols or is it deteriorating? Which scientist do you believe? Then he suggests that the research is really unnecessary. "In my opinion, if people are watching television four hours every day and they say they can't stop it, and also say that it seems to be programming them in some way and they are seeing their kids go dead, then really, I deeply feel there is no need to study television. This evidence is what lawyers call 'prima facie' proof. The only question is how to deal with it" (p. 161). Yet he later condemns scientists for having failed to study important topics about television effects (p. 163). His argument seems to be somewhat nonlinear. Goldsen argues further that research is manipulative and improper because it is often conducted without the permission of the viewer-subjects and may be used for commercial purposes which are not really in the viewers' interest. Altogether they paint a rather curious picture of what science is and what it can do.

Each of these books argues that it is important to understand the nature of television in order to defend oneself from its pervasive control. The same argument might be applied to readers of these books—even a vague understanding of the nature of the scientific method is helpful in putting their arguments in perspective. One of the most obvious points, as noted above, is that none has attempted to actually *review* the scientific literature. That would involve a rigorous comprehensive and rather dull exercise, but also a balanced and representative sample of findings. Also the extensive anecdotal evidence the authors take from personal experiences and interviews is hardly representative of the public response to television. Mander mentions that after one magazine article about his research on the negative effects of television was published, he got 250 letters from sympathetic viewers, most of whom felt as he did. Indeed, it is a self-reinforcing process.

Another curious phenomenon is the assumption of effects. Goldsen, for example, goes into considerable detail describing the content of prime-time entertainment programming and daytime soap operas. The language she uses to present her findings carries a strong implication that this particular content must have significant effects on the audience, but the issue is never addressed directly. Also, each of the authors makes a great deal of the fact that Americans spend many hours a day watching television. And, again, implicit in their language is the notion that each additional minute of viewing must be associated with an equivalent increase in effect. True, the findings about content and viewing behavior are interesting, but the demonstration of actual effects requires a more complex research design. A final problem of causal inference is more of a result of the style of writing than a matter of interpreting research. It is an issue which comes up frequently in television criticism. Most critics simply equate mass culture and television. They ignore the possibility that parallel phenomena are occurring in other media and in other spheres of modern life. Goldsen, for example, focuses on commercialism, but seems strangely blind to its manifestations in the print media and other cultural activities. Winn and Mander find the inactivity and passivity of television viewing a particular source of concern but ignore its relevance to other media. This final issue is most clearly a problem for Mander, who seems to project on the medium of television all the ills of industrialized society.

If the weakness of these books is an unsophisticated use of research findings, their strength lies in the important and often subtle issues they raise about potential media effects. Mander and Winn argue that the effect of television is not dependent upon its content, but involves a more complex process of psychological dependence. It is not what you watch, but the act of watching. Indeed, their extension of McLuhan's insight should receive more serious attention among researchers. Further research need not restrict itself to television, however. The analysis should include the print media and emerging technologies such as video discs. A second and probably more difficult issue to research is the hypothesis that television drama desensitizes viewers, making them less aware of their natural environment, sapping their ability to respond emotionally to real-world violence. It is an easy point to raise with a few well-chosen anecdotes, but an especially difficult challenge for the research community. Finally, the argument about the cultural pervasiveness and lack of diversity in television programming is an important issue which calls for comparative research. These books are strangely ethnocentric. None of the authors seem aware of the striking variety of television programming available around the world and alternative systems of control and regulation of the industry. True, because of the economies of scale, a great deal of American television is being shown elsewhere in the world, but American domination of the world's airwaves is decreasing. Other television systems in both developed and developing countries are exploring a diversity of formats and styles of programming, the study of which would make an important contribution to the literature critical of American television. Again, perhaps cable technology holds special promise. Hopefully, cable's new "television of abundance" will greatly expand the availability of foreign programming.

Each of these books is strongly critical of the American television industry and each expresses skepticism about the possibility of reform. Winn and Mander's answer is to banish the set from the house. Goldsen suggests learning more about the nature of the medium as a defense. Apparently, carefully balanced and scientifically documented books on television do not sell very well. It is likely we will see more of this mix of moral outrage and selective research summaries in the future. Ironically, these authors may find themselves in the position not unlike the competing networks, as an increasingly large number of television critics battle for the attention of the audience in head-to-head competition. They may find their voices rising, their anecdotes becoming more perverse, and their language more extreme. The treatment of science is not likely to fare well in such an environment.

## WHAT'S NEWS?

One way sociologists study social organizations (newspapers and television newsrooms, for example) is simply to hang around one. They call it "participant observation." Permission is sought from the authorities in charge and the scholar simply shows up and begins to watch the goings on, perhaps taking occasional notes. According to scholarly tradition, participant observers are candid about the fact that they are gathering data for research, but they are supposed to be as unobtrusive as possible in order to not unduly influence the social processes they are studying. Actually it is often surprisingly easy to be unobtrusive in the hubbub of organizational activities. An observer's presence is soon forgotten, or more often, taken for granted. But participant observers are not actually participants. In the newsroom they would never become involved in the writing or editing of news, but they are free to interact informally with those who do, asking the journalists, for example, about their decision to cover a story in a certain way. This intuitive and nontechnical approach to research is usually a healthy corrective to the more systematic and narrowly focused forms of data collection such as survey research or content analysis.

With the increasingly dominant role of television in the flow of news to the American citizenry, we might expect sociologists in increasing numbers to be lurking about newsrooms and studios around the country. Sure enough, a number of scholars have been busy. In 1973, Edward Jay Epstein's doctoral dissertation, based on participant observation at the news operations of all three of the networks but focusing primarily on NBC, was published under the title *News from Nowhere* (Vintage, 1973, $1.95). *Creating Reality: How TV News Distorts Events* by David Altheide, based on a study of production of local news on California stations, was published in 1976 (Sage, $6.95). This year two additional major studies were published. The field work for both actually goes back to 1965 and 1966, predating both the Epstein and Altheide books. The studies are Gaye Tuchman's *Making News: A Study of the Construction of Reality* (Free Press, 1978, $13.95), and Herbert J. Gans's *Deciding What's News* (Pantheon, 1979, $15).

Epstein's *News from Nowhere* sets the tone for this literature. It is a persuasive analysis of how the organizational, economic, and technological factors of television news production influence the selection and presentation of news stories. It has been widely read and tremendously influential. In effect, it sets up a very real challenge to further studies—what else can we learn from stalking about the country's newsrooms? Of course observers in different newsrooms or under unique circumstances are likely to find different aspects of the system emphasized. Surprisingly, however, Gans, whose field work spans the period 1965 to 1978, and who observed both television and magazine newsrooms, was struck by the similarities rather than differences over time and the different settings. The real issue is the perspective of the participant observer. These observers, like the journalists they study, must be extremely selective in filtering incidents and fragments of speech into the final written report. A comparison of these research studies tells us as much about the perspectives and abilities of their respective authors as the different newsrooms they studied. Reading Tuchman and Altheide, one might conclude that Epstein had indeed covered the central points and that these additional studies were primarily repetitive and derivative. Altheide's study is the most disappointing. More bombastic in tone and limited in scope, he seems least able to rise above the details of his field notes to draw broader conclusions about the processes he witnessed. He notes, for example, one incident in which technical problems prevent the filming of a cat rescue without ever addressing the question of why local news crews get such assignments in the first place. His argument that television ratings have undue influence on news decisions confuses the issue of the statistical reliability of ratings with the more subtle point of the effect of competition for audiences on news judgment. His review of the coverage of the Eagleton affair in 1972 demonstrates, perhaps unintentionally, an important point about the analysis of newsmaking. He argues that because of structural factors (a slow news week in August and the journalistic inclination to simplify), reporters focused unduly on Eagleton's mental health, and reflected an unsophisticated understanding of the nature of mental illness while ignoring other important elements of the Eagleton candidacy, such as his position on the issues. Although it is presumably based on a structural analysis of newsmaking, this is actually a straightforward dispute about news judgment. Because of the obvious possibility of assuming presidential powers and control of the nation's nuclear capacity, the issue of Eagleton's mental health had obvious and direct political relevance. Altheide's huffy critique illustrates dramatically that scholars may be able to clarify for the rest of us how decision making in such organizations operates; but he is hardly in a position to dictate new definitions of newsworthiness.

A unique element in Tuchman's approach to the study of news is an attempt to draw on the insights of several scholarly traditions, including the sociology of organizations, ethnomethodology, and Marxism. Unfortunately the result is a somewhat awkward mix. The analytic constructs she borrows seem overly simplified and often ill-suited to the subject of her field observations. An interested reader might do better to follow her footnotes for references to more complete works reflecting these perspectives. For the most part her conclusions parallel Epstein's. She presents an interesting but brief analysis of the news coverage of the women's movement in one chapter. It is, however, a topic itself worthy of book-length treatment.

It is Gans's *Deciding What's News,* however, which clearly establishes that there are a number of fresh insights yet to be drawn about the role of the news media in our society. Gans starts with an intriguing content analysis which explores the relative emphasis of the "CBS Evening News" and *Newsweek* magazine on well-known public officials and business leaders, as opposed to relative "unknowns" such as protesters, crime victims, and average citizens. He presents a revealing analysis of the treatment of social class and ideology in the American media. His chapter on cultural values in the news moves far beyond Epstein's work to explore such central American values as "responsible capitalism," "small town pastoralism," and "individualism" which, because of their omnipresence, tend to escape the attention of consumers of news in our culture.

The bulk of his study, like the others, draws heavily on his field experience in various newsrooms. The themes of the routinization of news processing and the development of interpersonal ties between reporters and sources are again emphasized. The final section of his book, however, is most interesting and likely to be more controversial. It most clearly sets this book off in the competition. It is an impressively detailed series of recommendations for the nurturance of what he calls "multiperspectival news." This new approach to news would be national in scope but would not simple-mindedly equate the nation with the federal government, would avoid the top-down perspective which judges events from the views of high officials, and would include the views of citizens from various walks of life likely to be affected by new policies. One of the most intriguing and radical elements of his recommendations is the concept of the establishment of a national Endowment for News, modeled loosely on the federal agencies which help support independent scholarship and entrepreneurship in the arts and humanities. Overall Gans's book is an impressive use of sociological theory to organize and interpret what might otherwise be, like several of the other books, a series of newsroom anecdotes.

## RECENT RESEARCH FINDINGS

Two ongoing studies of television and its audience have released updated reports this year. The Roper Organization, in cooperation with the Television Information Office, has been monitoring media use and public attitudes. Their report is entitled, "Public Perceptions of Television and Other Mass Media: A 20-year Review, 1959-1978." One of the most intriguing trends they describe is a substantial growth in public reliance on television for news. Part of this growth is no doubt due to the fact that over this period there has been a 10 percent growth in the number of households with television, until 1963 the nightly network news was only 15 minutes, and local news has been expanded in many markets as well. Roper's question is, "First, I would like to ask you where you usually get most of your news about what's going on in the world today—from the newspaper or radio or television or magazines or talking to people or where?" This trend line including the most recent survey is reproduced in Figure 1. The Figure reveals that growth in reliance as a news source may have stabilized somewhat in recent years. If there is to be continued growth, it may be a result of the expanded news coverage available through cable. Twenty percent of our nation's households are already hooked up and many systems have a 24-hour headline service. Discussions are now underway concerning establishment of a full-time, full-service national cable news channel to be distributed via satellite to local cable systems. Ultimately, of course, the distinction between newspapers and television is likely to become blurred. Newspapers eventually will be electronically delivered and we will have the choice of viewing "paper" on the screen or having our sets print out a "hard copy" on paper to take with us to the office.

*Figure 1*
**Reliance on Television for News**

| Sources of most news: | 12/59 % | 11/61 % | 11/63 % | 11/64 % | 1/67 % | 11/68 % | 1/71 % | 11/72 % | 11/74 % | 11/76 % | 12/78 % |
|---|---|---|---|---|---|---|---|---|---|---|---|
| Television | 51 | 52 | 55 | 58 | 64 | 59 | 60 | 64 | 65 | 64 | 67 |
| Newspapers | 57 | 57 | 53 | 56 | 55 | 49 | 48 | 50 | 47 | 49 | 49 |
| Radio | 34 | 34 | 29 | 26 | 28 | 25 | 23 | 21 | 21 | 19 | 20 |
| Magazines | 8 | 9 | 6 | 8 | 7 | 7 | 5 | 6 | 4 | 7 | 5 |
| People | 4 | 5 | 4 | 5 | 4 | 5 | 4 | 4 | 4 | 5 | 5 |

A second major ongoing study has been conducted by George Gerbner and Larry Gross at the University of Pennsylvania. They have been monitoring the level of violence in television by analyzing a random sample of programming each year since 1967. Their working definition of violence is "the overt expression of physical force against self or other, or compelling action against one's will upon pain of being hurt or being killed or actually hurting or killing." Their definition has been criticized as being unduly broad and failing to separate out violence in comic and dramatic contexts. Their latest data are reported in Figure 2. As a partial corrective to the issue of dramatic context, we have sepa-

*Figure 2*
**Trends in Television Violence**

| % of Programs Containing Violence | 1967 | 1968 | 1969 | 1970 | 1971 | 1972 | 1973 | 74-75* | 75-76* | 1976 | 1977** | 1978 |
|---|---|---|---|---|---|---|---|---|---|---|---|---|
| All Primetime | 75.0 | 75.4 | 70.3 | 62.3 | 75.8 | 71.7 | 59.7 | 72.2 | 68.7 | 80.3 | 69.8 | 74.6 |
| Action Programs | 97.3 | 96.9 | 96.0 | 95.8 | 96.8 | 100.0 | 92.9 | 94.4 | 94.6 | 92.9 | 90.7 | 90.0 |
| Comic Tone | 50.0 | 47.8 | 38.1 | 50.0 | 60.0 | 35.0 | 75.0 | 26.3 | 32.4 | 63.6 | 53.8 | 56.3 |
| All Weekend-Daytime | 93.8 | 93.3 | 98.2 | 96.0 | 87.8 | 90.0 | 94.6 | 93.5 | 90.2 | 100.0 | 90.6 | 97.9 |
| **Rate per Hour of Violence** | | | | | | | | | | | | |
| All Primetime | 5.9 | 4.4 | 4.0 | 3.7 | 4.3 | 5.2 | 4.9 | 5.4 | 6.0 | 6.1 | 5.5 | 4.5 |
| Action Programs | 7.7 | 5.6 | 6.1 | 5.6 | 5.2 | 7.3 | 7.3 | 6.9 | 7.2 | 8.1 | 7.5 | 5.2 |
| Comic Tone | 3.2 | 3.2 | 2.2 | 1.7 | 2.3 | 1.9 | 1.1 | 3.2 | 3.1 | 4.0 | 4.3 | 6.3 |
| All Weekend—Daytime | 21.6 | 22.9 | 28.4 | 22.5 | 16.2 | 15.8 | 13.2 | 12.2 | 14.2 | 22.4 | 15.6 | 25.0 |

*These figures are based upon two samples—one from the Fall and one from the Spring.
**The Fall 1977 sample consists of two weeks of prime-time and one weekend morning network dramatic programs.
Data & Chart assembled especially for *Television Annual* 1978-79.

rated out the violence level for action and comedy programs, as well as the total for prime time and children's programming (weekend daytime which, as it turns out, is primarily cartoons). Their full research report breaks the data down by network and reveals that at one time or another and in one category or another, each of the networks has held the lead in the amount of violence. Overall the picture is one of stability with moderate, seemingly rhythmic fluctuation from year to year. Apparently critics of television violence have not been especially effective in changing the character of the medium. Again, cable may be the source of the most dramatic shift in programming, the violence as well as sexual content, as unedited motion pictures and specialized cable programming become more readily available to the home viewing audience.

# PUBLIC TELEVISION

by Michael Ambrosino*

ONE of the documents you'll be dealing with tomorrow states that, "The basic purpose of public broadcasting is to deliver programs to an audience. About this there is little debate."

*Michael Ambrosino gave testimony to the Carnegie II Commission while he was executive producer of the PBS program "Nova." This is an edited version of his testimony. He is currently

I would like to debate that.

I realize that the writer probably meant to say "to create and deliver programs," but he used only the word "deliver." Often, when people talk about public broadcasting, they talk about a *delivery* system.

Sadly, many public TV administrators might consider public television a delivery system. It should be a system that *creates* and delivers. It is not a library, though many interpreted Carnegie I that way.

If literary allusions are necessary, public television should be considered a publishing house, not a library. Publishers and their editors seek out the best minds and deal with complex ideas. They generate books and then see that they are distributed. I doubt that the publisher of the *New York Times* sees his company as an organization that merely delivers papers, or Atlantic Press or Random House a delivery system for books.

It is not a small difference and it is central to your activity for the next year.

Instead of looking at the public broadcasting system from the top down, please look at it from the bottom up. Please take the point of view of the individual trying to create a program, and seek an answer to his or her needs. Come up with your answers from *that* point of view rather than thinking you will have succeeded if you once again reorganize the Corporation for Public Broadcasting (CPB) and the Public Broadcasting Service (PBS).

About 80 people in the United States are the creators of the schedule that's on public broadcasting today. They are not the managers or fund raisers. They are the producers and executive producers of the continuing series and specials on the air. They attend few meetings and are rarely heard from. You could be their voice.

Today, I'd like to present a few ideas about how programs are made and say a few things about "Nova" as a good model.

First, people make programs—people who are alert and curious about the world, people who are dealing with people on the street and in the universities, people who are traveling, reading books, and going to concerts: active, intelligent, curious people who are in touch with other people and ideas.

Secondly, good programs are made with people, not with abstract ideas. It is very difficult to make a program about "liberty." I thought that the late Charles Frankel's attempt was as good as I had seen, but it is very difficult to make programs about abstractions.

Thirdly, understanding a process makes good programs. A producer *must* understand the process of politics in order to make a program like "MacNeil/Lehrer." You must understand the process of science to make a "Nova." The producer then employs those processes. The core of our program-making is following scientists in the recreating of the processes of discovery.

Fourth, producers need opportunity. It is that little extra cash that a station has that allows its management to say, "Okay, it may take a year

president of his own independent production company in Boston called Public Broadcasting Associates.

to do this. . .work at it, play with it, come up with the idea and see if it will work."

Fifth, there also must be some sense of continuity. The hundreds of people who worked on the "Adams Chronicles" were disbanded. Virginia Kassel (who conceived the idea for the miniseries) might get them back three or four years later but she'd never get the same *team* back.

In "Nova" we planned and hired so that we could build a team and not have to begin over and over again. Continuity is essential, but it is not built into any funding arrangement that presently exists in public broadcasting.

Sixth, there should also be a possibility for refreshment and growth. My Corporation for Public Broadcasting Fellowship which was spent at BBC was directly responsible for "Nova." It was the most exceptional professional experience of my life and I think CPB got value for its money.

Instead of merely purchasing more BBC shows, or starting a new United States series without any help at all, "Nova" created a continuing series with a planned counterpart at BBC. We immediately had a series of international scope and standard, all at a lower per-program cost. WGBH of Boston now produces 50 percent of "Nova" and the rest are co-produced with BBC.

The development of "Nova" was supported by WGBH because they had the extra cash to do so and the interest in seeing it done. Boston seemed a natural place for science and television to come together. The funding was deceptively easy. We asked six people for money and four said yes. I've been raising money for the last six months for "Odyssey." The first two requests were positive and I've had 38 no's (later to stretch to 52).

We planned to have four funders for "Nova" because having four funders meant no bosses. Dealing with the controversy and having multiple funders like Polaroid, Carnegie, NSF, and CPB gave us the best possible protection.

The best, with exception of Station Program Cooperative (SPC)— the funding arm of PBS. I take issue with those who condemn SPC. I find having 156 bosses a joy! Stations might disagree with our program on plutonium or bombing but still feel it necessary to buy the total series. "Nova" was purchased year after year, after year, after year.

My interest goes beyond making programs. I want to make series. I see a raft of new series coming which could use the "Nova" concept in the arts as well as the sciences.

A few areas of concern.

First, look at the system from my angle, not yours and not from the system's angle. Instead of seeing how you can clean up CPB or PBS please figure out what creative individuals need in order to make programs and then create structures to meet these needs. Individuals rather than institutions make programs. Institutions must be created that will support those individuals!

Second, push for full funding rather than partial funding of programs and program development. Everybody tries to stretch the little money that they have: corporations, foundations, CPB, NEA, NEH. Everybody will give you a little bit. That means that you spend months fund-raising. I have put one-half to three-quarters of a year of my own salary into the development of my new series. Fortunately the National Endowment for the humanities supported the first year-and-a-half of my research.

Third, you must deal with the lack of coordination between the funding and the distribution of programs. It is insane to think of a restaurant menu being made up by farmers. With the present arrangement, people all over the country come up with ideas. There is no coordination as to *when* they are done or *how* they are done. There is no coordination between the CPB's giving of money and the PBS' scheduling. "America," "Civilization," and "The Ascent of Man" were not made simultaneously. They are very carefully staggered so that individuals and experience could go from one to the other, and so that funds could be used efficiently.

My fourth concern is the "step-by-step process." Although at times it can be helpful to film on a trial basis, with experienced people it can be inordinately wasteful. Producers of large series at BBC know that they are developing and planning in an atmosphere of positive affirmation.

The Bronowski series was going to fly if Adrian and Bronowski could make it fly. If they couldn't, it would die. From the beginning it was known that the end result was "go." The way you hired, the way you traveled, the way you thought was to make something occur, not to create a proposal. Film is made on celluloid and fights you. Film planning is of the moment and requires a positive, determined attitude, not a long continuing wait-and-see atmosphere.

Point five, beware of the concept of the block grant if it means small blocks. That would be little better than the system we presently have.


Questions?

HELLER: Thank you for that extraordinarily informative and thought-provoking presentation. What I'd like to know is, if you don't use the block grants, how do you keep an "Adams Chronicles" staff together for the next venture?

AMBROSINO: While the "Adams Chronicles" is in the process of being made, the "core" staff should know that something will come in the future. Some of that "core" can begin the future planning.

The core of "Nova" is together. The core of "Nova" has developed three new series, one on technology, another on animal behavior, and a third on the history of medicine. The individuals within the group cause a ferment. A good series is a training ground.

JOHNSON: Is there, in your judgment, any concern about the belief that the person or company who underwrites also dictates programs?

AMBROSINO: Not in mine. I've had no problems with either Exxon or Polaroid. We've done some of the most controversial programs in the "Nova" series (with their backing). If you want to talk about some other agencies afterwards . . . The corporation obviously has its reasons for doing what it does. But underwriting within "Nova" has never been a concern in terms of dictation.

JOHNSON: I wonder if the lack of direct dictation or involvement has any relationship to the success of a program. For example, "Nova" in my judgment would be classified as successful, whereas some independently produced programs have difficulty getting underwriting (and) having time to survive that period of becoming successful.

AMBROSINO: I think you've answered your own question. If the idea, the individual, and the backing are weak, someone wishing to have influence can have it.

JOHNSON: You see, the assumption here is that if it isn't successful it's weak, and I'm not making that assumption. My concern is the kinds of problems you may have had in trying to get funded and approved.

BAILEY: We've had a discussion before on the topic I'm about to ask you about, but it has really to do with theories about genius. One assumption is that genius is a tiny constant in the universe and will overcome all obstacles. It doesn't make any difference what you have in its way, it'll come through, it'll unfold itself.

The other extreme is you throw a lot of money around and genius comes up like weeds. Middle ground says that genius can be cultivated like good melons. Good soil, fertilizer, production management, and you can get a whole series of advance quality control. It makes a whale of a difference if we are going to give the attention which I think we ought to give, as partly the result of your eloquence, to the software production problems and the individualization of some of this, and I wonder if you can help us.

AMBROSINO: I wish you'd asked me about truth. (Laughter)

With "Nova" we were given a mandate for success. If the first 13 didn't make it we weren't going to get the chance for any others.

When BBC creates a series (unless it has a real tomato on its hands), it is willing to carry it through to a third season. You will see the title change, the executive producer change, and the staff change as it tries to work through that process.

You can prepare ideas, proposals, and pilots, but you've got to put a show on the air to work it out properly.

I don't know the answer to genius. If you collect enough intelligent people, and have a system that allows that process of development and allows for failures . . . then you're going to get some successes.

Public broadcasting expects much more. "Feeling Good" is put on the air and tries to work through its problems, but doesn't get the chance.

BAILEY: Assuming you can't be cloned, what are the ways in which the society goes about the business of cultivating the kind of talent that you and few others represent?

AMBROSINO: Go back to the BBC model again. The key word is activity. A lot of people doing things. A lot of people getting training.

On "Nova" we had a producer, an associate producer, and a production assistant per show. When we would do research, *three* people would be involved. Very expensive. Almost wasteful. But we trained people! In my mind that associate producer was next season's producer, and that PA was next season's associate producer.

Go to Kensington House (at BBC) and sit with 150 people in the club and tell them you're doing a show about water. Fifteen will tell you you're crazy and another fifteen will give you ideas for your program. A lot of people in action is the way you cultivate talent. No think-tank arrangements; I think the best TV laboratories are on the air at 9:00 P.M. on Tuesday nights.

DUNCAN: "Nova" originated at WGBH?

AMBROSINO: Right.

DUNCAN: To me that's part of the formula . . .

AMBROSINO: Right.

DUNCAN: And Michael Rice's ability to set his priorities to nurture something like that. You mention block grants. It would seem to me that having that luxury of a Program Manager who makes that kind of choice and who allows you the freedom to really develop a series makes a lot of difference in how it works out.

AMBROSINO: It was essential. The decisions on the corporate level, the cash, the freedom to play for the year and see if it would work or not, were essential to the creation of 'Nova.''

These projects were being developed during that year. One was "Nova," one was "Dying," one was a series of east-west programs in Massachusetts. In case they *all* failed, the station had reserved $100,000 for me to resume my own local documentary series.

That kind of support meant that I could succeed because I always had something to fall back on.

MASON: Listening to you "look at the system not from the top down, but from the bottom up," I've been wondering if I understand how you might feel about a strong network.

Did I get the impression from you that you don't think the SPC is necessary, that for instance that "Nova" would have gone on the air with the SPC, if the system were funded strictly through the stations and the SPC. But that would not have been a deterrent to "Nova."

AMBROSINO: Yes, I support a fourth network, I think that Carnegie I was misinterpreted and people spoke about "grass-roots" television and did not wish to push a fourth network much to our detriment. I believe very much in a strong PBS network. I want programs like "Nova" to be run in most of the cities at the same time if possible.

Second, I think SPC is very beneficial for a series that has made its mark. It is not the place where the system supports new series.

If you look at a list of programs in production, "The American Short Story"; "Odyssey"; a television series on history; four hour television programs on "The Scarlet Letter"; eight programs of dramatic adaptions of Fitzgerald's life; a documentary film on pre-colonial Williamsburg, a whole host of things—all very inventive ideas and developments—all coming out of NEH, not CBS.

In many ways the program manager of next year's season is Steve Rabin of the National Endowment for the Humanities. (Laughter)

EVANS: Mike, in some ways I would characterize you as a brilliant insider. You're a lucky person who's very creative and has the support of a huge, well, a large station compared to a lot of people who have power and authority over money, and I wonder if you can put yourself back a few years and answer a question that worries me. How do you deal with the brilliant outsiders? I once talked to an independent producer who said to me, "it's all a Tong war to get your idea on. And, by God, what we don't want is a centralized CPB system efficiently managed, tightly constructed—power relationship up and down the line. But just put a lot of funders out there and I'll find it, and put my idea through, and put it on the air." I just wondered how you would answer the question of the brilliant outsiders.

AMBROSINO: Go back to "Nova" as the model. "Nova" was meant to help change public broadcasting and I'd like to see more like it done. The strand allows you to make, coproduce, purchase, remake, commission the brilliant outsider. I'd like to see other such strands made.

I have not seen Widner's ("Plutonium") film. I don't know whether it's good or bad. Obviously he is a very provocative film-maker. But don't think spreading money on the waters is going to do the job unless network access is determined at the time the grant is made. Otherwise it's hypocrisy.

I also question individual programs being commissioned without some editorial overseeing.

EVANS: Unless your concept of what public television was and ought to be and what's seen on the air were different than what is now—that it was to be a controversial colliding medium of ideas and excitement and confrontation even, instead of a kind of "Nova" presentation of the scientific issues—an entirely different kind of medium.

AMBROSINO: True, the Bronowski series had a tough time being sold in America. Many corporations said, "that's not science."

At BBC they have a science series, a technology series, an archeology series, an anthropology series, a social science series—public affairs, and world affairs, and it just goes on and on. Each year a *personal* series is made. It is what Bronowski thought science *should* be. Bronowski's ideas had a chance.

HELLER: Well, on behalf of the Commission and its staff, let me thank you very much for what as I said is very thought-provoking, certainly very stimulating. I'm sure that we go out of here with a few more ideas than we came in before your appearance. Thanks again.

# SHAKESPEARE

**Lee Winfrey**[*]

ENGLAND exported six plays by William Shakespeare to the United States during the 1978-79 television season. Amid the small change of typical TV fare, they glittered like Shylock's ducats.

The British Broadcasting Corporation (BBC) budgeted $10 million to produce all of Shakespeare's 37 plays over a 6-year period, using English talent exclusively. Three American business firms—Exxon, Metropolitan Life Insurance, and Morgan Guaranty Trust—chipped in another $3.6 million to bring the productions to this country.

For the Public Broadcasting Service (PBS), which is telecasting the series here, the price is an incredible bargain. It works out to less than

[*]Lee Winfrey is a television columnist with the *Philadelphia Inquirer* and the Knight-Ridder news service.

$100,000 per play, less than half the cost of a typical episode of "Happy Days" or "Laverne and Shirley."

The first six plays aired at two-week intervals during February, March, and April 1979. One was a luminous success, one an unfortunate failure. The other four, which looked as though they will probably be typical of the series as a whole, were more than adequate video representations of the work of the world's greatest playwright.

The most admirable and eloquent of the plays was *Richard II*. Derek Jacobi turned in a peerless performance as the doomed king.

Shakespeare's genius in writing the English language is apparent everywhere in the words of Richard. Seldom has speech approached the sound of music so closely as in the wails and sighs of the last of the Plantagenet kings.

Richard's moods and motives range from capriciousness and hubris, through wastefulness and greed, to sorrow and despair. It is impossible to admire Richard's character, but Jacobi compelled attention to his every syllable. For Jacobi, *Richard II* was the finest role in his career.

The 40-year-old actor was previously best known in this country for his TV work in the title role of *I, Claudius*. His characterization of Richard II was the finest male performance so far in the Shakespeare series.

A notable virtue of the premiere season was the scrupulous attention given to the many occasions in which Shakespeare puts major speeches into the mouths of secondary characters.

For example, probably the most famous speech in *Richard II* is given to John of Gaunt, the Duke of Lancaster. This is the legendary tribute to England that includes the phrases ". . . this sceptred isle . . . this blessed plot . . ." On TV, Sir John Gielgud, one of the greatest Shakespearean actors of the past half-century, gave this great oration an impeccable reading.

The only failure among the first half-dozen Shakespeare plays was *Romeo and Juliet*. Of the four most important roles, one was inadequately projected and another miserably mishandled.

As Juliet, 14-year-old Rebecca Saire was handed a role beyond the reach of her experience. At least another decade lies between her and the ability to play a praiseworthy Juliet.

Shakespeare specified in the text of this play that Juliet is 13 years old. Hence the casting of the adolescent Miss Saire. The resulting accuracy in looks, however, was not enough to compensate for the short reach of her present talent.

The poorest performance in *Romeo and Juliet*, however, and the one absolutely fatal to the production, was Anthony Andrews as Mercutio. This role is so powerful that Elizabethan dramatist John Dryden thought Shakespeare was forced to kill Mercutio in the middle of the play because he was on the verge of dominating the entire proceeding.

There was no danger of Andrews's Mercutio taking over anything, save perhaps a ship of fools. Entire lines of Mercutio's were obliterated amid Andrews's expostulations, gasps, and trills. Among the missing parts were almost the whole of Mercutio's most touching speech, his charming description of Queen Mab.

Patrick Ryecart made a handsome and eloquent Romeo. As Juliet's nurse, Celia Johnson was superb. But their virtues were insufficient to save this TV production, whose overall quality fell short of Franco Zeffirelli's 1968 movie of *Romeo and Juliet* which starred Leonard Whiting and Olivia Hussey in the title roles.

The finest female performance during the series' first season was Helen Mirren as Rosalind in *As You Like It.*

Rosalind is one of Shakespeare's most admirable women. Although she spends more than half of *As You Like It* disguised as a boy, she is still everything that is wonderful in womankind: witty, warm, charming, loving, intelligent, and realistic, to mention only a few of her virtues.

Miss Mirren is one of the best Shakespearean actresses in England. Her performance as Rosalind was classically good, likely to be studied for years as a model for aspiring actresses.

Despite the profusion of spoken delights that Shakespeare lavished upon Rosalind, the most famous passage in the play is probably Jaques's speech about the seven ages of man, the one that begins "All the world's a stage, and all the men and women merely players." Richard Pasco gave the speech a varied and fascinating reading while he walked around a campfire in the Forest of Arden.

In the premiere play of the series, Pasco played Brutus in *Julius Caesar.* In the way that the best English actors can so convincingly make up and comport themselves to play different roles, Pasco was brave and dignified as Brutus, cynical and dissolute as Jaques. He was so disparate in looks and style that one would scarcely realize without reading a list of the casts that the same player essayed both roles.

In *Julius Caesar*, Pasco made an excellent Brutus. His diction is impeccable, musical and rolling, firm and clear. Delivering Shakespearean lines well demands the breath control of an opera singer. Pasco is a fine working model of how to do it.

Pasco's work was the key factor in making *Julius Caesar* a success, since Brutus speaks five times as many lines in the play as Caesar. Despite its title, *Julius Caesar* is not really about the murdered monarch, since he makes only three brief appearances and is murdered in the middle of the play.

Nevertheless Charles Gray made a memorable Caesar, suggesting both his majestic power and his growing vanity.

Keith Mitchell was a little too old to be a proper Marc Antony. He really should have been more of the age of Marlon Brando at the time Brando played this role in the famous 1953 movie production of *Julius Caesar.*

But Mitchell's rendition of Marc Antony's funeral oration ("Friends, Romans, countrymen, lend me your ears!") was a shrewd and telling piece of stagecraft, adroit and persuasive. And, sitting his steed on the battlefield of Philippi, Mitchell struck a properly martial pose.

*Measure for Measure,* which has defeated many a cast in the 375 years since it was written, took its toll on another band of players on TV last spring. Shakespeare's final comedy has a long last act that is unbelievable and practically unplayable.

But, undismayed by dubious material, an excellent cast made the video production about as close to successful as is possible. In particular, Kate Nelligan wrung the last extractable ounce of sympathy from the role of Isabella—the most stiff and smug of all of Shakespeare's heroines.

As Angelo, Tim Pigott-Smith was extremely able, bringing this hanging judge and secret sinner to life no matter what the mood.

Dark was the background as Angelo and Isabella played off their conflict, struggling over Isabella's virginity in two tense encounters that comprise the two best scenes in the play. Much of the play took place in a prison brilliantly conceived by set-designer Stuart Walker, whose work on *Romeo and Juliet* was also distinguished.

The staging of *Measure for Measure*, which augmented the appeal of the play, was in noteworthy contrast to *As You Like It,* whose outdoor setting sometimes dissipated precision and occasionally blurred the acting.

The premiere season closed appropriately with *Henry VIII*, the last play that Shakespeare wrote. Since it was beautiful to look at, with much pomp and pagaentry and royal marching about, the BBC capitalized upon this virtue by giving it a handsome mounting.

Three English castles were used: Penshurst Place, Hever Castle, and Leeds Castle. The costumes by Alun Hughes were as opulent as the surroundings.

Unhappily, John Stride didn't pack the heft to make a good Henry VIII. When he should have been angry, he seemed only petulant. He seemed merely shifty, rather than complex.

Part of the problem was that an aging Shakespeare, only three years away from his death, did not etch the character of Henry in sharp detail. Stride only added to the weakness of the role.

Timothy West, previously seen on TV in a miniseries as England's King Edward VII, played Cardinal Wolsey masterfully. Director Keven Billington wisely gave West full room to work, often letting the camera remain upon his expressive face even when other characters were speaking.

Particularly admirable was West's reading of Wolsey's finest speech, the most famous soliloquy in the play, the one where the cashiered cardinal broods upon his fall: "Farewell, a long farewell to all my greatness . . ."

Claire Bloom was magnificent as Queen Katharine, claiming place with Miss Mirren and Miss Nelligan as the three women who most luminously ornamented the Shakespearean season. Shakespeare wrote of Katharine in terms of highest praise, and the artistic assurance of Miss Bloom made every line of adulation seem fair comment.

Executive producer Cedric Messina, who is in charge of the series, deserves the thanks of everyone who loves Shakespeare. The fidelity and craftsmanship with which he has worked so far argue convincingly that the Bard is in good hands.

Messina has admirably resisted the contemporary tendency, dismally exemplified in so many productions by Joseph Papp and others, to try to make Shakespeare more palatable by bringing the settings more up-to-date. Thankfully, Messina serves Shakespeare straight, costuming the plays according to their proper times, surely the right way to do a series which will later enter many classrooms via video cassettes.

Aside from erring in his choice of a Juliet, which was an understandable experiment, Messina has been generally sure-handed in the casting of major roles. The acting has been on a high plateau with enough peaks like Jacobi's Richard II to compel confidence in Messina's future judgment.

On television, a medium where much of the product is not worth watching once much less seeing again, the Shakespeare series is truly a landmark, an assembling of artistry praiseworthy in both ambition and execution.

# "60 MINUTES" ON TRIAL

### by Michael Kramer*

ANYONE who believes that the press is always fair probably believes that inflation is simply a temporary nightmare. Most of us journalists are just regular folks. We have families to feed and mortgages to pay off and biases that color our individual views of the world. We would like people to believe that we become "objective" when we hit the street. Too often, we don't. Too often, as Tocqueville said, reporters "appeal to the passions of (their) readers; (abandoning) principles to assail the characters of individuals." Too often, journalistic morals take a backseat to "the story." And that story had better be good. As H. L. Mencken wrote, "You must give a good show to get a crowd, and a good show means one with slaughter in it."

It is exactly this reality that underlies the recent Supreme Court decision involving the right of an aggrieved party to question a reporter's biases, to probe his mind in an attempt to understand the editorial process. Reporters conditioned to absolute freedom via the First Amendment are in a state of mental collapse; "chilling," says Wicker of the *Times*, a "mighty blow," echoes Wieghart of the *Daily News*. These critics have a point. But . . .

Were the press to have its way, could it roam unchecked across the nation with no adequate redress available for those who feel unjustly accused? As it stands now, "public figures" (a term of increasingly wide latitude) are hard-pressed to sue successfully for libel. The landmark Supreme Court case of 1964 (*New York Times* v. *Sullivan*) held that even if a newspaper published an untrue charge against a public official that damaged his character or financial interests, a suit for damages had to prove not only a falsehood but "actual malice" on the part of the publisher—that the newspaper or radio or TV station had made the charge public with the knowledge that it was false or with reckless disregard of whether it was false. In the latest case, involving CBS's "60 Minutes" and its segment implying that Lieutenant Colonel Anthony Herbert may have lied about his reporting of war crimes in Vietnam, the Supreme Court asked and answered a very simple question: How can a defendant prove malice if he cannot examine the editorial process that results in the article or television reporting to which he objects?

*Michael Kramer is a contributing writer for *New York* magazine. This essay originally appeared in that magazine on May 7, 1979.

The Herbert case offers us a chance to see how the editorial process really works—at least, in this instance, at "60 Minutes."

Colonel Herbert is one of America's genuine war heroes. During the Korean conflict he was the country's most decorated fighting man. After his tour in Vietnam, he wrote a best-seller, *Soldier,* revealing the war crimes by Americans he had witnessed and the cover-up he claimed had followed. Needless to say, the army was not pleased. Then "60 Minutes" aired "The Selling of Colonel Herbert" in 1973, implying that Herbert himself "could be brutal with captured enemy prisoners."

Part of the inside story of the making of the "60 Minutes" show is revealed in over 3,000 pages of testimony taken thus far in the Herbert case. With the exception of Robert Friedman (writing in *More* magazine two years ago), no one has bothered to examine the sworn statements. Some highlights from Friedman's article:

Barry Lando, the segment's producer, had first suggested a *pro-*Herbert broadcast. It was rejected; nothing new, said Lando's bosses. In his own words Lando says that, at that time, he was under pressure from the network to "turn out a solid story as quickly as possible." Shortly thereafter Lando proposed an *anti-*Herbert, and therefore pro-army story; it was accepted. It is important to understand that, at the time, CBS itself felt uncomfortable with growing charges by the Nixon administration that the network's reporting had an antigovernment bias. CBS president Frank Stanton had even met at one point with presidential hatchet man Chuck Colson and, according to Colson, who had secretly recorded the confrontation, Stanton "volunteered to help us" in fashioning White House coverage.

On November 28, 1972, Lando met with an army spokesman to seek cooperation on the Herbert story. According to a "Memorandum for the Record" written by the officer with whom Lando spoke, "Lando's stated premise is that Herbert is a liar." It also warned, "He has stated that if he can't develop a sufficient number of incidents in which Herbert's account cannot be debunked, then there will be no story."

Interviews, with army personnel, in Lando's possession reveal numerous pieces of information damaging not to Herbert but to his army accusers. Herbert contends this material was deliberately not broadcast. In addition, in the final version of the show, correspondent Mike Wallace claimed that Herbert failed to report war crimes until 17 months after he was relieved of his command and only after the My Lai revelations had stunned the country. Yet Lando's notes indicate he had evidence to the contrary.

In an ironic twist rivaling the Nixon tapes, while Wallace and Lando were interviewing officers on-camera at the Pentagon, the army was surreptitiously recording the proceedings. When the CBS cameras were turned off, the Pentagon kept rolling and recorded Wallace saying: "Ideally, if we can get somebody on the film to say, 'I don't know whether (Herbert) reported (atrocities) but he is capable of doing that sort of thing himself.'"

The question in all of this is whether the conduct of "60 Minutes" adds up to malice aforethought and whether further inquiry into states of mind is warranted. The Supreme Court has now said that these questions can indeed be asked.

The decision represents a serious dilemma for the press, one aspect of which is the possibility of nuisance suits capable of draining a news organization's financial resources. But the Supreme Court has decided that the alternative is even more onerous—that it would, in effect, deny Colonel Herbert and other Colonel Herberts to come a fair and thorough hearing.

# THEN YOU TAKE THE SLAUSON CUTOFF TO THE CARSON NATIONAL MONUMENT. . .

## By Dick Hobson*

"MR. CARSON won't be able to see you today," his right-hand person had phoned. "Mr. Carson has a cold." Indeed, Carson's "Tonight Show" monologue the night before did have a nasal sound to it. "These jokes are coming out of a head where I can't even hear them myself," he'd told the audience. "I may be very fortunate." (Laughter.)

"How many of you know about the Academy Award nominations?" he pushed on. "*Heaven Can Wait* won eight nominations. That's the picture where Warren Beatty plays a man who dies and comes back. I die and come back two or three times a week and I didn't get any Academy Award nominations." (Laughter.) He didn't mention that he'd be emceeing the Oscar ceremonies for the first time this year. Solo emceeing, at that—inheriting Bob Hope's mantle.

But he did manage to brag a bit: "I'm kinda proud of this—I made the cover of *Rolling Stone* this month." (Applause.) "I've never done that before. I'm thinking of becoming the first punk comedian—Johnny Funny." (Laughter.) The youth-oriented *Rolling Stone*, in fact, pronounced him "a true show-business legend."

At 53, Johnny Carson, America's King of the Midnight Quip, is apparently slipping into a new role as a national monument. Harvard's Hasty Pudding Club elected him its Man of the Year. Even the august *New Yorker*, in a profile by Kenneth Tynan, conferred "cynosure status" upon his sharply tailored shoulders. "Long—or, at least, as long as the air at the summit continues to nourish and elate him—may he stay there," went the effusive tag line.

The Quip King's right-hand personage, Drue Wilson, swung open the door to his book-jammed hideaway atop the "Tonight Show" stage, revealing a mere wraith of a wizard, watery of eye, and still sniffling. "Forgive me," Carson said. "I'm so full of antibiotics I'm about a half-beat behind."

"Mr. Carson, to get straight to the matter at hand, I've been assigned to do a piece on 'The Avuncularization of Johnny Carson,' and I postulate that your 'avuncular period' got started three years ago when you went back to Nebraska to deliver the commencement address at

*Dick Hobson is a contributing editor to *Los Angeles* magazine. This essay originally appeared in that magazine in April 1979.

your old alma mater, Norfolk High School. 'How to Get to Be 50 Years of Age Without Going Bananas,' was the title of your speech, I believe. Do you concur?"

"Quite frankly, I don't consider being in my early 50s *old*."

"How about 'avuncular,' then? Uncle Walter of CBS News is thought to be avuncular."

"Well, he's *old*! I don't feel old. I suspect when I get to be 60 I won't feel so old either."

"I gather you've followed the research showing that every grown man passes through certain age-linked periods that determine his marriage and career problems—the midlife transition, the middle-adult era, the age-50 transition, and so on. Now, taking note of the 17 seasons you have been doing the "Tonight Show" can you see them as falling into certain periods?"

"No, it just all blends together, really."

"Well, you know the famous midlife crisis of one's early 40s. Can't you recall having one of your own?"

"Not really. I don't feel that way as far as age goes. As George Burns will tell you, he's probably having the biggest years of his entire professional career in the last few years, from 78 on. And Jack Benny, who was a good friend of mine, was working in nightclubs at 77, doing two shows a night. Jeez, Bob Hope was on the show last week, and he's like a kid running around. He's 76 going on 77, but I don't think anybody considers Bob Hope an elderly man. In the entertainment business, nobody comes in and tells you that it's time now to get your gold watch."

"Maybe your midlife crisis is still to come. What about the place of origin of the show? Doesn't the New York period—the first 10 years from 1962 to 1972—seem to you different from the California period?"

"No, I've never felt that where we do the show is that particularly important. I still have people who think we do the show in New York, believe it or not. Somebody the other day said, 'How long are you going to be out here?' I said, 'I beg your pardon.' He said, 'I thought you did the show from New York!'"

"Well, how about your anniversary telecasts where you collect all the best bits? Take your fifth-anniversary show; didn't you feel that those first five years constituted a kind of an entity?"

"Yeah, in a way, because I remember when the show started I was standing backstage and somebody said, 'You know, you'll do this show and a week'll go by and a year'll go by and all of a sudden 10 years'll go by,' and I just looked at him like he must be insane. Because Steve Allen only did it for two-and-a-half years, and Jack Paar went screaming into the woods talking to a moose after about four years."

"And the tenth anniversary, didn't it make a mark?"

"Yeah, in a way, because I remember when we got to 10 years I considered maybe dropping out or going somewhere else. If I hadn't cut back on my time, there is no way I could have continued. But the history of the show to me is all kind of a blur."

"How about standout events like Tiny Tim's wedding?"

"Well, I can remember Con Edison in New York saying they noticed it in the electrical output because people were staying up to watch that wedding."

"Did the periods with different producers seem distinctive? Or different band leaders?"

"I don't think of it that way."

"How about with your various spouses? Do you relate it to your private life?"

"No, I really don't. Am I going to wreck your thesis here?"

"You are determined not to have a midlife crisis, I can see that."

"Well, the show just goes on, and although there probably have been changes in me and my attitude over the years, I don't see it because I'm too close to it."

"How about confrontations and struggles with the network at contract-renewal time? Those could be landmarks."

"Those weren't really terrible things. I don't think I've ever been guilty of trying to hold the network up. The press always looks at it that way. They never see it from the entertainer's side."

"Do you feel that in the earlier days you had more strictly show-biz types as guests on the show?"

"Probably. I think we mix 'em better now."

"What about the topicality of your monologue over the years? Any change?"

"I think the monologues are probably a little more barbed now, probably a little more incisive on the political situation."

"Your treatment of current events like Vietnam seemed more delicate, shall we say, than today."

"Yeah, because in those times it was extremely difficult to know how to handle that humorously. You can tell from night to night and week to week the mood of the audience. For example, during the Watergate period you could see the whole country turn around to anti-Nixon very quickly, in just a couple of weeks. Right now, Carter's popularity is probably at an all-time low."

"Your availability to the press seems to have changed from available to unavailable back to available."

"Yeah, I think I got turned off when I'd see things in print that I'd never said and never done. I think interviewers see what they want to see. I remember once I did a thing for *Look* with Betty Rollin. We were playing somewhere in St. Louis and I had taken my son with me and we were riding back to the hotel. My son had said, 'Dad, how far is it to so-and-so?' and her line was, 'Mr. Carson didn't answer.' Well, that makes you sound like an ass! Now, I might not have heard him. Those kinda things I have never understood. And, as you well know, there are a lot of writers who simply want to do a hatchet job."

"Well, Mr. Carson, I guess I'll have to let you off the hook."

"I wish I could have been of more help to you on this midlife business, but I don't see it that way. Maybe I'm too close to it. I've got to go down now and do a sketch rehearsal. I hope this hasn't been too goddam dull."

"It's been, uh, useful."

"That's a nice, nebulous copout word. As I said, my brain is not working 100 percent today. Thanks for stopping by."

# AND NOW FOR A FEW WORDS . . .

### by Alan M. Kriegsman*

THE biggest mystery on television these days isn't to be found in the gumshoe series, but in the ever-enthralling realm of commercial advertisement. It might be entitled: "The Case of The Vicarious Husband." But more anon.

The last thing the people who concoct TV ads want to do is to make waves. On the other hand, they spend their working lives rebounding from the waves made by others, including their competitors. It follows that styles and trends in TV commercials tend to run in cycles. When the "hot" idea of the moment is scientific-looking analysis, for instance, then every other ad is apt to feature a bespectacled septuagenarian in a white coat explaining how the extra added ingredient in his pain-reliever works overtime to deliver instant surcease.

There was a long while, more or less coincident—and not accidentally, either—with the Watergate era, when the on-location, cinema-verité testimonial descended upon the tube like a plague. Mike in hand, the pitchman would corner his "unsolicited" prey in, say, a laundromat, where she (these subjects being almost always female for all-too-obvious reasons) could be prodded into gushing endorsements of Cold Power or the newest bleach or whatever else was going down at the time. Such recitations were marked by awkward pauses, ungrammatical constructions, colloquialisms, and faulty sentence structure intended to assure us of the realism of the scene, despite the patently staged look. Watching seven or eight of these in a row was sufficient to give one a terminal case of ring-around-the-collar. But like everything else on television, the fad passed and the new ones took its place.

Remember Mrs. Marsh, the Colgate babysitter, the skinny lady with the teeth (one had visions of Central Casting sending out a call for a woman of homey, ingratiating manner and a set of incisors of maximum size and visibility) who lectured the kiddies on the importance of frequent and regular scrubbing? Why, not long ago she was so omnipresent on our screens she seemed practically a member of the family. Her zeal was disarming, but one suspects her emaciated appearance may have been due to excessive dental prophylaxis, say, 47 times every hour. In any case we miss her pearly presence, for she seems now to have retreated into the mists of television Nirvana—maybe she brushed herself out of existence.

As to current trends, what's come to the fore recently is an overbearingly paternalistic approach in which the sponsor is presented as a benevolent, all-seeing, all-knowing father figure, who will lead us benighted souls to salvation—these ads often have an air of confessional or religious conversion about them. The unspoken creed behind them is: What's good for the Pickmark and Grumble is even better for The American Family.

One such goes more or less like this: An offscreen voice says, "We're fooling Mrs. Conworthy . . ." (The "we" is ambiguous—you see, you and me out there in viewerland are brought in as accomplices to this conspiracy; it makes one feel practically like a stockholder.) ". . . We've told her we've taken the whitener out of Final Touch."

On screen we see the aghast face of the homemaker who exclaims,

---

*Alan Kriegsman is a writer for *The Washington Post*. This essay originally appeared in that newspaper on April 29, 1979.

"Put it baghck!" (The word is "back," but it's pronounced in the accents of some regional argot impossible to render orthographically.)

"If my little boy goes around in gray, dingy undershirts," she continues, "how's that going to look? What kind of a mother am I?"

This question is not answered in the course of the commercial, thus prompting some research on the subject. It has been established independently that Pat Boone, Mick Jagger, and Robert Redford ran around in notoriously gray, dingy undershirts, and that, by way of contrast, Charles Manson's undershirts were sparkling white. Yet, curiously, in the opinion of objective experts, these facts seem to have had relatively little bearing on the competency or efficiency of the respective mothers. This would seem to suggest that factors other than whiteness of undershirt may be involved here.

In any case, all is set right. Our unseen patriarch assures the despairing woman that it was all in jest, that they wouldn't dream of removing the whitener because that's what makes the product so special.

Now we see a face of beaming relief, as she declares. "I'm pleased, I'm tickled to death."

But the ad that illustrates the trend most poignantly—and the one that brings us finally to our mystery—is the White Cloud series. Of course, one can understand the predicament of the advertisers when it comes to the topic of the downiness of toilet tissue.

One can see the Madison Avenue brain trust trying desperately to come up with ways to put the matter with a proper degree of delicacy and tact, and yet still get the message across. After all, the welfare of the Great American Sitzfleisch is at stake.

Charmin solved the problem charmingly (no pun intended) by intimating that their product is so irresistibly pliant that even the hard-shelled store manager, Mr. Whipple (of course, we know him for a softie at a glance), cannot prevent himself from cuddling and fondling the wrapped rolls of tissue right off the shelf.

The current White Cloud commercials, however, are composed in the manner of a catechism or inquisition. A woman is seated at a table. Facing her, his back to us, is Big Brother announcer. He asks her if her husband cares about softness in bathroom tissue—we can smell a setup a mile away. She replies, offhandedly, "No, he doesn't care." "Well let's see," says Mr. Smartypants; and at this point he indicates a TV set at the end of the table. He clicks a switch, and a masculine figure appears on the screen, also sitting at a table upon which are two rolls of guess what. "Who's that?" he demands. The woman looks at the screen. "That's my husband, tee-hee, tee-hee, tee-hee." (These admissions are always accompanied by inexplicable bouts of uncontrollable giggling.)

The husband is next asked which of the two brands in front of him he preferred; and when he tells us White Cloud, he is further importuned for his reasons. "Because it's softer." Now the inquisitor turns and pounces on the defenseless spouse, closing an insidious trap. "You told us your husband doesn't care about softness," he says, in the patronizing tone one uses with infants caught in a fib. The epiphany is at hand, the conversion complete. Under his further goading she confesses her error and promises henceforth to purchase only the Right-

and-True product. And why? "Because I want to please my husband."

It's probably unnecessary to bore the reader with the details of a study of husbands who have used brands other than White Cloud over the years, but who have, quite unaccountably, been pleased by their wives anyhow, possibly by different sorts of ministrations—who knows what wiles women may have?

We come now, however, to our strange puzzle: Why is the husband seen on a TV set? Why is he not there in the flesh, at the same table as his wife, to present his testimony?

There is the possibility, of course, as some of you may already have surmised, that this man is not the real husband at all, that the real husband may be bound and gagged in some closet somewhere, vainly trying to scream out his preference for another brand, while a cleverly disguised actor, abetted by video distortions, passes himself off as the genuine article.

The likely reason is that the sponsor is smarter than the rest of us after all in having realized that for a public reared on television, real life, compared to TV, isn't convincing enough—it doesn't sell. If we don't see it on TV, we don't "buy it."

It's one of the most bewildering paradoxes of contemporary society that television, possibly the medium most easily subject to distortion, manipulation, and misrepresentation of reality, has become for many of us the one absolute test of authenticity, of what's real.

We used to say, "I read it in the papers," and that sufficed to prove that something actually happened, but "I saw it on TV" has a thousand times the force because seeing is believing. Add to that the authoritative tone of TV announcers and admen, seen or unseen, and the vast reach of electronic broadcasting, and you've got the possibility of conning scores of millions at the speed of light.

The husband in this commercial is seen on TV because that's the way to certify his credibility for the wife and, doubly, for us, the audience. She sees him on television; we see him on a TV screen within a TV screen—it's television squared, twice as convincing. Maybe the next step will be an infinite regress of TV screens, at the apex of which we'll see—ourselves, surrounded by all the choice wares of the marketplace.

# APPENDICES

# NETWORK PRIME-TIME LOGS

Following are daily program listings for the prime-time viewing hours of each day from June 1, 1978 through May 31, 1979. All times given are Eastern Time. Listings for the Public Broadcasting Service (PBS) reflect scheduling of the network feed of programming from Washington, D.C., and these programs are not necessarily aired in the same sequence or on the same days by all public television stations. (Key: A stands for ABC, C for CBS, N for NBC, P for PBS, S for Special, and M for Movie.)

**Thursday, June 1, 1978**
**8:00**
N) CHiPs
C) The Waltons
A) Welcome Back, Kotter
P) Once upon a Classic
**8:30**
A) Operation Petticoat
P) In Search of the Real America
**9:00**
N) James at 16
C) Hawaii Five-0
A) Barney Miller
P) World: "Who Pays for Paradise?"
**9:30**
A) Fish
**10:00**
N) What Really Happened to the Class of '65?
C) Barnaby Jones
A) Baretta
P) Masterpiece Theatre: *Our Mutual Friend*

**Friday, June 2, 1978**
**8:00**
N) CPO Sharkey
C) The Adventures of Wonder Woman
A) *Roll of Thunder Hear My Cry,* Part 1 (S)
P) Washington Week in Review
**8:30**
N) Chico and the Man
P) Wall Street Week
**9:00**
N) The Rockford Files
C) NBA Basketball
A) ABC Theatre: *Eleanor and Franklin,* Part 1 (S)
P) Firing Line
**10:00**
N) Quincy
P) Austin City Limits

**Saturday, June 3, 1978**
**8:00**
N) The Bionic Woman
C) The Bob Newhart Show
A) *Roll of Thunder Hear My Cry,* Part 2 (S)
P) Old Friends, New Friends
**8:30**
C) Baby . . . I'm Back!
P) In Performance at Wolf Trap: "Verdi's 'Requiem' "
**9:00**
N) *Rafferty and the Highway Hustlers* (M)
C) America Salutes Richard Rodgers (S)
A) ABC Theatre: *Eleanor and Franklin,* Part 2 (S)
**10:00**
P) Soundstage

**Sunday, June 4, 1978**
**7:00**
N) Wonderful World of Disney
C) 60 Minutes
A) *Roll of Thunder Hear My Cry,* Part 3 (S)
**8:00**
N) Project U.F.O.
C) Rhoda
A) ABC Theatre: *Eleanor and Franklin,* Part 3 (S)
P) Previn and the Pittsburgh
**8:30**
C) On Our Own
**9:00**
N) *Top Secret* (M)
C) All in the Family
P) Masterpiece Theatre: *Poldark*
**9:30**
C) The Tony Awards (S)
**10:00**
P) Youth Unemployment: A Question of Survival (S)

**Monday, June 5, 1978**
**8:00**
N) Little House on the Prairie
C) The Jeffersons
A) Baseball
P) Consumer Survival Kit
**8:30**
C) Good Times
P) Turnabout
**9:00**
N) *Our Town* (S)
C) M*A*S*H
P) Welfare (S)
**9:30**
C) One Day at a Time
**10:00**
C) Lou Grant

**Tuesday, June 6, 1978**
**8:00**
N) Man from Atlantis
C) *National Velvet,* Part 1 (M)
A) Happy Days
P) Jacques Lipchitz (S)
**8:30**
A) Laverne & Shirley
**9:00**
N) *The Snow Beast* (M)
C) *The Spikes Gang* (M)
A) Three's Company
P) Affair in the Air
**9:30**
A) Carter Country
**10:00**
A) 20/20
P) George Crumb: Voice of the Whole (S)

**Wednesday, June 7, 1978**
**8:00**
N) Grizzly Adams
C) CBS News Special: "What Happened to Cambodia" (S)
A) Eight Is Enough
P) Nova: "The Tsetse Trap"

**9:00**
N) David Frost Headliners
C) NBA Basketball
A) Charlie's Angels
P) Great Performances: *Romeo and Juliet*
**10:00**
N) Police Woman
A) Starsky & Hutch

**Thursday, June 8, 1978**
N) CHiPs
C) The Waltons
A) Welcome Back, Kotter
P) Once upon a Classic
**8:30**
A) Operation Petticoat
**9:00**
N) James at 16
C) Hawaii Five-0
A) Barney Miller
P) Solzhenitsyn at Harvard (S)
**9:30**
A) Fish
**10:00**
N) Billion Dollar Bubble (S)
C) Barnaby Jones
A) Are You a Missing Heir? (S)
P) Masterpiece Theatre: *Poldark*

**Friday, June 9, 1978**
**8:00**
N) CPO Sharkey
C) The Adventures of Wonder Woman
A) Boxing
P) Washington Week in Review
**8:30**
N) Chico and the Man
P) Wall Street Week
**9:00**
N) The Rockford Files
C) The Incredible Hulk
P) Firing Line
**10:00**
N) Quincy
C) Husbands, Wives, and Lovers
P) Austin City Limits

**Saturday, June 10, 1978**
**8:00**
N) The Bionic Woman
C) The Bob Newhart Show
A) McNamara's Band (S)
P) Old Friends, New Friends
**8:30**
C) Baby . . . I'm Back!
P) In Performance at Wolf Trap: "Martha Graham Dance Company"

**9:00**
N) *Sharon, Portrait of a Mistress* (M)
C) *The Vanishing Point* (M)
A) The Love Boat
**10:00**
A) Fantasy Island
P) Soundstage

**Sunday, June 11, 1978**
**7:00**
N) Wonderful World of Disney
C) 60 Minutes
A) The Hardy Boys
**8:00**
N) *Fire* (M)
C) Circus of the Stars (S)
A) 1968: A Crack in Time (S)
P) Previn and the Pittsburgh
**9:00**
A) *Shoot Out* (M)
P) Masterpiece Theatre: *Poldark*
**10:00**
C) All in the Family
P) Nova: "The Tsetse Trap"
**10:30**
C) Alice

**Monday, June 12, 1978**
**8:00**
N) Little House on the Prairie
C) The Jeffersons
A) Baseball
P) Consumer Survival Kit
**8:30**
C) Good Times
P) Turnabout
**9:00**
N) *Love Is Not Enough* (M)
C) M*A*S*H
P) Meat (S)
**9:30**
C) One Day at a Time
**10:00**
C) Lou Grant

**Tuesday, June 13, 1978**
**8:00**
N) *Raid on Entebbe* (M)
C) *National Velvet*, Part 2 (M)
A) Happy Days
P) In Search of the Real America
**8:30**
A) Laverne & Shirley
**9:00**
C) *Play It Again, Sam* (M)
A) Three's Company
P) Minnesota Orchestra Anniversary (S)
**9:30**
A) Carter Country

**10:00**
A) 20/20

**Wednesday, June 14, 1978**
N) Grizzly Adams
C) The Carol Burnett Show
A) Eight Is Enough
P) Nova: "Memories from Eden"
**9:00**
N) David Frost Headliners
C) *Up the Sandbox* (M)
A) Charlie's Angels
P) Great Performances: "The Norman Conquests," Part 1
**10:00**
N) Police Woman
A) Starsky & Hutch

**Thursday, June 15, 1978**
**8:00**
N) CHiPs
C) The Angry Taxpayer (S)
A) Welcome Back, Kotter
P) Once upon a Classic
**8:30**
A) What's Happening!
P) In Search of the Real America
**9:00**
N) James at 16
C) Hawaii Five-0
A) Barney Miller
P) World: "Chachaji, My Poor Relation"
**9:30**
A) *The Lords of Flatbush* (M)
**10:00**
N) What Really Happened to the Class of '65?
C) Barnaby Jones
P) Masterpiece Theatre: *Poldark*

**Friday, June 16, 1978**
**8:00**
N) Tax Revolt (S)
C) The Adventures of Wonder Woman
A) Tabitha
P) Washington Week in Review
**8:30**
A) Operation Petticoat
P) Wall Street Week
**9:00**
N) The Rockford Files
C) The Incredible Hulk
A) *Terror in the Wax Museum* (M)
P) Firing Line
**10:00**
N) Quincy
C) Husbands, Wives, and Lovers
P) Austin City Limits

**Saturday, June 17, 1978**
**8:00**
N) The Bionic Woman
C) The Bob Newhart Show
A) The Love Boat
P) Old Friends, New Friends
**8:30**
C) Baby . . . I'm Back!
P) In Performance at Wolf Trap:
   *Roberto Devereaux*
**9:00**
N) *Sex and the Married Woman* (M)
C) *For Better, For Worse* (M)
A) ABC Presents Tomorrow's Stars
   (S)

**Sunday, June 18, 1978**
**7:00**
N) Wonderful World of Disney
C) 60 Minutes
A) The Hardy Boys
**8:00**
N) *Earthquake* (M)
C) Rhoda
A) Lucan
P) Previn and the Pittsburgh
**8:30**
C) On Our Own
**9:00**
C) All in the Family
A) *White Line Fever* (M)
P) Masterpiece Theatre: *Poldark*
**9:30**
C) Alice
**10:00**
C) Gypsy in My Soul (S)
P) Nova: "Memories from Eden"

**Monday, June 19, 1978**
**8:00**
N) Little House on the Prairie
C) The Jeffersons
A) Baseball
P) Consumer Survival Kit
**8:30**
C) Good Times
P) Turnabout
**9:00**
N) *Just a Little Inconvenience* (M)
C) M*A*S*H
P) The Rosenberg-Sobell Case
   Revisited (S)
**9:30**
C) One Day at a Time
**10:00**
C) Lou Grant
**10:30**
P) Anyone for Tennyson?

**Tuesday, June 20, 1978**
**8:00**
N) The Man from Atlantis
C) CBS Reports (S)
A) Happy Days
P) James Michener's World
**8:30**
A) Laverne & Shirley
**9:00**
N) *Scott Joplin: King of Ragtime* (M)
C) *Escape from Bogen County* (M)
A) Three's Company
P) Good Mornin' Blues
**9:30**
A) Carter Country
**10:00**
A) 20/20
P) The Unwanted (S)

**Wednesday, June 21, 1978**
**8:00**
N) Grizzly Adams
C) The Carol Burnett Show
A) Eight Is Enough
P) Nova: "A Whisper from Space"
**9:00**
N) David Frost Headliners
C) *The Great Brinks Robbery* (M)
A) Charlie's Angels
P) Great Performances: "The
   Norman Conquests," Part 2
**10:00**
N) Police Woman
A) Starsky & Hutch
**10:30**
P) Book Beat

**Thursday, June 22, 1978**
**8:00**
N) CHiPs
C) The Waltons
A) Welcome Back, Kotter
P) Once upon a Classic
**8:30**
A) What's Happening!
P) In Search of the Real America
**9:00**
N) James at 16
C) The People's Command
   Performance (S)
A) Barney Miller
P) The Advocates
**9:30**
A) *Phase IV* (M)
**10:00**
N) What Really Happened to the
   Class of '65?
P) Masterpiece Theatre: *Poldark*

**Friday, June 23, 1978**
**8:00**
N) CPO Sharkey
C) The Adventures of Wonder
   Woman
A) Tabitha
P) Washington Week in Review
**8:30**
A) Operation Petticoat
P) Wall Street Week
**9:00**
C) The Incredible Hulk
A) *Forty Carats* (M)
P) Firing Line
**10:00**
N) Quincy
C) Husbands, Wives, and Lovers
P) Austin City Limits

**Saturday, June 24, 1978**
**8:00**
N) The Bionic Woman
C) The Bob Newhart Show
A) Free Country
P) Old Friends, New Friends
**8:30**
C) Baby . . . I'm Back!
A) Snavely
P) In Performance at Wolf Trap: *La
   Traviata*
**9:00**
A) *Sensitive, Passionate Man* (M)
C) *The Secret of Santa Vittoria* (M)
A) The Love Boat
**10:00**
A) Fantasy Island

**Sunday, June 25, 1978**
**7:00**
N) Wonderful World of Disney
C) 60 Minutes
A) The Hardy Boys
**8:00**
N) Project U.F.O.
C) Rhoda
A) Lucan
P) Previn and the Pittsburgh
**8:30**
C) On Our Own
**9:00**
N) Police Story
C) All in the Family
A) *The Last Tenant* (M)
P) Masterpiece Theatre: *Poldark*
**9:30**
C) Alice
**10:00**
C) Switch
P) Nova: "A Whisper from Space"

**Monday, June 26, 1978**
**8:00**
N) Little House on the Prairie
C) The Jeffersons
A) Baseball
P) Consumer Survival Kit
**8:30**
C) Good Times
P) Turnabout
**9:00**
N) *The Girl from Petrovka* (M)
C) M*A*S*H
P) Canal Zone (S)
**9:30**
C) One Day at a Time
**10:00**
C) Lou Grant

**Tuesday, June 27, 1978**
**8:00**
N) The Man from Atlantis
C) *Where the Lilies Bloom,* Part 1
   (M)
A) Happy Days
P) National Geographic Special:
   "Strange Creatures of the Night"
   (S)
**8:30**
A) Laverne & Shirley
**9:00**
N) *Big Bob Johnson and His
   Fantastic Speed Circus* (M)
C) *In the Heat of the Night* (M)
A) Three's Company
P) The Priceless Treasures of
   Dresden (S)
**9:30**
A) Carter Country
**10:00**
A) 20/20
P) College Can Be Killing (S)

**Wednesday, June 28, 1978**
**8:00**
N) Clappers
C) The Carol Burnett Show
A) Eight Is Enough
P) After Bakke, Who Gets Ahead? (S)
**8:30**
N) The Bakke Decision (S)
**9:00**
N) David Frost Headliners
C) *Rancho Deluxe* (M)
A) Charlie's Angels
P) Great Performances: "The
   Norman Conquests," Part 3
**10:00**
N) NBC Reports: "Escape from
   Madness" (S)
A) ABC News Closeup: "Juvenile
   Crime" (S)

**Thursday, June 29, 1978**
N) CHiPs
C) The Waltons
A) Welcome Back, Kotter
P) Once upon a Classic
**8:30**
A) What's Happening!
**9:00**
N) James at 16
C) Hawaii Five-0
A) Barney Miller
P) World: "Bogota, One Day"
**9:30**
A) *S*P*Y*S* (M)
**10:00**
N) What Really Happened to the
   Class of '65?
C) Barnaby Jones
**10:30**
P) Masterpiece Theatre: *Poldark*

**Friday, June 30, 1978**
**8:00**
N) CPO Sharkey
C) The Adventures of Wonder
   Woman
A) Tabitha
P) Washington Week in Review
**8:30**
N) Chico and the Man
A) Operation Petticoat
P) Wall Street Week
**9:00**
N) The Rockford Files
C) The Incredible Hulk
A) Young Joe, the Forgotten
   Kennedy (S)
P) Firing Line
**10:00**
N) Quincy
C) Husbands, Wives, and Lovers
P) No Way to Run a Government (S)

**Saturday, July 1, 1978**
**8:00**
N) The Bionic Woman
C) The Bob Newhart Show
A) Free Country
P) Old Friends, New Friends
**8:30**
C) Baby . . . I'm Back!
A) ABC Saturday Comedy Special
   (S)
P) In Performance at Wolf Trap :
   "Fat Tuesday and All That Jazz"
**9:00**
N) *The War Between the Tates* (M)
C) *Conrack* (M)
A) The Love Boat

**10:00**
A) Fantasy Island
P) New Orleans Concerto

**Sunday, July 2, 1978**
**7:00**
N) Wonderful World of Disney
C) 60 Minutes
A) The Hardy Boys
**8:00**
N) Project U.F.O.
C) Rhoda
A) Lucan
P) Previn and the Pittsburgh
**8:30**
C) On Our Own
**9:00**
N) *Once an Eagle,* Part 1 (M)
C) All in the Family
A) *Custer of the West* (M)
P) Masterpiece Theatre: *Poldark*
**9:30**
C) Alice
**10:00**
C) Switch
P) Nova: "Alaska, the Closing
   Frontier"

**Monday, July 3, 1978**
**8:00**
N) Little House on the Prairie
C) The Jeffersons
A) Baseball
P) Consumer Survival Kit
**8:30**
C) Good Times
P) Turnabout
**9:00**
N) *Once an Eagle,* Part 2 (M)
C) M*A*S*H
P) Opera Theatre: "The Santa Fe
   Opera"
**9:30**
C) One Day at a Time
**10:00**
C) Lou Grant
P) Star of India: Iron Lady of the
   Seas (S)
**10:30**
P) Anyone for Tennyson?

**Tuesday, July 4, 1978**
**8:00**
N) The Man from Atlantis
C) *Where the Lilies Bloom,* Part 2
   (M)
A) Happy Days
P) Evening at Pops: "On The
   Esplanade"

**8:30**
A) Laverne & Shirley
**9:00**
N) *Once An Eagle,* Part 3 (M)
C) *Pocket Money* (M)
A) Three's Company
**9:30**
A) Carter Country
P) Phil Ochs Memorial Concert (S)
**10:00**
A) 20/20

**Wednesday, July 5, 1978**
**8:00**
N) Grizzly Adams
C) The Carol Burnett Show
A) Eight Is Enough
P) Nova: "In the Event of Catastrophe"
**9:00**
N) David Frost Headliners
C) *Tom and Joann* (M)
A) Charlie's Angels
P) Great Performances: "Julliard String Quartet"
**10:00**
N) Police Woman
C) CBS Reports (S)
A) Starsky & Hutch

**Thursday, July 6, 1978**
**8:00**
N) CHiPs
C) The Waltons
A) Welcome Back, Kotter
P) Once upon a Classic
**8:30**
A) What's Happening!
P) In Search of the Real America
**9:00**
N) James at 15
C) Hawaii Five-0
A) Barney Miller
P) The Advocates
**9:30**
A) *Ash Wednesday* (M)
**10:00**
C) Barnaby Jones
P) Masterpiece Theatre: *Poldark*

**Friday, July 7, 1978**
**8:00**
N) CPO Sharkey
C) The Adventures of Wonder Woman
A) Tabitha
P) Washington Week in Review
**8:30**
N) Chico and the Man
A) Operation Petticoat
P) Wall Street Week

**9:00**
N) The Rockford Files
A) *Fat City* (M)
P) Firing Line
**9:30**
C) *Bank Shot* (M)
**10:00**
N) Quincy
P) Austin City Limits

**Saturday, July 8, 1978**
**8:00**
N) The Bionic Woman
C) The Bob Newhart Show
A) Free Country
P) Great Performances: "Copland Conducts Copland"
**8:30**
C) Baby . . . I'm Back!
A) ABC Comedy Special (S)
**9:00**
N) *The Hindenberg* (M)
C) *The French Connection* (M)
A) The Love Boat
P) In Performance at Wolf Trap: "Benny Goodman"
**10:00**
A) Fantasy Island
P) In Performance at Wolf Trap: "Bonnie Raitt and Mose Allison"

**Sunday, July 9, 1978**
**7:00**
N) Wonderful World of Disney
C) 60 Minutes
A) The Hardy Boys
**8:00**
N) Project U.F.O.
C) Rhoda
A) How the West Was Won
P) Evening at Pops: "Henry Mancini"
**8:30**
C) On Our Own
**9:00**
N) Columbo: *Make Me a Perfect Murder* (M)
C) All in the Family
A) *Darling Lili* (M)
P) Masterpiece Theatre: *Poldark*
**9:30**
C) Alice
**10:00**
C) Switch
P) Faces of Communism

**Monday, July 10, 1978**
**8:00**
N) Little House on the Prairie
C) The Jeffersons

A) Laverne & Shirley
P) Consumer Survival Kit
**8:30**
C) Good Times
P) Turnabout
**9:00**
N) *Girl in the Empty Grave* (M)
C) M*A*S*H
A) Three's Company
P) Opera Theatre: *Falstaff*
**9:30**
C) One Day at a Time
A) Carter Country
**10:00**
C) Lou Grant
A) 20/20

**Tuesday, July 11, 1978**
**8:00**
N) The Man from Atlantis
C) *West Side Story* (M)
A) Happy Days
P) National Geographic Special: "The Volga" (S)
**8:30**
A) All-Star Baseball Game
**9:00**
N) *The Death of Richie* (M)
P) Jerusalem Peace (S)
**10:00**
P) Music in Jerusalem (S)

**Wednesday, July 12, 1978**
**8:00**
N) Grizzly Adams
C) The Carol Burnett Show
A) Eight Is Enough
P) Nova: "The Green Machine"
**9:00**
N) The Black Sheep Squadron
C) *Daddy I Don't Like It Like This* (M)
A) Charlie's Angels
P) Secret Service (S)
**10:00**
N) Police Woman
A) Starsky & Hutch

**Thursday, July 13, 1978**
**8:00**
N) CHiPs
C) The Waltons
A) Welcome Back, Kotter
P) Once upon a Classic
**8:30**
A) What's Happening!
P) In Search of the Real America
**9:00**
N) James at 15
C) Hawaii Five-0
A) *Return to Fantasy Island* (M)

P) World: "Three Days in Szechuan"
**10:00**
N) What Really Happened to the Class of '65?
C) Barnaby Jones
P) Masterpiece Theatre: *Poldark*

## Friday, July 14, 1978
**8:00**
N) CPO Sharkey
C) *Scalawag* (M)
A) *The Last Dinosaur* (M)
P) Washington Week in Review
**8:30**
N) Chico and the Man
P) Wall Street Week
**9:00**
N) The Rockford Files
P) From Paris with Love: An Evening of French TV (S)
**10:00**
N) Quincy
C) The Business of Newspapers (S)
A) ABC News Closeup: "Asbestos, the Dusty Way to Death"

## Saturday, July 15, 1978
**8:00**
N) The Bionic Woman
C) The Bob Newhart Show
A) Free Country
P) Great Performances: "Solti Conducts Mendelsohn"
**8:30**
C) Baby . . . I'm Back!
A) Harvey Korman
**9:00**
N) *In the Matter of Karen Ann Quinlan* (M)
C) *Fear Is the Key* (M)
A) The Love Boat
P) Hollywood Television Theatre: *And the Soul Shall Dance*
**10:00**
A) The Rock Rainbow (S)
**10:30**
P) The Night of the Empty Chairs (S)

## Sunday, July 16, 1978
**7:00**
N) Wonderful World of Disney
C) 60 Minutes
A) The Hardy Boys
**8:00**
N) Project U.F.O.
C) Rhoda
A) How the West Was Won
P) Evening at Pops: "Lionel Hampton"
**8:30**
C) On Our Own

**9:00**
N) *Seventh Avenue,* Part 1 (M)
C) All in the Family
A) *The Take* (M)
P) Masterpiece Theatre: *Poldark*
**9:30**
C) Alice
**10:00**
C) Switch
P) Faces of Communism

## Monday, July 17, 1978
**8:00**
N) Little House on the Prairie
C) The Jeffersons
A) Baseball
P) Consumer Survival Kit
**8:30**
C) Good Times
P) Turnabout
**9:00**
N) *Seventh Avenue,* Part 2 (M)
C) M*A*S*H
P) Opera Theatre: *The Yeomen of the Guard*
**9:30**
C) One Day at a Time
**10:00**
C) Lou Grant

## Tuesday, July 18, 1978
**8:00**
N) The Man from Atlantis
C) *Tom Sawyer,* Part 1 (M)
A) Happy Days
P) Guale (S)
**8:30**
A) Laverne & Shirley
**9:00**
N) *Seventh Avenue,* Part 3 (M)
C) *The Magnificent Seven Ride* (M)
A) Three's Company
P) Mr. Speaker: A Portrait of Tip O'Neil
**9:30**
A) Carter Country
**10:00**
A) 20/20
P) North Star: Mark di Suvero (S)

## Wednesday, July 19, 1978
**8:00**
N) Grizzly Adams
C) The Carol Burnett Show
A) Eight Is Enough
P) Nova: "Alaska, the Closing Frontier"
**9:00**
N) Black Sheep Squadron
C) *T.R. Baskin* (M)
A) Charlie's Angels

P) Great Performances: *The Prince of Hamburg*
**10:00**
N) Police Woman
A) Starsky & Hutch

## Thursday, July 20, 1978
**8:00**
N) President Carter Press Conference
C) President Carter Press Conference
A) President Carter Press Conference
P) Once upon a Classic
**8:30**
P) In Search of the Real America
**9:00**
N) CHiPs
A) Barney Miller
P) The Advocates
**9:30**
A) *A Minute to Pray, a Second to Die* (M)
**10:00**
N) NBC Reports: "I Want It All Now" (S)
C) Hawaii Five-0
P) Masterpiece Theatre: *Poldark*

## Friday, July 21, 1978
**8:00**
N) CPO Sharkey
C) The Adventures of Wonder Woman
A) Tabitha
P) Washington Week in Review
**8:30**
N) Chico and the Man
A) Operation Petticoat
P) Wall Street Week
**9:00**
N) The Rockford Files
C) *The Comedy Company* (M)
A) *Telethon* (M)
P) Evening at Pops: "Lionel Hampton"
**10:00**
N) Quincy
P) Firing Line

## Saturday, July 22, 1978
**8:00**
N) The Bionic Woman
C) The Bob Newhart Show
A) Free Country
P) Great Performances: "Tchaikovsky Symphony"

**8:30**

C) Baby . . . I'm Back!
A) ABC Comedy Special (S)

**9:00**

N) *The Reivers* (M)
C) Barnaby Jones
A) The Love Boat
P) In Performance at Wolf Trap: "Kostelanitz and Menuhin"

**10:00**

A) Fantasy Island
P) *The Plough and the Stars* (M)

**Sunday, July 23, 1978**

**7:00**

N) Wonderful World of Disney
C) 60 Minutes
A) U.S. Women's Open Golf

**8:00**

N) *Amelia Earhart* (M)
C) Rhoda
A) How the West Was Won
P) Evening at Pops: "Glen Campbell"

**8:30**

C) Alice

**9:00**

C) All in the Family
A) *Gold* (M)
P) Masterpiece Theatre: *Poldark*

**10:00**

C) Switch
P) Faces of Communism

**Monday, July 24, 1978**

**8:00**

N) Little House on the Prairie
C) The Jeffersons
A) Baseball
P) Consumer Survival Kit

**8:30**

C) Good Times
P) Turnabout

**9:00**

N) *Adam at 6 A.M.* (M)
C) Miss Universe Beauty Pageant (S)
P) Opera Theatre: *The Flying Dutchman*

**Tuesday, July 25, 1978**

**8:00**

N) The Man from Atlantis
C) *Tom Sawyer,* Part 2 (M)
A) Happy Days
P) National Geographic Special: "Voyage of the Herculea" (S)

**8:30**

A) Laverne & Shirley

**9:00**

N) *Emergency: Survival on a Charter* (M)
C) *Man on a Swing* (M)
A) Three's Company

**9:30**

A) Carter Country
P) Of Race and Blood

**10:00**

A) 20/20

**Wednesday, July 26, 1978**

**8:00**

N) Grizzly Adams
C) Funny Business (S)
A) Eight Is Enough
P) Nova: "Children of the Forest"

**9:00**

N) Black Sheep Squadron
A) Charlie's Angels
P) Great Performances: *Waiting for Godot*

**10:00**

N) Police Woman
C) CBS Reports: "The Fire Next Door" (S)
A) Starsky & Hutch

**Thursday, July 27, 1978**

**8:00**

N) CHiPs
C) The Waltons
A) Welcome Back, Kotter
P) Once upon a Classic

**8:30**

A) What's Happening!
P) In Search of the Real America

**9:00**

N) James at 15
C) Hawaii Five-0
A) Barney Miller
P) World: "North Korea"

**9:30**

A) *Claudine* (M)

**10:00**

N) What Really Happened to the Class of '65?
C) Barnaby Jones
P) Masterpiece Theatre: *Poldark*

**Friday, July 28, 1978**

**8:00**

N) CPO Sharkey
C) The Adventures of Wonder Woman
A) Tabitha
P) Washington Week in Review

**8:30**

N) CPO Sharkey
A) Operation Petticoat
P) Wall Street Week

**9:00**

N) The Rockford Files
C) *The Private Life of Sherlock Holmes* (M)
A) *Beautiful, but Deadly* (M)
P) Evening at Pops: "Glen Campbell"

**10:00**

P) Firing Line

**Saturday, July 29, 1978**

**8:00**

N) The Bionic Woman
C) The Bob Newhart Show
A) Krofft Comedy Hour (S)
P) Great Performances: "Chopin"

**8:30**

C) Baby . . . I'm Back!

**9:00**

N) *The Rhinemann Exchange,* Part 1 (M)
C) *Juggernaut* (M)
A) The Love Boat
P) In Performance at Wolf Trap: "Conservatory Ragtime Ensemble"

**10:00**

A) Fantasy Island
P) *As You Like It* (M)

**Sunday, July 30, 1978**

**7:00**

N) Wonderful World of Disney
C) 60 Minutes
A) The Hardy Boys

**8:00**

N) Project U.F.O.
C) Rhoda
A) How the West Was Won
P) Evening at Pops: "Itzhak Perlman"

**8:30**

C) On Our Own

**9:00**

N) *The Rhinemann Exchange,* Part 2 (M)
C) All in the Family
A) *The Friends of Eddie Coyle* M)
P) Masterpiece Theatre: *Poldark*

**9:30**

C) Alice

**10:00**

C) Switch
P) Faces of Communism

**Monday, July 31, 1978**
**8:00**
N) Little House on the Prairie
C) The Jeffersons
A) Baseball
P) Consumer Survival Kit
**8:30**
C) Good Times
P) Turnabout
**9:00**
C) M*A*S*H
P) Opera Theatre: *The Gondoliers*
**9:30**
N) Columbo: *Murder under Glass* (M)
C) One Day at a Time
**10:00**
C) Lou Grant

**Tuesday, August 1, 1978**
**8:00**
N) *Contract on Cherry Street* (M)
C) Shipshape (S)
A) Happy Days
P) Masterpiece Theatre: *Anna Karenina*
**8:30**
C) *The Russians Are Coming* (M)
A) Laverne & Shirley
**9:00**
A) Three's Company
P) The Edelin Conviction (S)
**9:30**
A) Carter Country
**10:00**
A) 20/20

**Wednesday, August 2, 1978**
**8:00**
N) *The Adventures of Frontier Freemont* (M)
C) The Carol Burnett Show
A) Eight is Enough
P) Masterpiece Theatre: *Anna Karenina*
**9:00**
C) *The Conversation* (M)
A) Charlie's Angels
P) Out of Our Father's House
**10:00**
N) Police Woman
A) Starsky & Hutch
P) Architecture Odyssey (S)

**Thursday, August 3, 1978**
**8:00**
N) Tut, the Boy King (S)
C) The Waltons

A) Welcome Back, Kotter
P) Once upon a Classic
**8:30**
A) What's Happening!
P) In Search of the Real America
**9:00**
N) The Rockford Files
C) Hawaii Five-0
A) Barney Miller
P) The Advocates
**9:30**
A) Harvey Korman
**10:00**
C) Barnaby Jones
A) ABC News Closeup: "Arson"
P) Masterpiece Theatre: *Poldark*

**Friday, August 4, 1978**
**8:00**
N) Black Sheep Squadron
C) Horton Hears a Who (S)
A) Tabitha
P) Washington Week in Review
**8:30**
C) The Lorax (S)
A) Operation Petticoat
P) Wall Street Week
**9:00**
N) The Rockford Files
C) *A Warm December* (M)
A) *Take the Money and Run* (M)
P) Evening at Pops: "Itzhak Perlman"
**10:00**
N) Quincy
P) Firing Line

**Saturday, August 5, 1978**
**8:00**
N) The Bionic Woman
C) The Bob Newhart Show
A) The Archie Special (S)
P) Great Performances: "Philadelphia Orchestra"
**8:30**
C) Baby . . . I'm Back!
**9:00**
N) *The Land that Time Forgot* (M)
C) *Burn* (M)
A) The Love Boat
P) In Performance at Wolf Trap: "Dionne Warwick"
**10:00**
A) Fantasy Island
P) *Hamlet* (M)

**Sunday, August 6, 1978**
**7:00**
N) Wonderful World of Disney

C) 60 Minutes
A) PGA Golf
**8:00**
N) Project U.F.O.
C) Pope Paul News Special (S)
A) How the West Was Won
P) Evening at Pops: "Tony Bennett"
**8:30**
C) Rhoda
**9:00**
N) Police Story
C) All in the Family
A) *Anything for Love* (M)
P) Masterpiece Theatre: *Poldark*
**9:30**
C) Alice
**10:00**
C) Switch
P) Bill Moyers' Journal

**Monday, August 7, 1978**
**8:00**
N) Little House on the Prairie
C) The Jeffersons
A) Baseball
P) Masterpiece Theatre: *Anna Karenina*
**8:30**
C) Good Times
**9:00**
C) M*A*S*H
P) Opera Theatre: *Albert Herring*
**9:30**
N) Columbo: *How to Dial a Murder* (M)
C) One Day at a Time
**10:00**
C) Lou Grant

**Tuesday, August 8, 1978**
**8:00**
N) Just for Laughs
C) *Charlotte's Web*, Part 1 (M)
A) Happy Days
P) Masterpiece Theatre: *Anna Karenina*
**8:30**
A) Laverne & Shirley
**9:00**
N) *The Deadly Game* (M)
C) *Hell Boats* (M)
A) Three's Company
P) The People vs. Inez Garcia (S)
**9:30**
A) Carter Country
**10:00**
A) 20/20
P) Mystery Murals of Baja California

**Wednesday, August 9, 1978**
**8:00**
N) *Peter Lundy and the Medicine
Hat Stallion* (M)
C) The Carol Burnett Show
A) Eight Is Enough
P) Masterpiece Theatre: *Anna
Karenina*
**9:00**
C) *The Hawaiians* (M)
A) Sinatra and Friends (S)
P) Great Performances: *The Royal
Family*
**10:00**
N) Police Woman
A) Barbara Walters Summer Special
(S)

**Thursday, August 10, 1978**
**8:00**
N) CHiPs
C) The Waltons
A) Welcome Back, Kotter
P) Once upon a Classic
**8:30**
A) What's Happening!
**9:00**
N) Richie Brockelman, Private Eye
C) Hawaii Five-0
A) Barney Miller
P) World: "Black's Britannica"
**9:30**
A) *For Pete's Sake* (M)
**10:00**
N) Operation Runaway
C) Barnaby Jones
P) Masterpiece Theatre: *Poldark*

**Friday, August 11, 1978**
**8:00**
N) Black Sheep Squadron
C) The Adventures of Wonder
Woman
A) Tabitha
P) Washington Week in Review
**8:30**
A) Operation Petticoat
P) Wall Street Week
**9:00**
N) The Rockford Files
C) The Incredible Hulk
A) *Three on a Date* (M)
P) Evening at Pops: "Tony Bennett"
**10:00**
N) Quincy
C) Sparrow (S)
P) Firing Line

**Saturday, August 12, 1978**
**8:00**
N) The Bionic Woman
C) The Bob Newhart Show
A) Family
P) Great Performances: "Brahms
'Symphony # 4' "
**8:30**
C) Baby . . . I'm Back!
**9:00**
N) *Lacy and the Mississippi Queen*
(M)
C) *A Girl Called Hatter Fox* (M)
A) The Love Boat
P) In Performance at Wolf Trap:
"The World Series of Jazz"
**10:00**
A) Fantasy Island
P) *Richard III* (M)

**Sunday, August 13, 1978**
**7:00**
N) Wonderful World of Disney
C) 60 Minutes
A) The Hardy Boys
**8:00**
N) Project U.F.O.
C) Rhoda
A) How the West Was Won
P) Evening at Pops: "Claude Kipnis
Mime Theater"
**8:30**
C) On Our Own
**9:00**
N) Police Story
C) All in the Family
A) *Newman's Law* (M)
P) Masterpiece Theatre: *Poldark*
**9:30**
C) Alice
**10:00**
C) Switch
P) Bill Moyers' Journal

**Monday, August 14, 1978**
**8:00**
N) Little House on the Prairie
C) The Jeffersons
A) Baseball
P) Masterpiece Theatre: *Anna
Karenina*
**8:30**
C) Good Times
**9:00**
N) *Breakout* (M)
C) M°A°S°H
P) Opera Theatre: *Transformations*
**9:30**
C) One Day at a Time

**10:00**
C) Lou Grant
**10:30**
P) Renoir (S)

**Tuesday, August 15, 1978**
**8:00**
N) Just for Laughs
C) *Charlotte's Web,* Part 2 (M)
A) Happy Days
P) Masterpiece Theatre: *Anna
Karenina*
**8:30**
A) Laverne & Shirley
**9:00**
N) *My Name Is Nobody* (M)
C) Festival of the Stars: Mexico (S)
A) Three's Company
P) TV on Trial (S)
**9:30**
A) Carter Country
**10:00**
A) 20/20

**Wednesday, August 16, 1978**
**8:00**
N) *The Beasts Are in the Streets* (M)
C) *Down Home* (M)
A) Eight Is Enough
P) Masterpiece Theatre: *Anna
Karenina*
**9:00**
C) *The Deadly Trap* (M)
A) Charlie's Angels
P) Great Performances: "The Arcata
Promise"
**10:00**
N) Police Woman
A) Starsky & Hutch
**10:30**
P) John Cage (S)

**Thursday, August 17, 1978**
**8:00**
N) CHiPs
C) The Waltons
A) Welcome Back, Kotter
P) Once upon a Classic
**8:30**
A) What's Happening!
**9:00**
N) Richie Brockelman, Private Eye
C) Hawaii Five-0
A) Barney Miller
P) Southie (S)
**9:30**
A) *Mother, Jugs, and Speed* (M)

**10:00**
N) Operation Runaway
C) Barnaby Jones
P) Masterpiece Theatre: *Poldark*

**Friday, August 18, 1978**
**8:00**
N) Black Sheep Squadron
C) The Adventures of Wonder
   Woman
A) Tabitha
P) Washington Week in Review
**8:30**
A) Operation Petticoat
P) Wall Street Week
**9:00**
N) The Rockford Files
C) The Incredible Hulk
A) NFL Football
P) Drum Corps International (S)
**10:00**
N) Quincy
C) Winner Take All (S)

**Saturday, August 19, 1978**
**8:00**
N) The Bionic Woman
C) The Bob Newhart Show
A) Family
P) Renoir (S)
**8:30**
C) Friends
P) In Performance at Wolf Trap:
   "Sarah Vaughan"
**9:00**
N) *Something Big* (M)
C) *Come Back Charleston Blue* (M)
A) The Love Boat
**10:00**
A) Fantasy Island

**Sunday, August 20, 1978**
**7:00**
N) NFL Football Preview
C) 60 Minutes
A) The Hardy Boys
**7:30**
N) Wonderful World of Disney
**8:00**
C) Rhoda
A) How the West Was Won
P) Evening at Pops: "Ben Vereen"
**8:30**
N) Project U.F.O.
C) On Our Own
**9:00**
C) All in the Family
A) *Joe Kidd* (M)
P) Masterpiece Theatre: *Poldark*

**9:30**
N) Police Story
C) Alice
**10:00**
C) Switch
P) Bill Moyers' Journal

**Monday, August 21, 1978**
**8:00**
N) Little House on the Prairie
C) The Jeffersons
A) Baseball
P) Masterpiece Theatre: *Anna
   Karenina*
**8:30**
C) Good Times
**9:00**
N) *Sgt. Matlovich vs. the U.S. Air
   Force* (M)
C) M*A*S*H
P) In Performance at Wolf Trap:
   "Tex Beneke, Helen O'Connell,
   Bob Eberly"
**9:30**
C) One Day at a Time
**10:00**
C) Lou Grant

**Tuesday, August 22, 1978**
**8:00**
N) TV in the Fabulous Fifties (S)
C) Public Schools, Part 1 (S)
A) Happy Days
P) Masterpiece Theatre: *Anna
   Karenina*
**8:30**
A) Laverne & Shirley
**9:00**
C) *Capone* (M)
A) Three's Company
P) In Performance at Wolf Trap:
   "Pete Seeger and Arlo Guthrie"
**9:30**
N) Steve Lawrence and Eydie Gorme
   (S)
A) Carter Country
**10:00**
A) 20/20

**Wednesday, August 23,1978**
**8:00**
N) *Willy Wonka and the Chocolate
   Factory* (M)
C) Public Schools, Part 2 (S)
A) Eight Is Enough
P) National Geographic Special:
   "The Great Whales" (S)
**9:00**
C) *The Parallax View* (M)
A) Charlie's Angels

P) The Joffrey Ballet (S)
**10:00**
N) Police Woman
A) Starsky & Hutch
**10:30**
P) Freddie Hubbard: Club Date (S)

**Thursday, August 24, 1978**
**8:00**
N) CHiPs
C) Public Schools, Part 2 (S)
A) Welcome Back, Kotter
P) Once upon a Classic
**8:30**
A) What's Happening!
**9:00**
N) Richie Brockelman, Private Eye
C) Hawaii Five-0
A) Barney Miller
**9:30**
A) *Vega$* (M)
**10:00**
N) Operation Runaway
C) Barnaby Jones

**Friday, August 25, 1978**
**8:00**
N) Black Sheep Squadron
C) The Adventures of Wonder
   Woman
A) Tabitha
P) Washington Week in Review
**8:30**
A) Operation Petticoat
P) Bernstein 60th Birthday
   Celebration (S)
**9:00**
N) The Rockford Files
C) 1968 (S)
A) NFL Exhibition Game
**10:00**
N) Quincy

**Saturday, August 26, 1978**
**8:00**
N) Pope John Paul (S)
C) Pope John Paul (S)
A) College Football Preview
P) Live From the Grand Ole Opry
   (S)
**8:30**
C) Wilder & Wilder
**9:00**
N) NFL Exhibition Football Game
C) *Mary Jane Harper Cried Last
   Night* (M)
A) The Love Boat
**10:00**
A) Fantasy Island

**Sunday, August 27, 1978**
**7:00**
N) Wonderful World of Disney
C) 60 Minutes
A) Flight of the Double Eagle II (S)
**8:00**
N) Project U.F.O.
C) The Body Human: The Miracle Months (S)
A) How the West Was Won
P) Evening at Pops: "Angel Romero"
**9:00**
N) Police Story
C) All in the Family
A) *Murder at the World Series* (M)
P) Masterpiece Theatre: *Poldark*
**9:30**
C) Alice
**10:00**
N) Paul Anka in Monte Carlo (S)
P) A Day to Remember: August 28, 1963 (S)
**10:30**
P) Bill Moyers' Journal

**Monday, August 28, 1978**
**8:00**
N) Little House on the Prairie
C) The Jeffersons
A) Baseball
P) Evenings at Pops
**8:30**
C) M*A*S*H
**9:00**
C) Flying High
P) National Geographic Special: "The Great Whales" (S)
**10:00**
N) Quincy
P) Bill Moyers' Journal

**Tuesday, August 29, 1978**
**8:00**
N) Memories of Elvis (S)
C) The Leningrad Ice Show (S)
A) Happy Days
P) *The Belle of Amherst* (S)
**8:30**
A) Laverne & Shirley
**9:00**
C) *The Amazing Howard Hughes,* Part 1 (M)
A) Three's Company
**9:30**
A) Carter Country
**10:00**
A) 20/20

**Wednesday, August 30, 1978**
**8:00**
N) *The Day of the Dolphin* (M)
C) The Funny World of Fred and Bunni
A) Eight Is Enough
P) OHO: Zoo Gorilla (S)
**8:00**
C) *The Amazing Howard Hughes,* Part 2 (M)
A) Charlie's Angels
P) Great Performances: *Sarah*
**10:00**
N) Police Woman
A) Starsky & Hutch

**Thursday, August 31, 1978**
**8:00**
N) CHiPs
C) The Waltons
A) Welcome Back, Kotter
P) Once upon a Classic
**8:30**
A) What's Happening!
P) Damien
**9:00**
N) *Dirty Harry* (M)
A) Barney Miller
P) Masterpiece Theatre: *Poldark*
**9:30**
A) Soap
**10:00**
C) Barnaby Jones

**Friday, September 1, 1978**
**8:00**
N) Columbo: *The Conspirators* (M)
C) The New Adventures of Wonder Woman
A) All-Star Saturday (S)
P) Washington Week in Review
**8:30**
P) Wall Street Week
**9:00**
C) The Incredible Hulk
A) *At the Earth's Core* (M)
P) Evening at Pops: "Angel Romero"
**10:00**
N) The Rockford Files
C) CBS Reports (S)
P) Firing Line

**Saturday, September 2, 1978**
**8:00**
N) The Bionic Woman
C) The Bob Newhart Show
A) The Love Boat
P) Great Performances: "The Cleveland Orchestra"
**8:30**
C) The Plant Family

**9:00**
N) *Gable and Lombard* (M)
C) *The Life and Times of Judge Roy Bean* (M)
A) NCAA Football
P) Harry S. Truman: Plain Speaking (S)
**10:00**
P) *Fires on the Plain* (M)

**Sunday, September 3, 1978**
**7:00**
N) Wonderful World of Disney
C) 60 Minutes
A) John Denver Special (S)
**8:00**
N) Project U.F.O.
C) Rhoda
P) Evening at Pops: "Jean-Pierre Rampal"
**8:30**
C) All in the Family
**9:00**
N) Police Story
A) *The New Maverick* (M)
P) Masterpiece Theatre: *The Mayor of Casterbridge*
**9:30**
C) Alice
**10:00**
C) Switch
P) *The Pallisers*

**Monday, September 4, 1978**
**8:00**
N) Little House on the Prairie
C) The Jeffersons
A) The Thirty-six Most Beautiful Girls in Texas (S)
P) Once upon a Classic
**9:00**
A) Monday Nite Football
P) Opera Theatre: *Trouble in Tahiti*
**9:30**
C) M*A*S*H
**10:00**
N) Quincy
C) Lou Grant
P) *The Pallisers*

**Tuesday, September 5, 1978**
**8:00**
N) *Little Mo* (M)
C) The Amazing Spiderman
A) Laverne & Shirley
P) James Michener's World
**9:00**
C) *Happily Ever After* (M)
A) *Roots,* Part 1
P) Antonia: Portrait of a Woman (S)

**10:00**
P) *The Pallisers*

**Wednesday, September 6, 1978**
**8:00**
N) Sharks: The Death Machines (S)
C) Dr. Strange (S)
A) Eight Is Enough
P) The Time of Your Life
**9:00**
N) Dick Clark's Live Wednesday
A) *Roots,* Part 2
**10:00**
C) The Incredible Hulk
P) *The Pallisers*

**Thursday, September 7, 1978**
**8:00**
N) The Waverly Wonders
C) The Waltons
A) *Roots,* Part 3
P) Once upon a Classic
**8:30**
P) Eric Hoffer: The Crowded Life
(S)
**9:00**
N) Grandpa Goes to Washington
C) Hawaii Five-0
**10:00**
N) Lifeline
C) Barnaby Jones
P) *The Pallisers*

**Friday, September 8, 1978**
**8:00**
N) The Bay City Rollers Meet the
Saturday Superstars (S)
C) The New Adventures of Wonder
Woman
A) Happy Days
P) Washington Week in Review
**8:30**
P) Wall Street Week
**9:00**
N) Eddie Capra Mysteries
C) Something for Joey (S)
A) *Roots,* Part 4
P) Masterpiece Theatre: *The Mayor
of Casterbridge*
**10:00**
P) *The Pallisers*

**Saturday, September 9, 1978**
**8:00**
N) Us against the World (S)
C) The Paper Chase
A) NCAA Football
P) Great Performances: "Trail
Blazers of Modern Dance"

**9:00**
C) *Magnum Force* (M)
A) The Love Boat
P) A Good Dissonance Like a Man
(S)
**10:00**
N) The Miss America Pageant (S)
A) Elvis: Love Me Tender (S)
P) *The Magician* (M)

**Sunday, September 10, 1978**
**7:00**
N) Wonderful World of Disney
C) U.S. Open Tennis
A) 20/20
**8:00**
N) *Sword of Justice* (M)
A) *Roots,* Part 5
P) Evening at Pops: "Clamma Dale"
**8:30**
C) 60 Minutes
**9:00**
P) Masterpiece Theatre: *The Mayor
of Casterbridge*
**9:30**
C) Alice
**10:00**
N) Weekend
C) Kaz
P) *The Pallisers*

**Monday, September 11, 1978**
**8:00**
N) Little House on the Prairie
C) The Jeffersons
A) Welcome Back, Kotter
P) Once upon a Classic
**8:30**
C) Good Times
**9:00**
N) *The Critical List,* Part 1 (M)
C) M*A*S*H
A) Monday Nite Football
P) Opera Theatre: "The World of
Victor Herbert"
**9:30**
C) One Day at a Time
**10:00**
C) Lou Grant
P) *The Pallisers*

**Tuesday, September 12, 1978**
**8:00**
N) Canine Hall of Fame (S)
C) The Amazing Spiderman
A) Happy Days
P) James Michener's World
**9:00**
N) *The Critical List,* Part 2 (M)

C) *Hondo* (M)
A) Three's Company
P) Los Angeles Philharmonic at the
Hollywood Bowl (S)
**9:30**
A) Taxi!
**10:00**
A) Starsky & Hutch
P) *The Pallisers*

**Wednesday, September 13, 1978**
**8:00**
N) Wonderful World of Disney 25th
Anniversary Show (S)
C) The Popeye Show (S)
A) Eight Is Enough
P) Great Performances: *Tosca*
**8:30**
C) *Buffalo Bill and the Indians* (M)
**9:00**
A) Charlie's Angels
**10:00**
N) W.E.B.
**10:30**
P) *The Pallisers*

**Thursday, September 14, 1978**
**8:00**
N) *Clone Master* (M)
C) The Waltons
A) Mork & Mindy
P) Once upon a Classic
**8:30**
P) Thracium: Gold (S)
**9:00**
C) Hawaii Five-0
A) Barney Miller
P) In Performance at Wolf Trap:
"Cleo Laine and John
Dankworth"
**10:00**
N) W.E.B.
C) Barnaby Jones
A) Soap
P) *The Pallisers*

**Friday, September 15, 1978**
**8:00**
N) *Starship Invasions* (M)
C) The Incredible Hulk
A) Ali-Spinks Heavyweight Boxing
P) Washington Week in Review
**8:30**
P) Wall Street Week
**9:00**
C) *Grand Theft Auto* (M)
P) Masterpiece Theatre: *The Mayor
of Casterbridge*
**9:30**
N) Quincy

**10:00**
P) *The Pallisers*

**Saturday, September 16, 1978**
**8:00**
N) CHiPs
C) Good Times
A) The Love Boat
P) Great Performances: "The Joffrey Ballet"
**9:00**
N) *King Kong*, Part 1 (M)
C) *The Islander* (M)
P) The Long Search
**10:00**
A) Fantasy Island
P) *Port of Call* (M)

**Sunday, September 17, 1978**
**7:00**
N) Wonderful World of Disney
C) The NFL Today
A) Lassie, Part 1 (S)
**7:30**
C) 60 Minutes
**8:00**
A) Battlestar Galactica
P) Evening at Pops: "Noel Parenti"
**8:30**
C) The Emmy Awards (S)
**9:00**
N) *King Kong*, Part 2 (M)
P) Masterpiece Theatre: *The Mayor of Casterbridge*
**10:00**
P) Mstislav Rostropovich at the White House (S)

**Monday, September 18, 1978**
**8:00**
N) President Carter's Address to Congress
C) President Carter's Address to Congress
A) President Carter's Address to Congress
P) President Carter's Address to Congress
**8:30**
N) Little House on the Prairie
C) WKRP in Cincinnati
A) Carter Speech Analysis
**9:00**
C) People
A) Monday Nite Football
P) Opera Theatre: *Jack, a Flash Fantasy*
**9:30**
N) *Audrey Rose* (M)
C) M°A°S°H

**10:00**
C) One Day at a Time
P) *The Pallisers*
**10:30**
C) Carter Speech Analysis

**Tuesday, September 19, 1978**
**8:00**
N) Grandpa Goes to Washington
C) The Paper Chase
A) Happy Days
P) James Michener's World
**8:30**
A) Laverne & Shirley
**9:00**
N) *Airport '77*, Part 1 (M)
C) *The Shootist* (M)
A) Three's Company
P) Union Maids (S)
**9:30**
A) Taxi!
**10:00**
A) Starsky & Hutch
P) *The Pallisers*

**Wednesday, September 20, 1978**
**8:00**
N) Dick Clark's Live Wednesday
C) The Jeffersons
A) Eight Is Enough
P) Echoes of Silver (S)
**8:30**
C) In the Beginning
**9:00**
N) *Airport '77*, Part 2 (M)
C) *Are You in the House Alone?* (M)
A) Charlie's Angels
P) Great Performances: "N.Y. Philharmonic"
**10:00**
A) Vega$
P) *The Pallisers*

**Thursday, September 21, 1978**
**8:00**
N) Project U.F.O.
C) The Waltons
A) Mork & Mindy
P) Once upon a Classic
**8:30**
A) What's Happening!
**9:00**
N) Quincy
A) Barney Miller
P) In Performance at Wolf Trap: "Galina and Valerie Panov"
**9:30**
A) Soap
**10:00**
N) W.E.B.
C) Barnaby Jones

A) Family
**10:00**
P) *The Pallisers*

**Friday, September 22, 1978**
**8:00**
N) The Waverly Wonders
C) The New Adventures of Wonder Woman
A) Donny & Marie
P) Washington Week in Review
**8:30**
N) Who's Watching the Kids?
P) Wall Street Week
**9:00**
N) The Rockford Files
C) The Incredible Hulk
A) *The Bad News Bears* (M)
P) Masterpiece Theatre: *The Mayor of Casterbridge*
**10:00**
N) Eddie Capra Mysteries
P) *The Pallisers*

**Saturday, September 23, 1978**
**8:00**
N) CHiPs
C) Rhoda
A) Carter Country
P) Great Performances: "The Pennsylvania Ballet"
**8:30**
C) Good Times
A) Apple Pie
**9:00**
N) *Burnt Offerings* (M)
C) The American Girls
A) The Love Boat
P) The Long Search
**10:00**
C) Dallas
A) Fantasy Island
P) *The Virgin Spring* (M)

**Sunday, September 24, 1978**
**7:00**
N) Wonderful World of Disney
C) 60 Minutes
A) Lassie, Part 2 (S)
**8:00**
C) Mary Tyler Moore
A) Battlestar Galactica
P) Evening at Pops: "Steven DeGroote"
**9:00**
N) *The Other Side of the Mountain* (M)
C) All in the Family
A) NFL Football
P) Masterpiece Theatre: *The Mayor of Casterbridge*

**9:30**
C) Alice
**10:00**
C) Kaz
P) *The Pallisers*

**Monday, September 25, 1978**
**8:00**
N) Little House on the Prairie
C) WKRP in Cincinnati
A) Welcome Back, Kotter
P) Live from the Met: *Otello*
**8:30**
C) People
A) Operation Petticoat
**9:00**
N) *Overboard* (M)
C) M*A*S*H
A) Monday Nite Football
**9:30**
C) One Day at a Time
**10:00**
C) Lou Grant

**Tuesday, September 26, 1978**
**8:00**
N) Grandpa Goes to Washington
C) The Paper Chase
A) Happy Days
P) James Michener's World
**8:30**
A) Laverne & Shirley
**9:00**
N) *Battered* (M)
C) *One in a Million: The Ron LeFlore Story* (M)
A) Three's Company
P) Mark Russell Comedy Special (S)
**9:30**
A) Taxi!
P) Me and Stella (S)
**10:00**
A) Starsky & Hutch
P) *The Pallisers*

**Wednesday, September 27, 1978**
**8:00**
N) Dick Clark's Live Wednesday
C) The Jeffersons
A) Eight Is Enough
P) The Berlin Philharmonic (S)
**8:30**
C) In the Beginning
**9:00**
N) *Zuma Beach* (M)
C) *Three Days of the Condor* (M)
A) Charlie's Angels
P) Making Television Dance

**10:00**
A) Vega$
P) *The Pallisers*

**Thursday, September 28, 1978**
**8:00**
N) Project U.F.O.
C) The Waltons
A) Mork & Mindy
P) Once upon a Classic
**8:30**
A) What's Happening!
P) The Islander
**9:00**
N) Quincy
C) Hawaii Five-0
A) Barney Miller
P) Previn and the Pittsburgh
**9:30**
A) Soap
**10:00**
N) W.E.B.
C) Barnaby Jones
A) Family
P) *The Pallisers*

**Friday, September 29, 1978**
**8:00**
N) The Waverly Wonders
C) The New Adventures of Wonder Woman
A) Donny & Marie
P) Washington Week in Review
**8:30**
N) Who's Watching the Kids?
P) Wall Street Week
**9:00**
N) The Rockford Files
C) The Incredible Hulk
A) G. E. Anniversary Special (S)
P) Masterpiece Theatre: *The Mayor of Casterbridge*
**10:00**
N) Eddie Capra Mysteries
C) Flying High
P) A Conversation with Earl Warren (S)

**Saturday, September 30, 1978**
**8:00**
N) CHiPs
C) Rhoda
A) Carter Country
P) Great Performances: "Twyla Tharp"
**8:30**
C) Good Times
A) Apple Pie

**9:00**
N) *The Missouri Breaks* (M)
C) The American Girls
A) The Love Boat
P) The Long Search
**10:00**
C) Dallas
A) Fantasy Island
P) *Wild Strawberries* (M)

**Sunday, October 1, 1978**
**7:00**
N) Wonderful World of Disney
C) 60 Minutes
A) The Hardy Boys
P) Bix Beiderbecke Memorial (S)
**8:00**
N) Centennial
C) Mary Tyler Moore
A) Battlestar Galactica
P) Opium, Part 1: The Warlords (S)
**9:00**
C) All in the Family
A) *The Users* (M)
P) Masterpiece Theatre: *The Mayor of Casterbridge*
**9:30**
C) Alice
**10:00**
C) Kaz
P) Trans-America Open Tennis

**Monday, October 2, 1978**
**8:00**
N) Little House on the Prairie
C) WKRP in Cincinnati
A) Welcome Back, Kotter
P) Opium, Part 2: The Politicians (S)
**8:30**
C) People
**9:00**
N) *Little Women,* Part 1 (M)
C) M*A*S*H
A) Monday Nite Football
P) Trans-America Open Tennis
**9:30**
C) One Day at a Time
**10:00**
C) Lou Grant

**Tuesday, October 3, 1978**
**8:00**
N) Grandpa Goes to Washington
C) The Paper Chase
A) Baseball Playoffs
P) Opium, Part 3: The White Powder Opera (S)
**9:00**
N) *Little Women,* Part 2 (M)
C) *Carrie* (M)
P) *Pumping Iron* (M)

**Wednesday, October 4, 1978**
**8:00**
N) Dick Clark's Live Wednesday
C) The Jeffersons
A) Baseball Playoffs
P) Great Performances: *The Turk in Italy*
**8:30**
C) In the Beginning
**9:00**
N) *BJ and the Bear* (M)
C) *Network* (M)

**Thursday, October 5, 1978**
**8:00**
N) Project U.F.O.
C) A Salute to American Imagination (S)
A) Happy Days
P) Nova: "Hitler's Secret Weapon"
**8:30**
A) Mork & Mindy
**9:00**
N) Quincy
A) Three's Company
P) In Performance at Wolf Trap: "Peter Seeger and Arlo Guthrie"
**9:30**
A) Taxi!
**10:00**
N) W.E.B.
C) Hawaii Five-0
A) Barney Miller
**10:30**
A) Soap

**Friday, October 6, 1978**
**8:00**
N) The Waverly Wonders
C) The New Adventures of Wonder Woman
A) Baseball Playoffs
P) Washington Week in Review
**8:30**
N) Who's Watching the Kids?
P) Wall Street Week
**9:00**
N) The Rockford Files
C) The Incredible Hulk
P) Congressional Outlook
**9:30**
P) Turnabout
**10:00**
N) Eddie Capra Mysteries
C) Flying High
P) Masterpiece Theatre: *The Mayor of Casterbridge*

**Saturday, October 7, 1978**
**8:00**
N) CHiPs
C) Rhoda
A) Baseball Playoffs
P) Once upon a Classic
**8:30**
C) Good Times
P) Julia Child & Company
**9:00**
N) Sword of Justice
C) The American Girls
P) The Long Search
**10:00**
C) Dallas
P) Island Holiday Tennis

**Sunday, October 8, 1978**
**7:00**
N) Wonderful World of Disney
C) 60 Minutes
A) The Hardy Boys
**8:00**
N) Centennial
C) Mary Tyler Moore
A) Battlestar Galactica
P) Leontyne Price at the White House (S)
**9:00**
C) All in the Family
A) *The Gumball Rally* (M)
P) Masterpiece Theatre: *The Mayor of Casterbridge*
**9:30**
C) Alice
**10:00**
N) Lifeline
C) Kaz
P) *Pumping Iron* (M)

**Monday, October 9, 1978**
**8:00**
N) Little House on the Prairie
C) WKRP in Cincinnati
A) Welcome Back, Kotter
P) Evening at Symphony: "Stravinsky 'Violin Concerto'"
**8:30**
C) M*A*S*H
A) Operation Petticoat
**9:00**
N) *Secrets of Three Hungry Wives* (M)
A) Monday Nite Football
P) Visions: "Charlie Smith and Fritter Tree"
**9:30**
C) Country Music Association Awards
P) Economically Speaking

**Tuesday, October 10, 1978**
**8:00**
N) Baseball World Series
C) The Paper Chase
A) Happy Days
P) Soundstage: "Leo Sayer"
**8:30**
A) Laverne & Shirley
**9:00**
C) *Once Is Not Enough* (M)
A) Three's Company
P) Word Is Out (S)
**9:30**
A) Taxi!
**10:00**
A) Starsky & Hutch

**Wednesday, October 11, 1978**
**8:00**
N) Baseball World Series
C) The Jeffersons
A) Eight Is Enough
P) Marie Curie
**8:30**
C) In the Beginning
**9:00**
C) *Lifeguard* (M)
A) Charlie's Angels
P) Great Performances: "Verna, USO Girl"
**10:00**
A) Vega$

**Thursday, October 12, 1978**
**8:00**
N) Project U.F.O.
C) The Waltons
A) Mork & Mindy
P) Nova: "One Small Step"
**8:30**
A) What's Happening!
**9:00**
N) Quincy
C) Hawaii Five-0
A) Barney Miller
P) Three by Four (S)
**9:30**
A) Soap
**10:00**
N) Weekend
C) Barnaby Jones
A) Family
P) Sneak Preview
**10:30**
P) The Reel West (S)

**Friday, October 13, 1978**
**8:00**
N) Baseball World Series

C) The New Adventures of Wonder
   Woman
A) Donny & Marie
P) Washington Week in Review
**8:30**
P) Wall Street Week
**9:00**
C) The Incredible Hulk
A) *A Guide for the Married Woman*
   (M)
P) Congressional Outlook
**9:30**
P) Turnabout
**10:00**
C) Flying High
P) Masterpiece Theatre: *The Mayor
   of Casterbridge*

**Saturday, October 14, 1978**
**8:00**
N) CHiPs
C) Rhoda
A) The Osmond Brothers
P) Once upon a Classic
**8:30**
C) Good Times
P) Julia Child & Company
**9:00**
N) *Rescue from Gilligan's Island*
   Part 1 (M)
C) The American Girls
A) The Love Boat
P) The Long Search
**10:00**
N) Sword of Justice
C) Dallas
A) Fantasy Island
P) The Champions, Part 1 (S)

**Sunday, October 15, 1978**
**7:00**
N) Baseball World Series
C) 60 Minutes
A) The Hardy Boys
**7:30**
N) Wonderful World of Disney
**8:00**
C) All in the Family
A) Battlestar Galactica
P) The Champions, Part 2 (S)
**8:30**
N) Bob Hope Special (S)
C) Alice
**9:00**
C) Dallas
A) *Mother, Jugs, and Speed* (M)
P) Masterpiece Theatre: *The Mayor
   of Casterbridge*
**10:00**
N) Lifeline
C) Kaz
P) Word Is Out (S)

**Monday, October 16, 1978**
**8:00**
N) Little House on the Prairie
C) WKRP in Cincinnati
A) Welcome Back, Kotter
P) Evening at Pops: "Berlioz
   *Beatrice et Benedict,* Act I"
**8:30**
C) People
A) Pope John Paul II Special (S)
**9:00**
C) M*A*S*H
A) Monday Nite Football
P) Visions: "Escape"
**9:30**
N) *Human Feelings* (M)
C) One Day at a Time
**10:00**
C) Lou Grant
**10:30**
P) Economically Speaking

**Tuesday, October 17, 1978**
**8:00**
N) Baseball World Series
C) The Paper Chase
A) Happy Days
P) Soundstage
**8:30**
A) Laverne & Shirley
**9:00**
C) *The Great Scout and Cathouse
   Thursday* (M)
A) Three's Company
P) Sinai Field Mission (S)
**9:30**
A) Taxi!
**10:00**
A) Starsky & Hutch

**Wednesday, October 18, 1978**
**8:00**
N) *Little Big Man* (M)
C) The Jeffersons
A) Eight Is Enough
P) Marie Curie
**8:30**
C) In the Beginning
**9:00**
C) *McClintock!* (M)
A) Charlie's Angels
P) Great Performances: "Dance in
   America"
**10:00**
A) Vega$

**Thursday, October 19, 1978**
**8:00**
N) Dick Clark's Live from
   Hollywood (S)
C) The Waltons

A) Mork & Mindy
P) Nova: "The Final Frontier"
**8:30**
A) Operation Petticoat
**9:00**
N) Quincy
C) Hawaii Five-0
A) Barney Miller
P) Ormandy and His Orchestra: A
   Japanese Odyssey (S)
**9:30**
A) Soap
**10:00**
N) Sword of Justice
C) Barnaby Jones
A) Family

**Friday, October 20, 1978**
**8:00**
N) Project U.F.O.
C) The New Adventures of Wonder
   Woman
A) Donny & Marie
P) Washington Week in Review
**8:30**
P) Wall Street Week
**9:00**
N) The Rockford Files
C) The Incredible Hulk
A) *More than Friends* (M)
P) Congressional Outlook
**9:30**
P) Turnabout
**10:00**
N) Eddie Capra Mysteries
C) Flying High
P) Masterpiece Theatre: *The Mayor
   of Casterbridge*

**Saturday, October 21, 1978**
**8:00**
N) CHiPs
C) Rhoda
A) Welcome Back, Kotter
P) Once upon a Classic
**8:30**
C) Good Times
A) Carter Country
P) Julia Child & Company
**9:00**
N) *Rescue from Gilligan's Island,*
   Part 2 (M)
C) The American Girls
A) The Love Boat
P) The Long Search
**10:00**
N) Sword of Justice
C) Dallas
A) Fantasy Island
P) The Champions, Part 2 (S)

**Sunday, October 22, 1978**
**7:00**
N) Wonderful World of Disney
C) 60 Minutes
A) The Hardy Boys
**8:00**
N) Hee Haw 10th Anniversary (S)
C) All in the Family
A) Battlestar Galactica
P) The California Reich (S)
**8:30**
C) Alice
**9:00**
C) *Like Mom, Like Me* (M)
A) *Final Chapter: Walking Tall* (M)
P) Masterpiece Theatre: *The Duchess of Duke Street*
**10:00**
N) Lifeline
P) Sinai Field Mission (S)

**Monday, October 23, 1978**
**8:00**
N) Little House on the Prairie
C) WKRP in Cincinnati
A) Ohio State Fair Special (S)
P) Evening at Pops: "Berlioz *Beatrice et Benedict,* Act II"
**8:30**
C) People
**9:00**
N) *Katie: Portrait of a Centerfold* (M)
C) M*A*S*H
A) Monday Nite Football
P) Visions: "Fans of the Kosko Show"
**9:30**
C) One Day at a Time
**10:00**
C) Lou Grant
**10:30**
P) Economically Speaking

**Tuesday, October 24, 1978**
**8:00**
N) Grandpa Goes to Washington
C) *Papillon* (M)
A) Happy Days
P) Soundstage
**8:30**
A) Laverne & Shirley
**9:00**
N) *Donner Pass: The Road to Survival* (M)
A) Three's Company
P) U.N. Day Concert (S)
**9:30**
A) Taxi!
**10:00**
N) President Carter's Address on the Economy

C) President Carter's Address on the Economy
A) President Carter's Address on the Economy
P) President Carter's Address on the Economy
**10:30**
A) Starsky & Hutch

**Wednesday, October 25, 1978**
**8:00**
N) Dick Clark's Live Wednesday
C) Bugs Bunny Halloween Special (S)
A) Eight Is Enough
P) Marie Curie
**8:30**
C) Fat Albert Halloween Special (S)
**9:00**
N) *Desperate Women* (M)
C) *The Grass Is Always Greener over the Septic Tank* (M)
A) Charlie's Angels
P) Great Performances: *The Collection*
**10:00**
A) Vega$

**Thursday, October 26, 1978**
**8:00**
N) *Cotton Candy* (M)
C) The Waltons
A) Dr. Seuss Special (S)
P) Nova: "The Great Wine Revolution"
**8:30**
A) NFL Football
**9:00**
C) Hawaii Five-0
P) Grease Band
**10:00**
N) Quincy
C) Barnaby Jones
P) Sneak Preview
**10:30**
P) Pompeii: Frozen in Fire (S)

**Friday, October 27, 1978**
**8:00**
N) Who's Watching the Kids?
C) The Magic of David Copperfield (S)
A) Donny & Marie
P) Washington Week in Review
**8:30**
N) Republican Party Reply to President Carter
P) Wall Street Week
**9:00**
N) The Rockford Files

C) The Incredible Hulk
A) *Possession* (M)
P) Congressional Outlook
**9:30**
P) Turnabout
**10:00**
N) Eddie Capra Mysteries
C) Flying High
P) Masterpiece Theatre: *The Duchess of Duke Street*

**Saturday, October 28, 1978**
**8:00**
N) *KISS Meets the Phantom* (M)
C) Rhoda
A) Welcome Back, Kotter
P) Once upon a Classic
**8:30**
C) *Cahill, U.S. Marshall* (M)
A) Carter Country
P) Julia Child & Company
**9:00**
A) The Love Boat
P) The Long Search
**10:00**
N) Sword of Justice
A) Fantasy Island
P) The California Reich (S)
**10:30**
C) Republican Party Reply to President Carter

**Sunday, October 29, 1978**
**7:00**
N) Wonderful World of Disney
C) 60 Minutes
A) The Hardy Boys
**8:00**
N) Centennial
C) All in the Family
A) Battlestar Galactica
P) F.Y.I.: "Prison Reform"
**8:30**
C) Alice
**9:00**
C) Kaz
A) *Crash* (M)
P) Masterpiece Theatre: *The Duchess of Duke Street*
**10:00**
N) Lifeline
C) Dallas
P) Bad Boys (S)

**Monday, October 30, 1978**
**8:00**
N) Little House on the Prairie
C) *It's the Great Pumpkin, Charlie Brown* (S)

A) ABC News Closeup: "Terror in the Promised Land"
P) Elections '78
**8:30**
C) Puff the Magic Dragon (S)
P) Evening at Symphony: "Respighi"
**9:00**
N) *Summer of My German Soldier* (M)
C) M*A*S*H
A) Monday Nite Football
**9:30**
C) WKRP in Cincinnati
P) Visions: "Blessings"
**10:00**
C) Lou Grant

**Tuesday, October 31, 1978**
**8:00**
N) Grandpa Goes to Washington
C) The Paper Chase
A) Happy Days
P) Election '78
**8:30**
A) Laverne & Shirley
P) Soundstage
**9:00**
N) *Stranger in Our House* (M)
C) *Devil Dog: The Hound of Hell* (M)
A) Three's Company
**9:30**
A) Taxi!
P) Great Performances: *Dracula*
**10:00**
A) Starsky & Hutch

**Wednesday, November 1, 1978**
**8:00**
N) Dick Clark's Live Wednesday
C) The Jeffersons
A) Eight Is Enough
P) Election '78
**8:30**
P) Marie Curie
**9:00**
N) *Thou Shalt Not Commit Adultery* (M)
C) *Gator* (M)
A) Charlie's Angels
**9:30**
P) *Macbeth* (S)
**10:00**
A) Vega$

**Thursday, November 2, 1978**
**8:00**
N) Project U.F.O.
C) The Waltons

A) Mork & Mindy
P) Election '78
**8:30**
A) What's Happening!
P) Nova: "Alaska, the Closing Frontier"
**9:00**
N) Quincy
C) Cinderella at the Palace (S)
A) Barney Miller
**9:30**
A) Soap
P) In Performance at Wolf Trap: "Chuck Mangione"
**10:00**
N) David Cassidy, Man Undercover
A) Family

**Friday, November 3, 1978**
**8:00**
N) Diff'rent Strokes
C) The New Adventures of Wonder Woman
A) Happy Days
P) Washington Week in Review
**8:30**
N) Who's Watching the Kids?
A) Welcome Back, Kotter
P) Election '78
**9:00**
N) The Rockford Files
C) The Incredible Hulk
A) *How to Pick Up Girls* (M)
P) Wall Street Week
**9:30**
P) Congressional Outlook
**10:00**
N) Eddie Capra Mysteries
C) Flying High
P) Turnabout
**10:30**
P) Masterpiece Theatre: *The Duchess of Duke Street*

**Saturday, November 4, 1978**
**8:00**
N) CHiPs
C) The Jeffersons
A) The Love Boat
P) Once upon a Classic
**8:30**
P) Julia Child & Company
C) *The Poseidon Adventure* (M)
**9:00**
N) Centennial
P) The Long Search
**9:30**
A) Fantasy Island
**10:00**
P) F.Y.I.: "Tax Reform"

**Sunday, November 5, 1978**
**7:00**
N) Wonderful World of Disney
C) 60 Minutes
A) The Hardy Boys
**8:00**
N) *The Time Machine* (M)
C) All in the Family
A) *The Sting* (M)
P) Election '78
**8:30**
C) Alice
**9:00**
C) Kaz
P) Masterpiece Theatre: *The Duchess of Duke Street*
**10:00**
N) Lifeline
C) Dallas
P) Great Performances: *Dracula*

**Monday, November 6, 1978**
**8:00**
N) Little House on the Prairie
C) WKRP in Cincinnati
A) All Star Family Feud (S)
P) Evening at Symphony
**8:30**
C) People
**9:00**
N) *Rainbow* (M)
C) M*A*S*H
A) Monday Nite Football
P) Visions: "Liza's Pioneer Diary"
**9:30**
C) One Day at a Time
**10:00**
C) Lou Grant
**10:30**
P) Economically Speaking

**Tuesday, November 7, 1978**
**7:00**
C) Elections Coverage
N) Elections Coverage
A) Elections Coverage
**8:00**
P) Soundstage
**9:00**
P) *Seven Beauties* (M)

**Wednesday, November 8, 1978**
**8:00**
N) Dick Clark's Live Wednesday
C) The Jeffersons
A) Eight Is Enough
P) Marie Curie
**8:30**
C) Good Times

**9:00**
N) *Return to Macon County* (M)
C) *First You Cry* (M)
A) Charlie's Angels
P) Great Performances: *The Good Doctor*
**10:00**
A) Vega$
**10:30**
P) Portrait of a Nurse

**Thursday, November 9, 1978**
**8:00**
N) *Li'l Abner in Dogpatch Today* (S)
C) The Waltons
A) Mork & Mindy
P) Nova: "Arms for South Africa"
**8:30**
A) What's Happening!
**9:00**
N) Quincy
C) Hawaii Five-0
A) Barney Miller
P) Geraldine Fitzgerald at Reno Sweeney's (S)
**9:30**
A) Soap
**10:00**
N) David Cassidy, Man Undercover
C) Barnaby Jones
A) Family
P) Sneak Preview
**10:30**
P) Show on the Road

**Friday, November 10, 1978**
**8:00**
N) Diff'rent Strokes
C) The New Adventures of Wonder Woman
A) Boxing (S)
P) Washington Week in Review
**8:30**
N) Who's Watching the Kids?
P) Wall Street Week
**9:00**
N) The Rockford Files
C) The Incredible Hulk
P) Congressional Outlook
**9:30**
P) Turnabout
**10:00**
N) Eddie Capra Mysteries
C) American Girls
P) Masterpiece Theatre: *The Duchess of Duke Street*

**Saturday, November 11, 1978**
**8:00**
N) CHiPs

C) Alice
A) Welcome Back, Kotter
P) Once upon a Classic
**8:30**
C) Rhoda
A) Carter Country
P) Julia Child & Company
**9:00**
N) Centennial
C) Hollywood Diamond Jubilee (S)
A) The Love Boat
P) The Long Search
**10:00**
A) Fantasy Island
P) Geraldine Fitzgerald at Reno Sweeney's (S)

**Sunday, November 12, 1978**
**7:00**
N) Wonderful World of Disney
C) 60 Minutes
A) Pat Boone Thanksgiving Special (S)
P) Up in Rosebud Country
**8:00**
C) *The Word,* Part 1 (M)
A) Battlestar Galactica
P) The Global Paper: "The Fight for Food," Part 1
**9:00**
N) *Ode to Billy Joe* (M)
A) Monday Nite Football
P) Masterpiece Theatre: *The Duchess of Duke Street*
**10:00**
C) Dallas
P) *Seven Beauties* (M)

**Monday November 13, 1978**
**8:00**
N) Little House on the Prairie
C) M*A*S*H
A) Lucan
P) The Global Paper: "The Fight for Food," Part 2
**8:30**
C) One Day at a Time
**9:00**
N) *Betrayal* (M)
C) *The Word,* Part 2 (M)
A) Monday Nite Football
P) Bill Moyers' Journal
**10:00**
P) Visions: "Blackout"

**Tuesday, November 14, 1978**
**8:00**
N) Lifeline
C) The Paper Chase
A) Happy Days

P) Soundstage
**8:30**
A) Laverne & Shirley
**9:00**
N) *Lady of the House* (M)
C) *The Word,* Part 3 (M)
A) Three's Company
P) *Distant Thunder* (M)
**9:30**
A) Taxi!
**10:00**
A) Starsky & Hutch

**Wednesday, November 15, 1978**
**8:00**
N) Dick Clark's Live Wednesday
C) *A Charlie Brown Thanksgiving* (S)
A) Eight Is Enough
P) Elections '78
**8:30**
C) *How Bugs Bunny Won the West* (S)
**9:00**
N) *Bud and Lou* (M)
C) *The Word,* Part 4 (M)
A) Charlie's Angels
P) Great Performances: *A Month in the Country*
**10:00**
A) Vega$
P) Race War in Rhodesia (S)

**Thursday, November 16, 1978**
**8:00**
N) Lifeline
C) The Waltons
A) Mork & Mindy
P) Nova: "A Whisper from Space"
**8:30**
A) What's Happening!
**9:00**
N) Quincy
C) Hawaii Five-0
A) Pearl, Part 1
P) Global Paper Forum
**9:30**
P) The Harpsichord Maker (S)
**10:00**
N) David Cassidy, Man Undercover
C) Barnaby Jones

**Friday, November 17, 1978**
**8:00**
N) Diff'rent Strokes
C) The Star Wars Holiday Special (S)
A) The Love Boat
P) Washington Week in Review
**8:30**
N) The Rockford Files
P) Wall Street Week

**9:00**
A) Pearl, Part 2
P) Congressional Outlook
**9:30**
N) Hallmark Hall of Fame: *Return Engagement* (S)
P) Turnabout
**10:00**
C) Flying High
P) Masterpiece Theatre: *The Duchess of Duke Street*

**Saturday, November 18, 1978**
**8:00**
N) CHiPs
C) *The Bible* (M)
A) Battle of the Network Stars (S)
P) Once upon a Classic
**8:30**
P) Julia Child & Company
**9:00**
N) Frankie and Annette
P) The Long Search
**10:00**
N) Lifeline
A) Fantasy Island
P) Elections '78

**Sunday, November 19, 1978**
**7:00**
N) Wonderful World of Disney
C) 60 Minutes
A) The Hardy Boys
**8:00**
C) All in the Family
A) Battlestar Galactica
P) The New Klan (S)
**8:30**
N) Heroes of the Bible
C) Alice
**9:00**
C) Lucy Comes to Nashville (S)
A) Pearl, Part 3
P) Masterpiece Theatre: *The Duchess of Duke Street*
**10:00**
C) Dallas
P) *Distant Thunder* (M)

**Monday, November 20, 1978**
**8:00**
N) Little House on the Prairie
C) Bobby Vinton's Rock 'n' Rollers (S)
A) Lucan
P) Evening at Symphony
**9:00**
N) Heroes of the Bible
C) M*A*S*H
A) Monday Nite Football

P) Visions: "The Dancing Bear"
**9:30**
C) One Day at a Time
**10:00**
C) Lou Grant
**10:30**
P) Economically Speaking

**Tuesday, November 21, 1978**
**8:00**
N) Heroes of the Bible
C) The Paper Chase
A) Happy Days
P) Great Performances: "Live from the Met: *The Bartered Bride*"
**8:30**
A) Laverne & Shirley
**9:00**
C) *The Pirate,* Part 1 (M)
A) Three's Company
**9:30**
A) Taxi!
**10:00**
N) Dean Martin Special
A) Starsky & Hutch

**Wednesday, November 22, 1978**
**8:00**
N) Heroes of the Bible
C) Bugs Bunny
A) Eight Is Enough
P) Wild Horses, Broken Wings (S)
**8:30**
C) The Jeffersons
**9:00**
C) *The Pirate,* Part 2 (M)
A) Charlie's Angels
P) Great Performances: "Thank You, Comrades"
**10:00**
N) Steve Martin Special (S)
A) Vega$
P) Every Tub on Its Own Bottom

**Thursday, November 23, 1978**
**8:00**
N) *The Thief of Baghdad* (M)
C) The Waltons
A) Mork & Mindy
P) Nova: "The Desert's Edge"
**8:30**
A) What's Happening!
**9:00**
C) Hawaii Five-0
A) Barney Miller
P) Sing-Sing Thanksgiving (S)
**9:30**
A) Soap
**10:00**
N) David Cassidy, Man Undercover
C) Barnaby Jones

A) Family
**10:30**
P) Sneak Preview

**Friday, November 24, 1978**
**8:00**
N) Diff'rent Strokes
C) The New Adventures of Wonder Woman
A) Donny & Marie
P) Washington Week in Review
**8:30**
N) Who's Watching the Kids?
P) Wall Street Week
**9:00**
N) The Rockford Files
C) The Incredible Hulk
A) *Fun with Dick and Jane* (M)
P) Congressional Outlook
**9:30**
P) Turnabout
**10:00**
C) Flying High
P) Masterpiece Theatre: *The Duchess of Duke Street*

**Saturday, November 25, 1978**
**8:00**
N) CHiPs
C) The Amazing Spiderman
A) Welcome Back, Kotter
P) Once upon a Classic
**8:30**
A) Carter Country
P) Julia Child & Company
**9:00**
N) Dick Clark's Good Old Days (S)
C) *Orca, the Killer Whale* (M)
A) The Love Boat
P) The Long Search
**10:00**
A) Fantasy Island
P) The New Klan (S)

**Sunday, November 26, 1978**
**7:00**
N) Wonderful World of Disney
C) 60 Minutes
A) The Hardy Boys
**8:00**
N) *A Fire in the Sky* (M)
C) All in the Family
A) Battlestar Galactica
P) James Michener's World
**8:30**
C) Alice
**9:00**
C) Kaz
A) *A Question of Love* (M)
P) Masterpiece Theatre: *The Duchess of Duke Street*

**10:00**
C) Dallas
P) Affair in the Air

**Monday, November 27, 1978**
**8:00**
N) Little House on the Prairie
C) The White Shadow
A) Lucan
P) Evening at Symphony
**9:00**
N) *And I Alone Survived* (M)
C) M*A*S*H
A) Monday Nite Football
P) Visions: "Gold Watch"
**9:30**
C) One Day at a Time
**10:00**
C) Lou Grant
**10:30**
P) Economically Speaking

**Tuesday, November 28, 1978**
**8:00**
N) *Patton* (M)
C) The Paper Chase
A) Happy Days
P) Soundstage
**8:30**
A) Laverne & Shirley
**9:00**
C) *High Ballin'* (M)
A) Three's Company
P) *Harlan County, U.S.A.* (M)
**9:30**
A) Taxi!
**10:00**
A) Starsky & Hutch

**Wednesday, November 29, 1978**
**8:00**
N) Dick Clark's Live Wednesday
C) Fat Albert (S)
A) Eight Is Enough
P) F.Y.I.: "Drugs in America"
**8:30**
C) The Jeffersons
**9:00**
N) *Someone Is Watching Me* (M)
C) *Billy Jack* (M)
P) Great Performances:
   "Choreography by Balanchine"
**10:00**
A) Barbara Walters Special
P) Findhorn

**Thursday, November 30, 1978**
**8:00**
N) Project U.F.O.
C) *Frosty the Snowman* (S)

A) Mork & Mindy
P) Nova: "Still Waters"
**8:30**
C) *Raggedy Ann and Andy* (S)
A) What's Happening!
**9:00**
N) Quincy
C) Hawaii Five-0
A) Barney Miller
P) Here to Make Music
**9:30**
A) Soap
**10:00**
N) Hallmark Hall of Fame: "Fame"
C) Barnaby Jones
A) 20/20
P) We Ain't What We Was

**Friday, December 1, 1978**
**8:00**
N) *Winnie the Pooh* (S)
C) The New Adventures of Wonder
   Woman
A) Donny & Marie
P) Washington Week in Review
**8:30**
N) Diff'rent Strokes
P) Wall Street Week
**9:00**
N) The Rockford Files
C) The Incredible Hulk
A) NCAA Football
P) Congressional Outlook
**9:30**
P) Turnabout
**10:00**
N) Eddie Capra Mysteries
C) Flying High
P) Masterpiece Theatre: *The
   Duchess of Duke Street*

**Saturday, December 2, 1978**
**8:00**
N) CHiPs
C) Rhoda
A) Welcome Back, Kotter
P) Once upon a Classic
**8:30**
C) Good Times
A) Carter Country
**9:00**
N) *The Story of Christmas* (S)
C) *Outside Chance* (M)
A) The Love Boat
P) The Long Search
**10:00**
N) Weekend
A) Fantasy Island
P) F.Y.I.: "Drugs in America"

**Sunday, December 3, 1978**
**7:00**
N) Wonderful World of Disney
C) 60 Minutes
A) The Hardy Boys
**8:00**
N) Bob Hope Special (S)
C) All in the Family
A) Battlestar Galactica
P) Christmas Eve on Sesame Street
   (S)
**8:30**
C) Alice
**9:00**
N) Centennial
C) Kaz
A) NFL Football
P) Masterpiece Theatre: *The
   Duchess of Duke Street*
**10:00**
C) Dallas
P) *Harlan County, U.S.A.* (M)

**Monday, December 4, 1978**
**8:00**
N) Little House on the Prairie
C) The White Shadow
A) Lucan
P) Evening at Symphony
**9:00**
N) *Suddenly Love* (M)
C) M*A*S*H
A) Monday Nite Football
P) Visions: "Alambrista"
**10:00**
C) Lou Grant

**Tuesday, December 5, 1978**
**8:00**
N) Grandpa Goes to Washington
C) The Paper Chase
A) Happy Days
P) Soundstage Anniversary Special
   (S)
**8:30**
A) Laverne & Shirley
**9:00**
N) My Husband Is Missing
C) America Salutes the Performing
   Arts (S)
A) Three's Company
P) *Monty Python and the Holy Grail*
   (M)
**9:30**
A) Taxi!
**10:00**
A) ABC News Closeup: "Psychic
   Phenomena"
**10:30**
P) The Forgotten Frontier

**Wednesday, December 6, 1978**

**8:00**
N) Dick Clark's Live Wednesday
C) *Rudolph the Red-Nosed Reindeer* (S)
A) Eight Is Enough
P) The Cousteau Odyssey: "Blind Prophets of Easter Island"

**9:00**
N) *Steel Cowboy* (M)
C) Bing Crosby: The Christmas Years (S)
A) Charlie's Angels
P) Great Performances: *Mourning Becomes Electra,* Part 1

**10:00**
C) The Johnny Cash Christmas Show (S)
A) Vega$
P) The Spirit of Pusinatawney (S)

**Thursday, December 7, 1978**

**8:00**
N) Project U.F.O.
C) The Waltons
A) *Benji* (S)
P) Nova: "Light of the 21st Century"

**8:30**
A) *The Pink Panther's Christmas Special* (S)

**9:00**
N) Quincy
C) A Country Christmas (S)
A) Barney Miller
P) Mornin' Blues

**9:30**
A) Soap

**10:00**
N) David Cassidy, Man Undercover
C) Tribute to Jimmy Stewart (S)
A) Family
P) Sneak Preview

**10:30**
P) Elizabethan Christmas Celebration (S)

**Friday, December 8, 1978**

**8:00**
N) Diff'rent Strokes
C) A Special Sesame Street Christmas (S)
A) Donny & Marie
P) Washington Week in Review

**8:30**
N) Who's Watching the Kids?
P) Wall Street Week

**9:00**
N) The Rockford Files
C) Young and Foolish (S)

A) *The Gift of Love* (M)
P) Golda Meir

**10:00**
N) Eddie Capra Mysteries
C) Flying High
P) Davis Cup Tennis

**Saturday, December 9, 1978**

**8:00**
N) CHiPs
C) Rhoda
A) *Rudolph's Shiny New Year* (S)
P) Once upon a Classic

**8:30**
C) Good Times
P) Julia Child & Company

**9:00**
N) Dean Martin Special (S)
C) *A Real American Hero* (M)
A) The Love Boat
P) The Long Search

**10:00**
N) Weekend
A) Fantasy Island
P) The Cousteau Odyssey: "The Blind Prophets of Easter Island"

**Sunday, December 10, 1978**

**7:00**
N) Wonderful World of Disney
C) 60 Minutes
A) *Santa Claus Is Coming to Town* (S)
P) Fifth Annual Bach Festival

**8:00**
N) Centennial
C) All in the Family
A) Jackie Gleason's Christmas (S)
P) Living Sands of Namib

**9:00**
C) Circus of the Stars (S)
A) ABC Theatre: *The Gathering* (S)
P) Masterpiece Theatre: *The Duchess of Duke Street*

**10:00**
N) NBC Reports: "Marijuana"
P) *Monty Python and the Holy Grail* (M)

**Monday, December 11, 1978**

**8:00**
N) The Flintstones (S)
C) The White Shadow
A) *The Year Without Santa Claus* (S)
P) Evening at Symphony

**9:00**
N) *A Woman Called Moses,* Part 1 (M)
C) M*A*S*H
A) Monday Nite Football

P) Visions: "The Brothers"

**9:30**
C) One Day at a Time

**10:00**
C) Lou Grant

**10:30**
P) Economically Speaking

**Tuesday, December 12, 1978**

**8:00**
N) Grandpa Goes to Washington
C) The Paper Chase
A) Happy Days
P) Soundstage

**8:30**
A) Laverne & Shirley

**9:00**
N) *A Woman Called Moses,* Part 2 (M)
C) *The Jordan Chance* (M)
A) Three's Company
P) Nobel Prize Ceremonies (S)

**9:30**
A) Taxi!

**10:00**
A) Starsky & Hutch

**Wednesday, December 13, 1978**

**8:00**
N) *The New Adventures of Heidi* (M)
C) The Jeffersons
A) *Frosty's Winter Wonderland* (S)
P) A Place for Dreams (S)

**8:30**
C) Good Times
A) *Nestor, the Christmas Donkey* (S)

**9:00**
C) *Lovey, a Circle of Children,* Part II (M)
A) Perry Como's Christmas (S)
P) Great Performances: *Mourning Becomes Electra,* Part 2

**10:00**
N) Dick Clark's Live Wednesday
A) Christmas at the Grand Ole Opry (S)
P) Elizabeth Swados: The Girl with the Incredible Feeling (S)

**Thursday, December 14, 1978**

**8:00**
N) Doug Henning's World of Magic (S)
C) The Waltons
A) Mork & Mindy
P) Nova: "The Tsetse Trap"

**8:30**
A) What's Happening!

**9:00**
N) Holiday Tribute to Radio City Music Hall (S)
C) Hawaii Five-0
A) Barney Miller
P) In Performance at Wolf Trap: "Leonard Bernstein's 60th Birthday"
**9:30**
A) Soap
**10:00**
C) Barnaby Jones
A) A Conversation with the Carters (S)

**Friday, December 15, 1978**
**8:00**
N) Diff'rent Strokes
C) The New Adventures of Wonder Woman
A) Donny & Marie
P) Washington Week in Review
**8:30**
N) Who's Watching the Kids?
P) Wall Street Week
**9:00**
N) Eddie Capra Mysteries
C) The Incredible Hulk
A) *The Long Journey Back* (M)
P) Congressional Outlook
**9:30**
P) Turnabout
**10:00**
C) Flying High
P) Masterpiece Theatre: *The Duchess of Duke Street*

**Saturday, December 16, 1978**
**8:00**
N) CHiPs
C) Dr. Seuss Christmas Special (S)
A) Welcome Back, Kotter
P) Once upon a Classic
**8:30**
C) The Tiny Tree (S)
A) Carter Country
P) Julia Child & Company
**9:00**
N) Lifeline
C) *Who'll Save Our Children?* (M)
A) The Love Boat
P) Like The Wind (S)
**10:00**
N) Weekend
A) Fantasy Island
P) The Living Sands of Namib (S)

**Sunday, December 17, 1978**
**7:00**
N) Hallmark Hall of Fame: *Stubby Pringle's Christmas*

C) 60 Minutes
A) Who Are the Debolts? (S)
P) Fifth Annual Bach Festival II
**8:00**
N) *The Winds of Kitty Hawk* (M)
C) All in the Family
A) Battlestar Galactica
P) Simple Gifts: Six Episodes for Christmas (S)
**9:00**
C) Kaz
A) *The Nativity* (M)
P) Masterpiece Theatre: *The Duchess of Duke Street*
**10:00**
N) Sword of Justice
C) Dallas
P) *Hester Street* (M)

**Monday, December 18, 1978**
**8:00**
N) Little House on the Prairie
C) *A Charlie Brown Christmas* (S)
A) 20/20
P) Evening at Symphony
**8:30**
C) *'Twas the Night Before Christmas* (S)
**9:00**
C) M*A*S*H
A) Monday Nite Football
**9:30**
N) *The Deerslayer* (M)
C) One Day at a Time
P) Visions: "The Great Cherub Knitwear Strike"
**10:00**
C) Lou Grant

**Tuesday, December 19, 1978**
**8:00**
N) *The Bear Who Slept Through Christmas* (S)
C) CBS Reports: "A Turning Point in History"
A) Happy Days
P) Great Performances: "Live From the Met: *Tosca*"
**8:30**
N) *Once Upon a Starry Night* (S)
A) Laverne & Shirley
**9:00**
C) *The Millionaire* (M)
A) The Carpenter's Christmas (S)
**10:00**
N) Mac Davis Christmas Special (S)
A) Starsky & Hutch

**Wednesday, December 20, 1978**
**8:00**
N) Dick Clark's Live Wednesday

C) The Jeffersons
A) Eight Is Enough
P) Christmas Snows, Christmas Winds (S)
**8:30**
C) Good Times
P) A Christmas Celebration (S)
**9:00**
N) *Ishi* (M)
C) *A Christmas to Remember* (M)
A) Charlie's Angels
P) Great Performances: *Mourning Becomes Electra,* Part 3
**10:00**
A) Vega$
P) Wonder Anew (S)

**Thursday, December 21, 1978**
**8:00**
N) *The Little Drummer Boy* (S)
C) The Waltons
A) Mork & Mindy
P) Christmas Eve on Sesame Street (S)
**8:30**
N) *The Gift of the Magi* (S)
A) What's Happening!
**9:00**
C) Hawaii Five-0
A) Barney Miller
P) Christmas Heritage (S)
**9:30**
A) Soap
**10:00**
N) David Cassidy, Man Undercover
C) Barnaby Jones
A) Family
P) Sneak Preview
**10:30**
P) Sing We Noel (S)

**Friday, December 22, 1978**
**8:00**
N) Bob Hope Special (S)
C) The New Adventures of Wonder Woman
A) John Davidson Christmas Special
P) Washington Week in Review
**8:30**
P) Wall Street Week
**9:00**
N) The Rockford Files
C) The Incredible Hulk
A) Eight Is Enough
P) Congressional Outlook
**9:30**
P) Turnabout

10:00
N) Eddie Capra Mysteries
C) Flying High
P) Masterpiece Theatre: *The Duchess of Duke Street*

**Saturday, December 23, 1978**
8:00
N) *The Stingiest Man in Town* (S)
C) *The Homecoming: A Christmas Story* (S)
A) Welcome Back, Kotter
P) Once upon a Classic
8:30
A) Carter Country
9:00
N) Lifeline
A) The Love Boat
P) Simple Gifts: Six Episodes for Christmas (S)
10:00
N) Weekend
C) CBS Reports: "But What about the Children?" (S)
A) Fantasy Island
P) Christmas Snows, Christmas Winds (S)
10:30
P) A Christmas Celebration (S)

**Sunday, December 24, 1978**
7:00
N) *Amahl and the Night Visitors* (S)
C) 60 Minutes
A) The Vatican Midnight Mass (S)
P) The Mirecourt Trio (S)
8:00
N) *Huck Finn* (M)
C) *The Nutcracker Suite* (S)
A) Battlestar Galactica
P) Christmas Heritage (S)
9:00
A) *It Happened One Christmas* (M)
P) Masterpiece Theatre: *The Duchess of Duke Street*
9:30
C) Alice
10:00
N) Sword of Justice
C) Dallas
P) Evening at Symphony: Handel's "Messiah"

**Monday, December 25, 1978**
8:00
N) Little House on the Prairie
C) The White Shadow
A) Fast-Lane Blues (S)
P) Evening at Symphony

9:00
N) *Sunshine Christmas* (S)
C) M*A*S*H
A) *Green Eyes* (M)
9:30
C) One Day at a Time
P) Visions: "Pleasantville"
10:00
C) Lou Grant
10:30
P) Economically Speaking

**Tuesday, December 26, 1978**
8:00
N) Grandpa Goes to Washington
C) CBS Reports: "Any Place but Here" (S)
A) Happy Days
P) Soundstage
8:30
A) Laverne & Shirley
9:00
N) *The Christmas Miracle in Caulfield, U.S.A.* (S)
C) *Terror Out of the Sky* (M)
A) Three's Company
P) *Hedda* (M)
9:30
A) Taxi!
10:00
A) Starsky & Hutch

**Wednesday, December 27, 1978**
8:00
N) Dick Clark's Live Wednesday
C) *Les Miserables* (M)
A) Eight Is Enough
P) Mark Russell Comedy Special (S)
8:30
P) The Wages of Congress
9:00
N) *Car Wash* (M)
A) Charlie's Angels
P) Great Performances: *Mourning Becomes Electra*, Part 4
10:00
A) ABC News Closeup: "Human Rights"
P) Willa Cather's America (S)

**Thursday, December 28, 1978**
8:00
N) Project U.F.O.
C) The Waltons
A) Mork & Mindy
P) F.Y.I.: "The Last Colony: Washington, D.C."
8:30
A) What's Happening!

9:00
N) Quincy
C) Hawaii Five-0
A) Barney Miller
P) The Van Cliburn Piano Competition (S)
9:30
A) Almost Heaven (S)
10:00
N) David Cassidy, Man Undercover
C) Barnaby Jones
A) Family
P) The Priceless Treasures of Dresden (S)

**Friday, December 29, 1978**
8:00
N) Diff'rent Strokes
C) The New Adventures of Wonder Woman
A) Donny & Marie
P) Washington Week in Review
8:30
P) Wall Street Week
9:00
N) The Rockford Files
C) The Incredible Hulk
A) The Gator Bowl
P) Congressional Outlook
9:30
P) Turnabout
10:00
N) Quincy
C) Flying High
P) Masterpiece Theatre: *The Duchess of Duke Street*

**Saturday, December 30, 1978**
8:00
N) The King Orange Parade (S)
C) The Amazing Spiderman
A) Welcome Back, Kotter
P) Once upon a Classic
8:30
A) Carter Country
9:00
N) Lifeline
C) *The Demon Seed* (M)
A) The Love Boat
P) *Hedda* (M)
10:00
N) Weekend
A) Fantasy Island

**Sunday, December 31, 1978**
7:00
N) Wonderful World of Disney
C) The NFL Today
A) The Hardy Boys

**8:00**
N) *Greatest Rescues of "Emergency"* (M)
C) 60 Minutes
A) Battlestar Galactica
P) Championship Ice Skating (S)
**9:00**
C) All in the Family
A) *Mrs. Sundance Rides Again* (M)
P) Masterpiece Theatre: *The Duchess of Duke Street*
**9:30**
C) Alice
**10:00**
N) Sword of Justice
C) Kaz
P) A Birthday Party for Josef Strauss (S)

## Monday, January 1, 1979
**8:00**
N) The Orange Bowl
C) The White Shadow
A) Rona Barrett Special (S)
P) Evening at Symphony
**9:00**
C) M*A*S*H
A) *Breaking Up* (M)
**9:30**
C) One Day at a Time
P) Visions: "If I Could See from Where I Stood"
**10:00**
C) Lou Grant

## Tuesday, January 2, 1979
N) The American Family: An Endangered Species? (S)
C) *The Incredible Journey of Dr. Meg Laurel* (M)
A) Happy Days
P) Soundstage
**8:30**
A) Laverne & Shirley
**9:00**
A) Three's Company
P) Hollywood Television Theatre: *The Last of Mrs. Lincoln*
**9:30**
A) Taxi!
**10:00**
A) Starsky & Hutch

## Wednesday, January 3, 1979
**8:00**
N) Tony Orlando Special
C) The Jeffersons
A) Eight Is Enough

P) The Cousteau Odyssey: "Search for the Britannic"
**8:30**
C) Good Times
**9:00**
N) *Pleasure Cove* (M)
C) *Some Kind of Miracle* (M)
A) Charlie's Angels
P) Great Performances: *Mourning Becomes Electra*, Part 4
**10:00**
A) Vega$
P) Bartelby the Scrivener

## Thursday, January 4, 1979
**8:00**
N) Project U.F.O.
C) The Waltons
A) Mork & Mindy
P) Nova: "The Black Tide"
**8:30**
A) What's Happening!
**9:00**
N) Quincy
C) Hawaii Five-0
A) Barney Miller
P) Here to Make Music
**9:30**
A) Soap
**10:00**
N) David Cassidy, Man Undercover
C) Barnaby Jones
A) Family
P) Sneak Preview
**10:30**
P) Alton Dehsner at 80 (S)

## Friday, January 5, 1979
**8:00**
N) Diff'rent Strokes
C) *Happy Birthday Charlie Brown* (S)
A) Donny & Marie
P) Washington Week in Review
**8:30**
N) Joe and Valerie
P) Wall Street Week
**9:00**
N) The Rockford Files
C) People's Command Performance (S)
A) *Killer Grizzly* (M)
P) Congressional Outlook
**9:30**
P) Turnabout
**10:00**
N) Eddie Capra Mysteries
P) Masterpiece Theatre: *The Duchess of Duke Street*

## Saturday, January 6, 1979
**8:00**
N) CHiPs
C) Mr. Billion
A) Welcome Back, Kotter
P) Once upon a Classic
**8:30**
A) Carter Country
**9:00**
N) *The Eiger Sanction* (M)
A) The Love Boat
**10:00**
C) A Conversation with Walter Cronkite and Eric Sevareid (S)
A) Fantasy Island
P) The Making of a Myth

## Sunday, January 7, 1979
**7:00**
N) Wonderful World of Disney
C) NFL Football
A) The Hardy Boys
**8:00**
N) The Sea Gypsies
A) The Two-Five (S)
P) National Geographic Special: "Gold" (S)
**8:30**
C) 60 Minutes
**9:00**
A) *You Only Live Twice* (M)
P) Masterpiece Theatre: *The Duchess of Duke Street*
**9:30**
C) All in the Family
**10:00**
N) Weekend
C) Dallas
P) We Interrupt the Year 1978 (S)

## Monday, January 8, 1979
**8:00**
N) Little House on the Prairie
C) *It's Your First Kiss Charlie Brown* (S)
A) 20/20
P) Evening at Symphony
**8:30**
C) The White Shadow
**9:00**
N) *Amateur Night* (M)
A) *A Small Town in Texas* (M)
**9:30**
C) M*A*S*H
P) Visions: "Ladies in Waiting"
**10:00**
C) Lou Grant

**Tuesday, January 9, 1979**
**8:00**
N) Grandpa Goes to Washington
C) The Paper Chase
A) Happy Days
P) Soundstage
**8:30**
A) Laverne & Shirley
**9:00**
N) Airport '75 (M)
C) *Rio Lobo* (M)
A) Three's Company
P) *Malcolm Lowry* (M)
**9:30**
A) Taxi!
**10:00**
A) Starsky & Hutch

**Wednesday, January 10, 1979**
**8:00**
N) A Gift of Song
C) The Jeffersons
A) Eight Is Enough
P) Great Performances: *Beyond the Horizon*
**8:30**
C) Monte Carlo Circus (S)
**9:00**
A) Charlie's Angels
**9:30**
N) The Best of "Saturday Night Live" (S)
C) Entertainer of the Year Awards (S)
**10:00**
A) Vega$
P) National Geographic Special: "Gold" (S)

**Thursday, January 11, 1979**
**8:00**
N) Mark Twain's America (S)
C) The Waltons
A) Mork & Mindy
P) Nova: "The Long Walk of Fred Young"
**8:30**
A) What's Happening!
**9:00**
N) Quincy
C) Barnaby Jones
A) Barney Miller
P) Raised in Anger (S)
**9:30**
A) Soap
**10:00**
N) NBC Reports: "China" (S)
A) Family
P) Jacques Lipchitz (S)

**Friday, January 12, 1979**
**8:00**
N) Diff'rent Strokes
C) The New Adventures of Wonder Woman
A) Donny & Marie
P) Washington Week in Review
**8:30**
N) Joe and Valerie
P) Wall Street Week
**9:00**
N) The Rockford Files
C) The Incredible Hulk
A) The American Music Awards (S)
P) Congressional Outlook
**9:30**
P) Turnabout
**10:00**
N) Eddie Capra Mysteries
P) Masterpiece Theatre: *The Duchess of Duke Street*

**Saturday, January 13, 1979**
**8:00**
N) CHiPs
C) The White Shadow
A) Welcome Back, Kotter
P) Once upon a Classic
**8:30**
A) Carter Country
P) Julia Child & Company
**9:00**
N) *Stuntmen* (M)
C) Champions: A Love Story
A) The Love Boat
P) In Performance at Wolf Trap: "Sarah Vaughan"
**10:00**
A) Fantasy Island

**Sunday, January 14, 1979**
**7:00**
N) Wonderful World of Disney
C) 60 Minutes
A) The Hardy Boys
**8:00**
N) Centennial
C) All in the Family
A) Battlestar Galactica
P) Once upon a Classic
**8:30**
C) Alice
**9:00**
C) Kaz
A) *The Dallas Cowboys Cheerleaders* (M)
P) Masterpiece Theatre: *The Duchess of Duke Street*

**10:00**
N) Weekend
C) Dallas
P) Nova: "The Long Walk of Fred Young"

**Monday, January 15, 1979**
**8:00**
N) Little House on the Prairie
C) The Tim Conway Show (S)
A) Mork & Mindy
P) Solti Conducts Music from Russia (S)
**9:00**
N) *Charleston* (M)
C) M*A*S*H
A) How the West Was Won
P) Tribute to Martin Luther King (S)
**9:30**
C) WKRP in Cincinnati
**10:00**
C) Lou Grant

**Tuesday, January 16, 1979**
**8:00**
N) Grandpa Goes to Washington
C) CBS Reports: "The Boat People"
A) Happy Days
P) Soundstage
**8:30**
A) Laverne & Shirley
**9:00**
N) *Murder in Music City* (M)
C) *Sky Riders* (M)
A) Three's Company
P) *Special Section* (M)
**9:30**
A) Taxi!
**10:00**
A) Starsky & Hutch

**Wednesday, January 17, 1979**
**8:00**
N) *The People That Time Forgot* (M)
C) The Incredible Hulk
A) Eight Is Enough
P) The Talking Walls of Pompeii (S)
**9:00**
C) One Day at a Time
P) Great Performances: "The N.Y. Philharmonic"
**10:00**
N) The Amazing World of Psychic Phenomena (S)
C) Kaz
A) Vega$
**10:30**
P) Thieves of Time

**Thursday, January 18, 1979**
**8:00**
N) The Challenge of the Super
Heroes (S)
C) The Waltons
A) Mork & Mindy
P) Nova: "B. F. Skinner and the
Good Life"
**8:30**
A) Delta House
**9:00**
N) Quincy
C) Hawaii Five-0
A) Barney Miller
P) Palestine, Part 1 (S)
**9:30**
A) Soap
**10:00**
N) David Cassidy, Man Undercover
C) Barnaby Jones
A) Family
**10:30**
P) Sneak Preview

**Friday, January 19, 1979**
**8:00**
N) Diff'rent Strokes
C) *Captain America* (M)
A) Donny & Marie
P) Washington Week in Review
**8:30**
N) Joe and Valerie
P) Wall Street Week
**9:00**
N) The Rockford Files
A) *Last Cry for Help* (M)
P) Congressional Outlook
**9:30**
P) Turnabout
**10:00**
N) Dean Martin Special (S)
C) The Paper Chase
P) Masterpiece Theatre: *The
Duchess of Duke Street*

**Saturday, January 20, 1979**
**8:00**
N) CHiPS
C) The White Shadow
A) The Love Boat
P) Great Performances: "Live from
The Met: *Luisa Miller*"
**9:00**
N) Superbowl Saturday Night (S)
C) *W. W. and the Dixie Dance Kings*
(M)
A) *Salvage I* (M)

**Sunday, January 21, 1979**
**7:00**
N) Super Bowl

C) 60 Minutes
A) *The Puppy Who Wanted a Boy* (S)
**7:30**
A) Benji Special (S)
**8:00**
N) Brothers and Sisters
C) All in the Family
A) Battlestar Galactica
P) Rizzo (S)
**8:30**
C) Alice
**9:00**
N) Centennial
C) *Black Sunday* (M)
A) *The Longest Yard* (M)
P) Masterpiece Theatre: *The
Duchess of Duke Street*
**10:00**
P) Nova

**Monday, January 22, 1979**
**8:00**
N) Little House on the Prairie
C) George Burns Special (S)
A) Fantasy Island
P) Pavarotti and Sutherland Recital
(S)
**9:00**
C) M*A*S*H
A) How the West Was Won
**9:30**
N) *The Institute for Revenge* (M)
C) WKRP in Cincinnati
**10:00**
C) Lou Grant

**Tuesday, January 23, 1979**
**8:00**
N) *Midway,* Part 1 (M)
C) Iran (S)
A) Happy Days
P) Soundstage
**8:30**
A) Laverne & Shirley
**9:00**
N) President Carter: State of the
Union Address
C) President Carter: State of the
Union Address
A) President Carter: State of the
Union Address
P) President Carter: State of the
Union Address
**10:00**
N) *Midway,* Part 2 (M)
C) Flying High
A) Three's Company
P) North Star: Mark di Suvero (S)
**10:30**
A) Starsky & Hutch

**Wednesday, January 24, 1979**
**8:00**
N) *Mandrake* (M)
C) The Incredible Hulk
A) Eight Is Enough
P) Great Performances: *Ah,
Wilderness*
**9:00**
C) One Day at a Time
A) Charlie's Angels
**9:30**
C) The Jeffersons
**10:00**
N) California Girls
C) Kaz
A) Vega$
P) Rizzo (S)
**10:30**
N) Republican Reply to President
Carter's Address

**Thursday, January 25, 1979**
**8:00**
N) Super Heroes' Roast
C) The Waltons
A) Mork & Mindy
P) Nova: "The Mind Machines"
**8:30**
A) What's Happening!
**9:00**
N) Quincy
C) Hawaii Five-0
A) Barney Miller
P) Palestine, Part 2 (S)
**10:00**
N) The Rockford Files
C) Barnaby Jones
A) Family
**10:30**
P) John Cage

**Friday, January 26, 1979**
**8:00**
N) Diff'rent Strokes
C) The New Adventures of Wonder
Woman
A) All Star Family Feud (S)
P) Washington Week in Review
**8:30**
N) Brothers and Sisters
P) Wall Street Week
**9:00**
N) Turnabout
C) The Dukes of Hazzard
A) *The Pink Panther Strikes Again*
(M)
P) Congressional Outlook
**9:30**
N) Hello Larry
P) Turnabout

**10:00**
N) Sweepstakes
C) Dallas
P) Masterpiece Theatre: *The Duchess of Duke Street*

**Saturday, January 27, 1979**
**8:00**
N) CHiPs
C) The White Shadow
A) Delta House
P) Once upon a Classic
**8:30**
A) The Love Boat
P) Julia Child & Company
**9:00**
N) *The Sentinel* (M)
C) *Fighting Mad* (M)
P) In Performance at Wolf Trap: "Tex Beneke, Helen O'Connell, Bob Eberly"
**9:30**
A) Fantasy Island
**10:30**
A) Republican Reply to President Carter's Address

**Sunday, January 28, 1979**
**7:00**
N) Wonderful World of Disney
C) 60 Minutes
A) The Osmond Family Hour
**8:00**
N) Centennial
C) All in the Family
A) Battlestar Galactica
P) National Geographic Special: "Hong Kong"
**8:30**
C) Alice
**9:00**
C) *And Your Name Is Jonah* (M)
A) *Taxi Driver* (M)
P) Masterpiece Theatre: *The Duchess of Duke Street*
**10:00**
N) Bob Hope Special (S)
P) The Energy War, Part 1 (S)

**Monday, January 29, 1979**
**8:00**
N) *Backstairs at the White House,* Part 1 (M)
C) M*A*S*H
A) Salvage I
P) Solti Conducts Berlioz
**8:30**
C) WKRP in Cincinnati
**9:00**
C) *The Corn Is Green* (M)

A) Pro Bowl Football
P) America Entertains Deng Xioping (S)
**10:00**
P) The Energy War, Part 2 (S)

**Tuesday, January 30, 1979**
**8:00**
N) Mark Twain's America (S)
C) Republican Reply to President Carter's Address
A) Happy Days
P) Soundstage
**8:30**
A) Laverne & Shirley
**9:00**
N) *The Triangle Factory Fire Scandal* (M)
C) *Big Jake* (M)
A) Three's Company
P) The Energy War, Part 3 (S)
**9:30**
A) Taxi!
**10:00**
A) Starsky & Hutch

**Wednesday, January 31, 1979**
**8:00**
N) Circus Highlights (S)
C) The Incredible Hulk
A) Eight Is Enough
P) Great Performances: "Vanessa"
**9:00**
N) *Viva Kneivel* (M)
C) One Day at a Time
A) Charlie's Angels
**10:00**
C) Kaz
A) Vega$
P) National Geographic Special: "Hong Kong"

**Thursday, February 1, 1979**
**8:00**
N) Circus Super Heroes (S)
C) *Mr. Horn,* Part 1 (S)
A) Mork & Mindy
P) Nova: "Cashing in on the Ocean"
**8:30**
A) Makin' It
**9:00**
N) Quincy
A) Barney Miller
P) Palestine, Part 3 (S)
**9:30**
A) Soap
**10:00**
C) Barnaby Jones
A) Family

**10:30**
P) Sneak Preview

**Friday, February 2, 1979**
**8:00**
N) Diff'rent Strokes
C) The New Adventures of Wonder Woman
A) Happy Days
P) Washington Week in Review
**8:30**
N) Brothers and Sisters
A) Makin' It
P) Wall Street Week
**9:00**
N) Turnabout
C) The Dukes of Hazzard
A) *The Girls in the Office* (M)
P) Congressional Outlook
**9:30**
N) Hello Larry
P) Turnabout
**10:00**
N) Sweepstakes
C) Dallas
P) Masterpiece Theatre: *The Duchess of Duke Street*

**Saturday, February 3, 1979**
**8:00**
N) CHiPs
C) *Mr. Horn,* Part 2 (S)
A) Delta House
P) Once upon a Classic
**8:30**
A) Welcome Back, Kotter
P) Julia Child & Company
**9:00**
N) Centennial
A) The Love Boat
P) Leontyne Price at the White House (S)
**10:00**
C) Liberace: A Valentine Special (S)
P) *Pumping Iron* (M)

**Sunday, February 4, 1979**
**7:00**
N) Wonderful World of Disney
C) 60 Minutes
A) *The Bad News Bears* (M)
**8:00**
N) Centennial
C) *Rocky* (M)
P) To Mrs. Brown: A Daughter
**9:00**
A) *The Way We Were* (M)
P) Masterpiece Theatre: *Country Matters*

**10:00**
P) Nova: "Cashing in on the Ocean"
**10:30**
C) Co-ed Fever

**Monday, February 5, 1979**
**8:00**
N) Little House on the Prairie
C) All in the Family
A) Salvage
P) Bill Moyers' Journal
**8:30**
C) Alice
**9:00**
N) *Backstairs at the White House,* Part 2 (M)
C) M*A*S*H
A) How the West Was Won
P) Academy Leaders
**9:30**
C) WKRP in Cincinnati
**10:00**
C) Lou Grant
P) Austin City Limits

**Tuesday, February 6, 1979**
**8:00**
N) *Two-Minute Warning* (M)
C) The Horror Show (S)
A) Happy Days
P) *On the Town* (M)
**8:30**
A) Laverne & Shirley
**9:00**
A) Three's Company
**9:30**
A) Taxi!
**10:00**
C) The Paper Chase
A) Starsky & Hutch
P) Du Pont Awards Ceremonies (S)

**Wednesday, February 7, 1979**
**8:00**
N) Supertrain
C) The Amazing Spider Man
A) Charlie's Angels
P) Great Performances: "Solti on Tour"
**9:00**
C) One Day at a Time
**9:30**
C) The Jeffersons
P) Langston (S)
**10:00**
N) Quincy
C) Kaz
A) Vega$
P) Roots, Rock, Reggae (S)

**Thursday, February 8, 1979**
**8:00**
N) Little Women
C) The Waltons
A) Mork & Mindy
P) Nova: "Patterns from the Past"
**8:30**
A) Angie
**9:00**
N) Women in White, Part 1
C) Hawaii Five-0
A) Barney Miller
P) World: "Solzhenitsyn's Children . . . Are Making a Lot of Noise in Paris"
**9:30**
A) Soap
**10:00**
C) Barnaby Jones
A) Family
P) Here to Make Music

**Friday, February 9, 1979**
**8:00**
N) Diff'rent Strokes
C) *Be My Valentine, Charlie Brown* (S)
A) Makin' It
P) Washington Week in Review
**8:30**
N) Brothers and Sisters
C) *Rikki-Tikki-Tavi* (S)
A) What's Happening!
P) Wall Street Week
**9:00**
N) Turnabout
C) The Dukes of Hazzard
A) The Heroes of Rock 'n' Roll (S)
P) Congressional Outlook
**9:30**
N) Hello Larry
P) Turnabout
**10:00**
N) Sweepstakes
C) Dallas
P) Bill Moyers Talks with Prince Sihanouk (S)

**Saturday, February 10, 1979**
**8:00**
N) BJ and the Bear
C) The White Shadow
A) Delta House
P) Once upon a Classic
**8:30**
A) Welcome Back, Kotter
**9:00**
C) *Flatbed Annie & Sweetpie: Lady Truckers* (M)
A) The Love Boat

P) *The Merry Widow* (S)
**9:30**
N) The Rockford Files
**10:00**
A) Fantasy Island
**10:30**
P) Chinese New Year Special (S)

**Sunday, February 11, 1979**
**7:00**
N) Wonderful World of Disney
C) *Gone With the Wind,* Part 1 (M)
A) The Osmond Family Hour
**8:00**
N) *One Flew Over the Cuckoo's Nest* (M)
A) *Elvis* (M)
P) Dragons of Paradise (S)
**9:00**
P) Masterpiece Theatre: *Country Matters*
**10:00**
N) Weekend
C) 60 Minutes
P) World Special: "Papua New Guinea: Finally a Nation"

**Monday, February 12, 1979**
**8:00**
N) Little House on the Prairie
C) *Gone With the Wind,* Part 2 (M)
A) All Star Family Feud
P) Bill Moyers' Journal
**9:00**
N) *Backstairs at the White House,* Part 3 (M)
A) How the West Was Won
P) Academy Leaders
**10:00**
C) Lou Grant
P) Austin City Limits

**Tuesday, February 13, 1979**
**8:00**
N) *Tentacles* (M)
C) *Crisis in Mid-air* (M)
A) Happy Days
P) Soundstage
**8:30**
A) Laverne & Shirley
**9:00**
A) Three's Company
P) *Kiss Me, Kate* (M)
**9:30**
A) Taxi!
**10:00**
N) Circus Challenge: America vs. the World (S)
C) The Paper Chase
A) Starsky & Hutch

**Wednesday, February 14, 1979**
**8:00**
N) Supertrain
C) Bugs Bunny's Valentine (S)
A) Eight Is Enough
P) The Shakespeare Plays: *Julius Caesar* (S)
**8:30**
C) *The Popeye Valentine Special* (S)
**9:00**
N) *From Here to Eternity,* Part 1 (M)
C) M*A*S*H
A) Charlie's Angels
**9:30**
C) One Day at a Time
**10:00**
C) Dolly and Carol in Nashville (S)
A) Vega$

**Thursday, February 15, 1979**
**8:00**
N) Little Women
C) The Waltons
A) Mork & Mindy
P) Nova: "Memories from Eden"
**8:30**
A) Angie
**9:00**
N) Quincy
C) Grammy Awards Special (S)
A) Three's Company
P) World: "Getting Elected in Papua, New Guinea"
**9:30**
A) Taxi!
**10:00**
N) Women in White, Part 2
A) Barney Miller
P) Sneak Preview
**10:30**
A) Soap
P) All for One

**Friday, February 16, 1979**
**8:00**
N) Diff'rent Strokes
C) The New Adventures of Wonder Woman
A) Makin' It
P) Washington Week in Review
**8:30**
N) Hello Larry
A) What's Happening!
P) Wall Street Week
**9:00**
N) Brothers and Sisters
C) The Dukes of Hazzard
A) *Shampoo* (M)

**9:30**
N) Turnabout
P) Turnabout
**10:00**
N) Sweepstakes
C) Dallas
P) Masterpiece Theatre: *Country Matters*

**Saturday, February 17, 1979**
**8:00**
N) CHiPs
C) The White Shadow
A) The Love Boat
P) Once upon a Classic
**8:30**
P) Julia Child & Company
**9:00**
N) BJ and the Bear
C) *Murder by Natural Causes* (M)
P) Skating Spectacular (S)
**9:30**
A) Fantasy Island
**10:00**
N) The Rockford Files
P) *Man on the Roof* (M)

**Sunday, February 18, 1979**
**7:00**
N) Wonderful World of Disney
C) 60 Minutes
A) The Osmond Family Hour
**8:00**
N) *American Graffiti* (M)
C) All in the Family
A) *Roots, The Next Generations,* Part 1
P) F.Y.I.: "The Legacy of Vietnam"
**8:30**
C) Alice
**9:00**
C) *Marathon Man* (M)
P) Masterpiece Theatre: *Country Matters*
**10:00**
N) Weekend
A) Battlestar Galactica
P) Volvo Tennis Classic

**Monday, February 19, 1979**
**8:00**
N) Little House on the Prairie
C) The New Adventures of Wonder Woman
A) *Roots: The Next Generations,* Part 2
P) Bill Moyers' Journal
**9:00**
N) *Backstairs at the White House,* Part 4 (M)

C) M*A*S*H
P) Academy Leaders
**9:30**
C) WKRP in Cincinnati
**10:00**
C) Lou Grant
A) Salvage
P) Austin City Limits

**Tuesday, February 20, 1979**
**8:00**
N) *The Eagle Has Landed* (M)
C) *White Lightning* (M)
A) Happy Days
P) The Cousteau Odyssey: "Calypso's Search for Atlantis," Part 1
**8:30**
A) Laverne & Shirley
**9:00**
A) *Roots: The Next Generations,* Part 3
P) *Silk Stockings* (M)
**10:00**
C) The Paper Chase

**Wednesday, February 21, 1979**
**8:00**
N) Supertrain
C) The Amazing Spider Man
A) Eight Is Enough
P) Great Performances: *Fidelio*
**9:00**
N) *From Here to Eternity,* Part 2 (M)
C) One Day at a Time
A) *Roots: The Next Generations,* Part 4
**9:30**
C) The Jeffersons
**10:00**
C) Kaz
**10:30**
P) Monet (S)

**Thursday, February 22, 1979**
**8:00**
N) Little Women
C) The Waltons
A) Mork & Mindy
P) Nova: "The Invisible Flame"
**8:30**
A) Angie
**9:00**
N) Quincy
C) Hawaii Five-0
A) *Roots: The Next Generations,* Part 5
P) World: "Inside Europe, the Shirt Off Your Back"

**10:00**
N) Women in White, Part 3
C) Barnaby Jones
P) Always for Pleasure

**Friday, February 23, 1979**
**8:00**
N) Diff'rent Strokes
C) The Incredible Hulk
A) Makin' It
P) Washington Week in Review
**8:30**
N) Hello Larry
A) What's Happening!
P) Wall Street Week
**9:00**
N) Brothers and Sisters
C) The Dukes of Hazzard
A) *Roots: The Next Generations,*
 Part 6
P) Congressional Outlook
**9:30**
N) Sweepstakes
P) Turnabout
**10:00**
C) Dallas
P) Masterpiece Theatre: *Country
 Matters*

**Saturday, February 24, 1979**
**8:00**
N) CHiPs
C) The White Shadow
A) Delta House
P) Once upon a Classic
**8:30**
A) Welcome Back, Kotter
P) Julia Child & Company
**9:00**
N) BJ and the Bear
C) *Silent Victory: The Kitty O'Neil
 Story* (M)
A) The Love Boat
P) Mehta and His Music: A Tour
 Triumph (S)
**10:00**
N) The Rockford Files
A) Fantasy Island
**10:30**
P) In Performance at Wolf Trap:
 "Fat Tuesday and All That Jazz"

**Sunday, February 25, 1979**
**7:00**
N) *The Sound of Music* (M)
C) 60 Minutes
A) Battlestar Galactica
**8:00**
C) All in the Family
P) Paul Jacobs and the Nuclear Gang
 (S)

**8:30**
C) Alice
**9:00**
C) Celebrity Challenge of the Sexes
 (S)
A) *Roots: The Next Generations,*
 Part 7
P) Masterpiece Theatre: *Country
 Matters*
**10:00**
P) Nova: "The Invisible Flame"
**10:30**
N) Weekend

**Monday, February 26, 1979**
**8:00**
N) Little House on the Prairie
C) Billy
A) Salvage
P) Bill Moyers' Journal
**8:30**
C) Flatbush
P) Mark Russell Comedy Special (S)
**9:00**
N) Mrs. Columbo
C) M*A*S*H
A) How The West Was Won
P) Academy Leaders
**9:30**
C) WKRP in Cincinnati
**10:00**
C) Lou Grant
P) Austin City Limits

**Tuesday, February 27, 1979**
**8:00**
N) Cliffhangers
C) *Woman at West Point* (M)
A) Happy Days
P) The Cousteau Odyssey: "The
 Search for Atlantis," Part 2
**8:30**
A) Laverne & Shirley
**9:00**
N) *The Drowning Pool* (M)
A) Three's Company
P) *The Great Caruso* (M)
**9:30**
A) Taxi!
**10:00**
C) The Paper Chase
A) 20/20

**Wednesday, February 28, 1979**
**8:00**
N) Supertrain
C) Married: The First Year
A) Eight Is Enough

P) The Shakespeare Plays: *As You
 Like It* (S)
**9:00**
N) *From Here to Eternity,* Part 3 (M)
C) One Day at a Time
A) Charlie's Angels
**9:30**
C) The Jeffersons
**10:00**
C) Kaz
A) Vega$
**10:30**
P) Special: Governor Brown and the
 Tax Revolt (S)

**Thursday, March 1, 1979**
**8:00**
N) Leopard of the Wild (S)
C) The Waltons
A) Mork & Mindy
P) Nova: "The End of the Rainbow"
**8:30**
A) Angie
**9:00**
N) Quincy
C) Hawaii Five-0
A) Barney Miller
P) World: "Chachaji, My Poor
 Relation"
**9:30**
A) Soap
**10:00**
N) Mrs. Columbo
C) Barnaby Jones
A) Family
P) Sneak Preview
**10:30**
P) Fluorocarbons: The Unfinished
 Agenda (S)

**Friday, March 2, 1979**
**8:00**
N) Diff'rent Strokes
C) The Incredible Hulk
A) Makin' It
P) Washington Week in Review
**8:30**
N) American Youth Awards (S)
A) What's Happening!
P) Wall Street Week
**9:00**
C) *Day of the Animals* (M)
A) *Baby Blue Marine* (M)
P) Congressional Outlook
**9:30**
N) Hello Larry
P) Turnabout
**10:00**
N) Sweepstakes
P) Masterpiece Theatre: *Country
 Matters*

**Saturday, March 3, 1979**
**8:00**
N) CHiPs
C) *Across the Great Divide* (M)
P) Live from the Grand Ole Opry (S)
**8:30**
A) Welcome Back, Kotter
**9:00**
N) The Rockford Files
A) The Love Boat
**10:00**
C) Boston and Kilbride (S)
A) Fantasy Island

**Sunday, March 4, 1979**
**7:00**
N) Wonderful World of Disney
C) 60 Minutes
A) The Osmond Family Hour
**8:00**
C) 200th Episode of All in the
Family (S)
A) *The Ordeal of Patty Hearst* (M)
P) National Geographic Special:
"Last Stand in Eden"
**9:00**
N) *Jeremiah Johnson* (M)
P) Masterpiece Theatre: *Country
Matters*
**9:30**
C) Just Friends
**10:00**
C) The Mary Tyler Moore Hour
P) Nova: "The End of the Rainbow"

**Monday, March 5, 1979**
**8:00**
N) Little House on the Prairie
C) Billy
A) Salvage
P) Bill Moyers' Journal
**8:30**
C) Flatbush
**9:00**
N) *Jennifer: A Woman's Story* (M)
C) M*A*S*H
A) How the West Was Won
P) Academy Leaders
**9:30**
C) WKRP in Cincinnati
**10:00**
C) Lou Grant
P) Austin City Limits

**Tuesday, March 6, 1979**
**8:00**
N) Cliff Hangers

C) CBS Reports: "Inside the Union"
(S)
A) Happy Days
P) The Cousteau Odyssey: "Time
Bomb at Fifty Fathoms"
**8:30**
A) Laverne & Shirley
**9:00**
N) *Gold of the Amazon Women* (M)
C) *Coach* (M)
A) Three's Company
P) *High Society* (M)
**9:30**
A) Taxi!
**10:00**
A) Starsky & Hutch

**Wednesday, March 7, 1979**
**8:00**
N) Cher (S)
C) Married: The First Year
A) Eight Is Enough
P) Great Performances: "Balanchine
IV"
**9:00**
N) *Studs Lonigan*, Part 1
C) One Day at a Time
A) Charlie's Angels
**9:30**
C) The Jeffersons
P) Celebration of Strauss (S)
**10:00**
C) Kaz
A) Vega$
**10:30**
P) The Four Freshmen in Concert
(S)

**Thursday, March 8, 1979**
**8:00**
N) *Little Women*
C) The Waltons
A) Mork & Mindy
P) Nova: "The Beersheva
Experiment"
**8:30**
A) John Denver (S)
**9:00**
N) Quincy
C) People's Choice Awards
P) World: "The Search for Sandra
Laing"
**9:30**
A) Soap
**10:00**
A) Family
P) Wild Horses, Broken Wings

**Friday, March 9, 1979**
**8:00**
N) Diff'rent Strokes
C) The Incredible Hulk
A) Makin' It
P) Washington Week in Review
**9:30**
N) Hello Larry
A) What's Happening!
P) Wall Street Week
**9:00**
N) Brothers and Sisters
C) The Dukes of Hazzard
A) *The Child Stealer* (M)
P) Echoes of Silver
**9:30**
N) Turnabout
P) Turnabout
**10:00**
N) Sweepstakes
C) Dallas
P) Masterpiece Theatre: *Country
Matters*

**Saturday, March 10, 1979**
**8:00**
N) CHiPs
C) The New Adventures of Wonder
Woman
A) Delta House
P) Once upon a Classic
**8:30**
A) ABC News Closeup: "The Middle
East" (S)
P) Julia Child & Company
**9:00**
N) BJ and the Bear
C) *Death Wish* (M)
A) The Love Boat
P) *The Band Wagon* (M)
**10:00**
N) The Rockford Files
A) Fantasy Island

**Sunday, March 11, 1979**
**7:00**
N) *Airport '77* (M)
C) 60 Minutes
A) The Osmond Family Hour
**8:00**
C) All in the Family
A) Battlestar Galactica
P) Andres Segovia at the White
House (S)
**8:30**
C) Alice
**9:00**
A) Starsky & Hutch
P) Masterpiece Theatre: *Lillie*

**9:30**
C) Just Friends
**10:00**
N) Weekend
C) The Mary Tyler Moore Hour
P) Horowitz Live . . . Encore (S)

**Monday, March 12, 1979**
**8:00**
N) Little House on the Prairie
C) Billy
A) Salvage
P) Bill Moyers' Journal
**8:30**
C) Flatbush
**9:00**
N) *Too Far to Go* (M)
C) M*A*S*H
A) How the West Was Won
P) Academy Leaders
**9:30**
C) Salute to Alfred Hitchcock (S)
**10:00**
P) Austin City Limits

**Tuesday, March 13, 1979**
**8:00**
N) Cliff Hangers
C) The Middle East (S)
A) Happy Days
P) Einstein's Universe (S)
**8:30**
A) Laverne & Shirley
**9:00**
N) *Checkered Flag or Crash* (M)
C) *Zorro* (M)
A) Three's Company
**9:30**
A) The Ropers
**10:00**
A) Barbara Walters Special (S)
P) *Singin' in the Rain* (M)

**Wednesday, March 14, 1979**
**8:00**
N) Supertrain
C) Married: The First Year
A) Eight Is Enough
P) The Shakespeare Plays: *Romeo and Juliet* (S)
**9:00**
N) *Studs Lonigan*, Part 2 (M)
C) One Day at a Time
A) Charlie's Angels
**9:30**
C) The Jeffersons
**10:00**
C) Salute to Pearl Bailey (S)
A) Vega$

**Thursday, March 15, 1979**
**8:00**
N) Harris & Company
C) The Waltons
A) Mork & Mindy
P) Nova: "Einstein"
**8:30**
A) Angie
**9:00**
N) Quincy
C) Hawaii Five-0
A) Barney Miller
P) World: "Inside Europe: F-16"
**9:30**
A) Soap
**10:00**
N) Mrs. Columbo
C) Barnaby Jones
A) Family
P) Sneak Preview
**10:30**
P) Echoes of Silver

**Friday, March 16, 1979**
**8:00**
N) Diff'rent Strokes
C) The Incredible Hulk
A) Makin' It
P) Washington Week in Review
**8:30**
N) Hello Larry
A) What's Happening!
P) Wall Street Week
**9:00**
N) Brothers and Sisters
C) The Dukes of Hazzard
A) *The Cracker Factory* (M)
P) America at the Movies (S)
**9:30**
N) *Rafferty and the Highway Hustlers* (M)
**10:00**
C) Dallas

**Saturday, March 18, 1979**
**8:00**
N) CHiPs
C) The New Adventures of Wonder Woman
A) Delta House
P) American Pop: The Great Singers (S)
**8:30**
A) Welcome Back, Kotter
**9:00**
N) BJ and the Bear
C) *Willa* (M)
A) The Love Boat
**10:00**
N) The Rockford Files

A) Fantasy Island

**Sunday, March 18, 1979**
**7:00**
N) Greatest Heroes of the Bible
C) 60 Minutes
A) The Osmond Family Hour
**8:00**
N) Wonderful World of Disney
C) All in the Family
A) Battlestar Galactica
P) Arthur Fiedler: Call Me Maestro (S)
**8:30**
C) One Day at a Time
**9:00**
C) Alice
A) *The Jericho Mile* (M)
P) Masterpiece Theatre: *Lillie*
**9:30**
C) Just Friends
**10:00**
N) Weekend
C) The Mary Tyler Moore Hour
P) Grand Finale (S)

**Monday, March 19, 1979**
**8:00**
N) Little House on the Prairie
C) *You're the Greatest, Charlie Brown* (S)
A) Salvage
P) Bill Moyers' Journal
**8:30**
C) The White Shadow
**9:00**
N) *Fast Friends* (M)
A) How the West Was Won
P) Academy Leaders
**9:30**
C) WKRP in Cincinnati
**10:00**
C) Lou Grant
P) Austin City Limits

**Tuesday, March 20, 1979**
**8:00**
N) Cliff Hangers
C) The Paper Chase
A) Happy Days
P) Up in Rosebud Country
**8:30**
A) Laverne & Shirley
**9:00**
N) Superstunt 2 (S)
C) *Red Sun* (M)
A) Three's Company
P) Grand Jury: An Institution Under Fire (S)
**9:30**
A) 13 Queens Boulevard

**10:00**
A) The Ropers
**10:30**
A) Bizarre
P) The Islander

**Wednesday, March 21, 1979**
**8:00**
N) Killer of the Plains
C) Married: The First Year
A) Eight Is Enough
P) Great Performances: *Madame Butterfly*
**9:00**
N) *Studs Lonigan,* Part 3 (M)
C) The Jeffersons
A) Charlie's Angels
**10:00**
C) Kaz
A) 20/20

**Thursday, March 22, 1979**
**8:00**
N) Harris & Company
C) The Waltons
A) Mork & Mindy
P) Nova: "The Insect Alternative"
**8:30**
A) Angie
**9:00**
N) Quincy
C) Hawaii Five-0
A) Barney Miller
P) World: "The Clouded Window"
**9:30**
A) Delta House
**10:00**
N) Mrs. Columbo
C) Barnaby Jones
A) Family
P) Here to Make Music

**Friday, March 23, 1979**
**8:00**
N) Diff'rent Strokes
C) *The Wizard of Oz* (M)
A) What's Happening!
P) Washington Week in Review
**8:30**
N) Hello Larry
A) Boxing
P) Wall Street Week
**9:00**
N) Brothers and Sisters
P) Congressional Outlook
**9:30**
N) Turnabout
P) Turnabout
**10:00**
N) Sweepstakes

C) Dallas
P) Masterpiece Theatre: *Lillie*

**Saturday, March 24, 1979**
**8:00**
N) Dracula '79 (S)
C) The Bad News Bears
A) Paul Lynde Special (S)
P) Once upon a Classic
**8:30**
C) Billy
P) Julia Child & Company
₃**9:00**
N) BJ and the Bear
C) *No Other Love* (M)
A) The Love Boat
P) Arthur Fiedler : Call Me Maestro (S)
**10:00**
N) The Rockford Files
A) Fantasy Island
P) Up in Rosebud County

**Sunday, March 25, 1979**
**7:00**
N) Wonderful World of Disney
C) 60 Minutes
A) Friends
**8:00**
N) *Sooner or Later* (M)
C) All in the Family
A) *The Ten Commandments* (M)
P) Work: Is It Worth It? (S)
**8:30**
C) One Day at a Time
**9:00**
C) Alice
P) Masterpiece Theatre: *Lillie*
**9:30**
C) Just Friends
**10:00**
N) Weekend
C) The Mary Tyler Moore Hour
P) Nova: The Insect Alternative (S)

**Monday, March 26, 1979**
**8:00**
N) Little House on the Prairie
C) The White Shadow
A) The Captain and Tennille (S)
P) Bill Moyers' Journal
**9:00**
N) NCAA Basketball
C) M*A*S*H
A) All American Women (S)
P) Academy Leaders
**9:30**
C) WKRP in Cincinnati
**10:00**
C) Lou Grant

P) Austin City Limits

**Tuesday, March 27, 1979**
N) Cliff Hangers
C) The Paper Chase
A) Happy Days
P) Cleveland Orchestra 60th Anniversary Special (S)
**8:30**
A) The Mackenzies of Paradise Cove
**9:00**
N) *The Dark Secret of Harvest Home,* Part 1 (M)
C) *Moonshine County Express* (M)
P) Methadone: An American Way of Dealing
**9:30**
A) Three's Company
**10:00**
A) The Ropers
**10:30**
A) 13 Queens Boulevard
P) Pompeii: Frozen in Time (S)

**Wednesday, March 28, 1979**
**8:00**
N) Brothers and Sisters
C) The Jeffersons
A) Eight Is Enough
P) The Shakespeare Plays: *Richard II* (S)
**8:30**
N) *The Dark Secret of Harvest Home,* Part 2 (M)
C) Miss Winslow and Son
**9:00**
C) *Dear Detective* (M)
A) Charlie's Angels
**10:00**
A) Vega$

**Thursday, March 29, 1979**
**8:00**
N) Harris and Company
C) *The Chisholms,* Part 1 (S)
A) Mork & Mindy
P) Nova: "The Keys to Paradise"
**8:30**
A) Angie
**9:00**
N) Quincy
A) Barney Miller
P) The Chinese Way
**9:30**
A) Carter Country
**10:00**
N) Mrs. Columbo
C) Barnaby Jones
A) ABC News Closeup: "Toxic Waste" (S)
P) Sneak Preview

**10:30**
P) The Reel West

**Friday, March 30, 1979**
**8:00**
N) Diff'rent Strokes
C) The Incredible Hulk
A) Family
P) Washington Week in Review
**8:30**
P) Wall Street Week
**9:00**
N) Brothers and Sisters
C) The Dukes of Hazzard
A) *You Light up My Life* (M)
P) The Diplomatic Style of Andrew Young (S)
**9:30**
N) Sweepstakes
P) Turnabout
**10:00**
C) Danger at Three Mile Island (S)
P) Masterpiece Theatre: *Lillie*
**10:30**
N) Nuclear Risk (S)

**Saturday, March 31, 1979**
**8:00**
N) CHiPs
C) The Bad News Bears
A) What's Happening!
P) Once upon a Classic
**8:30**
C) Billy
A) Delta House
P) Julia Child & Company
**9:00**
N) BJ and the Bear
C) *Hustle* (M)
A) The Love Boat
P) Cleveland Orchestra 60th Anniversary Special (S)
**10:00**
A) Fantasy Island
P) Methadone: An American Way of Dealing (S)

**Sunday, April 1, 1979**
**7:00**
N) Wonderful World of Disney
C) 60 Minutes
A) Friends
**8:00**
N) *Jesus of Nazareth,* Part 1 (M)
C) *The Lion, the Witch, and the Wardrobe,* Part 1 (S)
A) Battlestar Galactica
P) National Geographic Special: "The Tigris Expedition"

**9:00**
C) Alice
A) *From Russia with Love* (M)
P) Masterpiece Theatre: *Lillie*
**9:30**
C) Just Friends
**10:00**
N) Weekend
C) The Mary Tyler Moore Hour
P) Nova: "The Keys to Paradise"

**Monday, April 2, 1979**
**8:00**
N) Little House on the Prairie
C) *The Lion, the Witch, and the Wardrobe,* Part 2 (S)
A) Salvage
P) Bill Moyers' Journal
**9:00**
N) *Jesus of Nazareth,* Part 2 (M)
C) M*A*S*H
A) How the West Was Won
P) *The Scarlet Letter,* Part 1
**9:30**
C) WKRP in Cincinnati
**10:00**
C) Lou Grant
P) Austin City Limits

**Tuesday, April 3, 1979**
N) Cliff Hangers
C) CBS Reports: "How Much for the Handicapped?" (S)
A) Happy Days
P) Previn and the Pittsburgh
**8:30**
A) Laverne & Shirley
**9:00**
N) *Jesus of Nazareth,* Part 3 (M)
C) *The Darker Side of Terror* (M)
A) Three's Company
P) *The Scarlet Letter,* Part 2
**9:30**
A) Taxi!
**10:00**
A) The Ropers
P) Black Man's Land: "White Man's Country"
**10:30**
A) 13 Queens Boulevard

**Wednesday, April 4, 1979**
**8:00**
N) Happy Birthday, Donald Duck (S)
C) The Jeffersons
A) The Mackenzies of Paradise Cove
P) Great Performances: "Ormandy and the Philadelphia Orchestra"
**8:30**
C) Miss Winslow and Son

**9:00**
N) *Wheels,* Part 1 (M)
C) Dear Detective
A) Charlie's Angels
P) *The Scarlet Letter,* Part 3
**10:00**
C) Kaz
A) Vega$
P) Black Man's Land: "Mau Mau"

**Thursday, April 5, 1979**
**8:00**
N) Harris & Company
C) *The Chisholms,* Part 2 (S)
A) Mork & Mindy
P) Nova: "The Road to Happiness"
**8:30**
A) Delta House
**9:00**
N) President Carter's Address on Energy
C) President Carter's Address on Energy
A) President Carter's Address on Energy
P) *The Scarlet Letter,* Part 4
**9:30**
N) The Duke
C) Hawaii Five-0
A) Barney Miller
**10:00**
A) Carter Country
P) Black Man's Land: "Kenyatta"
**10:30**
A) Doctors' Private Lives

**Friday, April 6, 1979**
**8:00**
N) Diff'rent Strokes
C) The Incredible Hulk
A) Family
P) Washington Week in Review
**8:30**
N) Hello Larry
P) Wall Street Week
**9:00**
N) Brothers and Sisters
C) The Dukes of Hazzard
A) *The Little Girl Who Lives Down the Lane* (M)
P) National Geographic Special: "The Tigris Expedition" (S)
**10:00**
C) Dallas
P) Masterpiece Theatre: *Lillie*

**Saturday, April 7, 1979**
**8:00**
N) CHiPs

C) The Bad News Bears
A) What's Happening!
P) Once upon a Classic
**8:30**
C) *The First Easter Rabbit* (S)
A) Delta House
P) Julia Child & Company
**9:00**
N) BJ and the Bear
C) *The Seeding of Sarah Burns* (M)
A) The Love Boat
P) Who Killed Martin Luther King? (S)
**10:00**
N) Supertrain
A) Fantasy Island
P) Great Performances: "Ormandy and the Philadelphia Orchestra"

**Sunday, April 8, 1979**
**7:00**
N) Wonderful World of Disney
C) 60 Minutes
A) Friends
**8:00**
N) *Jesus of Nazareth,* Part 4 (M)
C) All in the Family
A) Battlestar Galactica
P) The Cousteau Odyssey: "Diving for Roman Plunder"
**8:30**
C) One Day at a Time
**9:00**
C) Alice
A) *Thunderbolt and Lightfoot* (M)
P) Masterpiece Theatre: *Lillie*
**9:30**
C) Just Friends
**10:00**
N) Weekend
C) The Mary Tyler Moore Hour
P) Nova: "The Road to Happiness"

**Monday, April 9, 1979**
**8:00**
N) Little House on the Prairie
C) *It's the Easter Beagle, Charlie Brown* (S)
A) Perry Como's Springtime Special (S)
P) Bill Moyers' Journal
**8:30**
C) The White Shadow
**9:00**
N) *Deliverance* (M)
A) The Cheryl Ladd Special (S)
P) Academy Leaders
**9:30**
C) Lou Grant

**10:00**
A) Academy Awards Ceremonies (S)
P) Austin City Limits
**10:30**
C) Energy: Other Views (S)

**Tuesday, April 10, 1979**
**8:00**
N) Cliff Hangers
C) *Here Comes Peter Cottontail* (S)
A) Happy Days
P) Previn and the Pittsburgh
**8:30**
A) Laverne & Shirley
**9:00**
N) *Legend of the Golden Gun* (M)
C) *Deadman's Curve* (M)
A) Three's Company
P) Library of Congress (S)
**9:30**
A) Taxi!
**10:00**
A) The Ropers
**10:30**
A) 13 Queens Boulevard

**Wednesday, April 11, 1979**
**8:00**
N) On Vacation with Mickey Mouse and Friends (S)
C) The Jeffersons
A) The Mackenzies of Paradise Cove
P) The Shakespeare Plays: *Measure for Measure* (S)
**8:30**
C) Miss Winslow and Son
**9:00**
N) *Wheels,* Part 2 (M)
C) Dear Detective
A) Charlie's Angels
**10:00**
C) Kaz
A) The Hal Linden Special (S)

**Thursday, April 12, 1979**
**8:00**
N) Whodunnit?
C) *The Chisholms,* Part 3 (S)
A) Mork & Mindy
P) Nova: "Icarus' Children"
**8:30**
N) Highcliff Manor
A) Angie
**9:00**
N) Quincy
C) A Special Kenny Rogers (S)
A) Barney Miller
P) World: "Bogota, One Day"
**9:30**
A) Carter Country

**10:00**
C) Barnaby Jones
A) Doctors' Private Lives
**10:30**
P) Sneak Preview

**Friday, April 13, 1979**
**8:00**
N) Diff'rent Strokes
C) *The Bugs Bunny Easter Special* (S)
A) Family
P) Washington Week in Review
**8:30**
N) Hello Larry
P) Wall Street Week
**9:00**
N) The Rockford Files
C) The Dukes of Hazzard
A) *Like Normal People* (M)
P) Royal Heritage
**10:00**
N) The Duke
C) Dallas
P) Masterpiece Theatre: *Lillie*

**Saturday, April 14, 1979**
**8:00**
N) CHiPs
C) America's Junior Miss Pageant (S)
A) *The Easter Bunny Is Coming to Town* (S)
P) Once upon a Classic
**9:00**
N) BJ and the Bear
C) *Cold Turkey* (M)
A) The Love Boat
P) The Do-It-Yourself Messiah (S)
**10:00**
N) Supertrain
P) The Cousteau Odyssey: "Diving for Roman Plunder"

**Sunday, April 15, 1979**
**7:00**
N) Wonderful World of Disney
C) 60 Minutes
A) Friends
**8:00**
N) *With Six You Get Egg Roll* (M)
C) All in the Family
A) Pat Boone and Family Easter Special (S)
P) Baryshnikov at the White House
**8:30**
C) One Day at a Time
**9:00**
C) Alice
A) *The Billion Dollar Threat* (M)
P) Masterpiece Theatre: *Lillie*

**9:30**
C) Just Friends
**10:00**
N) Weekend
C) The Mary Tyler Moore Hour
P) Nova: "Icarus' Children"

**Monday, April 16, 1979**
**8:00**
N) Little House on the Prairie
C) Collegiate Cheerleading
Championships (S)
A) Salvage
P) Bill Moyers' Journal
**9:00**
N) *The Prisoner of Second Avenue*
(M)
A) How the West Was Won
P) Academy Leaders
**9:30**
C) M*A*S*H
**10:00**
C) Lou Grant
P) Boston Marathon '79

**Tuesday, April 17, 1979**
**8:00**
N) Cliff Hangers
C) The Paper Chase
A) Happy Days
P) Previn and the Pittsburgh
**8:30**
A) Laverne & Shirley
**9:00**
N) *Hard Times* (M)
C) Transplant (S)
A) Three's Company
P) Off Your Duff (S)
**9:30**
A) Taxi!
**10:00**
A) The Ropers
**10:30**
A) 13 Queens Boulevard

**Wednesday, April 18, 1979**
**8:00**
N) Real People
C) The Jeffersons
A) Eight Is Enough
P) Great Performances: "Bernstein
Conducts Mahler"
**8:30**
C) Miss Winslow and Son
**9:00**
N) *Wheels,* Part 3 (M)
C) Dear Detective
A) Charlie's Angels

**9:30**
P) The Great Mid-West Hot Air
Balloon Rally
**10:00**
C) Kaz
A) Vega$
P) Who Remembers Mama? (S)

**Thursday, April 19, 1979**
**8:00**
N) Whodunnit?
C) *The Chisholms,* Part 4 (S)
A) Mork & Mindy
P) Nova: "Across the Silence
Barrier"
**8:30**
N) Highcliff Manor
A) Angie
**9:00**
N) Quincy
A) Barney Miller
P) World: "The Nayba Connection"
**9:30**
A) Carter Country
**10:00**
N) Sgt. T.K. Yu
C) Barnaby Jones
A) Doctors' Private Lives
P) One of the Missing

**Friday, April 20, 1979**
**8:00**
N) Diff'rent Strokes
C) The Incredible Hulk
A) Family
P) Washington Week in Review
**8:30**
N) Hello Larry
P) Wall Street Week
**9:00**
N) The Rockford Files
C) The Dukes of Hazzard
A) *Drive-In* (M)
P) Royal Heritage
**10:00**
N) The Duke
C) Dallas
P) Masterpiece Theatre: *Lillie*

**Saturday, April 21, 1979**
**8:00**
N) Olympathon '79 (S)
C) The Bad News Bears
A) What's Happening!
P) Once upon a Classic
**8:00**
C) Billy
A) Delta House
P) California's Public Workers: A
Time of Crisis (S)

**9:00**
C) *Uptown Saturday Night* (M)
A) The Love Boat
P) Off Your Duff (S)
**10:00**
A) ABC News Closeup: "Men Under
Siege: Life with Modern Women"
(S)
P) Who Remembers Mama? (S)

**Sunday, April 22, 1979**
**7:00**
N) Wonderful World of Disney
C) 60 Minutes
A) Friends
**8:00**
N) *Rooster Cogburn and the Lady*
(M)
C) All in the Family
A) *Friendly Firs* (M)
P) F.Y.I.
**8:30**
C) One Day at a Time
**9:00**
C) Alice
P) Masterpiece Theatre: *Lillie*
**9:30**
C) Just Friends
**10:00**
N) Weekend
C) The Mary Tyler Moore Hour
P) Nova: "Across the Silence
Barrier"

**Monday, April 23, 1979**
**8:00**
N) Little House on the Prairie
C) The White Shadow
A) Dorothy Hamill's Corner of the
Sky (S)
P) Bill Moyers' Journal
**9:00**
N) *Sanctuary of Fear* (M)
C) M*A*S*H
A) How the West Was Won
P) Generation on the Wind (S)
**9:30**
C) WKRP in Cincinnati
**10:00**
C) Lou Grant
P) Austin City Limits

**Tuesday, April 24, 1979**
**8:00**
N) Cliff Hangers
C) The Paper Chase
A) Happy Days
P) Previn and the Pittsburgh
**8:30**
A) Laverne & Shirley

**9:00**
N) *Against a Crooked Sky* (M)
C) *The Deserter* (M)
A) Three's Company
P) An Americanism: Joe McCarthy
**9:30**
A) Taxi!
**10:00**
A) 20/20
**10:30**
P) The Great Mid-West Hot Air Balloon Rally (S)

**Wednesday, April 25, 1979**
**8:00**
N) Real People
C) The Jeffersons
A) Eight Is Enough
P) The Shakespeare Plays: *Henry VIII* (S)
**8:30**
C) Miss Winslow and Son
**9:00**
N) *Mustang Country* (M)
C) *You Can't Go Home Again* (M)
A) Charlie's Angels
**10:00**
A) Vega$

**Thursday, April 26, 1979**
**8:00**
N) Whodunnit?
C) Time Express
A) Mork & Mindy
P) Nova: "A Desert Place"
**8:30**
N) Highcliff Manor
A) Angie
**9:00**
N) Quincy
C) Hawaii Five-0
A) Barney Miller
P) World: "Cuba, Sport, and Revolution"
**9:30**
A) Carter Country
**10:00**
N) Presenting Susan Anton
C) Barnaby Jones
A) Doctors' Private Lives
P) Sneak Preview
**10:30**
P) California Public Workers: A Time of Crisis (S)

**Friday, April 27, 1979**
**8:00**
N) Diff'rent Strokes
C) The Incredible Hulk
A) The Mackenzies of Paradise Cove
P) Washington Week in Review

**8:30**
N) Hello Larry
P) Wall Street Week
**9:00**
N) The Rockford Files
A) *With This Ring* (M)
P) Royal Heritage
**10:00**
N) The Duke
C) CBS Reports: "The Boston Symphony Goes to China" (S)
P) Masterpiece Theatre: *Lillie*

**Saturday, April 28, 1979**
**8:00**
N) CHiPs
C) The Bad News Bears
A) What's Happening!
P) Once upon a Classic
**8:30**
C) Billy
A) Delta House
P) Three American Goldsmiths (S)
**9:00**
N) BJ and the Bear
C) *I Know Why the Caged Bird Sings* (M)
A) The Love Boat
P) An Act of Congress
**10:00**
N) Supertrain
A) Fantasy Island
P) Generation on the Wind (S)

**Sunday, April 29, 1979**
**7:00**
N) Wonderful World of Disney
C) 60 Minutes
A) John Denver's Rocky Mountain Reunion (S)
**8:00**
N) *Swashbuckler* (M)
C) All in the Family
A) Battlestar Galactica
P) Global Paper: "The Fight for Food," Part 1
**8:30**
C) One Day at a Time
**9:00**
C) Alice
A) *The Master Gunfighter* (M)
P) Masterpiece Theatre: *Lillie*
**9:30**
C) Just Friends
**10:00**
N) College Sports, Inc.: Big Money on Campus (S)
C) The Mary Tyler Moore Hour
P) Nova: "A Desert Place"

**Monday, April 30, 1979**
**8:00**
N) Little House on the Prairie
C) The White Shadow
A) *Beach Patrol* (M)
P) Bill Moyers' Journal
**9:00**
C) Miss U.S.A. Pageant (S)
P) Global Paper: "The Fight for Food," Part 2
**9:30**
N) *Macon County Line* (M)
A) *Samurai* (M)
**10:00**
P) Austin City Limits

**Tuesday, May 1, 1979**
**8:00**
N) Cliff Hangers
C) CBS Reports: "Three Mile Island" (S)
A) Happy Days
P) Evening at Pops
**8:30**
A) Laverne & Shirley
**9:00**
N) *Stay Hungry* (M)
C) *Fraternity Row* (M)
A) Three's Company
P) Global Paper: "Waging Peace"
**9:30**
A) Taxi!
**10:00**
A) Starsky & Hutch

**Wednesday, May 2, 1979**
**8:00**
N) Real People
C) The Jeffersons
A) Eight Is Enough
P) Great Performances: "*Sleeping Beauty:* American Ballet Theatre'
**8:30**
C) Miss Winslow and Son
**9:00**
N) Academy of Country Music Awards Ceremonies (S)
C) *Torn Between Two Lovers* (M)
A) Charlie's Angels
**10:00**
A) Vega$

**Thursday, May 3, 1979**
**8:00**
N) Highcliff Manor
C) Time Express
A) Mork & Mindy
P) Nova: "The Still Waters"

**8:30**
N) *Castaways from Gilligan's Island* (M)
A) Mork & Mindy
**9:00**
C) Hawaii Five-0
A) *Ike,* Part 1 (M)
P) World: "Australia, the Lucky Continent"
**10:00**
N) Presenting Susan Anton
C) Barnaby Jones
P) Inflation Special (S)

**Friday, May 4, 1979**
**8:00**
N) Diff'rent Strokes
C) The Incredible Hulk
A) The Mackenzies of Paradise Cove
P) Washington Week in Review
**8:30**
N) Steve Martin Special (S)
P) Wall Street Week
**9:00**
C) The Dukes of Hazzard
A) *Ike,* Part 2 (M)
P) Royal Heritage
**9:30**
N) The Best of "Saturday Night Live," Part 2 (S)
**10:00**
C) Dallas
P) Masterpiece Theatre: *Lillie*

**Saturday, May 5, 1979**
**8:00**
N) CHiPs
C) The Bad News Bears
A) Roy Clark Special (S)
P) Once upon a Classic
**8:30**
C) The Beane's of Boston
P) Forgotten Frontier (S)
**9:00**
N) BJ and the Bear
C) *Take a Hard Ride* (M)
A) The Love Boat
P) Cross Country (S)
**10:00**
N) Supertrain
A) Fantasy Island

**Sunday, May 6, 1979**
**7:00**
N) Wonderful World of Disney
C) 60 Minutes
A) The Osmond Family Hour
**8:00**
C) All in the Family
A) Fantasy Island

P) Close to Home (S)
**8:30**
C) One Day at a Time
**9:00**
N) *The Poseidon Adventure* (M)
C) Alice
A) *Ike,* Part 3 (M)
P) Masterpiece Theatre: *Lillie*
**9:30**
C) Just Friends
**10:00**
C) The Mary Tyler Moore Hour
P) Nova: "The Still Waters"

**Monday, May 7, 1979**
**8:00**
N) *Rollercoaster* (M)
C) The White Shadow
A) Battle of the Network Stars (S)
P) Bill Moyers' Journal
**9:00**
C) M*A*S*H
P) *The Prime of Miss Jean Brodie*
**9:30**
C) WKRP in Cincinnati
**10:00**
C) Lou Grant
A) Playboy 25th Anniversary (S)
P) The Originals: "Women in Art"
**10:30**
N) Whodunnit?

**Tuesday, May 8, 1979**
**8:00**
N) Greatest Heroes of the Bible
C) The Paper Chase
A) Happy Days
P) Previn and the Pittsburgh
**8:30**
A) Laverne & Shirley
**9:00**
N) *Hanging by a Thread,* Part 1 (M)
C) *Anatomy of a Seduction* (M)
A) Three's Company
P) Alexander's Bachtime Band (S)
**9:30**
A) Taxi!
**10:00**
A) Starsky & Hutch
P) La La Making It In L.A. (S)

**Wednesday, May 9, 1979**
**8:00**
N) Real People
C) The Wild Wild West Revisited (S)
A) Eight Is Enough
P) The Long Search
**9:00**
N) *Hanging by a Thread,* Part 2 (M)
P) Great Performances: "The Paul Taylor Dance Company"

**10:00**
C) Johnny Cash Springtime Special (S)
A) Vega$
P) Once a Daughter (S)

**Thursday, May 10, 1979**
**8:00**
N) Hizzoner
C) Time Express
A) Mork & Mindy
P) Nova: "A Whisper from Space"
**8:30**
N) Whodunnit?
A) Angie
**9:00**
N) Chevy Chase Special (S)
C) Hawaii Five-0
A) Barney Miller
P) World: "Inside Europe: Chain Reaction"
**9:30**
A) Carter Country
**10:00**
N) Presenting Susan Anton
C) Barnaby Jones
A) Family
P) Sneak Preview
**10:30**
P) Pearls: Mako (S)

**Friday, May 11, 1979**
**8:00**
N) Diff'rent Strokes
C) The Incredible Hulk
A) *Power Man* (M)
P) Washington Week in Review
**8:30**
P) Wall Street Week
**9:00**
N) Dean Martin Special (S)
C) The Dukes of Hazzard
P) Royal Heritage
**9:30**
A) *Night Rider* (M)
**10:00**
C) Dallas
P) Masterpiece Theatre: *Lillie*

**Saturday, May 12, 1979**
**8:00**
N) CHiPs
C) The Bad News Bears
A) Paul Lynde Special (S)
P) Once upon a Classic
**8:30**
C) Bugs Bunny
P) Irish Treasures (S)
**9:00**
C) *The Ultimate Imposter* (M)
A) The Love Boat
P) *The Prime of Miss Jean Brodie*

**10:00**
N) BJ and the Bear
A) Fantasy Island
P) The Best of Families: Generations

**Sunday, May 13, 1979**
**7:00**
N) Wonderful World of Disney
C) 60 Minutes
A) The Osmond Family Hour
**8:00**
C) All in the Family
A) Fantasy Island
P) Over Easy: "Four Alone: The Older Woman in America" (S)
**8:30**
C) One Day at a Time
**9:00**
N) *The Cassandra Crossing* (M)
C) *Strangers* (M)
A) *Butch Cassidy and the Sundance Kid* (M)
P) Masterpiece Theatre: *Lillie*
**10:00**
P) The Three Mile Island Syndrome (S)

**Monday, May 14, 1979**
**8:00**
N) London Palladium Anniversary Special (S)
C) Snoopy, Come Home (S)
A) Salvage
P) Bill Moyers' Journal
**9:00**
N) *Son Rise: Miracle of Love* (M)
A) Television Annual 1978-79 (S)
P) *The Prime of Miss Jean Brodie*
**9:30**
C) M*A*S*H
**10:00**
C) Lou Grant
P) The Originals: "Women in Art"

**Tuesday, May 15, 1979**
**8:00**
N) Greatest Heroes of the Bible
C) The Paper Chase
A) Happy Days
P) Previn and the Pittsburgh
**8:30**
A) Laverne & Shirley
**9:00**
N) *The Sacketts,* Part 1 (M)
C) *Walking through Fire* (M)
A) Three's Company
P) From China to Us (S)
**9:30**
A) Taxi!
**10:00**
A) Starsky & Hutch

**10:30**
P) Irish Treasures (S)

**Wednesday, May 16, 1979**
**8:00**
N) Real People
C) The Muppets Go Hollywood (S)
A) Eight Is Enough
P) The Long Search
**9:00**
N) *The Sacketts,* Part 2 (M)
C) *You Can't Take It with You* (S)
A) Charlie's Angels
P) Great Performances: "The Eliot Feld Dance Company"
**10:00**
A) Vega$
P) George Segal (S)

**Thursday, May 17, 1979**
**8:00**
N) Hizzoner
C) Time Express
A) Mork & Mindy
P) Nova: "The New Healers"
**8:30**
N) Whodunnit?
A) Angie
**9:00**
N) Quincy
C) Hawaii Five-0
A) Barney Miller
P) Views of Asia
**9:30**
A) Carter Country
**10:00**
N) Presenting Susan Anton
C) Barnaby Jones
A) Family
P) Gravity Is My Enemy (S)
**10:30**
P) Appalachian Moods (S)

**Friday, May 18, 1979**
**8:00**
N) Diff'rent Strokes
C) The Leif Garrett Special (S)
A) The Mackenzies of Paradise Cove
P) Washington Week in Review
**9:30**
N) Hello Larry
P) Wall Street Week
**9:00**
N) The Rockford Files
C) The Dukes of Hazzard
A) *Return of the Mod Squad* (M)
P) Royal Heritage
**10:00**
N) The Duke
C) Dallas
P) Masterpiece Theatre: *Lillie*

**Saturday, May, 19, 1979**
**8:00**
N) CHiPs
C) The Bad News Bears
A) The Love Boat
P) Once upon a Classic
**8:30**
C) The Hobbitt
**9:00**
N) BJ and the Bear
P) *The Prime of Miss Jean Brodie*
**9:30**
A) Fantasy Island
**10:00**
N) The Nightingales
C) Steeltown (S)
P) The Best of Families: The Bridge

**Sunday, May 20, 1979**
**7:00**
N) Wonderful World of Disney
C) 60 Minutes
A) The Osmond Family Hour
**8:00**
N) *A Man Called Intrepid,* Part 1 (S)
C) *Blind Ambition,* Part 1 (S)
A) The Guinness Book of Records (S)
P) Rites of Spring (S)
**9:00**
A) *Love's Savage Fury* (M)
P) Masterpiece Theatre: *Lillie*
**10:00**
N) Glen Campbell Special (S)
C) Shirley Maclaine Special (S)
P) Nova: "The New Healers"

**Monday, May 21, 1979**
**8:00**
N) Little House on the Prairie
C) The Body Human (S)
A) Salvage
P) Bill Moyers' Journal
**9:00**
N) *A Man Called Intrepid,* Part 2 (S)
C) *Blind Ambition,* Part 2 (S)
A) *Vacation in Hell* (M)
P) *The Prime of Miss Jean Brodie*
**10:00**
P) The Originals: "Women in Art"
**10:30**
P) The Originals: "Writers in America"

**Tuesday, May 22, 1979**
**8:00**
N) Greatest Heroes of the Bible
C) The Paper Chase
A) Happy Days
P) Previn and the Pittsburgh
**8:30**
A) Laverne & Shirley

**9:00**
N) *A Man Called Intrepid,* Part 3 (S)
C) *Blind Ambition,* Part 3 (S)
A) Three's Company
P) Lewis Mumford: Toward Human Architecture (S)
**9:30**
A) Taxi!
**10:00**
A) Helen Reddy
**10:30**
P) Gravity Is My Enemy

**Wednesday, May 23, 1979**
**8:00**
N) Real People
C) Rocky's People (S)
A) Eight Is Enough
P) The Long Search
**8:30**
C) Good Times
**9:00**
N) *Police Story* (M)
C) *Blind Ambition,* Part 4 (S)
A) Barry Manilow Special (S)
P) Great Performances: "Balanchine," Part 2
**10:00**
A) Vega$
P) The Heifetz Concert (S)

**Thursday, May 24, 1979**
**8:00**
N) Hizzoner
C) The Waltons
A) Mork & Mindy
P) Nova: "Black Tide"
**8:30**
N) Comedy Theater
C) Hawaii Five-0
A) Barney Miller
P) Views of Asia
**9:30**
A) Carter Country
**10:00**
C) Barnaby Jones
A) Alan King Special (S)
P) Sneak Preview
**10:30**
P) Cat (S)

**Friday, May 25, 1979**
**8:00**
N) Diff'rent Strokes
C) The Incredible Hulk
A) Welcome Back, Kotter
P) Washington Week in Review
**8:30**
N) Hello Larry
P) Wall Street Week

**9:00**
N) The Rockford Files
C) The Dukes of Hazzard
A) *Hot Rod* (M)
P) Royal Heritage
**10:00**
C) Dallas
P) Masterpiece Theatre: *Lillie*

**Saturday, May 26, 1979**
**8:00**
N) CHiPs
C) The Bad News Bears
A) The Love Boat
P) Meeting of Minds
**8:30**
C) *A Boy Named Charlie Brown* (S)
**9:00**
N) BJ and the Bear
P) *The Prime of Miss Jean Brodie*
**9:30**
C) *The Lords of Flatbush* (M)
A) Fantasy Island
**10:00**
N) Buffalo Soldier (S)
P) The Best of Families

**Sunday, May 27, 1979**
**7:00**
N) Wonderful World of Disney
C) 60 Minutes
A) The Osmond Family Hour
**8:00**
C) All in the Family
A) Charlie's Angels
P) The Cousteau Odyssey: "Mediterranean: Cradle or Coffin?"
**8:30**
C) One Day at a Time
**9:00**
N) *The Best Place to Be,* Part 1 (M)
C) *Dummy* (M)
A) Indy 500 Auto Race
P) Masterpiece Theatre: *Lillie*
**10:00**
P) Italian Open Tennis Finals

**Monday, May 28, 1979**
**8:00**
N) Little House on the Prairie
C) The New Adventures of Wonder Woman
A) Salvage
P) Bill Moyers' Journal
**9:00**
N) *The Best Place to Be,* Part 2 (M)
C) M*A*S*H
A) *The House on Garibaldi Street* (S)
P) *The Prime of Miss Jean Brodie*

**10:00**
C) Lou Grant
P) The Originals: "Women in Art"
**10:30**
P) The Originals: "Writers in America"

**Tuesday, May 29, 1979**
**8:00**
N) Runaways
C) The New Adventures of Wonder Woman
A) Happy Days
P) Previn and the Pittsburgh
**8:30**
A) Laverne & Shirley
**9:00**
N) *The Revengers* (M)
C) *The Survival of Dana* (M)
A) Three's Company
P) An Apple, an Orange (S)
**9:30**
A) Taxi!
**10:00**
A) Barbara Walters Special (S)
**10:30**
P) Run America, Run (S)

**Wednesday, May 30, 1979**
**8:00**
N) Bob Hope Special
C) The Jeffersons
A) Eight Is Enough
P) The Long Search
**8:30**
C) Good Times
**9:00**
C) *Stunt Seven* (M)
A) Charlie's Angels
P) Great Performances: "Martha Graham"
**9:30**
N) *This Man Stands Alone* (M)
**10:30**
P) Estampa Flamenia

**Thursday, May 31, 1979**
**8:00**
N) Hizzoner
C) The Waltons
A) Mork & Mindy
P) Nova: "The Long Walk of Fred Young"
**8:30**
N) Piper's Pets
A) Angie

**9:00**

N)  *The Innocent and the Damned,*
    Part 1 (S)
C)  Hawaii Five-0
A)  Barney Miller
P)  Views of Asia

**9:30**

A)  Carter Country

**10:00**

C)  Barnaby Jones
A)  20/20
P)  The Cousteau Odyssey:
    "Mediterranean: Cradle or
    Coffin?"

# NETWORK PRIME-TIME RATINGS

The following charts show the ranking of the top fifteen programs as reported in the bi-weekly Nielsen Television Index Reports for the two-week period ending each quarter of our "television year" (June 1, 1978 to May 31, 1979). Data is reprinted by permission of A.C. Nielsen Company.

**National TV Nielsen Ratings—Top Programs**
**Based on Nielsen Estimates for Two Weeks Ending February 25, 1978**
**Nielsen Average Audience**

### Total Persons

| Rank | Program | % U.S. | No. (000) |
|------|---------|--------|-----------|
| | | | Audiences |
| 1 | Mork & Mindy | 29.7 | 60,710 |
| 2 | Three's Company | 25.0 | 51,150 |
| 3 | Laverne & Shirley | 24.9 | 50,870 |
| 4 | Angie | 24.6 | 50,270 |
| 5 | Happy Days | 24.3 | 49,740 |
| 6 | *Roots: Next Generations (S)* | 22.6 | 46,330 |
| 7 | *Roots: Next Generations (S)* | 21.8 | 44,680 |
| 8 | *Roots: Next Generations (S)* | 21.7 | 44.370 |
| 9 | Eight Is Enough | 21.4 | 43,890 |
| 10 | *Roots: Next Generations (S)* | 20.9 | 42,800 |
| 11 | Taxi! | 19.7 | 40,240 |
| 12 | *Gone With the Wind,* Part 2 (S) | 19.7 | 40,230 |
| 13 | M°A°S°H | 18.0 | 36,800 |
| 14 | 60 Minutes | 17.7 | 36,280 |
| 15 | Diff'rent Strokes | 17.2 | 35,180 |

**National TV Nielsen Ratings—Top Programs**
**Based on Nielsen Estimates for Two Weeks Ending August 27, 1978**
**Nielsen Average Audience**

### Total Persons

| Rank | Program | % U.S. | No. (000) |
|------|---------|--------|-----------|
| | | | Audiences |
| 1 | Three's Company | 23.3 | 16,990 |
| 2 | M°A°S°H | 22.2 | 16,180 |
| 3 | One Day at a Time | 21.8 | 15,890 |
| 4 | Laverne & Shirley | 21.5 | 15,670 |
| 4 | Quincy | 21.5 | 15,670 |
| 6 | Alice | 21.4 | 15,600 |
| 7 | ABC Sunday Night Movie | 21.1 | 15,380 |
| 7 | Carter Country | 21.1 | 15,380 |
| 9 | Starsky and Hutch | 19.9 | 14,510 |
| 10 | Happy Days | 19.6 | 14,290 |
| 11 | All in the Family | 19.3 | 14,070 |
| 12 | Barnaby Jones | 19.2 | 14,000 |
| 13 | Charlie's Angels | 19.1 | 13,920 |
| 14 | Lou Grant | 19.0 | 13,850 |
| 15 | 60 Minutes | 17.9 | 13,050 |

**National TV Nielsen Ratings—Top Programs**
**Based on Nielsen Estimates for Two Weeks Ending November 26, 1978**
**Nielsen Average Audience**

### Total Persons

| | | Audiences | |
|---|---|---|---|
| Rank | Program | % U.S. | No. (000) |
| 1 | Mork & Mindy | 25.2 | 51,540 |
| 2 | Laverne & Shirley | 22.7 | 46,460 |
| 3 | Happy Days | 22.1 | 45,150 |
| 4 | Three's Company | 21.4 | 43,770 |
| 5 | Charlie's Angels | 20.9 | 42,750 |
| 6 | What's Happening! | 20.4 | 41,650 |
| 7 | Wonderful World of Disney | 19.3 | 39,450 |
| 8 | Alice | 19.1 | 39,180 |
| 9 | Eight Is Enough | 18.9 | 38,680 |
| 10 | Pearl(S) | 18.7 | 38,370 |
| 11 | M*A*S*H | 17.7 | 36,260 |
| 12 | 60 Minutes | 17.5 | 35,910 |
| 13 | Little House on the Prairie | 17.2 | 35,150 |
| 14 | Love Boat | 17.1 | 35,000 |
| 15 | Barney Miller | 16.9 | 34,680 |

**National TV Nielsen Ratings—Top Programs**
**Based on Nielsen Estimates for Two Weeks Ending May 27, 1979**
**Nielsen Average Audience**

### Households

| | | Audiences | |
|---|---|---|---|
| Rank | Program | % U.S. | No. (000) |
| 1 | Three's Company | 25.6 | 19,070 |
| 2 | Laverne & Shirley | 25.3 | 18,850 |
| 3 | ABC Monday Night Movie | 24.5 | 18,250 |
| 4 | ABC Sunday Night Movie | 23.2 | 17,280 |
| 5 | Mork & Mindy | 22.3 | 16,610 |
| 6 | Taxi! | 22.1 | 16,460 |
| 7 | The Body Human: The Sexes (S) | 21.8 | 16,240 |
| 8 | Dummy (S) | 21.7 | 16,170 |
| 9 | Happy Days | 21.6 | 16,090 |
| 9 | M*A*S*H | 21.6 | 16,090 |
| 9 | 3rd Barry Manilow Special (S) | 21.6 | 16,090 |
| 12 | Blind Ambition, Part 4 (S) | 21.2 | 15,790 |
| 13 | Angie | 21.1 | 15,720 |
| 14 | Guinness Book of World Records | 21.0 | 15,650 |
| 15 | 60 Minutes | 20.7 | 15,420 |
| 16 | Blind Ambition, Part 2 (S) | 20.5 | 15,270 |
| 17 | Barney Miller | 20.2 | 15,050 |
| 17 | Blind Ambition, Part 1(S) | 20.2 | 15,050 |
| 17 | Eight Is Enough | 20.2 | 15,050 |
| 17 | Snoopy Come Home (S) | 20.2 | 15,050 |
| 21 | Blind Ambition, Part 3 (S) | 20.0 | 14,900 |
| 22 | Carter Country | 19.8 | 14,750 |
| 23 | Young Guy Christian (S) | 19.7 | 14,680 |
| 24 | Charlie's Angels | 19.1 | 14,230 |
| 25 | Barnaby Jones | 19.0 | 14,160 |

| Rank | Program | % U.S. | No. (000) |
|---|---|---|---|
| | | Audiences | |
| 1 | Three's Company | 18.8 | 38,490 |
| 2 | Laverne & Shirley | 18.3 | 37,380 |
| 3 | Mork & Mindy | 16.6 | 33,920 |
| 4 | Taxi! | 15.9 | 32,550 |
| 5 | Dukes of Hazzard | 15.4 | 31,610 |
| 6 | Happy Days | 15.2 | 31,120 |
| 7 | M*A*S*H | 15.0 | 30,630 |
| 8 | Angie | 14.4 | 29,410 |
| 9 | Eight Is Enough | 14.2 | 29,030 |
| 10 | Barney Miller | 13.6 | 27,830 |
| 11 | Charlie's Angels | 13.5 | 27,690 |
| 12 | 60 Minutes | 13.3 | 27,170 |
| 13 | Carter Country | 12.8 | 26,240 |

# MILESTONES

Congressman Lionel Van Deerlin (D-Ca.) unveils the Communications Act of 1978—a proposal to overhaul the existing law. Fred Silverman begins work at NBC as president and chief executive officer.

**June-July 1978**

William Leonard, vice president CBS, Inc., Washington, D.C., named to succeed retiring Richard S. Salant as president of CBS News.

Judge Robert Dossee rules that the NBC program *Born Innocent* was not responsible for the assault of a nine-year-old girl which imitated the television show.

**August-September 1978**

Jane Cahill Pfeiffer, a former IBM vice president, named NBC chairman.

**October-November 1978**

"Sesame Street" opens its tenth season. An estimated 80 percent of U.S. households with children under six tune into the PBS-produced show.

"60 Minutes" is the most-watched program in the country for the first time in its 10-year history.

In Jonestown, Guyana, two NBC journalists—Don Harris and Bob Brown—were killed, among others, while investigating the fanatic People's Temple cult.

"Carnegie II" a 400-page report dealing with the future of public broadcasting, is released.

**December 1978-
January 1979**

FTC begins hearings on children's advertising. The FTC proposal is to limit and, in some cases, ban children's advertising.

Congressman Van Deerlin (D.-Ca.) introduces the latest version of a bill to overhaul the existing Communications law.

**February-March 1979**

February is the most expensive month of prime-time programming in history. Sunday, February 11, CBS ran *Gone With The Wind,* NBC ran *One Flew Over the Cuckoo's Nest,* and ABC ran *Elvis,* a three-part made-for-TV movie, during the 9:00-11:00 P.M. slot.

PBS announces it will broadcast all 37 of Shakespeare's plays over the next 6 years (produced by BBC).

*Roots: The Next Generations* (ABC) is billed as the biggest revenue-making miniseries ever. Seventy advertisers bought $21 million worth of advertising in a seven-day spread.

The new system for televising daily floor proceedings from the House of Representatives begins.

In a landmark case, Herbert vs. CBS, the U.S. Supreme Court rules that a public figure who sues for libel may ask about a journalist's thoughts, motivations, and internal editorial processes in an effort to determine whether the journalist acted maliciously.

**April-May 1979**

The U.S. Supreme Court strikes down the FCC regulation that requires cable systems to operate certain channels for public and private use.

For the first time ever, morning TV viewers watched something other than NBC's "Today Show." "Good Morning America" inched by with a 4.2 rating to "Today's" 4.1, according to Nielsen figures.

After 17 years as president of CBS News, Richard Salent joins NBC. Salant retired from CBS because of a forced-retirement policy.

Fred Pierce is named second-in-line for the presidency of ABC, Inc. He's currently president of ABC-TV.

University of Pennsylvania releases its tenth annual "Violence Profile." New findings show:

1. Violence in children's TV programming rose to near-record levels.
2. Women and minorities bear an unequal burden of victimization.
3. Children who watch more TV than others worry more about their own safety and are more likely to think that people are mean and selfish.

*"Let's watch NBC, for Fred Silverman's sake, the poor dear."*
(Drawing by Stevenson; © 1979 The New Yorker Magazine, Inc.)

# NECROLOGY

Bob Crane, 49, star of the former CBS-TV series now in syndication, "Hogan's Heroes," was found beaten to death in an apartment in Scottsdale, Arizona, where he was appearing in a dinner-theater play. (June 29, 1978)

Samuel Pottle, 44, resident composer and musical director of "Sesame Street," died of a heart attack in Great Barrington, Massachusetts. (July 4, 1978)

James Daly, 59, character actor in films and more than six hundred TV shows, died of an apparent heart attack in Nyack, New York. His most recent credit was in *Roots II*. He was also seen in *Overseas Assignment, Henry Adams, The Court Martial of Billy Mitchell, The Eagle and the Cage,* and *The Magnificent Yankee.* (July 4, 1978)

Television and nightclub comedian, Totie Fields, 48, died of a heart attack in Las Vegas. (August 2, 1978)

Frank Fontaine, 58, comic best known as "Crazy Guggenheim" on the Jackie Gleason Show, died of a heart attack in Spokane, Washington. (August 4, 1978)

Leon Levy, 83, broadcast pioneer who bought CBS' first affilate, WCAU (AM), Philadelphia, in 1925, with his brother, the late Isaac D. Levy, died at his home in Philadelphia. (August 9, 1978)

Gig Young, 60, film and television actor, shot and killed himself and his bride of three weeks in their New York City apartment. He appeared in the series "The Rogues," and "Gibbsville," and won an Academy Award for the 1969 film, *They Shoot Horses Don't They?* (October 19, 1978)

Norman Pincus, age unreported, producer of "The Real McCoys" and other television series, died in Los Angeles after a long illness. (October 30, 1978)

Robert Alan Arthur, born in New York, was a writer-producer. His short stories appeared in many magazines, including *The New Yorker, Harper's,* and *Esquire,* where he had a column in 1972 called "Hanging Out." He was a freelance dramatist from 1951-1958 and also served as vice president of Talent Associates—Paramount Ltd. His TV scripts include "Philco Playhouse" and "Mr. Peepers." (November 20, 1978)

Jack Soo, 63, who played the role of Sergeant Nick Yemana in ABC's "Barney Miller" series, died of cancer at the UCLA Medical Center, Los Angeles. (January 15, 1979)

Ted Cassidy, 46, television actor best known for his role as Lurch in the "Addams Family" television series, died of complications following open-heart surgery for a nonmalignant tumor in Los Angeles. Cassidy played Bigfoot in "The Six Million Dollar Man" series. (January 16, 1979)

Mr. Ed, television's "talking horse" died at the age of 33. Mr. Ed was the star of a television show in the 1960s that ran for five years. (March 9, 1979)

Paul Crabtree, 60, actor, writer, producer, and director. He wrote for "Kraft Television Theatre," "Philco Playhouse," "American Heritage Series," and "Studio One." His script for *The Pilot* was voted one of the seven best TV plays of 1956. He also wrote and directed "The Loretta Young Show." (March 21, 1979)

John Meston, 64, script writer who created the "Gunsmoke" television series, died of a cerebral hemorrhage in Tarzana, Arizona. (March 24, 1979)

Fred Coe, producer and director of more than 500 television shows, died in Los Angeles at the age of 65. He produced such programs as "Philco-Goodyear Playhouse" on NBC, the "Mr. Peepers" series, and several "Playhouse 90" dramas on CBS. (March 29, 1979)

Ethel Harper, 75, widely known as Aunt Jemima, died of a heart attack in Morristown, New Jersey. She appeared as the kerchiefed Aunt Jemima in Quaker Oats' advertising campaign for pancake mix during the 1950s. (March 31, 1979)

Milton Ager, 85, Broadway and movie songwriter of the '20s and '30s, died in Los Angeles. Ager composed "Happy Days Are Here Again," the Democrats' theme song, and "Ain't She Sweet?" in 1927 for his daughter, writer Shana Alexander. (May 6, 1979)

# AWARDS

## EMMY AWARDS 1977-78

Emmy Awards are presented by the Academy of Television Arts and Sciences
for excellence in all areas of television entertainment.

OUTSTANDING COMEDY SERIES: All in the Family (CBS)

OUTSTANDING DRAMA SERIES: The Rockford Files (NBC)

OUTSTANDING COMEDY-VARIETY OR MUSIC SERIES: The Muppet Show (syndicated)

OUTSTANDING LIMITED SERIES: *Holocaust* (NBC)

OUTSTANDING INFORMATION SERIES: The Body Human (CBS)

OUTSTANDING SPECIAL—DRAMA OR COMEDY: "The Gathering" (NBC)

OUTSTANDING SPECIAL—COMEDY-VARIETY OR MUSIC: "Bette Midler—Ole Red Hair Is
  Back" (NBC)

OUTSTANDING INFORMATION SPECIAL: "The Great Whales: National Geographic"
  (PBS)

OUTSTANDING CLASSICAL PROGRAM IN THE PERFORMING ARTS: "American Ballet
  Theatre: *Giselle* Live from Lincoln Center" (PBS)

OUTSTANDING LEAD ACTOR IN A COMEDY SERIES: Carroll O'Connor, All in the Family
  (CBS)

OUTSTANDING LEAD ACTOR IN A DRAMA SERIES: Edward Asner, Lou Grant (CBS)

OUTSTANDING LEAD ACTOR IN A LIMITED SERIES: Michael Moriarty, *Holocaust* (NBC)

OUTSTANDING LEAD ACTOR IN A DRAMA OR COMEDY SPECIAL: Fred Astaire, *A Family
  Upside Down* (NBC)

OUTSTANDING LEAD ACTOR FOR A SINGLE APPEARANCE IN A DRAMA OR COMEDY SE-
  RIES: Barnard Hughes, "Judge," Lou Grant (CBS)

OUTSTANDING LEAD ACTRESS IN A COMEDY SERIES: Jean Stapleton, All in the Family
  (CBS)

OUTSTANDING LEAD ACTRESS IN A DRAMA SERIES: Sada Thompson, Family (ABC)

OUTSTANDING LEAD ACTRESS IN A LIMITED SERIES: Meryl Streep, *Holocaust* (NBC)

OUTSTANDING LEAD ACTRESS IN A DRAMA OR COMEDY SPECIAL: Joanne Woodward,
  *See How She Runs,* General Electric Theater (CBS)

OUTSTANDING LEAD ACTRESS FOR A SINGLE APPEARANCE IN A DRAMA OR COMEDY
  SERIES: Rita Moreno, "The Paper Palace," The Rockford Files (NBC)

OUTSTANDING CONTINUING PERFORMANCE BY A SUPPORTING ACTOR IN A COMEDY
  SERIES: Rob Reiner, All in the Family (CBS)

OUTSTANDING CONTINUING PERFORMANCE BY A SUPPORTING ACTOR IN A DRAMA SE-
  RIES: Robert Vaughn, "Washington: Behind Closed Doors" (ABC)

OUTSTANDING CONTINUING OR SINGLE PERFORMANCE BY A SUPPORTING ACTOR IN
  VARIETY OR MUSIC: Tim Conway, The Carol Burnett Show (CBS)

OUTSTANDING PERFORMANCE BY A SUPPORTING ACTOR IN A COMEDY OR DRAMA SPE-
  CIAL: Howard Da Silva, "Verna: USO Girl," Great Performances (PBS)

OUTSTANDING SINGLE PERFORMANCE BY A SUPPORTING ACTOR IN A COMEDY OR
  DRAMA SERIES: Ricardo Montalban, How the West Was Won—Part Two (ABC)

OUTSTANDING CONTINUING PERFORMANCE BY A SUPPORTING ACTRESS IN A COMEDY
  SERIES: Julie Kavner, Rhoda (CBS)

OUTSTANDING CONTINUING PERFORMANCE BY A SUPPORTING ACTRESS IN A DRAMA
  SERIES: Nancy Marchand, Lou Grant (CBS)

OUTSTANDING CONTINUING OR SINGLE PERFORMANCE BY A SUPPORTING ACTRESS IN
  VARIETY OR MUSIC: Gilda Radner, NBC's Saturday Night Live (NBC)

OUTSTANDING PERFORMANCE BY A SUPPORTING ACTRESS IN A COMEDY OR DRAMA
  SPECIAL: Eva La Gallienne, "The Royal Family" (PBS)

OUTSTANDING SINGLE PERFORMANCE BY A SUPPORTING ACTRESS IN A COMEDY OR
  DRAMA SERIES: Blanche Baker, *Holocaust—Part One* (NBC)

OUTSTANDING DIRECTING IN A DRAMA SERIES (A SINGLE EPISODE OF A REGULAR OR
  LIMITED SERIES WITH CONTINUING CHARACTERS AND/OR THEME): Marvin J. Chom-
  sky, *Holocaust,* entire series (NBC)

OUTSTANDING DIRECTING IN A COMEDY SERIES (A SINGLE EPISODE OF A REGULAR OR LIMITED SERIES WITH CONTINUING CHARACTERS AND/OR THEME): Paul Bogart, "Edith's 50th Birthday," All in the Family (CBS)

OUTSTANDING DIRECTING IN A COMEDY-VARIETY OR MUSIC SERIES (A SINGLE EPISODE OF A REGULAR OR LIMITED SERIES): Dave Powers, The Carol Burnett Show, with Steve Martin and Betty White (CBS)

OUTSTANDING DIRECTING IN A COMEDY-VARIETY OR MUSIC SPECIAL: Dwight Hemion, "The Sentry Collection Presents Ben Vereen—His Roots" (ABC)

OUTSTANDING DIRECTING IN A SPECIAL PROGRAM—DRAMA OR COMEDY: David Lowell Rich, *The Defection of Simas Kudirka* (CBS)

OUTSTANDING WRITING IN A DRAMA SERIES: Gerald Green, *Holocaust* (NBC)

OUTSTANDING WRITING IN A COMEDY SERIES: Harve Broston, Barry Harman, Bob Schiller, and Bob Weiskopf, All in the Family (CBS)

OUTSTANDING WRITING IN A COMEDY-VARIETY OR MUSIC SERIES: Roger Beatty, Dick Clair, Tim Conway, Rick Hawkins, Robert Illes, Jeanna McMahon, Gene Perret, Bill Richmond, Liz Sage, Larry Siegel, Franelle Silver, Ed Simmons, and James Stain, The Carol Burnett Show (CBS)

OUTSTANDING WRITING IN A COMEDY-VARIETY OR MUSIC SPECIAL: Chevy Chase, Tom Davis, Al Franken, Charles Grodin, Lorne Michaels, Paul Simon, Lily Tomlin, and Alan Zweibel, "The Paul Simon Special" (NBC)

OUTSTANDING WRITING IN A SPECIAL PROGRAM—DRAMA OR COMEDY—ORIGINAL TELEPLAY: George Rubino, *The Last Tenant* (ABC)

OUTSTANDING WRITING IN A SPECIAL PROGRAM—DRAMA OR COMEDY—ADAPTATION: Caryl Ledner, *Mary White* (ABC)

OUTSTANDING EVENING CHILDREN'S SPECIAL: "Halloween Is Grinch Night" (ABC)

SPECIAL CLASSIFICATION OF OUTSTANDING PROGRAM ACHIEVEMENT: The Tonight Show, starring Johnny Carson (NBC)


## GEORGE FOSTER PEABODY AWARDS

George Foster Peabody Awards are presented by the Henry W. Grady School of Journalism and Mass Communications, University of Georgia, for the "most distinguished and meritorious public service rendered each year by radio and television."

Southern Baptist Radio and TV Commission, Fort Worth: "A River to the Sea"

CBS News: 30 Minutes, and "The Battle for South Africa"

Four D Productions Trisene Corp. and ABC-TV: Barney Miller

Bob Keeshan: Captain Kangaroo

KGO-TV San Francisco: "Old Age: Do Not Go Gentle"

KHET-TV Honolulu: "Damien"

KQED-TV San Francisco: "Over Easy"

MTM Productions and CBS-TV: Lou Grant

The Muppets: "For...high standards for family viewing"

Newsweek Broadcasting: "Cartoon-A-Torial"

Richard S. Salant: For "staunch defense of the first amendment"

Survival Anglia/World Wildlife Fund and NBC-TV: "Mysterious Castles of Clay"

Titus Productions and NBC-TV: *Holocaust*

Tomorrow Entertainment/Medcom Co. and CBS-TV: "The Body Human: The Vital Connection"

WAVE-TV Louisville, Ky.: "Whose Child Is This?"

WDVM-TV Washington: "Your Health and Your Wallet" and "Race War in Rhodesia"

WENH-TV Durham, N.H.: "Arts in New Hampshire"

WQED-TV Pittsburgh: *A Connecticut Yankee in King Arthur's Court*

## DUPONT-COLUMBIA AWARDS 1977-78

DuPont-Columbia Awards are presented by the Alfred I. duPont-Columbia Survey and Awards, Graduate School of Journalism, Columbia University, New York, for "outstanding performance in radio and television journalism."

KOOL-TV, Phoenix, Az.: "Water: Arizona's Most Precious Resource"
KPIX-TV, San Francisco: "Laser Con-Fusion"
WBBM-TV, Chicago: For Documentary Programming
WFAA-TV, Dallas: For Investigative Reporting
WGBH-TV, Boston: Nova series and "Chachaji: My Poor Relation"
WMHT-TV, Schenectady, N.Y.: Inside Albany series
WPLG-TV, Miami: For Investigative Reporting
The National Geographic Society and WQED-TV, Pittsburgh: "The Living Sands of Namib"
NBC-TV: NBC Reports: "Africa's Defiant White Tribe"

CITATIONS
KAIT-TV, Jonesboro, Ak.: "Crisis at the Crossing"
KENS-TV, San Antonio: ". . .And Justice for All"
WNET-TV, New York City: "The Originals: Women in Art—Georgia O'Keeffe"

SPECIAL AWARD

Richard Salant, President, CBS News

## CLIO/U.S. TELEVISION WINNERS 1979

Clio Awards are presented by the American TV and Radio Commercials Festival Group to companies for showing a high degree of excellence in advertising.

| | PRODUCT | TITLE | ENTRANT |
|---|---|---|---|
| OVERALL CAMPAIGN | McDonald's Restaurant | "Mary Ryan," "Spring Green," "Hot Stuff" | Needham, Harper & Steers, Chicago |
| TECHNIQUES | Polaroid Cameras | "Trick Shot" | The Polaroid Corporation, Cambridge, Ma. |
| | Georgia-Pacific | "TV ID Logo" | Aries Sound International, NY. |
| | Bubblicious | "Ultimate Bubble" | The Radio Band of America, NY. |
| | Pepsi-Cola | "Dancing Bottles" | BBDO, NY. |
| | Kentucky Fried Chicken | "America" | HEA Productions, NY. and Young & Rubicam, NY. |
| | Chemical Bank | "Neighborhoods" | HEA Productions, NY. |
| | Pan Am | "Theme" | HEA Productions, NY. |

| | | | |
|---|---|---|---|
| | Mobil One Oil | "Cold Weather" | Mathew Brady Films, NY. |
| | 3M Corporation | "Ivory Tower" | BBDO, NY. |
| ANIMATION | Jovan Sex Appeal For Men | "Frazetta" | J. Walter Thompson, Chicago |
| | Blitz Weinhard Beer | "Rancher" | Rick Levine Productions, NY. |
| | Hoffmann-LaRoche On Health Care | "Immunization" | Carl Borack Productions, Venice, Ca. |
| | Catholic Church of Maryland | "You Only Live Once" | Mathis, Burden & Charles, Baltimore |
| | The Church of Jesus Christ of Latter Day Saints/ Marriage Solidarity | "Try Again" | Bonneville Productions, Salt Lake City |
| | Polaroid One Step | "Funny Name" | The Polaroid Corporation Cambridge, Ma. |
| | Warner Brothers/ Superman | "Superman The Movie" | J. Walter Thompson, Chicago and R/Greenberg Associates,NY. |
| | Big Boy | "Open The Hangar" | Dick & Bert Productions, La. |
| | Minolta XG-7 | "Jump" | Dick Lavsky's Music House, NY. |

# GOOD READING ON TELEVISION

This is a selective listing of books on American television published in 1978 and through June of 1979. Given inflation, prices shown should be considered approximate. (P) indicates paperback edition available.

Anderson, Kent. *Television Fraud: The History and Implications of the Quiz Show Scandals.* Westport, Conn.: Greenwood Press, 1978. 226 pp. $18.95. Rise and fall of the big-money quiz shows of 1955-59 with fascinating behind-the-scenes information.

Barnouw, Erik. *The Sponsor: Notes on a Modern Potentate.* New York: Oxford University Press, 1978. 220 pp. $10.00. Development, current status, and problems/prospect of broadcast advertising and advertisers. Well written with many interesting examples.

Barrett, Marvin, ed. *Rich News, Poor News: Alfred I. DuPont-Columbia University Survey of Broadcast Journalism.* New York: Crowell, 1978. 244 pp. $12.95/5.95 (P). Latest edition (6th) in a biennial discussion and analysis of both network and local station broadcast news, concentrating on television.

Brooks, Tim, and Earle Marsh. *The Complete Directory to Prime Time Network TV Shows, 1946-Present.* New York: Ballantine Books, 1979. 848 pp. $19.95/9.95 (P). Perfect argument settler with details on network programs including for each: date on air, network, time on air, good descriptive paragraph, and cast. Best such guide available at present.

Carnegie Commission on the Future of Public Broadcasting. *A Public Trust.* New York: Bantam Books, 1979. 401 pp. $2.95 (P). Analysis of the organization, funding, and programs of public television and ways to improve the system, with some useful comparisons to commercial broadcasting.

Cole, Barry, and Mal Oettinger. *Reluctant Regulators: The FCC and the Broadcast Audience.* Reading, Mass.: Addison-Wesley, 1978. 355 pp. $6.95 (P). A very readable discussion of the major issues in broadcast regulation and who has the clout to affect the regulators and thus the outcome of the controversies. Best behind-the-scenes analysis of the Washington scene in some years.

Comstock, George, et al. *Television and Human Behavior.* New York: Columbia University Press, 1978. 581 pp. $16.95/9.95 (P). Comprehensive review of what is known of television's effects with emphasis on children and violence, general audience use of television, persuasion and politics, TV and the elderly.

Cowan, Geoffrey. *See No Evil: The Backstage Battle over Sex and Violence in Television.* New York: Simon and Schuster, 1979. 324 pp. $10.95. The broadcast networks and stations vs. the government vs. program producers over the "family viewing time" concept to lessen violence on the air. Good narrative on how the industry works—and works us over. Valuable record of a major controversy, told by a lawyer who played a key role.

Diamond, Edwin. *Good News, Bad News.* Cambridge, Mass.: MIT Press, 1978. 263 pp. $12.50. New campaign journalism (the 1972 campaign), news as entertainment and the effects of that approach, and comparison of the content and role of print broadcast news.

Epstein, Laurily Keir, ed. *Women and the News.* New York: Hastings House, 1978. 144 pp. $12.50. Coverage of women in the news, and role of women in the journalism business, including discussion of women's access to the media.

Fates, Gil. *What's My Line? The Inside History of TV's Most Famous Panel Show.* Englewood Cliffs, N.J.: Prentice-Hall, 1978. 239 pp. $9.95. As told by the show's producer for twenty-five years, concentrating on the people and events.

Gans, Herbert J. *Deciding What's News: A Study of CBS Evening News, NBC Nightly News, Newsweek & Time.* New York: Pantheon, 1979. 393 pp. $12.95. A sociologist seeks answers to the all-important question—who decides what is news, how, and with what effect on the news programs (and magazines)—and the audience.

Gates, Gary Paul. *Air Time: The Inside Story of CBS News.* New York: Harper & Row,

1978. 440 pp. $12.95. Everything you wanted to know about Walter, Eric, Mike, Dan, Roger, Harry, and those *behind* the cameras too.

Gianakos, Larry James. *Television Drama Series Programming: A Comprehensive Chronicle, 1959-1975.* Metuchen, N.J.: Scarecrow Press, 1978. 794 pp. $27.50. Detailed listings of episode titles, dates, and cast for prime-time network shows, including much pre-1959 data. A good supplement to Brooks and Marsh (above).

Halberstam, David. *The Powers That Be.* New York: Knopf, 1979. 771 pp. $15.00. Huge narrative of the development of *Time,* CBS News, and two newspapers (Washington *Post,* and Los Angeles *Times*), especially over past thirty years, and their effect on the nation's political and social life. Fascinating portraits of key figures.

Hamburg, Morton I. *All about Cable. Legal and Business Aspects of Cable and Pay Television.* New York: New York Law Journal, 1978. $37.50. The book provides a basic overview of what cable and pay television is about, covering problems such as copyright, obscenity, pole attachments, exclusivity, and franchising standards.

Harris, Jay S., ed. *TV Guide: The First 25 Years.* New York: Simon and Schuster, 1978. 317 pp. $14.95. Reprints both serious and trivial of articles on the rise of TV since 1953 as seen in the "weekly bible," plus a big selection of color pictures of *TV Guide* covers.

Kaye, Evelyn. *The ACT Guide to Children's Television or, How to Treat TV with TLC.* Boston: Beacon Press, 1979. 226 pp. $10.95/5.95(P). Activist guide to how the industry works and how best to keep track of what your kids watch . . . and shouldn't watch.

Krasnow, Erwin G., and Lawrence D. Longley. *The Politics of Broadcast Regulation.* 2d ed. New York: St. Martin's Press, 1978. 213 pp. $12.95/5.95 (P). Good discussion of the "players" in the regulation of broadcasting, including five case studies of how the players interact to create broadcasting policy.

Lachenbruch, David. *Videocassette Recorders. The Complete Home Guide.* New York: Everest House, 1979. An illustrated guide to understanding, selecting, and using videotape equipment.

Martin, James. *The Wired Society.* Englewood Cliffs, N.J.: Prentice-Hall, 1978. 300 pp. $12.95. How television fits into the exploding future technology which may soon make broadcasting as we know it obsolete.

Newcomb, Horace, ed. *Television: The Critical View.* 2d ed. New York: Oxford University Press, 1979. 557 pp. $5.95 (P). Serious collection of what many critics think of television content and role—both positive and negative.

Paley, William S. *As It Happened.* New York: Doubleday, 1979. 418 pp. $14.95. The founder of CBS tells his life story and also relates much of broadcasting's development, concentrating on programming and stars.

Price, Jonathan. *The Best Thing on TV: Commercials.* New York: Viking Press/Penguin Books, 1978. 184 pp. $17.95/8.95 (P). Author contends the ads are often more interesting than the programs. Here he details how they are made, the different types of ads, the people who make them—and appear in them—and provides examples of the best.

Simmons, Steven J. *The Fairness Doctrine and the Media.* Berkeley: University of California Press, 1978. 285 pp. $14.95. Serious study of the development, controversies, and prospects of the FCC regulations calling for equal treatment of different sides of controversial issues as discussed on radio and television.

Stein, Ben. *The View From Sunset Boulevard: America as Brought to You by the People Who Make Television.* New York: Basic Books, 1979. 156 pp. $8.95. The TV makers in this case are the leading producers of TV entertainment series living in Los Angeles. Stein, former TV critic for the *Wall Street Journal,* interviews many of them and comments on how their personal views affect the shows watched by millions. Provides some valuable insights.

Sterling, Christopher H. and John M. Kittross. *Stay Tuned: A Concise History of American Broadcasting.* Belmont, Calif.: Wadsworth, 1978. 562 pp. $19.95. The whole story including networks and stations, programs, the advertisers, educational broadcasting, changing technology, and government regulation, all broken into eight periods and interrelated with American life at the time.

# FOR FURTHER INFORMATION

For further information concerning any of the programs covered in this book, following are the addresses of the public information departments of each network:

NBC: Audience Services
National Broadcasting Company
30 Rockefeller Plaza
New York, NY 10020

CBS: Press Information
Columbia Broadcasting System
51 West 52nd Street
New York, NY 10019

ABC: Audience Information
American Broadcasting Company
1330 Avenue of the Americas
New York, NY 10019

PBS: Public Information
Public Broadcasting Service
475 L'Enfant Plaza WSW
Washington, D.C., 20024

# INDEX

Aaron Spelling Productions, Inc., 29, 35, 47
ABBA, 59
Abbott, Norman, 48
ABC Circle Films, 53
ABC Documentaries, 152
"ABC News Close-Up," 16
Abdo, Nick, 23
"Academy Leaders,"19
Ackroyd, David, 75
*Across the Great Divide*, 101
Adair, Peter, 67
*Adam at 6 A.M.*, 101
Adams, David C., 7
Adams, Edie, 80–81
Adams, Maud, 76
Adams, Steven, 39
"Adams Chronicles," 258, 259
Adelson, Gary, 27, 28
Adler, Mortimer, 22
advertising to children, 176–80, 319
"Afternoon Playhouse," 185
"Afterschool Specials," 16, 125, 181, 183–84
Ager, Milton, 324
Aiken, Charles, 29
*Airport '77*, 101
Ajaye, Franklyn, 105
Akins, Claude, 76
Akroyd, Dan, 56
Alan Landsburg Productions, 52
Albee, Denny, 127
Albert, Eddie, 78, 88, 109, 120
Albertson, Jack, 30, 78
Alcott, Louisa May, 53
Alda, Alan, 37
Aldrich, Adell, 79
Alexander, Denise, 127
Alexander, Jane, 16, 17, 88, 92
Ali, Muhammad, 167, 170–71
"Alice," 12, 13, 19, 59
Allen, Irwin, 83
Allen, Jay Presson, 41
Allen, Phillip R., 21
Allen, Steve, 269
Allen, Woody, 120
Allergro Film, 60
"All in the Family," 12, 13, 20, 198
"All My Children," 126, 199
"All Star Secrets," 125
Allwhit, Inc., 39
Allyson, June, 97, 99
Altheide, David, 253–54
Altman, Robert, 104
Amateau, Rod, 26, 108
*Amateur Night at the Dixie Bar and Grill*, 8, 74
"The Amazing Spider-Man," 13, 20
"America," 259
American Ballet Theatre, The, 19, 30
American Film Institute, The, 56
*American Film Institute Salute to Alfred Hitchcock*, 56
"American Girls, The," 13, 20
*American Graffiti*, 102
"American Short Story, The," 261
Ames, Rachel, 127
*Anatomy of a Seduction*, 74
Anderson, Cortland, 240
Anderson, John, 80
Anderson, Marian, 61
Anderson, Melissa Sue, 35, 96
Anderson, Michael, 114
Anderson, Richard Dean, 127
Andes, Keith, 98
*And I Alone Survived*, 75
Andrews, Anthony, 263
Andrews, Dana, 53
Andrews, Julie, 13, 57, 107
Andrews, Mark, 219
Andrews, Tige, 230
*And Your Name Is Jonah*, 75

Angelou, Maya, 84
"Angie," 12, 20
Angier, John, 38
*Animal House*, 12, 15, 25
Annakin, Kenneth, 92
Annis, Francesca, 18, 37
Ann-Margret, 64, 233
"Another World," 124, 126
Ansara, Michael, 51, 107
Anton, Susan, 15, 24
Antonacci, Greg, 36
Antonio, Lou, 93, 95
"Anyplace but Here," 17
*Anything for Love*, 102
"Apple Pie," 12, 21
Apstein, Ted, 126
Arango, Douglas, 23
Archer, Ann, 111
Archer, Anne, 92
Ardoin, John, 57
Ardolino, Emile, 56
Arledge, Roone, 133
Arley, Jean, 128
Armitage, George, 83
Armstrong, Bess, 84, 99
Armus, Burton, 47
Arnaz, Desi, Jr., 78, 84
Arness, James, 32, 110
Arnold, Danny, 22
Arnold, Nick, 44
Arrau, Claudio, 61
Artemis Productions, 62
Arthur, Karen, 77
Arthur, Robert Alan, 66, 323
Arum, Bob, 171
"Asbestos: The Way to Dusty Death," 16
"Ascent of Man, The," 259
Ashby, Hal, 117
Asher, Bill, 19
Asher, William, 28
Ashley, Elizabeth, 81, 115
*Ash Wednesday*, 102
*As It Happened* (Paley), 7
Asner, Ed, 63
*Aspen*, 14
Assante, Armand, 86
Astaire, Fred, 61
"As the World Turns," 126
Astin, Patty Duke, 55, 83
*As You Like It*, 42–43, 264, 265
At Long Last Love, 102
*At the Earth's Core*, 103
ATV, England, 63
Atwood, David, 27, 38
*Audrey Rose*, 103
Auerbach, Larry, 128
Austin, Ronald, 23
"Austin City Limits," 21
Avakian, Aram, 102
Avalon, Frankie, 120
Averback, Hy, 54, 90
Avildsen, John G., 116
Ayres, Lew, 53, 96

*Baby Blue Marine*, 103
Bach, Catherine, 26
Bachrach, Doro, 64
*Backstairs at the White House*, 17, 50
Backus, Jim, 93
Backus, Richard, 127
*Bad Boys*, 56
"Bad News Bears, The" (series), 14, 21
*Bad News Bears, The* (film), 103
Bagdikian, Ben H., 207
Baggetta, Vincent, 27
Bagni, Gwen, 50
Bail, Chuck, 110
Bailey, Pearl, 14
Bain, Bill, 37
Bain, Conrad, 14, 26

Baio, Scott, 49, 103
Baker, Diane, 62
Baker, Joe Don, 101, 106
Balanchine, George, 18, 30, 56, 61
Ball, Lucille, 34
Balsam, Martin, 88, 93, 94
Balsam, Talia, 96
Bancroft, Anne, 115
Banks, Seymour, 178
*Bank Shot, The*, 103
Barbeau, Adrienne, 78, 79, 93, 95
Barbour, John, 41
Barenboim, Daniel, 60
"Barnaby Jones," 13, 22
Barnes, Priscilla, 20, 97, 99
"Barney Miller," 12, 22, 59, 205
Barr, Julia, 126
Barrett, Ellen, 129
Barron, Evelyn, 66
Barrow, Bernard, 129
Barry Lowen Productions, 35
*Bartered Bride, The*, 18, 30
Bartlett, Juanita, 42
Baryshnikov, Mikhail, 30, 56
*Baryshnikov at the White House*, 56
Basinger, Kim, 86
Bates, Alan, 18, 37
Bates, H. E., 18, 37
Batten, Tony, 29
*Battered*, 8, 76
Battista, Lloyd, 128
"Battle for South Africa, The," 17
*Battle of Algiers*, 104
"Battlestar Galactica," 2, 5, 10, 12
Bauer, Charita, 127
Bauer, Jaime Lyn, 130
Bauer, Marion Dane, 184
Baxter, Anne, 87
Baxter-Birney, Meredith, 28, 53
BBC-TV, 19, 36, 37, 42, 43, 57
*Beach Patrol*, 76
Beatles, The, 60
Beaton, Alex, 26
Beatty, Ned, 8, 16, 82, 92, 121
Beatty, Roger, 58
Beatty, Warren, 117, 268
*Beautiful But Deadly*, 103
Beck, John, 97
Bedi, Kabir, 97
Bee Gees, The, 31, 59
Behar, Joe, 126
Bel Geddes, Barbara, 24
Bell, Dale, 41
Bell, William J., 126, 130
Bellamy, Earl, 77, 80
Bellamy, Ralph, 76, 78
Beller, Kathleen, 75
Bellwood, Pamela, 48
Belushi, John, 56, 231
Bendick, Robert, 29
Beneman, George, 47
Benjamin, Paul, 91
Benjamin, Richard, 59
Bennet, Joan, 96
Bennett, Harve, 42, 52
Bennett, Tony, 27
Bennett/Katleman Productions, Inc., 20, 42, 52
Bennewitz, Rich, 44
Bennion, Nicholas Harvaey, 62
Benny, Jack, 13, 14, 234, 269
Bensfield, Dick, 32, 39
Benson, Lucille, 89
Beradino, John, 127
Berg, Dick, 55
Bergen, Candice, 102, 121
Berger, Helmut, 102
Berger, Robert, 61
Bergman, Ingrid, 56
Bergmann, Ted, 38
Berlin, Irving, 65
Berlinger, Warren, 39
Bernau, Christopher, 127
Bernhardt, Melvin, 126

Bernie Kukoff/Jeff Harris, 39
Bernstein, Elmer, 52
Bernstein, Leonard, 61
Berry, Chuck, 60
Berry, Fred, 48
Berry, John, 106
Bertinelli, Valerie, 39
Bertram, Lanie, 128
Bessmertovna, Natalia, 59
Best, James, 26
*Best of Saturday Night Live, The*, 56
*Best Place to Be, The*, 50–51
*Betrayal*, 76
"Beverly Hillbillys," 13, 26
Beyer, John, 64
Bharucha, Cyrus H., 58
Biehn, Michael, 106
*Big Bob Johnson and his Fantastic Speed Circus*, 76
*Big Fix, The*, 230
Billingsley, Jennifer, 121
Billington, Kevin, 43, 265
*Billion Dollar Threat, The*, 76
Bill Melendez Productions, 57
"Bill Moyers' Journal," 17, 22, 145
"Billy," 13, 22
*Billy Liar*, 22
Bilson, Bruce, 21, 79
Bing, Rudolf, 57
Binns, Edward, 92
Bird, Larry, 167, 172
Birman, Len, 77
Birney, David, 95
Bixby, Bill, 32, 97
"BJ and the Bear," 23, 76
Black, John D. F., 78
Black, Karen, 53, 104
"Black's Brittania," 19
*Black Sunday*, 104
Blackwell, Charles, 66
Blaine, Vivian, 86
Blair, Linda, 96
Blakely, Colin, 115
Blakely, Ronee, 80
Blakely, Susan, 105
Blazo, John, 129
Blees, Robert, 41
*Blind Ambition*, 16, 51, 233
"Blind Prophets of Easter Island," 24
Blinn, William, 35, 44, 53, 92
Blinn/Thorpe Productions, 35
Bloom, Claire, 265
Bloom, Harold Jack, 41
Blye, Margaret, 108
"Boat People," 17
*Body Human: The Sexes, The*, 56–57
"Body Machine," 181
Bogart, Paul, 20
Bogdanovich, Peter, 102
Bolen, Lin, 48
Bolger, Ray, 97
Bolkan, Florinda, 55
Bologna, Joe, 97
Bolshoi Ballet, 59
Bombeck, Erma, 82
Bonerz, Peter, 21
Boni, John, 21
Bonner, Mary S., 126
Bono, Sonny, 89
Booke, Sorrell, 103
*Born Innocent*, 224, 321
Bosley, Tom, 31, 58, 98
Bostick, Cynthia, 127
Boston, Joe, 45
Boston Symphony Orchestra, 27, 28
Bostwick, Barry, 89
Bottoms, Timothy, 82, 116, 118
Bowen, Gary, 126
Boxleitner, Bruce, 83
Boyle, Peter, 119, 121

Watson, Vernee, 88
"Waverly Wonders, The," 15, 48
Waxman, Mark, 19
Way, Harry, 241
Wayne, David, 82
Wayne, John, 110, 118
Wayne, Patrick, 114
WCET (Cincinnati), 23
Weaver, Dennis, 54, 84, 85, 91
Weaver, Fritz, 104, 107
"W.E.B.," 15, 48
Webb, Jack, 41
Webster, Nicholas, 64
Weege, Rhinehold, 22
"Weekend," 10, 18, 143, 144, 159–60
"Weekend Specials," 181, 182
Weicker, Lowell, 177, 219
Weinberg, Peter, 57
Weinberger, Ed, 45
Weiss, Chuck, 126
Weiss, Don, 88
Welch, Ken, 58, 59
Welch, Mitzie, 58, 59
Welch, Raquel, 62, 112
Welch/Layton/Welch Productions, 59
"Welcome Back, Kotter," 13, 48, 205
Welles, Orson, 67
Wells, H.G., 97
Wells, Mary K., 126
Wendkos, Paul, 67, 76, 91, 110
Wenig, Patricia, 130
Werner, Peter, 76
West, Bernie, 33, 42, 46
West, Red, 26
West, Timothy, 19, 43, 265
West Side Story, 61
Westworld, 93
WETA (Washington), 47, 56
WGBH (Boston), 27, 28, 33, 37, 38, 42, 50, 65
Wharmby, Tony, 37
"What's Happening!" 12, 48

Whedon, Tom, 19
Whelan, Jill, 29
"Whew!" 125
White, Betty, 51
White, Bob, 127
White, Margita, 239, 242, 248
White, Phyllis, 127
Whitelaw, Jordan M., 27, 28
White Lightning, 121
"White Shadow, The," 7–8, 14, 48
Whiting, Leonard, 264
Whitman, Marina v. N., 27
Whitman, Stuart, 55
Whitmer, Margy, 63
Whitmore, James, 55
Whitmore, Stanford, 51
Whitney, Helen, 144
Whittemore, Hank, 57
Who Are the DeBolts? And Where Did They Get 19 Kids?, 8, 67
"Whodunnit?" 15, 49
Who Is Killing the Stuntmen?, 122
Who'll Save Our Children, 99
"Who's Right?" 181
"Who's Watching the Kids," 49, 198
WHYY (Philadelphia), 63
Wiard, William, 42
Widdoes, James, 25
"Wide World of Sports," 231
Widmark, Richard, 53, 116
Wilcox, Larry, 23
Wilder, Billy, 115
Wilder, John, 51
Wild Wild West Revisited, The, 99
Wilkes, Donna, 32
Willa, 99
Willard, Fred, 41
Williams, Bert, 65
Williams, Billy Dee, 116, 120
Williams, Cindy, 34, 96, 102, 106
Williams, Clarence, III, 93, 230
Williams, Dick Anthony, 67
Williams, Emlyn, 9, 16, 57
Williams, Jack, 37

Williams, Paul, 99
Williams, Robin, 12, 38
Williamson, Fred, 120
Williamson, Nicol, 83
Willis, Jack, 63, 95
Willmore, Joseph, 126
Wilson, Dave, 56
Wilson, Drue, 268
Wilson, Hugh, 49
Wilson, Ronald, 40
Winds of Kitty Hawk, The, 8, 100
Winer, Harry, 62
Winged Colt, The, 181
Winkler, Henry, 30–31, 67
Winn, Marie, 249, 250, 251, 252
Winner, Michael, 117
Winter, Edward, 41
Winters, Shelley, 80, 120
Wise, Herbert, 37, 43
Wise, Robert, 103
Witt, Kathryn, 29, 82
Witt, Paul Junger, 44
Witt/Thomas/Harris Productions, 44
"WKRP in Cincinnati," 13, 49
WNET-TV (New York), 22, 30, 40, 56, 57, 67
Wolf, Harry L., 41
Wolfe, Digby, 41
Wolfe, Thomas, 100
Wolper, David L., 54
Wolper Productions, 48
Woman Called Moses, A, 17, 67
Women at West Point, 100
"Women Inside," 22
Women in White, 55
"Wonderama," 182
Wonderful Town, 61
"Wonderful World of Disney, The," 14, 50
Wood, Jack, 126
Wood, Natalie, 16, 17, 52
Wood, Peter, 37
Woods, James, 75
Woodward, Joanne, 77

Wopat, Tom, 26
Word, The, 55
Word Is Out, 67
"World," 50, 146
"World News Tonight," 132, 133
"World of Disney," 143
WQED-TV (Pittsburgh), 29, 41, 63
WQLN (Erie, Pennsylvania), 27
WTTW (Chicago), 43, 44
Wyatt, Jane, 90
Wyman, Jane, 84
Wyndham, Victoria, 126
Wynn, Keenan, 106

Yani, Nicholas, 230
Yates, Peter, 112
"Yogi's Space Race," 182
York, Michael, 53
York, Susannah, 118
Yorkin, Bud, 46, 48
You Can't Go Home Again, 100
You Light Up My Life, 122
Young, Burt, 79
Young, Dr. Frederick, 38
Young, Gig, 323
Young, Michael, 182
Young, Robert, 14
Young, Robert Malcolm, 55
Young, Stephen, 111
"Young and the Restless, The," 124, 130
"Youth Terror; The View From Behind the Gun," 16

Zabriskie, Jay, 29
Zacharias, Steve, 48
Zagor, Michael, 35
Zaslow, Michael, 122, 127
Zeffirelli, Franco, 57, 264
Zerbe, Anthony, 86
Zimbalist, Efrem, Jr., 51, 96
Zimbalist, Stephanie, 87–88, 98
Zmed, Adrian, 28
Zukerman, Pinchas, 60
Zuma Beach, 101